FREEDOM'S VOICE
IN
POETRY AND SONG

FREEDOM'S VOICE
IN
POETRY AND SONG

Compiled and Edited by
Gillian B. Anderson

PART I
AN INVENTORY OF POLITICAL
AND PATRIOTIC LYRICS IN
COLONIAL AMERICAN NEWSPAPERS
1773-1783

PART II
SONG BOOK

Scholarly Resources Inc.
Wilmington, Delaware

Scholarly Resources, Inc.
104 Greenhill Avenue
Wilmington, Delaware 19805

Library of Congress Cataloging in Publication Data
Main entry under title:

Freedom's voice in poetry and song.

Includes index
CONTENTS: Pt. 1. An inventory of political and
patriotic lyrics in colonial American newspapers, 1773–
1783. — Pt. 2.   Song book.
1.   United States—History—Revolution, 1775–1783—
Poetry.   2. American poetry—Revolutionary period,
1775–1783.   3. Political poetry, American.   4. Patriotic
poetry, American.   5. United States—History—Revolution, 1775–1783—Songs and music.   6. Political ballads
and songs, American.   7. Patriotic music, American.
I. Anderson, Gillian B., 1943–
M1631.F73   784.7'1   77-78353
ISBN 0-8420-2124-8

TABLE OF CONTENTS

v

ACKNOWLEDGEMENTS

To my gift,
To Isabelle Cazeaux,
To Woody -- with whom I started a new life,
To Wayne and Louisa, Jane and Joel,
To the staff of the Library of Congress Music Division,
To Simone Reagor, Armen Tashdinian and Nancy Moses,
To the National Endowment for the Humanities Youthgrants,
To Shelly -- my midwife,
To Mary Ellen, Arlene, Susan and Gail --
    without whom I would never have finished,
To the C. T. Wagner Music Publishers,
To Crane Miller,
And to my husband:

Thank you.

                    Gill

THE SITUATION TO WHICH THIS WORK IS A RESPONSE

Often our understanding of history is limited when our access to original sources is limited. Music of the American Revolution is a case in point. For years, Americans have laboured under the erroneous impression that there was no music during the colonial period or that it was primitive. Bibliographic aids to the music have been few and have contributed to this impression. Charles Evans' American Bibliography[1] almost completely ignored American musical imprints, and Oscar Sonneck's Bibliography of Early American Secular Music[2] was limited to secular American imprints, most of which were post-Revolutionary. There has been no bibliographic control over sacred and secular music in manuscript, sacred music printed in America, songs whose lyrics were written or published apart from their music, and European imprints used in the colonies. In other words, bibliographic aids have been lacking for precisely those kinds of music that were most prevalent during the American Revolution. Most of the music was not printed in America, or if printed in America, it was sacred music. Like a vicious circle, the lack of bibliographic control has limited people's access to the music, has led to the impression that there was no music and has discouraged research in the area.

Access has also been limited by the nature of some of the music itself. For example, eighteenth century song texts were frequently written or published without the music. Either the music was so popular that it had been memorized, or the exact tune was not important. In any event, unlike formal concert music, it was part of an informal music making tradition. Having lost touch with this tradition, we must bring the music and lyrics back together if we are to understand them again as songs.

Unfortunately, there are a number of problems that make this matching difficult and thus limit our access to the songs. First, song lyrics without music are often indistinguishable from poems in regular or irregular metre. Less than 25% carry the notation "To the tune of...." or have a chorus. Some have the indication "Song" or "Hymn" in the title. Often there is no such distinction.

Second, even if it is determined that a lyric is a song text, what music is to be set to it is unclear. Sometimes a chorus line, like "Yankee Doodle," or repeated words, like "Vicar of Bray," or a first line or title provide the tune name. These kinds of clues are often not present, however. Even when they are, they are not useful unless the researcher has an intimate knowledge of the large eighteenth century song repertory. Moreover, tunes often have up to five different versions and can be found arranged for everything from solo fife to chamber orchestra and full chorus. The question of which version and which arrangement to use is almost always open, as is the whole question of performance practices.

Finally, locating music and lyrics is a problem because they are scattered throughout so many different sources. Finding and matching them involves going through newspapers, magazines, broadsides, songsters, diaries, letters, eighteenth century English and American manuscripts, printed instrumental tutors, dance collections, song collections, operas, oratorios, pantomimes and hymn books. With both lyrics and music spread everywhere and no bibliographic control over either, our access to and our understanding of this type of music is severely limited.

Yet this music was a substantial component of the musical scene during the War for Independence. We get an idea of the part such songs played from the following letter, dated July 11, 1779:

> Dear Sir,--- I heard an Irishman the other day, sing a very foolish ballad of three or four verses, yet its simplicity struck me, and I have, this rainy morning scribbled the enclosed... I send it to you that you may give it to some of your singing sergeants or to be introduced into the army, under the protection of at least a non-commissioned officer. It goes to the tune of an Irish lilt, which I have often heard the fifers play. I do not trouble you with it from any view of credit I shall gain by it---but you must know that I am a great friend to ballads, and believe that more can be achieved, by a few occasional simple songs, than by an hundred recommendations of Congress especially considering how few attend to or read them. This is not singular, for it is the case with the public acts of all governments. I wish often to see ballads dispersed among the soldiery, which, inspiring in them a thirst for glory, patience under their hardships, a love of their General, and submission to their officers, would animate them to a cheerful discharge of their duty, and prompt them to undergo their hardships with a soldierly patience and pleasure.[3]

This letter was written by Richard Peters, Secretary to the Board of War and later a member of the Continental Congress, to the Continental general, Anthony Wayne. Peters clearly valued such songs for their ability to express and inspire desirable feelings and their actual performance was an integral part of this end. His letter emphasizes that such songs are important for our understanding of early American music and of the Revolution itself.

ABOUT THE METHOD USED TO COLLECT THE MATERIAL IN THE INVENTORY AND SONGBOOK

The present work is a response to the situation sketched above. Other researchers are preparing bibliographies to American imprints of sacred music to 1820 (Richard Crawford), American songsters to 1820 (Irving Lowens) and secular American manuscripts to 1800 (James Fuld). This work attempts to provide bibliographic control over song lyrics published in the colonial newspapers apart from their music. It is an inventory to 1,455 lyrics that were or could have been songs. All were published in the colonial American newspapers from 1773 to 1783. Almost all are political and patriotic, that is, express sentiments about the colonies, the nation, Great Britain, France or Spain, or contain references to specific events or people. Unavoidably, non-political lyrics have crept in, as have lyrics which were probably strictly poems. A decision to make the sin of commission rather than omission has led to the inclusion of such questionable items in the inventory. It is perhaps unnecessary to add that

items were undoubtedly missed in the collection process, involving as
it did the inspection of almost 20,000 newspaper issues. (See the list
of newspapers consulted on page xi.) One should also remember that songs
about love or the seasons, for example, were purposely omitted.

After the lyrics were collected, they were inventoried according to
first lines, titles, chorus lines, tune names, repeated words or names,
author and place of supposed original publication. With these inventories
in hand and in mind, the process of matching lyrics to music began.

It would be impossible to list all the music that was looked at
during the research for this book. However, a general statement can
and should be made. The catalogues for printed and manuscript material in
the British Museum were consulted and a large number of items ordered on
microfilm. These microfilms are to be deposited in the Music Division of
the Library of Congress. American Secular Music Manuscripts to 1800, a
typescript inventory compiled by James Fuld, was consulted and many of the
manuscripts were also ordered on microfilm. Finally, a shelf by shelf,
page by page search through the Library of Congress holdings of English and
American music from the eighteenth century was made.

Anyone who has ever attempted this kind of matching work will appreciate
that memory more than science is required for recognizing the little clues
which lead to the identification of a lyric's tune. The volume of material
involved in the matching of these newspaper lyrics to their tunes was
enormous. Therefore, this work must be considered only a beginning.

THE ARRANGEMENT OF THE INVENTORY AND SONGBOOK EXPLAINED

The MAIN ENTRY SECTION of the inventory (pages 1-313) is arranged
alphabetically, first by colony, city and then newspaper. This arrangement
follows the standard established by Clarence Brigham in his History and
Bibliography of American Newspapers, 1690-1820 (Worcester: American
Antiquarian Society, 1947). The lyrics within each newspaper are arranged
chronologically. Each lyric has been given a Main Entry Number and is
described by the following information:

MAIN ENTRY NO.   Date of Publication, Issue No., Page, Column. (Twentieth
                     Century Location of Issue, Call No.)
                 First Line
                 Title, if given
                 Author of Lyrics, if given
                 Tune
                 Eighteenth Century Source, if reprinted from another
                     Eighteenth Century Publication, if indicated.

Brackets have been used to indicate information supplied by this editor.

An attempt has been made to maintain the original spelling, punctuation
and capitalization but the distinction between the various sizes of italics
and capital letters is not represented. Anyone familiar with the eighteenth
century's cavalier attitude toward these matters will appreciate the proofreading difficulties presented by the attempt to maintain the eighteenth
century's inconsistencies.

Rarely were lyrics spelled, punctuated or capitalized the same way if they appeared in more than one paper. Often even individual words were changed in various verses. Some lyrics even contained examples of creative spelling, that is, the same word spelled two or three different ways within one and the same lyric. In the face of such variety and such a relaxed attitude, the twentieth century mind freezes. The twentieth century proofreader turns pale and the author prays that what errors remain even after hours and hours of proofreading will be forgiven.

Following the MAIN ENTRY SECTION are CROSS INDICES by first line (page 315), title (page 370), author (page 426), tune (page 473), and eighteenth century source (page 513). In this section the reader will find how many newspapers carried a particular lyric and in what chronological order it appeared. The varieties of spelling, punctuation and capitalization made it necessary to list only one version of each first line, title or author. A reader wishing to quote a lyric from a specific newspaper should use the version found in the main entry section, not that in the cross indices section.

The TUNE INDEX contains the following:

NAME OF TUNE: alternate names.

MAIN ENTRY NO. Name of tune
      IN:
      Eighteenth Century Source, page no. Title of Song.
       "First Line" (Twentieth Century Location of Music,
       Call No.)

The tune index was set up to maximize its clarity and usefullness for the average reader. Eighteenth century tunes often went under a variety of names. Thus, the common name with all its alternatives is listed above each entry. It is set off visually by being in capital letters. Cross references to the alternate names are found throughout the tune index. The spelling and capitalization of the tune name after the main entry number has been standardized. Spelling, capitalization and punctuation of the eighteenth century source for the tune, its title, and first line follow that of the original version. A perusal of this section emphasizes the fact that only 25% of all the lyrics have been matched to a tune.

This work concludes with a SONGBOOK, containing 92 songs and 8 poems, arranged chronologically, selected to give both a representative sampling of sentiments and music. The music selected for the songbook was chosen for aesthetic reasons and reflects no rational bias whatever. In some cases the most frequently encountered version of a tune was chosen, but no attempt was made to use primarily American sources for the tunes. A short list of events from the War for Independence precedes the lyrics for each of the eleven years, and an index to proper names and events follows on page 863.

ABOUT THE MUSIC AND ITS SOURCES

With the exception of a small core of tunes, the eighteenth century repertory of popular music changed every ten or twelve years. Some pieces disappeared completely after being popular for a year or two. Some tune titles remained the same but were applied to new tunes; some old tunes were given new names. Some localities preserved very archaic or conservative traditions. Generally, all these things were going on simultaneously. Because of this flux, only two assumptions have been made for the purposes of this work. 1) Music in sources dated after 1790 is suspect. Tunes from such sources have been listed only if the sources are American manuscripts or if there is no other source for the music. 2) The distinction between English and American music did not begin to be pronounced until after 1790. Thus, music has been taken from both English and American sources. As many versions of the music as were found are listed in the Tune Index. Not only does this emphasize the variety of tunes, it also stresses our uncertainty about which versions were sung to which lyrics, if, in fact, some were sung at all.

Although much remains to be identified, every conceivable type of music is already represented in the Tune Index: folk tunes, fiddle tunes, theatre music, fife tunes, marches, hunting songs, choral music, opera arias, dialogues, and an oratorio. And this repertory does not overlap much with that preserved on broadsides or in certain manuscript tune books. All this data contradicts the assertion about the primitive nature of colonial music and music making. However, a word of caution is here in order. The lyrics are certain. The music is conjectural, as are the possible arrangements and performing forces. Furthermore, the presence of lyrics in a colonial newspaper does not mean that the music was ever performed in the colonies or even that the colonists were necessarily familiar with the music. It certainly means that they were interested in the words and sentiments expressed therein. It might mean that they were familiar with the music but not necessarily.

A good example of this point is ALEXANDER's Feast PARODIED, Main Entry 393. A keyboard-vocal score to Handel's Alexander's Feast has been found in Francis Hopkinson's music collection. He was a signer of the Declaration of Independence and America's first poet-composer. Presumably he was familiar with the Handel work and one might conjecure that other colonists were familiar with it too. The satire inherent in the parody to Alexander's Feast is partly musical, the setting of ridiculous words to Handel's marvelously well-crafted fugues. To ignore the music for the parody is to ignore the possibility that the American colonists did appreciate this aspect of the satire. However, the possibility is clearly speculative.

As elsewhere, the sin of commission rather than omission has been preferred and music that almost certainly was not available to the colonists has been listed in the Tune Index (William Boyce, Ode for His Majesty's Birthday, for example). It is important to realize that although the music to these lyrics has probably not been lost, we will never be able to say for sure which versions were used to perform them or if they were even performed at all. The uncertainty inherent in matching music to lyrics should not prevent us from attempting to identify or perform the music but the hypothetical nature of the attempt should not be lost sight of.

ABOUT THE VALUE OF POLITICAL AND PATRIOTIC SONGS

The special value of political and patriotic songs is their ability to present an entertaining kind of informal history. As suggested earlier by Richard Peters, this end is accomplished by the simplicity and vitality of their tunes and by the sentiments they communicate. Taken as a body, the lyrics convey a picture of emotional complexity. If, for example, one compares the songs by the rebels with those by the loyalists, one is struck by the similar, often ambivalent, feelings expressed by both sides. The figures on each side are not experienced just as doers of impressive deeds and heroic acts, as villains and heroes, good guys and bad, or formal figures with little in the way of common human characteristics. The lyrics remind us that these people were more than just the sum of their heroic or dastardly acts. They remind us that the colonists viciously or ferociously pursued their ideals with great regret or acted unselfishly out of self interest or could be heroic while afraid.

One is tempted to focus on the extraordinary and unique accomplishments of the Revolutionary era to the exclusion of all else. When performed with sympathy, these songs, and herein lies ther special significance, directly express the feelings of their authors: fear, hatred, hope, outrage, despair, sarcasm, horror and the yearning for peace. These feelings cut acorss the boundaries of two centuries, across differences in language, culture, society and the world. They lift the curtain of formality that has fallen around the figures of the Revolutionary era and reveal people like ourselves, faced with momentous decisions.

I hope that you will come away from this curtain raising with an increased sympathy and admiration for the people caught in the struggle for independence. After the 1976 celebration, I hope that this work will continue to be used as an educational and bibliographic tool. By providing access to this music, it will hopefully enlarge our understanding of the informal tradition of music making that existed during the American War for Independence.

Gillian B. Anderson
March, 1975

....

1   (Chicago, 1910). Evans also overlooked what Wonneck had included in his Bibliography of Early American Secular Music (Washington, D.C., 1905). It is especially regrettable that this oversight has been left uncorrected in the updated editions of Evans.

2   (Washington, D.C., 1905). Sonneck's contribution to the study of early American music is monumental. In addition to the Bibliography he published works about Yankee Doodle, America, Hail Columbia and the Star-Spangled Banner, the composers Francis Hopkinson and James Lyon, early concert life in the colonies and young republic, and early American opera.

3   I would like to thank Ms. Rosemary Plakas of the Library of Congress Bicentennial Committee for bringing this letter to my attention.

NEWSPAPERS CONSULTED AND NOT CONSULTED

The following list of newspapers was taken from Clarence S. Brigham, History and Bibliography of American Newspapers, 1690-1820 (Worcester: American Antiquarian Society, 1947).

1. Hartford, Connecticut Courant, 1764-1820.

    I saw all the issues in:
    1773: Except Nos. 427 and 460.
    1774.
    1775.
    1776.
    1777.
    1778.
    1779.
    1780.
    1781.
    1782.
    1783.

2. Hartford, The Freeman's Chronicle: or, the American Advertiser, September-December, 1783.

    I saw all the issues in:
    1783: except Nos. 9-18.

3. New Haven, Connecticut Journal, 1767-1820.

    I saw all the issues in:
    1773: except 271-9,282-6,288-99,301,303-6,308-11,314,318,320,323.
    1774: except nos. 325,332,339,345.
    1775: except nos. 390,402,426-428.
    1776: except nos. 429-35,437-42,444,446-49,453-54,459,464,471,476.
    1777: except no. 481.
    1778: except nos. 577,580,582,584.
    1779: except nos. 586,591,599,614,624,626,628,630-34.
    1780: except nos. 640,643,646-8,660;
    1781.
    1782: except nos. 740,779,791.
    1783: except nos. 817, 843-44.

4. New London, Connecticut Gazette, 1763-1820.

    I saw all the issues in:
    1773.
    1774.
    1775.
    1776.
    1777.
    1778.

1779.
1780.
1781.
1782.
1783.

5. Norwich, <u>Norwich Packet</u>, 1773-1802.

    I saw all the issues in:
    1773: except nos. 1-4.
    1774.
    1775: except nos. 92,98,99, 102-4.
    1776.
    1777: except nos. 198-212.
    1778.
    1779: except nos. 300-301.
    1780: except nos. 342?,343-44.
    1781: except nos. 412-13, 416.
    1782.
    1783: except no. 476.

6. St. Augustine, <u>The East-Florida Gazette</u>, 1783.

    I saw in:
    1783: only issue nos. 5,14 and 16.

7. Savannah, <u>The Gazette of the State of Georgia</u>, 1783-1788.

    I saw all the issues in:
    1783.

8. Savannah, <u>Georgia Gazette</u>, 1763-1776.

    I saw:
    1773: none of the issues.
    1774: all of the issues.
    1775: all the issues except nos. 592-7,600-1,604-5,616.

9. Savannah, <u>Georgia Gazette</u>, 1777-1778.

    I saw none of these issues.

10. Savannah, <u>Royal Georgia Gazette</u>, 1779-1782.

    I saw all the issues in:
    1779: except nos. 1-3,5-7,9-29,32-50.
    1780: except nos. 51-73,76-78,81-2,84,86-93.
    1781: except nos. 94-96.
    1782: except nos. 150-1,153-58,161-64,166-68.

11. Annapolis, <u>Maryland</u> <u>Gazette</u>, 1745-1820.

    I saw all the issues in:
    1773.
    1774.
    1775.
    1776: except no. 1609.
    1777.
    1778.
    1779.
    1780.
    1781.
    1782.
    1783.

12. Annapolis, <u>Maryland</u> <u>Gazette</u>, <u>and</u> <u>Annapolis</u> <u>Advertiser,</u> 1779.

    I saw only:
    1779: issue no 15.

13. Baltimore, <u>Dunlap's</u> <u>Maryland</u> <u>Gazette</u>, 1775-1778.

    I saw all the issues in:
    1775: except no. 19.
    1776: except nos. 38,44,55,58-9,76,78-9,81,83.
    1777: except nos. 89-93,119,127-130,133.
    1778: except nos. 159,166-8,174,184.

14. Baltimore, <u>Maryland</u> <u>Gazette</u>, 1778-1779, 1783-1792.

    I saw:
    1778: none of the issues.
    1779: only issue nos. 7-13,15-33.

15. Baltimore, <u>Maryland</u> <u>Journal</u>, 1773-1797.

    I saw all the issues in:
    1773: except nos. 7,8.
    1774: except nos. 23,24,27,28,36-8,40,42,44-6,51.
    1775: except nos. 57,60,64,66,80,100-1.
    1776: except nos. 116,120,125,128-9,146,149,151-55,158.
    1777: except no. 165.
    1778: except nos. 257,262.
    1779.
    1780: except nos. 359,361.
    1782: except no. 467.
    1783.

16. Boston, Continental Journal, 1776-1787.

    I saw all the issues in:
    1776.
    1777.
    1778.
    1779.
    1780.
    1781.
    1782.
    1783.

17. Boston, Boston Evening-Post, 1735-1775.

    I saw all the issues in:
    1773.
    1774.
    1775.

18. Boston, Evening Post, 1778-1780.

    I saw all the issues in:
    1778.
    1779.
    1780: except nos. 76,77,79.

19. Boston, Boston Evening-Post, 1781-1784.

    I saw all the issues in:
    1781.
    1782.
    1783.

20. Boston, Boston Gazette, 1719-1798.

    I saw all the issues in:
    1773.
    1774.
    1775.
    1776.
    1777.
    1778.
    1779: except nos. 1319,1320,1321.
    1780: except nos. 1323,1326,1330,1339,1343,1345,1347,1371-3,1375.
    1781: except nos. 1376,1379.
    1782.
    1783: except no. 1519.

21. Boston, _Independent Chronicle_, 1776-1820

     I saw all the issues in:
     1776.
     1777.
     1778.
     1779.
     1780.
     1781.
     1782.
     1783.

22. Boston, _Independent Ledger_, 1778-1786.

     I saw all the issues in:
     1778.
     1779.
     1780.
     1781.
     1782: except nos. 191,219.
     1783: except no. 309.

23. Boston, _Massachusetts Spy_, 1770-1775.

     I saw all the issues in:
     1773.
     1774.
     1775.

24. Boston, _New-England Chronicle_, 1776

     I saw all the issues.

25. Boston, _Boston News-Letter_, 1704-1776.

     I saw all issues in:
     1773: except nos. 3613.
     1774: except nos. 3698.
     1775: except nos. 3738-42,3745,3748-9,3753,3756,3758.
     1776: except nos. 3767,3768.

26. Boston, _Boston Post-Boy_, 1734-1775.

     I saw all issues in:
     1773.
     1774: except nos. 856,860.
     1775.

27. Cambridge, _New-England Chronicle_, 1775-76.

     I saw all issues in:
     1775.
     1776.

28. Newburyport, _Essex Journal_, 1773-1777.

    I saw all issues in:
    1773.
    1774.
    1775.
    1776.
    1777: except no. 163.

29. Salem, _American Gazette_, 1776.

    I saw all the issues.

30. Salem, _Essex Gazette_, 1768-1775.

    I saw all the issues in:
    1773.
    1774.
    1775.

31. Salem, _Salem Gazette_, 1774-1775.

    I saw none of these issues.

32. Salem, _Salem Gazette_, 1781.

    I saw all the issues in:
    1781: except nos. 24,30-1,34-6.

33. Salem, _Salem Gazette_, 1781-1785.

    I saw all the issues in:
    1781.
    1782.
    1783.

34. Springfield, _Massachusetts Gazette,_ 1782-1784.

    I saw all the issues in:
    1782.
    1783.

35. Worcester, _Massachusetts Herald,_ 1783

    I saw none of the issues.

36. Worcester, _Massachusetts Spy,_ 1775-1820.

    I saw all the issues in:
    1775.
    1776.
    1777: except nos.305,310,323-4,326-7,335.
    1778.
    1779.
    1780.

1781.
1782.
1783.

37.   Exeter, _Exeter Journal_, 1778-1779.

I saw all the issues in:
1778: except nos. 1,9,24,30,39.
1779: except nos. 46,48-9,54,60,68,75,81.

38.   Exeter, _New Hampshire Gazette_, 1776-1777.

I saw all issues in:
1776: except no. 8.
1777: except no. 57.

39.   Hanover, _Dresden Mercury_, 1779.

I **saw** only:
1779: issue nos. 11,14,15,20,22.

40.   Portsmouth, _Freeman's Journal_, 1776-1778.

I saw all the issues in:
1776.
1777.   (The numbering changed with the May 24, 1777 issue and
1778.   makes it unclear which numbers are missing thereafter.)

41.   Portsmouth, _New-Hampshire Gazette_, 1756-1820.

I saw all the issues in:
1773.
1774.
1775: except nos. 983,986-7,989-91,994-5,997-9.
1777: except nos. 1,2,3,25-9.
1778.
1779.
1780: except nos. 2209-2210,22014(sic),22018,22021,22022,22023,1255(sic)
        1260.
1781: except no. 1306.
1782.
1783.

42.   Bridgeton, _Plain Dealer_, 1775-1776.

I saw all the issues.

43.   Burlington, _New Jersey Gazette_, 1777-1778.

I saw all the issues in:
1777.
1778.

44. Chatham, <u>New-Jersey</u> <u>Journal</u>, 1779-1783.

I saw in:
1779: only issues 1,2,11,18.
1780: all issues except 47,54,72,78,91-3.
1781: all issues except 102,103,104.
1782: all issues except no. 153.
1783: all issues except 219,243-4,246-7.

45. New Brunswick, <u>Political</u> <u>Intelligencer</u>, 1783-1785.

I saw all the issues in:
1783: except nos. 1,4.

46. Newark, <u>New-York</u> <u>Gazette</u>, 1776.

I saw all the issues in 1776.

47. Trenton, <u>New-Jersey</u>, 1778-1786.

I saw all the issues in:
1778.
1779.
1780.
1781.
1782.
1783.

48. Albany, <u>New-York</u> <u>Gazetteer</u>, 1782-1784.

I saw all the issues in:
1782: except nos. 1-3,5-6,8-11,24.
1783: except nos. 32,34,37,39,41-44,46-50,53,55-6,58,60-1,
          63-5,68,72,76-7,79-81,83.

49. Fishkill, <u>New-York</u> <u>Packet</u>, 1777-1783.

I saw all the issues in:
1777: except nos. 36-8,41-3,45,47-51,54-7,61-3,65-8,71-5,83-4.
1778: except nos. 90,101,104,120.
1779: except nos. 124-5,129,133,137,140,154-55,157.
1780: except nos. 158-60,175,178-9.
1781.
1782.
1783: except nos. 321,328,330,333.

50. Kingston, <u>New</u> <u>York</u> <u>Journal</u>, 1777.

I saw all the issues.

51. New York, Constitutional Gazette, 1775-1776.

     I saw all issues in:
     1775: except nos. 1,2.
     1776: except nos. 52,108-110.

52. New York, New York Evening Post, 1782-1783.

     1782: I saw only issue 23.
     1783: I saw only issues 67,71,80 and 86.

53. New York, New-York Gazette, or Weekly Post-Boy, 1747-1773.

     1773: I saw only issues 1551,1555-6,1665(sic),1574,1576-7,July 12.

54. New York, New-York Gazette and Weekly Mercury, 1768-1783.

     I saw all issues in:
     1773.
     1774.
     1775.
     1776.
     1777.
     1778.
     1779.
     1780.
     1781.
     1782: except no. 1606.
     1783.

55. New York, New-York Gazetteer, 1783-1787.

     I saw only:
     1783: issue nos. 4 and 5.

56. New York, Independent Gazette, 1783-1784.

     I saw all issues in:
     1783: except nos. 1,2,3.

57. New York, Independent Journal,1783.

     I saw all the issues for 1783.

58. New York, Independent New-York Gazette, 1783.

     I saw all the issues for 1783.

59. New York, New-York Journal, 1766-1776.

     I saw all the issues in:
     1773: except no. 1610.

1774: except no. 1635.
1775.
1776: except nos. 1727,1735,1739,1742,1744.

60. New York, New York Mercury, 1779-1783.

I saw only:
1779: issue nos. 10,14,15.
1780: issue nos. 21,35,42,44,46.
1781: issue nos. 73,March 9, March 16, 87,89,CVIX.
1782: issue nos. 126,131,147,149.
1783: issue no. 211.

61. New York, New-York Morning Post, 1783-1792.

1783: I saw only issues 125,129,155,Nov.7,162.

62. New York, New York Packet, 1776.

I saw all the issues in:
1776: except no. 34.

63. New York, New York Packet, 1783.

1783: I saw only issues 341,342,343,344,345.

64. New York, Rivington's New York Gazette, 1777.

I saw all the issues in 1777.

65. New York, Rivington's New-York Gazette, 1783.

I saw all the issues in 1783.

66. New York, Rivington's New-York Gazetteer, 1773-1775.

I saw all the issues in:
1773.
1774.
1775.

67. New York, Rivington's New York Loyal Gazette, 1777.

I saw all the issues in 1777.

68. New York, Royal American Gazette, 1777-1783.

I saw all the issues in:
1777: except no. 5.
1778: except nos. 72,104.
1779: except nos. 137-140,219,221.
1780: except nos. 240-243,300(sic?),301(sic?),312.

I saw only:
1781: issues   359,March 3, March 6,March 13,March 27,April 19,
        May 1, June 5, August 14, August 16, September 4.
1782: issues January 24,May 28, June 11, July 9, July 23, October 22,
        November 28, December 3, December 10, December 19, December 26,
        December 31.
1783: issues January 2, February 11, April 15, April 17, April 22,
        April 24, April 29, May 1, May 6, May 8, May 13, May 15,
        May 20, May 22, May 27, July 17, July 22, July 31,
        August 7.

69. New York, Royal Gazette, 1777-1783.

     I saw all the issues in:
     1777.
     1778.
     1779.
     1780: except no. 389.
     1781.
     1782.
     1783.

70. New York, Town and Country Journal, 1783.

     1783: I saw only issues 4,12,December 11.

71. Poughkeepsie, New York Journal, 1778-1782.

     I saw all the issues in:
     1778.
     1779.
     1780.
     1781.
     1782.

72. New Bern, North-Carolina Gazette, 1768-1778.

     1773: I saw none of the issues.
     1774: I saw only issues for July 15 and September 2.
     1775: I saw only issues 312,316,318,322,323,330-2,344,December 22.
     1777: I saw only issues 383-97,399-406,408.
     1778: I saw all the issues except nos. 420,424,433,451,452.

73. New Bern, North Carolina Gazette, 1783-1784.

     I saw none of these issues.

74. Wilmington, Cape-Fear Mercury, 1769-1775.

     1773: I saw only issue no. 204.
     1774: I saw only issue nos. 223 and 266.
     1775: I saw only issue nos. 266-270.

75. Germantown, Germantowner Zeitung, 1762-1777.

    I saw only:
    1773: issue nos. 542,553,560.
    1774: issue nos. 572,583.
    1775: issue no. 598.
    1776: issue nos. 636,645,670.
    1777: issue nos. 688,689.
    1778: issue no. 733.

76. Lancaster, Lancaster Mercury, 1778-1779.

    I saw none of the issues.

77. Lancaster, Pennsylvania Packet, 1777-1778.

    I saw all the issues in:
    1777.
    1778.

78. Lancaster, Pennsylvanische Zeitungs-Blat, 1778.

    I saw all the issues from 1778.

79. Philadelphia, Allied Mercury, 1781.

    1781: I saw only issue no. 13.

80. Philadelphia, Freeman's Journal, 1781-1792.

    I saw all the issues in:
    1781.
    1782.
    1783.

81. Philadelphia, Gemeinnuetzige Philadelphische Correspondenz,1781-90.

    1781: I saw only issue nos. 14 and 18.
    1782: I saw none of these issues.
    1783: I saw none of these issues.

82. Philadelphia, Independent Gazetteer, 1782-1796.

    I saw all the issues in:
    1782.
    1783.

83. Philadelphia, Pennsylvania Chronicle, 1767-1774.

    I saw all the issues in:
    1773.
    1774.

84. Philadelphia, <u>Pennsylvania</u> <u>Evening</u> <u>Post</u>, 1775-1784.

I saw all the issues in:
1775.
1776.
1777.
1778.
1779.
1780.
1781.
1782: except no. 870.
1783.

85. Philadelphia, <u>Pennsylvania</u> <u>Gazette</u>, 1728-1815.

I saw all the issues in:
1773.
1774.
1775.
1776.
1777.
1778.
1779.
1780.
1781.
1782: except no. 2742.
1783.

86. Philadelphia, <u>Pennsylvania</u> <u>Journal</u>, 1742-1793.

I saw all the issues in:
1773.
1774.
1775.
1776.
1777: except nos. 1776,1808,1809.
1778.
1779: except no. 1810.
1780.
1781.
1782.
1783.

87. Philadelphia, <u>Pennsylvania</u> <u>Ledger</u>, 1775-1778.

I saw all the issues in:
1775.
1776.
1777.
1778.

88. Philadelphia, Pennsylvania Packet, 1771-1790.

I saw all the issues in:
1773.
1774.
1775.
1776.
1777.
1778: except no. July 11.
1779.
1780.
1781.
1782.
1783.

89. Philadelphia, Pennsylvanische Gazette, 1779.

I saw none of the issues.

90. Philadelphia, Pennsylvanische Staats-Courier, 1777-1778.

1777: I saw none of these issues.
1778: I saw only issue no. 745.

91. Philadelphia, Philadelphia Price Current, 1783.

1783: I saw only issue for Dec. 16.

92. Philadelphia, Royal Pennsylvania Gazette, 1778.

I saw all the issues in:
1783: except nos. 23,24,25.

93. Philadelphia, Philadelphisches Staatsregister, 1779-1781.

1779: I saw none of these issues.
1780: I saw only issue no. 26.
1781: I saw none of these issues.

94. Philadelphia, Story and Humphreys's Pennsylvania Mercury, 1775.

I saw all these issues.

95. Philadelphia, Wochentliche Philadelphische Staatsbote, 1762-1779.

I saw all the issues in:
1773.
1774.
1775.
1776.
1777.
1778.
1779.

96. Newport, <u>Newport</u> <u>Gazette</u>, 1777-1779.

I saw all the issues in:
1777: except nos. 1-7,19,23,26,37-8,43,46.
1778: except nos. 52,72-4,76-81,84-8,91-2,94-111.
1779: except nos. 113-124.

97. Newport, <u>Gazette</u> <u>Francoise</u>, 1780-1781.

I saw all the existing issues.

98. Newport, <u>Newport</u> <u>Mercury</u>, 1758-1820.

I saw all the issues in:
1773: except no. 798.
1774: except no. 851.
1775: except no. 894.
1776: except nos. 908,910,912-14,919,932,934-5,941,943-44,950-1,953-4.
1780: except nos. 956-68,970-77,979,981-2,985-6,989,992,994,996-8,
      1000,1002-3.
1781: except nos. 1005-6,1010-12,1015-16,1018-19,1021,1054.
1782: except nos. 1064,1103,1104.
1783: except nos. 1112,1114,1116-20,1123-24,1126-29,1131-32,1140,
      1151,1155.

99. Providence, <u>American</u> <u>Journal</u>, 1779-1781.

I saw all the issues in:
1779.
1780.
1781.

100. Providence, <u>Providence</u> <u>Gazette</u>, 1762-1820.

I saw all the issues in:
1773.
1774.
1775.
1776.
1777.
1778.
1779.
1780.
1781.
1782.
1783.

101. Charleston, <u>Chronicle</u> <u>of</u> <u>Liberty</u>, 1783.

I saw all the issues in 1783.

102. Charleston, <u>Charleston</u> Gazette, 1778-1780.

1778: I saw none of the issues.
1779: I saw only issue nos. 33,41 and 61.
1780: I saw only issue nos. 67,68.

103. Charleston, <u>Gazette</u> of the <u>State</u> of <u>South</u> Carolina, 1777-1780,
     1783-1785.

I saw all the issues in:
1777: except nos. 2180,2182.
1778: except nos. 2108,2117,2118.
1779: except nos. 2122,2123,2135,2136,2146,2150,2153,2154.
1780: except nos. 2158-62.
1783: except nos. 2180.

104. Charleston, <u>Royal</u> Gazette, 1781-1782.

I saw all the issues in:
1781.
1782: except nos. 152-3.

105. Charleston, <u>Royal</u> South-Carolina Gazette, 1781-1782.

1780: I saw only issue nos. 4,6,15,58,59,93,101,103,109,110,112.
1781: I saw only issue nos. 190 and 194.
1782: I saw only issue nos. 284,S,289,291,300-303,311,320-322,330,
      338,339.

106. Charleston, <u>South-Carolina</u> and <u>American</u> General Gazette, 1764-1781.

I saw in:
1773: only issue nos. 778 and 796.
I saw all the issues in:
1774: except nos. 798-800,802-812.
1775: except nos. 855,895-898.
1776: except nos. 903,912,920,922,924-926,931,934.
1777: except nos. 940,949,950,958,964,987,989.
1778: except nos. 1003,1034,1038.
1779: except nos. 1044,1055,1056,1062-65,1067,1069,1073,1081-2,1084.
1780.
1781.

107. Charleston, <u>South-Carolina</u> Gazette, 1732-1775.

I saw all the issues in:
1773.
1774: except nos. 2012.
1775: except nos. 2035,2048.

108. Charleston, <u>South-Carolina</u> Gazette; <u>and</u> Country Journal, 1765-1775.

I saw all the issues in:
1773: except no. 378.
1774: except nos. 423,429,451.
1775.

xxx

109. Charleston, <u>South-Carolina</u> <u>Gazette</u> <u>and</u> <u>General</u> <u>Advertiser</u>, 1783-1785.

I saw all the issues in:
1783: except nos. 66-74,80,83,86.

110. Charleston, <u>South</u> <u>Carolina</u> <u>Weekly</u> <u>Advertiser</u>, 1783.

I saw all of these issues.

111. Charleston, <u>South</u> <u>Carolina</u> <u>Weekly</u> <u>Gazette</u>, 1783-1786.

I saw none of these issues.

112. Jacksonburgh, <u>Gazette,</u> 1782.

I saw none of these issues.

113. Parker's Ferry, <u>South</u> <u>Carolina</u> <u>Gazette</u>, 1782.

I saw none of these issues.

114. Bennington, <u>Vermont</u> <u>Gazette</u>, 1780-1781.

I saw all the issues in 1783.

115. Westminster, <u>Vermont</u> <u>Gazette</u>, 1780-1781.

1780: I saw none of these issues.
1781: I saw only the issue for July 9, 1781.

116. Windsor, <u>Vermont</u> <u>Journal</u>, 1783-1820.

I saw all the issues in 1783.

117. Norfolk, <u>Virginia</u> <u>Gazette</u>, 1774-1775.

1774: I saw only issue nos. 5,6,8,9,11,12,18.
1775: I saw only issue nos. 37,38,55,56,July 5,59,62,63,64,66,68.

118. Norfolk, <u>Virginia</u> <u>Gazette</u>, 1775-1776.

1775: I saw only issue for November 25,
1776: I saw only issue for February 3.

119. Richmond, <u>Virginia</u> <u>Gazette</u>, 1780-1781.

1780: I saw only July 26 issue.
1781: I saw only March 31 issue.

120. Richmond, <u>Virginia</u> <u>Gazette</u> <u>and</u> <u>Independent</u> <u>Chronicle</u>, 1783-1789.

1783: I saw only issue nos. 14,15,18.

121. Richmond, _Virginia Gazette and Weekly Advertiser_, 1781-1797.

I saw all the issues in:
1781: except no. 1.
1782: except nos. 23,24,25,27,29,32,33,43,46,49-53.
1783: I saw only issue nos. 54,56,60,66,70,72,80,81,91,92,92(sic),
      93,95,96,97,98,99,100,102,103,105.

122. Richmond, _Virginia Gazette, or, the American Advertiser_, 1781-1786.

I saw all the issues in:
1781.
1782: except nos. 11,12,13,15,17.
1783: except nos. 79,86.

123. Williamsburg, _Virginia Gazette_ (Hunter,Royle,Purdie & Dixon,
      Dixon and Hunter), 1751-1778.

I saw all the issues in:
1773.
1774.
1775.
1776: except no. 1322.
1777.
1778: except nos. 1400-11,1413,1416-22,1425-35,1438,1442.

124. Williamsburg, _Virginia Gazette_ (Rind,Pinkney), 1766-1776.

I saw all the issues in:
1773.
1774: except nos. 404,407,416,417.
1775.
1776: except no. 507.

125. Williamsburg, _Virginia Gazette_ (Purdie,Clarkson and Davis),1775-80.

I saw all the issues in:
1775.
1776.
1777: except no. 152.
I saw in:
1778: only issue nos. 155,156,157,161,162,165,June 5,June 12,
          June 19, 171,177,185,186,187.
1779: only issue nos. 228,237,238,239,230(sic),231,233,234,235.
1780: only issue nos. 243,255,263,268,276,283.

126. Williamsburg, _Virginia Gazette_ (Dixon and Nicolson), 1779-1780.

I saw all the issues in:
1779.
1780: except nos. 47,78,93.

Abbreviations

DFO
Folger Shakespeare Library
201 E. Capitol St.
Washington, D.C. 20003

DLC
Library of Congress
Washington, D.C. 20540

GB/Lbm
British State Library [British Museum]
London, WCIB 3DG
ENGLAND

GB/Ob3
The Bodleian Library
Oxford OXI 3BG
ENGLAND

MB
Boston Public Library
Box 286
Boston, Mass. 02117

MdHi
Maryland Historical Society Library
201 W. Monument St.
Baltimore, Md. 21201

MSaE
James Duncan Phillips Library
Essex Institute
132-34 Essex St.
Salem, Mass. 01970

MWA
American Antiquarian Society Library
185 Salisbury St.
Worcester, Mass. 01609

NHi
New York Historical Society Library
170 Central Park W.
New York, N.Y. 10024

NJHi
New Jersey Historical Society Library
230 Broadway
Newark, N.J. 07104

NN
New York Public Library
Fifth Ave. and 42nd St.
New York, N.Y. 10018

NNC
Columbia University Library
535 W. 114th St.
New York, N.Y. 10027

Abbreviations

NNHi New York Historical Society
    See: NHi

PHi   Historical Society of Pennsylvania Library
    1300 Locust St.
    Philadelphia, Pa. 19107

PPL   Library Company of Philadelphia
    1314 Locust St.
    Philadelphia, Pa. 19107

RHi   Rhode Island Historical Society Library
    121 Hope St.
    Providence, R.I. 02906

RMEAN Readex Microprint Corporation, Early
    American Newspapers. [This is a standard
    microcard series, found in most major
    libraries.]

RPB   Brown University Libraries
    Prospect St.
    Providence, R.I. 02912

Vi   Virginia State Library
    Capitol St.
    Richmond, Va. 23219

ViW   Earl Gregg Swem Library
    College of William and Mary
    Williamsburg, Va. 23185

PART I
AN INVENTORY OF POLITICAL
AND PATRIOTIC LYRICS IN
COLONIAL AMERICAN NEWSPAPERS
1773-1783

CONNECTICUT

1. May 25, 1773, #439, p. 4, col. 1. (DLC 13)
   "Adieu New England's smiling Meads,"
   Farewell to America.
   Phillis Wheatley
   . . . . .
   . . . . .

2. June 1, 1773, #440, p. 4, col. 1. (DLC 13)
   "Ordain'd to tread the thorney Ground,"
   The Lawyer's Prayer.
   . . . . .
   . . . . .
   . . . . .

3. June 15, 1773, #442, p. 4, col. 1. (DLC 13)
   "WHEN Popery in Britain sway'd I've read,"
   . . . . .
   . . . . .
   . . . . .
   . . . . .

4. June 22, 1773, #443, p. 4, col. 1.   (DLC 13)
   "Sov'reign of All, whose Will ordains"
   On His MAJESTY's BIRTH-DAY, JUNE 4.
   . . . . .
   . . . . .
   . . . . .

5. July 6, 1773, #445, p. 4, col. 1.   (DLC 13)
   "A Monarch in my rustic bower,"
   The HERMIT's EMPIRE.
   . . . . .
   . . . . .
   . . . . .

6. Aug. 3, 1773, #449, p. 4, col. 1. (DLC 13)
   "IN antient times e'er frequent vice began,"
   A TALE.
   . . . . .
   . . . . .
   . . . . ., New Haven, 1772.

7. Sept. 28, 1773, #457, p. 3, col. 2. (DLC 13)
   "THUS fell barbarians: whose rapacious breast,"
   .....
   X.Y.
   .....
   .....

8. Oct. 5, 1773, #458, p. 4, col. 1. (DLC 13)
   "AS good Ezekiel on his bed"
   The DYING SAINT.
   .....
   .....
   .....

9. Dec. 28, 1773, #470, p. 4, col. 1. (DLC 13)
   "PArliament an Act has made"
   .....
   A daughter of Liberty
   .....
   .....

10. Feb. 8, 1774, #476, p. 4, col. 1. (DLC 14)
    "AS near beauteous BOSTON lying"
    A NEW SONG.
    BRITTANNO AMERICANUS
    "Hosier's Ghost"
    Pennsylvania Packet

11. March 1, 1774, #479, p. 4, col. 1. (DLC 14)
    "FAREWELL the Tea Board, with its gaudy Equipage,"
    A Lady's Adieu to her TEA-TABLE.
    .....
    .....
    .....

12. March 8, 1774, #480, p. 4, col. 1. (DLC 14)
    "TO years far distant, and to scenes more bright,"
    A PROPHECY of the future GLORY of AMERICA.
    .....
    .....
    .....

Connecticut, Hartford; Connecticut Courant, 1764-1820+

13. June 7, 1774, #493, p. 4, col. 1.   (DLC 14)
    "FREEDOM's Charms alike engage"
    A Favorite AIR.
    . . . . .
    . . . . .
    . . . . .

14. June 5 (sic July 5), 1774, #497, p. 4, col. 1.   (DLC 14)
    "TRAITORS would fix Rebellion's odius Name"
    . . . . .
    . . . . .
    . . . . .
    . . . . .

15. July 26, 1774, #500, p. 4, col. 1.   (DLC 14)
    "BEneath fair FREEDOM's banner, waving high,"
    . . . . .
    Philo Sappho.
    . . . . .
    Great-Barrington, 9th July, 1774.

16. August 2, 1774, #501, p. 4, col. 1.   (DLC 14)
    "THE muse, disgusted at an age and clime"
    Of the Prospect of Arts and Sciences in America.
    Dr. George Berkeley
    . . . . .
    . . . . .

17. August 9, 1774, #502, p. 4, col. 1.   (DLC 14)
    "HAIL LIBERTY! A Glorious word,"
    . . . . .
    . . . . .
    . . . . .
    . . . . .

18. August 23, 1774, #504, p. 4, col. 1.   (DLC 14)
    "YE Princes of the earth, ye mighty few,"
    On Tyrannical Government.
    . . . . .
    . . . . .
    . . . . .

19. Aug. 30, 1774, #505, p. 4, col. 1. (DLC 14)
     "VAIN are the sculptur'd effigies of Fame,"
     EPITAPH.
     .....
     .....
     .....

20. Sept. 12, 1774, #507, p. 4, col. 1. (DLC 14)
     "YOUR Colonel H[ancoc]k by neglect,"
     A General sample of Gubernatorial Eloquence, as lately
        exhibited to the Company of C[ADET]S.
     .....
     .....
     MASSACHUSETTS SPY

21. Sept. 26, 1774, #509, p. 4, col. 1. (DLC 14)
     "N[OR]TH:THOU canker wedded to my Breast,"
     A Dialogue between Frederick L[or]d N[or]th and his con-
        science, upon passing the Quebec Bill.
     .....
     .....
     BINGLEY's London Journal.

22. Oct. 3, 1774, #510, p. 4, col. 1. (DLC 14)
     "TO all the pretty Girls and Boys,"
     A PROCLAMATION.
     .....
     .....
     .....

23. Oct. 10, 1774, #511, p. 4, col. 1. (DLC 14)
     "O GOD of mercy bend thine ear,"
     A PRAYER for this Land under its present melancholy
        Circumstances.
     .....
     .....
     .....

24. Oct. 17, 1774, #512, p. 4, col. 1. (DLC 14)
     "OH! thou great Ruler of my Soul!"
     A DIALOGUE between two Friends, viz. An unlimited
        COMMANDER, now in America, and the D[evi]l.
     .....
     .....
     .....

Connecticut, Hartford; Connecticut Courant, 1764-1820+

25.   Oct. 31, 1774, #514, p. 4, col. 1. (DLC 14)
      "COME let us join the glorious Train,"
      A Liberty Song.
      PHILO SAPPHO, Oct. 12, 1774.
      . . . . .
      . . . . .

26.   Nov. 21, 1774, #517, p. 2, col. 1. (DLC 14)
      "SINCE an Assembly most unlawful,"
      A PROCLAMATION.
      . . . . .
      . . . . .
      . . . . .

27.   Dec. 19, 1774, #521 et al., p. 4, col. 1. (DLC 14)
      "THERE did (what signifies it when?)"
      The Story of ZEYN Alasman Prince of Balsora, in the Arabian
         Nights Entertainments, done into English Verse, with
         Additions and Imitations, in three Cantos.
      . . . . .
      . . . . .
      . . . . .

28.   Jan. 30, 1775, #527, p. 4, col. 3. (DLC 15)
      "FAIR Ladies, 'tis not very arch,"
      ADVERTISEMENT Addressed to the LADIES.
      William Beadle.
      . . . . .
      . . . . .

29.   March 6, 1775, #532, p. 4, col. 1. (DLC 15)
      "Alas! (said Cynthia, as she pour'd the Tea)"
      AN ELEGY.
      . . . . .
      . . . . .
      . . . . .

30.   [March 13], 1775, #533, p. 4, col. 1. (DLC 15)
      "WHEN De La Manca's famous Knight,"
      KNIGAT ERRANTRY. (sic)
      . . . . .
      . . . . .
      . . . . .

Connecticut, Hartford; Connecticut Courant, 1764-1820+

31. April 17, 1775, #538, p. 4, col. 1. (DLC 15)
    "WHAT instruments my friends, shall we employ"
    A DIALOGUE between the Pope, the Devil, and a Tory.
    .....
    .....
    .....

32. May 1, 1775, #540, p. 4, col. 1. (DLC 15)
    "HAPPY's the man, who unconstrained"
    An ODE on LIBERTY.
    .....
    .....
    .....

33. May 8, 1775, #541, p. 4, col. 1. (DLC 15)
    "THAT Seat of Science Athens, and Earths great Mistress
       Rome"
    A SONG compos'd by a SON of LIBERTY.
    Son of LIBERTY, Feb. 13, 1770.
    BRITISH GRANADIER.
    .....

34. May 22, 1775, #543, p. 4, col. 1. (DLC 15)
    "BRITONS, if you pant for glory,"
    ODE to INDEPENDENCE.
    .....
    .....
    .....

35. May 29, 1775, #544, p. 4, col. 1. (DLC 15)
    "WELCOME! once more"
    To the Friend of his Country and Mankind, Doctor BENJAMIN
       FRANKLIN, On his arrival from England, May 6th, 1775.
    .....
    .....
    Philadelphia, May 8, 1775.

36. June 19, 1775, #547, p. 4, col. 1. (DLC 15)
    "COME listen my cocks, to a brother and a friend,"
    The SAILORS ADDRESS.
    .....
    [Hearts of Oak]
    London Paper.

Connecticut, Hartford; Connecticut Courant, 1764-1820+

37. June 26, 1775, #548, p. 4, col. 1. (DLC 15)
     "WHERE now is Athens? Where the Grecian Name"
     . . . . .
     PHILOPATRIS.
     . . . . .
     . . . . .

38. July 17, 1775, #551, p. 4, col. 1. (DLC 15)
     "WHEREAS the Rebels hereabout,"
     Tom. Gage's PROCLAMATION, or Blustering Denunciation.
     TOM. GAGE, By command of Mother Cary, Thomas Flucker,
        Secretary.
     . . . . .
     . . . . .

39. August 7, 1775, #554, p. 4, col. 1. (DLC 15)
     "WHEREAS th' infatuated creatures"
     A PROCLAMATION.
     Thomas Gage
     . . . . .
     . . . . .

40. August 14, 1775, #555, p. 4, col. 1. (DLC 15)
     "WHEREAS th' infatuated creatures"
     A PROCLAMATION.
     Thomas Gage
     . . . . .
     . . . . .

41. Sept. 25, 1775, #561, p. 4, col. 1. (DLC 15)
     "WHENCE this wild uproar, Oh ye muses tell?"
     . . . . .
     . . . . .
     . . . . .
     . . . . .

42. March 4, 1776, #580, p. 4, col. 1. (DLC 16)
     "WHY should vain Mortals tremble at the sight of"
     The AMERICAN HERO.--A Saphic Ode.
     . . . . .
     [Bunker Hill, Music by Andrew Law]
     . . . . .

Connecticut, Hartford; Connecticut Courant, 1764-1820+

43.   April 22, 1776, #587, p. 4, col. 1.   (DLC 16)
      "PRAISE to that God who arch'd the sky,"
      A SONG for BOSTON, Upon the preceipitate (sic) Flight of
         the King's Troops out of Town.
      T.H.
      .....
      .....

44.   April 29, 1776, #588, p. 4, col. 1.   (DLC 16)
      "THE watry God, great Neptune, lay"
      The Watry God.   A new SONG.
      .....
      "The Watry God."
      .....

45.   Jan. 13, 1777, #625, p. 4, col. 1.   (DLC 17)
      "HOW does my breast with kindling raptures glow,"
      .....
      A young Lady of Fifteen
      .....
      .....

46.   Feb. 17, 1777, #630, p. 4, col. 1.   (DLC 17)
      "MY Lords, with your leave,"
      A New WAR SONG.
      Sir PETER PARKER.
      "Well met Brother Tar"
      .....

47.   April 7, 1777, #637, p. 2, col. 1.   (DLC 17)
      "YE wrong heads, and strong heads, attend to my strains;"
      THE HEADS, Or, the Year 1776.
      .....
      [Derry Down]
      (London) PUBLIC LEDGER.

48.   June 2, 1777, #645, p. 2, cols. 1-2.   (DLC 17)
      "WITHOUT wit, without wisdom, half stupid and drunk,"
      The EXPEDITION to DANBURY, under the command of General
         Tryon, to destroy the stores of Beef, Pork and Rum, SCENE,
         New York.
      COMUS.
      .....
      Philadelphia, May 12.

Connecticut, Hartford; Connecticut Courant, 1764-1820+

49. June 2, 1777, #645, p. 2, cols. 1-2. (DLC 17)
     "Let freedom and love be the glee of our song,"
     The EXPEDITION to DANBURY, under the command of General
        Tryon, to destroy the stores of Beef, Pork and Rum,
        SCENE, New York.
     COMUS.
     .....
     Philadelphia, May 12.

50. Aug. 4, 1777, #654, p. 3, col. 2. (DLC 17)
     "COME soldiers all in chorus join"
     On the Death of General MONTGOMERY.
     .....
     "Hark! Hark! the joy inspiring Horn," Favorite Hunting
        Song, sung by Mr. Taylor.
     .....

51. Aug. 11, 1777, #655, p. 3, col. 2. (DLC 17)
     "WHEN the great hero in arms himself array'd,"
     An ODE
     .....
     [Bunker-Hill?]
     .....

52. Sept. 1, 1777, #658, p. 4, col. 1. (DLC 17)
     "O Spirit of the truly brave,"
     An ODE, To the Memory of General MONTGOMERY.
     .....
     .....
     .....

53. Jan. 20, 1778, #678, p. 3, col. 2. (DLC 18)
     "AS Jack, the King's commander,"
     A SONG. On the Surrender of Lieutenant-General Burgoyne
        and his Army, to Major-General Gates.
     .....
     "My Daddy was in the Rebellion."
     .....

54. May 12, 1778, #694, p. 4, col. 1. (DLC 18)
     "AS late I travell'd o'er the plain,"
     DATE OBOLUM BELESARIO.
     .....
     .....
     .....

55.   June 9, 1778, #698, p. 4, col. 1. (DLC 18)
       "GIVE ear to my song, I'll not tell you a story,"
       The Halcyon Days of Old England; Or, The Wisdom of
         Administration demonstrated: A BALLAD.
       .....
       "Ye Medley of Mortals."
       London Evening Post.

56.   June 23, 1778, #700, p. 4, col. 1. (DLC 18)
       "WHEN valor directed by motives sincere"
       The TRUE SOLDIER. A New Song.
       .....
       "Black Sloven."
       .....

57.   Aug. 18, 1778, #708, p. 4, col. 1. (DLC Microfilm #997)
       "WHEN Satan first from Heaven's bright region fell"
       To Governor Johnstone, one of the British Commissioners,
         on his late letters and offers to bribe certain eminent
         characters in America, and threatening afterwards to
         appeal to the public.
       COMMON SENSE.
       .....
       PHILADELPHIA, July 27, 1778.

58.   Dec. 1, 1778, #723, p. 1, col. 1. (DLC 18)
       "THE rain pours down--the city looks forlorn,"
       To The KING of ENGLAND.--Wed., Nov. 11, 1778.
       COMMON SENSE.
       .....
       PHILADELPHIA.

59.   Jan. 19, 1779, #730, p. 4, col. 1. (DLC 19)
       "SHINE Phoebus, shine, to cheer the land,"
       NEWYEAR's-DAY, 1779.
       .....
       .....
       .....

60.   July 27, 1779, #757, p. 2, cols. 1-2. (DLC 19)
       "BY Collier George, Sir Commodore,"
       .....
       [An obstinate, unpardonable rebel. July 24, 1779.]
       .....
       .....

Connecticut, Hartford; Connecticut Courant, 1764-1820+

61.   Dec. 25, 1781, #883, p. 4, col. 1.   (DLC 21)
      "WHEN British troops first landed here,"
      CORNWALLIS Burgoyn'd.   A SONG.
      .....
      "Maggie Lauder."
      .....

62.   Jan. 8, 1782, #885, p. 4, col. 1.   (DLC 22)
      "CORNWALLIS led a country dance,"
      The DANCE
      .....
      "Yankey Doodle."
      .....

63.   Feb. 12, 1782, #890, p. 3, col. 2.   (DLC 22)
      "PRINCE William of the Brunswick race"
      The ROYAL ADVENTURER.
      .....
      .....
      .....

64.   Feb. 26, 1782, #892, p. 4, col. 1.   (DLC 22)
      AMIDST Belona's dire alarms,"
      SEASONABLE THOUGHTS.
      .....
      .....
      .....

65.   March 5, 1782, #893, p. 2, col. 2.   (DLC 22)
      "MY lords, I can hardly from weeping refrain,"
      [A SPEECH that should have been spoken by the king of the
        island of Britain to his parliament.]
      .....
      .....
      .....

66.   Sept. 17, 1782, #921, p. 4, col. 1.   (DLC 22)
      "THAT your honours petitioner's, tories by trade,"
      The REFUGEES PETITION to Sir Guy Carleton, [and] SIR
        GUY's ANSWER.
      .....
      .....
      .....

Connecticut, Hartford; Connecticut Courant, 1764-1820+

67. Dec. 30, 1783, #988, p. 4, col. 1.   (DLC Microfilm #997)
     "THE third and general State Convention,"
     .....
     .....
     .....
     MIDDLETOWN, December, 1783.

Connecticut, Hartford
The Freeman's Chronicle: or, the American Advertiser,
1783-1784.

68. Sept. 1, 1783, #1, p. 4, col. 1. (DLC Box 1, #11)
     "WELCOME! thrice welcome, to a rescu'd land,"
     To the AMERICAN ARMY.
     . . . . .
     . . . . .
     . . . . .

69. Sept. 8, 1783, #2, p. 4, cols. 1-2. (DLC Box 1, #11)
     "IN former days--no matter when--"
     The Lion, the Mastives and other Beasts. A FABLE.
     . . . . .
     . . . . .
     . . . . .

70. Sept. 15, 1783, #3, p. 4, col. 1. (DLC Box 1, #11)
     "OF all the leaders in the state"
     A SONG. On the wise Coalition compleated the 1st of
        April, 1783.
     . . . . .
     Nancy Dawson.
     . . . . .

71. Oct. 20, 1783, #8, p. 4, col. 1. (DLC Box 1, #11)
     "MONARCHS, 'tis true, should calm the storms of war,"
     THOUGHTS on PEACE.
     . . . . .
     . . . . .
     . . . . .

72. July 30, 1773, #302, p. 1, cols. 1-2. (DLC Box 2, #8)
     [Dear Sir,] "I Have your letter, shewing"
     .....
     .....
     .....
     The CORRESPONDENT, No. XXXIII. [May, 1773.]

73. Jan. 21, 1778, #536, p. 4, col. 1. (DLC 55)
     "Genius of Freedom! whether (sic) art thou fled?"
     .....
     .....
     .....
     YORK-TOWN, December 20.

74. April 21, 1778, #549, p. 4, col. 1. (DLC 55)
     "LET Rome, the glories of her Pompey tell,"
     A short PANEGYRIC, on his Excellency George Washington,
       Esq; Commander in Chief of the Army of the United States.
     .....
     .....
     .....

75. April 21, 1778, #549, p. 3, col. 3. (DLC 55)
     "'Tis Washington's Health--fill a Bumper all round,"
     The TOAST.
     .....
     ['Tis Washington's Health--fill a Bumper all round, Music
       by Francis Hopkinson]
     .....

76. May 6, 1778, #551, p. 3, col. 2. (DLC 55)
     "GREAT A, stands for Asses in Administration,"
     The Political A.B.C.
     .....
     .....
     .....

77. Aug.27, 1773, #511, p. 2, col. 2. (RMEAN, Card #33)
     "Who has e'er been at Versailles must needs know the King;"
     MUSICAL INTELLIGENCE EXTRAORDINARY. (Song in Praise of
        the King of France)
     .....
     Who has e'er been at Baldock must needs know the Mill
     .....

78. Aug. 27, 1773, #511, p. 2, col. 2. (RMEAN, Card #33)
     "Hanover, thou Land of Pleasure,"
     MUSICAL INTELLIGENCE EXTRAORDINARY. (AIR in PRAISE of
        HANOVER)
     .....
     AIR in PRAISE of HANOVER
     .....

79. Aug. 27, 1773, #511, p. 2, col. 2. (RMEAN, Card #33)
     "Then here's to thee, my boy Jack,"
     MUSICAL INTELLIGENCE EXTRAORDINARY. (grand Chorus)
     .....
     .....
     .....

80. Sept. 3, 1773, #512, p. 4, col. 1. (RMEAN, Card #33)
     "GENTEEL is my Damon, engaging his air,"
     .....
     Said to be by present Q[uee]n of Great Britain.
     [Genteel Damon]
     .....

81. Feb. 4, 1774, #534, p. 2, col. 1-2. (RMEAN, Card #35)
     "As near bounteous Boston lying"
     A NEW SONG
     BRITTANNO-AMERICANUS.
     Hosier's Ghost
     Pennsylvania Packet, Jan. 3, 1774.

82. Feb. 11, 1774, #535, p. 2, col. 3. (RMEAN, Card #35)
     "E'ER since the day that Adam fell,"
     .....
     JOE IRONY
     .....
     Massachusetts Spy.

Connecticut, New London; Connecticut Gazette, 1763-1820+

83. April 8, 1774, #543, p. 4, col. 1. (RMEAN, Card #35)
     "JUBA! a Name that carries in the Sound"
     In Answer to Juba's Rules for the LADIES of Connecticut.
        (See Gazette No. 524.)
     MARCIA
     .....
     .....

84. April 22, 1774, #545, p. 4, col. 1. (RMEAN, Card #36)
     "WHAT mortal but slandor, that serpent hath stung,"
     A Picture of Slander.
     .....
     .....
     .....

85. May 6, 1774, #547, p. 4, col. 1. (RMEAN, Card #36)
     "PERMIT a giddy trifling girl,"
     .....
     .....
     .....
     Massachusetts Spy.

86. May 13, 1774, #548, p. 4, col. 1. (RMEAN, Card #36)
     "OH despicable state of all that groan"
     .....
     .....
     .....
     .....

87. June 3, 1774, #551, p. 4, col. 1. (RMEAN, Card #36)
     "FREEDOM's Charms alike engage"
     A Favourite AIR.
     .....
     .....
     .....

88. July 15, 1774, #557, p. 4, col. 1. (RMEAN, Card #37)
     "ATTEND, ye Sons of Freedom, to the call,"
     On WILLIAM HORNBY's putting up the Sign of Dr. Franklin...
     .....
     .....
     Pennsylvania Journal.

89.   Aug. 19, 1774, #562, p. 4, col. 1.   (RMEAN, Card #37)
      "HAIL LIBERTY! A glorious word,"
      .....
      .....
      .....
      .....

90.   Aug. 26, 1774, #563, p. 4, col. 1.   (RMEAN, Card #37)
      "We men of coventry"
      The address of the Mayor and Corporation of Coventry, to
        Queen Elizabeth, on her paying them a visit.
      Z.
      .....
      Pennsylvania Packet.

91.   Sept. 9, 1774, #565, p. 2, col. 3.   (RMEAN, Card #37)
      "YOUR Colonel Hancock by neglect,"
      A General Sample of Gubernatorial Eloquence, as lately
        exhibited to the Company of Cad[et]s
      .....
      .....
      .....

92.   Sept. 23, 1774, #567, p. 4, col. 1.   (RMEAN, Card #37)
      "AMERICA! Thou fractious nation,"
      A PROCLAMATION.
      .....
      .....
      Virginia Gazette

93.   Sept. 30, 1774, #568, p. 4, col. 1.   (RMEAN, Card #37)
      "JUST is the Strife, in thy devoted Land"
      A THOUGHT on the present state of AMERICA.
      A Friend to LIBERTY, Aug. 24, 1774.
      .....
      .....

94.   Oct. 14, 1774, #570, p. 4, col. 1.   (RMEAN, Card #37)
      "FAREWELL the Tea-board with your gaudy attire,"
      A Lady's adieu to her Tea-Table.
      .....
      .....
      .....

Connecticut, New London; Connecticut Gazette, 1763-1820+

95. Nov. 4, 1774, #573, p. 4, col. 1. (RMEAN, Card #38)
     "O My baby, my baby,"
     A NEW SONG, Supposed to have been sung by Goody N[ort]h,
        by way of lullaby to the foundling brat, the Popish
        Quebec Bill.
     .....
     "O my kitten, my kitten."
     St. James's Chronicle.

96. Nov. 11, 1774, #574, p. 4, col. 1. (RMEAN, Card #38)
     "WHEN true religion supercedes grimace,"
     The Golden AGE Conditional.
     .....
     .....
     .....

97. Nov. 25, 1774, #576, p. 4, col. 1. (RMEAN, Card #38)
     "WHEN Britons first, by Heaven's command,"
     AN AMERICAN PARODY.
     .....
     "Rule Britannia"
     .....

98. Dec. 16, 1774, #579, p. 4, col. 1. (RMEAN, Card #38)
     "BRAVE race of men, who boldly shew's"
     On the Province of Massachusetts-Bay.
     .....
     .....
     .....

99. Dec. 23, 1774, #580, p. 4, col. 1. (DLC Box 3, #3)
     "WHEN tyrants o'er the continent were spread,"
     .....
     .....
     .....
     .....

100. Jan. 6, 1775, #582, p. 4, col. 1. (RMEAN, Card #38)
     "WHEN mighty Roast Beef was the Englishman's Food,"
     The Roast Beef of OLD-ENGLAND.
     .....
     [The Roast Beef of Old-England]
     .....

Connecticut, New London; Connecticut Gazette, 1763-1820+

101.   Jan. 20, 1775, #584, p. 4, col. 1.   (RMEAN, Card #38)
       "IN George the second's golden days,"
       The following parody on the Ballad of the Vicar of Bray.
       .....
       Vicar of Bray
       Massachusetts Spy.

102.   Jan. 27, 1775, #585, p. 4, col. 1.   (RMEAN, Card # 39)
       "LET others strive by servile arts to gain,"
       To GENERAL L----
       AMERICA
       .....
       New-York Journal

103.   Feb. 10, 1775, #587, p. 4, col. 1.   (RMEAN, Card #39)
       "BY art and surprize, my Lord swears he'll succeed,"
       .....
       Z.
       .....
       London Morning Chronicle.

104.   Feb. 24, 1775, #589, p. 4, col. 1.   (RMEAN, Card #39)
       "LET's look to Greece and Athens!"
       A New SONG.
       .....
       [British Grenadiers]
       .....

105.   March 3, 1775, #590, p. 4, col. 1.   (DLC Box 3, #3)
       "LOST is our old simplicity of times,"
       On the proceedings against America.
       .....
       .....
       London Magazine.

106.   March 17, 1775, #592, p. 4, col. 1.   (DLC Box 3, #3)
       "BRITONS, if you pant for glory,"
       ODE to INDEPENDENCE.
       .....
       .....
       From a London Magazine for Oct. 1774.

Connecticut, New London; Connecticut Gazette, 1763-1820+

107. April 14, 1775, #596, p. 4, col. 1. (DLC Box 3, #3)
      "SHall George our King, misled by wicked Knaves,"
      .....
      TOM WISHWELL.
      .....
      .....

108. May 5, 1775, #599, p. 4, col. 1. (RMEAN, Card #39)
      "ATTEND--these lines my loyal wish declare,"
      A LOYAL WISH.
      .....
      .....
      .....

109. May 12, 1775, #600, p. 4, col. 1. (RMEAN, Card #40)
      "WHEN party-spirit prevail'd a pace,"
      A FABLE.
      .....
      .....
      Massachusetts Spy, March 17.

110. May 19, 1775, #601, p. 4, col. 1. (RMEAN, Card #40)
      A while, fond Damon, prithee tarry,"
      .....
      [Female Reader]
      .....
      .....

111. May 26, 1775, #602, p. 4, col. 1. (DLC Box 3, #3)
      "HARK! 'tis FREEDOM that calls, come Patriots awake!"
      A SONG.
      .....
      "The ecchoing (sic) Horn"
      The Cambridge News-Paper.

112. June 9, 1775, #604, p. 4, col. 1. (DLC Box 3, #3)
      "ROUSE, rouse brave North America,"
      .....
      W---, May 27, 1775.
      .....
      .....

Connecticut, New London; Connecticut Gazette, 1763-1820+

113.   June 16, 1775, #605, p. 4, col. 1. (DLC Box 3, #3)
        "HAIL America, Hail! Still unrival'd in Fame,"
        A NEW SONG.
        . . . . .
        Hail Albion, fam'd Albion, &c.
        New-York.

114.   June 23, 1775, #606, p. 4, col. 1. (DLC Box 3, #3)
        "HAPPY's the man, who unconstrain'd"
        An ODE on LIBERTY.
        . . . . .
        . . . . .
        . . . . .

115.   June 30, 1775, #607, p. 4, col. 1. (RMEAN, Card #40)
        "BY my faith but I think ye're all makers of bulls,"
        The IRISHMAN's EPISTLE to the Officers and Troops of
            Boston.
        PADDY.
        . . . . .
        Pennsylvania Magazine, for May 1775.

116.   July 7, 1775, #608, p. 4, col. 1. (RMEAN, Card #40)
        "MEN of every size and station,"
        LIBERTY.
        . . . . .
        . . . . .
        From a Pennsylvania Paper.

117.   July 7, 1775, #608, p. 4, col. 1. (RMEAN, Card #40)
        "BROTHER Soldiers, all fight on,"
        The CHRISTIAN SOLDIER.
        . . . . .
        . . . . .
        . . . . .

118.   July 21, 1775, #610, p. 4, col. 1. (DLC Box 3, #3)
        "WHEREAS the Rebels here about,"
        Tom Gage's PROCLAMATION
        Tom Gage?
        . . . . .
        . . . . .

22

Connecticut, New London; Connecticut Gazette, 1763-1820+

119.   July 28, 1775, #611, p. 4, col. 1.   (RMEAN, Card #40)
        "AT length the Action is commenc'd,"
        .....
        [Diana]
        .....
        .....

120.   Dec. 22, 1775, #632, p. 1, col. 3.   (DLC Box 3, #3)
        "THO' some folks may tell us, it is not so clever"
        A SONG.
        A Soldier in the Continental Army
        The Black Sloven
        .....

121.   Dec. 29, 1775, #633, p. 3, cols. 2-3.   (DLC Box 3, #3)
        "AH me! what means my rising Soul!"
        On hearing Miss ----- sing.
        PHILO-MUSICUS.
        .....
        .....

122.   Feb. 2, 1776, #638, p. 4, col. 1.   (DLC Box 3, #4)
        "WHY should vain Mortals tremble at the sight of"
        The American HERO--A Saphic Ode.
        .....
        [Bunker-hill, Music by Andrew Law]
        .....

123.   Feb. 23, 1776, #641, p. 3, col. 2-3.   (RMEAN, Card #43)
        "SMILE, Massachusetts Smile,"
        .....
        ....., Sept. 21, 1773.
        "Smile Britannia, &."
        .....

124.   April 5, 1776, #647, p. 4, col. 1.   (RMEAN, Card #43)
        "I Claim no likeness to your motley songs,"
        THE ENVIOUS POET.
        .....
        .....
        .....

Connecticut, New London; Connecticut Gazette, 1763-1820+

125.   April 19, 1776, #649, p. 4, col. 1.   (RMEAN, Card #43)
        "THE watry God, great Neptune, lay"
        The watry God. A new SONG.
        .....
        The Watry God.
        .....

126.   June 28, 1776, #659, p. 4, col. 1.   (RMEAN, Card #44)
        "FROM North, tho' stormy winds may blow"
        .....
        .....
        .....
        .....

127.   Sept. 13, 1776, #670, p. 4, col. 1.   (RMEAN, Card #45)
        "SCOTCH Machiavel, in Tory spleen grown old,"
        A BON MOT of Dr. Price versified,....
        .....
        .....
        London Evening Post

128.   June 6, 1777, #708, p. 1, cols. 1-2.   (DLC #82)
        "WITHOUT wit, without wisdom, half stupid and drunk,"
        The EXPEDITION to DANBURY, under the Command of General
          TRYON, to destroy the stores of Beef, Pork & Rum.
        COMUS.
        .....
        Pennsylvania Gazette.

129.   July 18, 1777, #714, p. 4, col. 1.   (DLC #82)
        "COME my boys, let us sing"
        .....
        .....
        .....
        London Evening Post, March 20.

130.   Nov. 7, 1777, #730, p. 1, col. 2.   (RMEAN, Card #48)
        "NINE Thousand better Troops this War,"
        On a late secret EXPEDITION.
        .....
        .....
        .....

Connecticut, New London; Connecticut Gazette, 1763-1820+

131. June 12, 1778, #761, p. 2, col. 3.   (RMEAN, Card #50)
     "ONCE more our Rulers call a Fast,"
     .....
     Bishop Sternford, Feb. 7.
     .....
     LONDON EVENING POST.

132. July 3, 1778, #764, p. 3, cols. 2-3.   (DLC Box 3, #5)
     "HAIL joyful Day! which on our western Earth,"
     A short Reflection on the Anniversary of American Indepen-
        dency, July 4th, 1778.
     A NOVA-SCOTIA REFUGEE.
     .....
     Norwich, June 24th, 1778.

133. June 17, 1779, #814, p. 4, cols. 1-2.   (RMEAN, Card #53)
     "SEVEN marks the trifle of the rising States,"
     .....
     AN OBSERVER.
     .....
     Thomas's Massachusetts Spy.

134. Dec. 5, 1780, #891, p. 2, col. 3.   (RMEAN, Card #57)
     "TWAS Arnold's post, Sir Henry sought,"
     .....
     .....
     .....
     Pennsylvania Packet.

135. Jan. 4, 1782, #947, p. 1, cols. 1-2.   (RMEAN, Card #61)
     "'TWAS for the conquest nobly won,"
     An ODE. An humble Imitation of Dryden's Alexander's Feast.
     A SOUTHERN EXILE.
     .....
     Pennsylvania Packet.

136. March 15, 1782, #957, p. 4, col. 1.   (RMEAN, Card #61)
     "MY lords, I can hardly from weeping refrain,"
     A SPEECH that should have been spoken by the king of the
        Island of Britain to his ----(?) (Parliament?)
     .....
     .....
     .....

137. March 29, 1782, #959, p. 4, col. 1. (RMEAN, Card #61)
      "THERE was--and a very great fool,"
      A Merry SONG about MURDER, Published in London for the
         Anniversary of the GENERAL FAST (?) the 21st (?) of
         February, 1781, and hawk'd about the Streets by the
         Ballad-Singers.
      .....
      .....
      London.

138. May 17, 1782, #966, p. 4, col. 1. (RMEAN, Card #62)
      "LET those who will be proud and sneer,"
      A DIALOGUE at Hyde-Park Corner. [between Burgoyne and
         Cornwallis]
      .....
      .....
      .....

139. July 5, 1782, #973, p. 4, col. 1. (RMEAN, Card #62)
      "YE sons of Mars, attend,"
      A NEW SONG Written on the Celebration of the Birth of the
         Dauphin, at West-Point.
      .....
      [Restoration March]
      .....

140. Aug. 9, 1782, #978, p. 4, col. 2-3. (RMEAN, Card #63)
      "WHILE we are fighting our malicious foe,"
      Reflections on the illicit Trade
      PHILANTHROPOS
      .....
      .....

141. Oct. 11, 1782, #987, p. 4, col. 1. (DLC Box 3, folder 7)
      "I Sing of George's golden days,"
      WHO's the NOODLE. A NEW SONG.
      .....
      Qd's Blood Who's the NOODLE.
      London Advertiser.

Connecticut, New London; Connecticut Gazette, 1763-1820+

142. Jan. 24, 1783, #1002, p. 2, col. 3, p. 3, col. 1.
        (RMEAN, Card #64)
      "THE rising Sun his Race begun,"
      AN ODE. A friendly Wish for a happy New-Year, Jan. 1, 1783.
      . . . . .
      . . . . .
      . . . . .

143. May 30, 1783, #1020, p. 3, col. 1. (RMEAN, Card #65)
      "LONG has Columbia's crimson'd shore,"
      AN ODE FOR WASHINGTON.
      Young LADY
      . . . . .
      . . . . .

144. [June 6, 1783, #1021], p. 3, col. 1. (DLC Box 3, folder 8)
      ["Dearly beloved brethren"]/JOYFUL days at length have
        come!"
      . . . . .
      . . . . .
      . . . . .
      Maryland Gazette.

145. July 25, 1783, #1028, p. 4, col. 1. (RMEAN, Card #66)
      "THE Lord of Glory Reigns,"
      An HYMN of Praise to God, for the Freedom of the
        American States from British Tyranny
      . . . . .
      WORCESTER
      . . . . .

146. Dec. 12, 1783, #1048, p. 2, col. 3. (RMEAN, Card #67)
      "THEY come! they come! the Heroes come!"
      ODE, On the arrival of their Excellencies General
        Washington and Governor Clinton in New-York.
      . . . . . , Nov. 25, 1783.
      "He comes! He comes!"
      . . . . .

The Norwich Packet and the Connecticut, Massachusetts,
New Hampshire & Rhode Island Weekly Advertiser, 1773-1802

147. Dec. 2, 1773, #9, p. 3, col. 2.   (RMEAN, Card #1)
     "FREEDOM, Freedom, aloudly cries,"
     .....
     A Customer.
     .....
     .....

148. Feb. 24, 1774, #21, p. 3, col. 2.   (RMEAN, Card #2)
     "WHAT mortal but Slander, that serpent, hath stung,"
     A PICTURE of SLANDER.
     Rev. James de la Cour, D.D.
     .....
     .....

149. May 26, 1774, #34, p. 4, col. 1.   (RMEAN, Card #3)
     "WHILE fawning Sycophants the Nine implore,"
     To the glorious Defenders of LIBERTY.
     .....
     .....
     .....

150. May 26, 1774, #34, p. 14, col. 1.   (RMEAN, Card #3)
     "A Bag-wig of a jauntee air,"
     The BAG-WIG and the TOBACCO-PIPE.   A FABLE.
     .....
     .....
     .....

151. July 28, 1774, #43, p. 4, col. 1.   (DLC Box 3, folder 26)
     "NATIONS unborn shall curse the men who first"
     The Unnatural PARENT.
     .....
     .....
     .....

152. Aug. 4, 1774, #44, p. 4, col. 1.   (DLC Box 3, folder 26)
     "PEACE to thy royal shade, illustrious [KING]!"
     An ELEGY to the Memory of the late [KING].
     .....
     .....
     LONDON MERCURY.

153. Aug. 18, 1774, #46, p. 4, col. 1. (RMEAN, Card 4)
      "HAIL LIBERTY! A glorious word,"
      .....
      .....
      .....
      .....

154. Aug. 25, 1774, #47, p. 4, col. 1. (RMEAN, Card #4)
      "YE Princes of the earth, ye mighty few,"
      ON TYRANNICAL GOVERNMENT.
      .....
      .....
      .....

155. Oct. 20, 1774, #55, p. 4, col. 1. (RMEAN, Card #4)
      "GOD prosper long our liberty,"
      A PARODY on the SONG of CHEVY CHACE.
      .....
      Chevy Chace
      From the London Evening Post.

156. Nov. 3, 1774, #57, p. 4, col. 1 (RMEAN, Card #4)
      "WHEN Britons first, By Heaven's Command,"
      An AMERICAN PARODY on the Old Song of "RULE BRITANNIA."
      .....
      Rule Britannia
      .....

157. Nov. 10, 1774, #58, p. 4, cols. 2-3. (RMEAN, Card #4)
      "ADIEU, adieu, to SANS SOUCIE,"
      .....
      Lisbon, 10th March, 1789 (sic).
      .....
      .....

158. Dec. 1, 1774, #61, p. 4, col. 1. (RMEAN, Card #4A)
      "ATTEND your country's call, ye lovely fair,"
      To the WOMEN of AMERICA.
      .....
      .....
      .....

159. Dec. 22, 1774, #64, p. 4, col. 1. (RMEAN, Card #4A)
      "THE expences of war, and corruptions of peace,"
      SONG
      ....
      Derry Down
      From a late London Paper.

160. Dec. 29, 1774, #65, p. 3, col. 2. (RMEAN, Card #4A)
      "YE Ministers who every Hour,"
      ....
      ....
      ....
      From the NORTH BRITON (?)

161. Jan. 26, 1775, #69, p. 4, col. 1. (RMEAN, Card #4A)
      "WHY do we fast and hang the Head,"
      Paraphrase of 58th Chap. Isaiah, Verses 3-9.
      P.Z., Norwich, January 25, 1775.
      ....
      ....

162. Feb. 9, 1775, #71, p. 4, col. 1. (RMEAN, Card #4A)
      "BY art and surprize, my Lord swears he'll succeed,"
      ....
      ....
      ....
      From the London Morning Chronicle.

163. Feb. 23, 1775, #73, p. 4, col. 1. (RMEAN, Card #5)
      "WHAT is the cause of all the woes,"
      ....
      ....., Colchester, February 10, 1775.
      ....
      ....

164. Feb. 23, 1775, #73, p. 4, col. 1-2. (RMEAN, Card #5)
      "O MY baby, my baby,"
      A NEW SONG...Supposed to have been sung by Goody
        N[ort]h, by way of Lulla-by, to the foundling Popish
        Quebec Bill.
      ....
      O my Kitten, my Kitten.
      ....

165. March 2, 1775, #74, p. 4, col. 1. (RMEAN, Card #5)
     "LOST is our old simplicity of times,"
     On the Proceedings against America,
     .....
     .....
     From a late London Magazine.

166. March 9, 1775, #75, p. 4, col. 1. (mutilated.) (RMEAN,
       Card #5)
     "THERE is a nation on the earth,"
     .....
     A COUNTRYMAN
     .....
     From the Boston Evening Post.

167. March 30, 1775, #78, p. 4, col. 1. (RMEAN, Card #5)
     "What....(?) spring, or the sweet smelling rose?"
     On the LIBERTIES of the NATION.
     Ejus Sidney
     .....
     .....

168. April 20, 1775, #81, p. 4, col. 1. (RMEAN, Card #5)
     "FROM orchards of ample extent,"
     PAMONA: A Pastoral.
     .....
     .....
     .....

169. May 4, 1775, #83, p. 4, col. 1. (RMEAN, Card #5)
     "B[ute]! M[ansfield]! N[orth]! need I point out the men,"
     On the Infamous Triumvirate from whence our National
       Apprehensions arise.
     An Englishman.
     .....
     From the MIDDLESEX JOURNAL.

170. May 25, 1775, #86, p. 4, col. 1. (RMEAN, Card #6)
     "Beside Euphrates awful flood,"
     An ODE, on the 137th Psalm.
     .....
     .....
     .....

171. June 1, 1775, #87, p. 4, col. 1. (RMEAN, Card #6)
      "'TIS money makes the member vote,"
      A JUNTO SONG.
      .....
      A begging we will go, we'll go, &c.
      .....

172. June 15, 1775, #89, p. 4, col. 1. (RMEAN, Card #6)
      "YE heirs of freedom! glorius is your cause,"
      To the AMERICANS.
      CATO, April 18, 1775
      .....
      .....

173. June 26, 1775, #91, p. 4, col. 1. (RMEAN, Card #6)
      "COME listen my cocks, to a brother and friend,"
      The SAILOR's ADDRESS.
      .....
      [Hearts of Oak]
      A London Paper.

174. Aug. 28, 1775, #100, p. 4, col. 1. (RMEAN, Card #6)
      "AT length the Action is commenc'd,"
      .....
      .....
      .....
      .....

175. Oct. 30, 1775, #109, p. 4, col. 1. (RMEAN, Card #7)
      "TO him, on whom each future joy depends,"
      An EPISTLE from a Lady to her Husband, who embarked at
          Plymouth, on the American Expedition.
      .....
      .....
      .....

176. Jan. 22, 1776, #121, p. 4, col. 1. (RMEAN, Card #8)
      "AH! yet shall we wish horror hear,"
      An ODE for the NEW-YEAR.
      .....
      .....
      .....

177. July 15, 1776, #146, p. 4, col. 1.   (RMEAN, Card #10)
     "THE World's turn'd up side down throughout the Nation,"
     A PROLOGUE.
     .....
     .....
     .....

178. Aug. 19, 1776, #151, p. 4, col. 1.   (RMEAN, Card 11)
     "GREAT ruler of the earth and skies,"
     HYMN for National PEACE.
     .....
     .....
     .....

179. Sept. 9, 1776, #154, p. 4, col. 1.   (RMEAN, Card #11)
     "AUSPICIOUS hour! again the fav'ring muse"
     .....
     .....
     .....
     .....

180. Sept. 16, 1776, #155, p. 4, col. 1.   (RMEAN, Card #11)
     "COME all you brave soldiers, both valient and free,"
     ON INDEPENDENCE.
     .....
     .....
     .....

181. Oct. 7, 1776, #158, p. 4, col. 1.   (RMEAN, Card 11)
     "WHILE tyrants lift their impious hands,"
     An ODE. Suitable to the Times.
     .....
     .....
     .....

182. Oct. 14, 1776, #159, p. 4, col. 1.   (RMEAN, Card #11)
     "IF two of the same trade,"
     PEN, INK, and PAPER. A Fable.
     .....
     .....
     .....

183. Oct. 28, 1776, #161, p. 4, col. 1. (RMEAN, Card #12)
"WHY toils the world so eager after fame?"
The Vanity of Mortal Things.
......
......
......

184. Nov. 25, 1776, #165, p. 2, cols. 1-2. (RMEAN, Card #12)
"ALL hail G[e]rm[ai]ne, G[e]rm[ai]ne, all hail!"
ODE to Lord G[eorge] G[e]rm[ain]e
......
......
London

185. Nov. 25, 1776, #165, p. 4, col. 1. (RMEAN, Card #12)
"HAIL! O America!"
......
......
[God Save the King]
......

186. March 3, 1777, #179, p. 4, col. 1. (RMEAN, Card #13)
"MY Lords, with your leave,"
A NEW WAR SONG.
Sir Peter Parker
"Well met Brother Tar."
......

187. March 24, 1777, #182, p. 4, col. 1. (RMEAN, Card #13)
"BEHOLD the Man who had it in his Pow'r,"
IMPROMTO (sic) occasioned by seeing an inverted Picture
   of the British Tyrant.
......
......
......

188. March 31, 1777, #183, p. 4, col. 1. (RMEAN, Card #13)
"GALL'WAY has fled, and join'd the venal Howe,"
......
......
......
......

189. May 5(?), 1777, #188, p. 4, col. 1. (RMEAN, Card #14)
      "WHEN Heaven for hidden causes shakes the rod,"
      The TIMES. An ELEGY.
      .....
      .....
      .....

190. May 26, 1777, #191, p. 4, col. 1. (RMEAN, Card #14)
      "YE wrong heads, and strong heads, attend to my strains;"
      The HEADS, or the Year 1776.
      .....
      [Derry Down]
      London Public Ledger.

191. June 2, 1777, #192, p. 4, cols. 1-2. (RMEAN, Card #14)
      "WITHOUT wit, without wisdom, half stupid and drunk,"
      EXPEDITION to DANBURY, under the command of General
         TRYON, to destroy the stores of beef, pork and rum.
      COMUS, Philadelphia, May 12.
      .....
      .....

192. Dec. 15, 1777, #220, p. 1, cols. 1-2. (RMEAN, Card #16)
      "LET poets sing, in raptures high,"
      O TEMPORA! O MORES! CICERO.
      .....
      .....
      .....

193. Jan. 5, 1777 (sic for 1778), #223, p. 4, col. 1. (RMEAN,
         Card 16)
      "AS Mushrooms in a night are grown,"
      [Formose puer! nimium ne credo coleri.]
      .....
      .....
      .....

194. Jan. 5, 1777 (sic for 1778), #223, p. 4, col. 1. (RMEAN,
         Card 16)
      "IN nature's works, we here behold"
      .....
      A MECHANICK
      .....
      .....

195. March 23, 1778, #234, p. 1, cols. 1-2. (RMEAN, Card #17)
     "GALLANTS attend, and hear a friend,"
     British VALOUR displayed, in the BATTLE of the CAGS (sic).
     .....
     [Battle of the Kegs].
     .....

196. June 15, 1778, #246, p. 4, col. 1. (RMEAN, Card #18)
     "ONCE more our Rulers call a Fast,"
     .....
     .....
     .....
     London Evining (sic)-Post.

197. July 6, 1778, #249, p. 4, col. 1. (RMEAN, Card #18)
     "IN this, dear George, we both agree,"
     WASHING WEEK.
     .....
     .....
     .....

198. Aug. 17, 1778, #255, p. 4, col. 1. (RMEAN, Card #19)
     "WEST of th' old Atlantic, firm liberty stands?"
     THE GAMESTER. A new Song.
     .....
     A late worthy old lion, &.
     .....

199. Sept. 14, 1778, #259, p. 4, col. 1. (RMEAN, Card 19)(DLC Box
     "YE poor simple people, who foolishly think,"
     .....
     TOMAHAWK.
     A Cob'er there was, &.
     LONDON EVENING POST.

200. Dec. 14, 1778, #272, p. 4, col. 1. (RMEAN, Card #20)
     "'TIS Past:--ah! calm thy cares to rest!"
     The NEGRO's Dying Speech on his being executed for
        Rebellion in the island of Jamaica.
     .....
     .....
     .....

201.   Jan. 25, 1779, #279, p. 4, col. 1.   (RMEAN, Card #20)
        "YE Farmers all, with one accord,"
        The DEVIL and the FARMER.
        . . . . .
        . . . . .
        Independent Ledger.

202.   June 22, 1779, #298, p. 4, col. 1.   (RMEAN, Card #22)
        "SEVEN marks the crisis of the rising states,"
        . . . . .
        AN OBSERVER
        . . . . .
        . . . . .

203.   Aug. 10, 1779, #305, p. 4, col. 1.   (RMEAN, Card #23)
        "ENGLAND. I feel for what I'm sure you must,"
        A contrast between Sir William Howe and Sir Henry Clinton,
            dedicated to Lord North.
        . . . . .
        . . . . .
        New Jersey Journal.

204.   Aug. 24, 1779, #307, p. 4, col. 1.   (RMEAN, Card #23)
        "HARK! hear the trumpet's pleasing sound!"
        . . . . .
        . . . . .
        . . . . .
        Pennsylvania Gazette.

205.   Sept. 28, 1779, #312, p. 4, col. 2-3.   (RMEAN, Card #23)
        "JULY they say, the fifteenth day,"
        A NEW SONG.
        . . . . .
        "One night as Ned stept into bed,"
        . . . . .

206.   May 11, 1780, #345, p. 4, col. 1.   (RMEAN, Card #25)
        "I'm not high church nor low church, nor tory, nor whig,"
        . . . . .
        . . . . .
        [Derry Down]
        American Journal.

207. May 25, 1780, #347, p. 4, col. 1-2. (RMEAN, Card #25)
     "HENCE with the Lover who sighs o'er his wine,"
     THE VOLUNTEER BOYS.
     .....
     Let the Toast Pass.
     .....

208. June 1, 1780, #348, p. 4, col. 1. (RMEAN, Card #25)
     "THERE was, and a very great fool,"
     A merry Song about MURDER.
     .....
     .....
     Westminster Courant.

209. June 22, 1780, #351, p. 4, cols. 1-2. (RMEAN, Card #26)
     "ADIEU ye tow'ring spires, no more"
     ON A COUNTRY LIFE.
     .....
     .....
     .....

210. Jan. 9, 1781, #379, p. 4, col. 1. (RMEAN, Card #28)
     "SINCE Heav'n has bless'd us with a soil,"
     A NEW SONG.
     An American Sailor, in a British Prison.
     Rule, Britannia! &.
     .....

211. Jan. 16, 1781, #380, p. 4, col. 1. (RMEAN, Card #28)
     "THOU who in glory's shining track,"
     To General WASHINGTON, on the late Conspiracy.
     .....
     .....
     Virginia Gazette.

212. Nov. 29, 1781, #425, p. 4, cols. 1-2. (RMEAN, Card #31)
     "YE loyalists all, within the town,"
     A NEW-YORK ADDRESS. "To all honest hearts and sound
       bottoms."
     .....
     [Yankee-Doodle].
     .....

213. Dec. 20, 1781, #428, p. 3, col. 3. (RMEAN, Card #32)
"ON the day set apart to be cheerful and gay,"
[The Thanksgiving of 1781]
.....
"Who would have thought it?" Or, "The Thanksgiving of
1781."
.....

214. Jan. 3, 1782, #430, p. 3, cols. 2-3. (RMEAN, Card #32)
"HAIL, heav'n born muse! thy sire some godlike sage--"
[A Panegyric on the author of "The Thanksgiving of
1781."]
PHILOMEIDES.
All cry and no wool
.....

215. Feb. 28, 1782, #438, p. 4, cols. 1-2. (RMEAN, Card #32)
"ARISE! arise! your voices raise."
The TEMPLE of MINERVA. An Oratorial Entertainment.
[Francis Hopkinson]
[The Temple of Minerva; Francis Hopkinson, arr.]
Freeman's Journal.

216. May 23, 1782, #450, p. 4, cols. 1-2. (RMEAN, Card #33)
"O'ER the waste of waters cruising,"
.....
RUSTICUS, Dover, April 26, 1782.
The Tempest; or, Hosier's Ghost.
Freeman's Journal.

217. June 20, 1782, #454, p. 4, col. 1. (RMEAN, Card #33)
"WELCOME one Arnold to our shore,"
ODE addressed to General Arnold.
Lady Craven.
.....
A London Paper.

218. Sept. 26, 1782, #468, p. 3, col. 2. (RMEAN, Card #34)
"UNHAPPY day! it grieves me sore,"
.....
.....
.....
.....

219.   Dec. 18, 1783, #476, p. 4, col. 1.   (RMEAN, Card #35)
       ["A Soldier, a Soldier, a Soldier for me"]
       A Song
       .....
       .....
       .....

220.   Dec. 25, 1783, #477, p. 2, col. 3.   (RMEAN, Card #35)
       "AT this unwonted Hour, behold,"
       An ODE for Christmas Morn.
       .....
       .....
       .....

GEORGIA

Georgia, Savannah
Gazette of the State of Georgia, 1783-1788.

221.   March 6, 1783, #6, p. 4, col. 1.   (DLC #137)
        "The old Tory rout"
        .....
        .....
        .....
        Independent Gazetteer, or the Chronicle of Freedom,
          Philadelphia

222.   May 29, 1783, #18, p. 2, cols. 1-2.   (DLC Early State
          Records Supplement, Microfilm, 1551 GA.Na. Reel 13, Unit 1.)
        "TH' Assembly call'd the first of May,"
        REFLECTIONS.
        JAS. HERRIOT, Charlestown, 20th May, 1783.
        .....
        .....

223.   June 12, 1783, #20, p. 3, col. 2.   (DLC #137)
        "PEACE to thy royal shade, illustrious King!"
        ELEGY to the Memory of the late King.   Written in the
          Year 1775.
        A TRUE BRITON.
        .....
        .....

224.   Sept. 18, 1783, #34, p. 3, col. 2.   (DLC #137)
        ["Dearly beloved Brethren,]/"Joyful days at length have
          come!"
        .....
        .....
        .....
        Maryland Gazette.

225. April 6, 1774, #548, p. 4, col. 1. (DLC Early State
        Records Supplement, Microfilm 1551 Ga.Na. Reel 2,
        Unit 3)
     "PASS but a few short fleeting years,"
     ODE for the NEW YEAR, 1774.
     William Whitehead, Esq. Poet Laureat
     Set to music by Dr. Boyce, Master of the King's Band
        of Musicians-[Ode for the New Year, 1774]
     .....

226. Aug. 10, 1774, #566, p. 4, col. 2. (DLC Early State
        Records Supplement, Microfilm 1551 Ga.Na. Reel 2,
        Unit 3)
     "'Tis Strange how some mens tempers suit"
     .....
     .....
     .....
     .....

227. Aug. 24, 1774, #568, p. 2, col. 2, p. 3, col. 1. (DLC
        Early State Records Supplement, Microfilm 1551 Ga.
        Na. Reel 2, Unit 3)
     "HARK!----or does the Muse's ear"
     ODE for His MAJESTY's Birth-Day, June 4, 1774.
     William Whitehead, Esq. Poet Laureat.
     Set to Musick by Dr. Boyce-[Ode for his Majesty's
        Birthday, June 4, 1774]
     .....

228. Sept. 6, 1775, #622, p. 1, col. 2 & p. 2, col. 1. (DLC
        Early State Records Supplement, Microfilm 1551 Ga.Na.
        Reel 2, Unit 3)
     "YE Powers, who rule o'er States and Kings,"
     ODE for his Majesty's Birth-Day, 1775.
     .....
     [ODE for his Majesty's Birth-Day, 1775]
     .....

Georgia, Savannah
Royal Georgia Gazette, 1779-1782.

229.   Aug. 16, 1781, #129, p. 4, col. 3.   (DLC Early State
         Records Supplement, Microfilm 1551 Ga. Na., Reel 2,
         Unit 6)
       "STILL does the Rage of War prevail,"
       ODE for his MAJESTY's BIRTH-DAY, June 4, 1781.
       William Whitehead, Esq. Poet Laureat
       Set to Musick by Mr. Stanley, Master of the King's
         Band of Musicians.   [Ode for his Majesty's Birth-
         day, June 4, 1781]
       . . . . .

230.   Oct. 4, 1781, #136, p. 2, col. 3.   (DLC Early State
         Records Supplement, Microfilm 1551 Ga. Na. Reel 2,
         Unit 6)
       "COME join, my brave lads, come all from afar,"
       The VOLUNTEERS of AUGUSTA, A NEW SONG.
       . . . . .
       The Lilies of France.
       . . . . .

MARYLAND

231.   Jan. 28, 1773, #1429, p. 4, col. 1.   (DLC Microfilm 1181,
          1772-1782)
       "WHO has not heard, what few have seen"
       Ode to Sensibility. Address'd to Miss Lucy Clarius, a
          celebrated Toast.
       ["Joint Composition of three or four eminent Poets of
          this Province"]
       .....
       Printed in England.

232.   June 10, 1773, #1448, p. 4, col. 1.   (DLC Microfilm 1181,
          1772-1782)
       "THE pains you've been at and the things you have wrote,"
       A new Edition of a late Letter of Thanks to the First
          Citizen.
       Broomstick and Quoad.
       .....
       .....

233.   June 24, 1773, #1450, p. 4, cols. 1-3.   (DLC Microfilm
          1181, 1772-1782)
       "THAT I've 'merited well', no proof can require;"
       A new edition of the answer to the letter of thanks,
          address'd by the representatives of the city of
          Annapolis to the First Citizen, with notes.
       .....
       .....
       .....

234.   July 1, 1773, #1451, p. 5, col. 3.   (DLC Microfilm 1181
          1772-1782)
       "'TIS strange, in faith, 'tis passing strange,"
       On a Late DIVISION.
       EUGENIO
       .....
       .....

Maryland, Annapolis; Maryland Gazette, 1745-1820+.

235.   July 8, 1773, #1452, p. 4, col. 1. (DLC Microfilm
          1181, 1772-1782)
        "GREAT nature, Peale! that bade thy genius rise,"
        To Mr. Charles Peale, on his exquisite and celebrated
          picture of beauty, addressing itself to insensibility.
        CRITO
        .....
        .....

236.   Sept. 16, 1773, #1462, p. 4, col. 1. (DLC Microfilm
          1181, 1772-1782)
        "ALACK-a-day my muse has stray'd,"
        A PARAPHRASE of the Latin POEM in the week before last
          paper, attempted.
        .....
        The Archbishop of CANTERBURY.
        .....

237.   Nov. 18, 1773, #1471, p. 4, col. 1. (DLC Microfilm
          1181, 1772-1782)
        "WHY did I leave my cheerful home,"
        .....
        B.H., Frederick Town, November 3, 1773.
        .....
        .....

238.   Sept. 12, 1776, #1618, p. 3, col. 1. (DLC Microfilm
          1181, 1772-1782)
        "WHY throbs my heart? ah! -- whence that sigh!"
        On the death of Mr. WILLIAM STERET, who was killed in
          the engagement on Long-Island.
        .....
        .....
        .....

Maryland, Annapolis; Maryland Gazette, 1745-1820+.

239.   Oct. 24, 1776, #1624, p. 4, cols. 1-2.   (DLC Microfilm
            1181, 1772-1782)
        "AS round the globe I took my way,"
        The SONG of the MAN in the MOON.
        .....
        .....
        .....

240.   Jan. 28, 1780, #1725, p. 2, cols. 1-2.   (DLC Microfilm
            1181, 1772-1782)
        "WHERE flows the Severn, when her streams can flow,"
        A WINTER PASTORAL, Addressed to Mrs. LIVINGSTON.*
            *Lady of Walter Livingston, Esq; of the state of
            New-York.
        ....., Annapolis, January 21, 1780.
        .....
        .....

241.   Jan. 5, 1781, #1773, p. 2, col. 1.   (DLC Microfilm
            1181, 1772-1782)
        "ALL hail! Superior sex, exalted fair,"
        ["To those American LADIES, who have lately distinguished
            their patriotism..."]
        A SOLDIER
        .....
        .....

242.   June 14, 1781, #1796, p. 4, col. 1.   (DLC Microfilm
            1181, 1772-1782)
        [Ass:] "DEAR Ya, how nobly you and I,"
        A DIALOGUE. The Ass, the Yahoo, and Houyhnhnm.
        .....
        .....
        .....

243.   April 17, 1783, #1892, p. 4, col. 1.   (DLC Microfilm
            1181, 1780-1784)
        "CEASE that strepent trumpet's sound!--"
        ODE to PEACE.
        ....., Eastern Shore, Maryland, March 30, 1783.
        .....
        .....

48

Maryland, Annapolis; Maryland Gazette, 1745-1820+.

244.   April 17, 1783, #1892, p. 4, cols. 1-2. (DLC Microfilm
           1181, 1780-1784)
       ["Dearly beloved brethren"]/"JOYFUL days at length
           have come!"
       .....
       ...., April 10, 1783.
       .....
       .....

245.   April 24, 1783, #1893, p. 2, col. 1. (DLC Microfilm
           1181, 1780-1784)
       "Dearly beloved brethren, Let ye banjers play and
           bagpipes join"
       .....
       ...., April 17, 1783.
       .....
       .....

Maryland, Baltimore
Dunlap's Maryland Gazette; or The Baltimore General Advertiser,
1775-1778.

246. May 30, 1775, #5, p. 3, col. 3. (MdHi)
      "If he had lived in Ancient Pagan Days,"
      On seeing uncommon pains taken by Mr. Richard Carey, in
        forming the troops of Baltimore.
      ...., Baltimore, May 1st, 1775.
      .....
      .....

247. June 27, 1775, #9, p. 4, col. 1. (MdHi)
      "To you, Ye all inchanting Maids, belong,"
      To the LADIES.
      .....
      .....
      .....

248. June 27, 1775, #9, p. 4, col. 1. (MdHi)
      "Serene the Even, behold the PATRIOT TRAIN,"
      On seeing the BALTIMORE MILITIA reviewed.
      S.
      .....
      .....

249. Aug. 15, 1775, #16, p. 2, col. 2. (MdHi)
      "In a chariot of light from the regions of day,"
      LIBERTY TREE. A New Song.
      Atlanticus
      The Gods of the Greeks.
      .....

250. Oct. 17, 1775, #25, p. 4, col. 1. (MdHi)
      "Young Florimel, of gentle race,"
      LOVE and GLORY. A SONG. Written in better days, when
        Britain and her sons were happily and gloriously
        united against their ancient and natural enemies.
      .....
      [LOVE and GLORY.]
      .....

Maryland, Baltimore; Dunlap's Maryland Gazette; or The Baltimore
General Advertiser, 1775-1778.

251.   Oct. 17, 1775, #25, p. 4, col. 1.   (MdHi)
       "Oh despicable state of all that groan,"
       ON LIBERTY.
       .....
       .....
       .....

252.   Nov. 28, 1775, #31, p. 3, cols. 2-3.   (MdHi)
       "Shall venal chains th'aspiring soul detain?"
       AMBITION: an Elegy.
       M.
       .....
       .....

253.   Jan. 23, 1776, #39, p. 3, col. 1.   (MdHi)
       "Come join hand in hand, brave Americans all,"
       A SONG.
       .....
       Hearts of OAK.
       .....

254.   Feb. 13, 1776, #42, p. 4, col. 1.   (MdHi)
       "What mean those tears, that thus effusive flow,"
       [On Montgomery]
       .....
       .....
       .....

255.   April 9, 1776, #50, p. 3, col. 1.   (MdHi)
       "A Maid from affectation free,"
       On LIBERTY.
       S........ .
       .....
       .....

256.   April 30, 1776, #53, p. 3, cols. 1-2.   (MdHi)
       "Saint George for their Patron our ancestors chose,"
       A SONG.
       .....
       [Derry Down]
       .....

Maryland, Baltimore; Dunlap's Maryland Gazette; or The Baltimore
General Advertiser, 1775-1778.

257. Dec. 10, 1776, #85, p. 4, cols. 2-3. (MdHi)
      "Hark! The Goddess of fame,"
      An ODE addressed to the Freemen of America, and of
        PENNSYLVANIA in particular, on this dreadful crisis
        of affairs.
      . . . . .
      . . . . .
      . . . . .

258. March 4, 1777, #97, p. 4, col. 2. (MdHi)
      "My Lords, with your leave,"
      A New WAR SONG.
      Sir Peter Parker.
      "Well met, Brother Tar."
      Written and Printed in LONDON.

259. March 11, 1777, #98, p. 4, cols. 1-2. (MdHi)
      "How blest is he, who unconstrain'd,"
      THE SWEETS of LIBERTY. An ODE.
      P.
      [The Sweets of Liberty]
      . . . . .

260. April 29, 1777, #105, p. 4, col. 1. (MdHi)
      "The Morning air, my senses chear,"
      . . . . .
      W.C.D., Garrison Forest, April 24.
      . . . . .
      For the Maryland Gazette.

261. June 3, 1777, #110, p. 4, cols. 1-2. (MdHi)
      "Without wit, without wisdom, half stupid and drunk,"
      The EXPEDITION to Danbury...
      . . . . .
      . . . . .
      . . . . .

262. Nov. 4, 1777, #132, p. 2, cols. 2-3. (MdHi)
      "As Jack the King's Commander,"
      A NEW SONG.
      . . . . .
      [Lexington March]
      . . . . .

Maryland, Baltimore; Dunlap's Maryland Gazette; or The Baltimore
General Advertiser, 1775-1778.

263. Dec. 16, 1777, #138, p. 3, col. 4. (MdHi)
      "Tax'd as we are beyond our strength,"
      A certain Speech versified.
      . . . . .
      . . . . .
      (?) the London Public Advertiser, May 28.

264. Jan. 27, 1778, #144, p. 4, col. 1. (MdHi)
      "Hark! the drum beats To Arms -- to your girls laid
         adieu,"
      . . . . .
      Young Lady - PORTIA.
      . . . . .
      . . . . .

265. Feb. 17, 1778, #147, p. 4, col. 1. (MdHi)
      "Come, Youthful Muse, my breast inspire"
      HOPE. An ODE.
      H.
      . . . . .
      . . . . .

266. March 24, 1778, #152, p. 4, col. 1. (MdHi)
      "Gallants attend, and hear a friend"
      BRITISH VALOUR DISPLAYED: Or, the BATTLE of the KEGS.
      . . . . .
      [Battle of the Kegs].
      . . . . .

267.   June 13, 1783, #5, p. 4, col. 1.   (MdHi)
       "Let every age due honours pay,"
       The following VERSES.
       .....
       .....
       .....

268.   June 28, 1783, #7, p. 4, col. 1.   (DLC 227)
       "It must be so--farewel my native land!"
       The Tories Soliloquy.
       .....
       .....
       New-York Packet.

269.   July 4, 1783, #8, p. 4, col. 1.   (MdHi)
       "At length War's sanguine scenes are o'er,"
       On the PEACE: An ODE. Designed for Music.
       .....
       .....
       .....

270. May 10, 1775, #73, p. 3, col. 2. (MdHi)
      "Liberty! thou dearest child of Heaven,"
      An ADDRESS to LIBERTY.
      A VIRGINIAN.
      .....
      .....

271. May 17, 1775, #74, p. 3, col. 2. (MdHi)
      "Curs'd be the Wretch, that's bought and sold,"
      ON LIBERTY.
      A Marylander, Baltimore, May 17.
      [Curs'd be the Wretch, that's bought and sold]
      .....

272. July 26, 1775, #84, p. 3, col. 2. (MdHi)
      "What a court hath old ENGLAND of folly and sin,"
      FISH and TEA. A New SONG.
      .....
      [Derry Down]
      .....

273. Aug. 2, 1775, #85, p. 3, col. 2. (MdHi)
      "Americans be men, espouse the glorious cause,"
      ON LIBERTY.
      Corio Lanus.
      .....
      .....

274. Aug. 9, 1775, #86, p. 2, col. 1. (MdHi)
      "These mighty crimes will sure ere long provoke,"
      .....
      .....
      .....
      .....

275. Oct. 4, 1775, #94, p. 3, col. 2. (MdHi)
      "In a chariot of light from the regions of day,"
      LIBERTY TREE. A New Song.
      .....
      The Gods of the Greeks.
      .....

Maryland, Baltimore; Maryland Journal, and the Baltimore
Advertiser, 1773-1797

276. Nov. 1, 1775, #98, p. 1, col. 2. (MdHi)
      "In story, we're told,/That heroes of old,"
      .....
      .".....
      ["In story we're told how our Monarchs of old"]
      .....

277. Nov. 1, 1775, #98, p. 4, col. 1. (MdHi)
      "A kingdom that's fam'd for politeness and dress,"
      A REBUS.
      .....
      .....
      .....

278. Jan. 3, 1776, #107, p. 4, col. 1. (MdHi)
      "Whom should we fear, since God to us"
      .....
      .....
      .....
      .....

279. Jan. 24, 1776, #110, p. 3, col. 3. (MdHi)
      "Parent of all, Omnipotent"
      The Patriot's PRAYER.
      .....
      .....
      .....

280. Jan. 24, 1776, #110, p. 3, col. 3. (MdHi)
      "Freedom's charms alike engage,"
      On Freedom.
      .....
      .....
      .....

281. May 15, 1776, #126, p. 4, col. 1. (MdHi)
      "To years far distant, and to scenes more bright,"
      A Prophecy of the future GLORY of AMERICA.
      .....
      .....
      .....

Maryland, Baltimore; Maryland Journal, and the Baltimore
Advertiser, 1773-1797

282.   Aug. 21, 1776, #140, p. 3, col. 2. (MdHi)
       "Happy's the man who unconstrain'd,"
       Ode on LIBERTY.
       .....
       .....
       .....

283.   Jan. 21, 1777, #166, p. 2, col. 1-2. (MdHi)
       "My Lords, with your leave,"
       A New WAR SONG.
       Sir Peter Parker.
       "Well met, Brother Tar."
       .....

284.   Feb. 4, 1777, #169, p. 4, col. 1. (DLC 235)
       "WHEREAS our former declarations,"
       A PROCLAMATION, at the point of the sword,....
       .....
       .....
       Continental Journal, (printed at Boston) Jan. 2, 1777.

285.   Nov. 18, 1777, #211, p. 2, col. 3 and p. 3, col. 1. (DLC
          235)
       "WITH hearts, at York, as light as cork,"
       A SONG. On the Grand AMERICAN EXPEDITION, in the Year 1777.
       .....
       Kitty Fell.
       .....

286.   Dec. 9, 1777, #214, p. 4, col. 1. (DLC 235)
       "WHILST the saucy Buckskins bluster,"
       A NEW SONG.
       .....
       .....
       .....

287.   March 17, 1778, #228, p. 3, col. 1. (MdHi)
       "Here's a health to the States,"
       Toast given EXTEMPORE.
       A gentleman.
       .....
       .....
       .....

Maryland, Baltimore; Maryland Journal, and the Baltimore
Advertiser, 1773-1797

288.   May 12, 1778, #236, p. 2, col. 3. (MdHi)
       "God save America,"
       Song composed extempore on receiving the Treaties from
         France.
       . . . . .
       [God save the King]
       . . . . .

289.   June 16, 1778, #242, p. 3, col. 2. (DLC 236)
       "A WAR broke out in former days"
       The BIRDS, the BEASTS, and the BAT. A FABLE.
       . . . . .
       . . . . .
       . . . . .

290.   July 7, 1778, #245, p. 3, col. 2. (MdHi)
       "War! how I hate thy horrid name,"
       WAR!
       . . . . .
       . . . . .
       . . . . .

291.   Oct. 20, 1778, #260, p. 2, col. 1. (MdHi)
       "Let croakers croak, for croak they will,"
       On the Queen's Pregnancy of her Thirteenth Child.
       . . . . .
       . . . . .
       London Evening Post.

292.   Oct. 27, 1778, #263, p. 4, col. 1. (MdHi)
       "'Tis past: --ah! calm thy* cares to rest!"
       The NEGROE's Dying Speech on his being executed for
         Rebellion in the Island of Jamaica.
       B.E. Esquire.
       . . . . .
       . . . . .
       . . . . .

293.   May 25, 1779, #296, p. 4, col. 1. (MdHi)
       "Strange paradox among the fowl;"
       EPIGRAM on the Hawke Privateer taken by the Oseau.
       James De La Cour.
       . . . . .
       London Daily Advertiser.

Maryland, Baltimore; Maryland Journal, and the Baltimore
Advertiser, 1773-1797

294.   May 25, 1779, #296, p. 4, col. 1. (MdHi)
        "In vain BELLONA mounts the Gallic Gun."
        Epigram on the vestal taking the Bellona.
        .....
        .....
        London Daily Advertiser.

295.   May 25, 1779, #296, p. 4, col. 1. (MdHi)
        "The common soldier who has broke"
        An Epigram.
        .....
        .....
        London Evening Post.

296.   June 6, 1780, #350, p. 2, cols. 2-3. (MdHi)
        "I am glad my dear John, now to find that some laws,"
        New Song.
        .....
        Ballanamona oro.
        Maryland Journal (sic Gazette?)

297.   Feb. 20, 1781, #388, p. 2, col. 2. (MdHi)
        "When Alcides, the Son of Olympian Jove,"
        On General Washington.
        A Soldier, Feb. 11, 1781.
        The Highland March.
        .....

298.   April 23, 1782, #451, p. 4, col. 1. (MdHi)
        "How happy is he born or taught"
        The Happy Life, excellent old ballads.
        Sir Henry Watton, 1639.
        The Happy Life, [an excellent old Ballad...]
        .....

299.   April 30, 1782, #452, p. 4, col. 1. (MdHi)
        "Where'er thy impulse, goddess, beams,"
        ODE to INCLINATION.
        .....
        .....
        .....

Maryland, Baltimore; Maryland Journal, and the Baltimore
Advertiser, 1773-1797

300.   Dec. 10, 1782, #484, p. 4, col. 1.   (DLC Box 8, folder
          15)
       "THO' the fate of battle on to-morrow wait;"
       The Musical Interlude of the TOBACCO-BOX, or The SOLDIER's
          PLEDGE of LOVE.
       . . . . .
       Original music French, accompanyments by Dr. Arnold.
          [The Tobacco Box: or, the Soldier's Pledge of Love]
       A late London Paper.

301.   March 11, 1783, #497, p. 4, col. 1.   (MdHi)
       "The youth, who's destin'd by the muse"
       On EDUCATION.
       . . . . .
       . . . . .
       . . . . .

302.   April 1, 1783, #503, p. 4, col. 1.   (MdHi)
       "Blest Notes of PEACE! with Joy your Sound I hear,"
       LINES written on the Prospect of PEACE.
       A LADY of this State.
       . . . . .
       . . . . .

MASSACHUSETTS

303.   June 6, 1776, #2, p. 4, col. 1.   (RMEAN, Card #1)
       "COME ye valient sons of thunder,"
       The Soldier's Sentimental Toast.
       New-York, May 22, 1776.
       .....
       .....

304.   Jan. 2, 1777, #33, (sic for 32), p. 2, col. 2.   (RMEAN
          Card #3)
       "HONOURS like Sulpher, cure all Stains,"
       A LYRIC POSTSCRIPT, Addressed to Lord B---ring----n.
       ......
       ......
       London Public Advertiser.

305.   Jan. 30, 1777, #36, p. 3, col. 2.   (DLC 418)
       "AS Mars, great God of battles! lay,"
       A PARODY on "The Watry God"--occasioned by General
          WASHINGTON's late successes in the Jersies.
       ......
       Watry God.
       .....

306.   Feb. 12, 1778, #90, p. 4, col. 2.   (RMEAN, Card #7)
       "ONCE the Court of Great-Britain in parliament sat(?),"
       A SONG.
       ......
       Once the Gods of the Greeks, &c.
       .....

307.   Feb. 12, 1778, #90, p. 4, col. 2.   (RMEAN, Card #7)
       "SHOUT, shout America,"
       A SONG.
       .....
       Smile Britannia.
       .....

308.   March 26, 1778, #96, p. 4, cols. 1-2.   (DLC 419)
       "GALLANTS attends (sic), and hear a friend"
       BRITISH VALOUR DISPLAYED; or, The BATTLE of the KEGS.
       Mr. [Hopkinson], of Jersey.
       [Battle of the Kegs.].
       .....

309. Jan. 24, 1774, #2000, p. 2, col. 2. (DLC 276)
      "AS Near beauteous Boston lying"
      A NEW SONG.
      BRITTANNO-AMERICANUS.
      Hosier's Ghost.
      Pennsylvania Packet, Jan. 3, 1774.

310. Feb. 13, 1775, #2055, p. 4, col. 1. (DLC 277)
      "THERE is a Nation on the Earth,"
      .....
      A Countryman.
      .....
      .....

311. Feb. 20, 1775, #2056, p. 4, cols. 1-2. (DLC 277)
      [Majesty.] "COME you my Subjects let me know,"
      A CONFERENCE, Between his Britannic Majesty and his
          Subjects.
      A Countryman.
      .....
      .....

312. Oct. 17, 1778, #1, p. 4, col. 1. (DLC Box 11, folder 8)
      "WHILE virtue crown'd fair Albion's throne,"
      On the Rising glory of AMERICA.
      [T.Z.]
      .. ...
      .. ...

313. Oct. 31, 1778, #3, p. 4, col. 1. (DLC Box 11, folder 8)
      "HAIL ye gallant sons of freedom,"
      To the AMERICAN ARMY.
      Young Lady in the country.
      .. ...
      .. ...

314. Nov. 21, 1778, #6, p. 4, col. 1. (MWA)
      "Hail happy Freedom, whose reviving Ray,"
      .. ...
      .. ...
      .. ...
      .. ...

315. Dec. 5, 1778, #8, p. 4, col. 1. (MWA)
      "BRITANNA (sic) was sick, for a doctor they sent,"
      The STATE QUACKS.
      .. ...
      .. ...
      From a late London Magazine.

316. Feb. 27, 1779, #20, p. 4, col. 1. (DLC 428)
      "ATTEND while he sings"
      .. ...
      E.
      .. ...
      .. ...

317. April 17, 1779, #27, p. 4, col. 1. (DLC 428)
      "IN virtue's cause to draw a daring pen,"
      On Good and Ill Nature.
      .. ...
      .. ...
      .. ...

Massachusetts, Boston; The Evening Post; and the General
Advertiser, 1778-1780

318.   May 22, 1779, #32, p. 4, col. 1.   (MWA)
        "Of Bray the vicar long I've been"
        The Vicar of Bray.   A Ballad.
        .....
        Turncoat.
        .....

319.   June 12, 1779, #35, p. 4, col. 1.   (DLC 428)
        "FOR George the Third I turn'd my coat,"
        The Vicar of Bray.
        .....
        [The Vicar of Bray]
        .....

320.   July 10, 1779, #39, p. 4, col. 1.   (DLC 428)
        "OF all the ages ever known,"
        The present AGE.
        .....
        .....
        .....

321.   Aug. 7, 1779, #43, p. 4, cols. 1-2.   (DLC 428)
        "ENGLAND, I feel for what I'm sure you must,"
        A Contrast between Sir William Howe and Sir Henry Clinton,
           dedicated to Lord North.
        .....
        .....
        NEW-JERSEY JOURNAL.

322.   Aug. 21, 1779, #45, p. 1, col. 3.   (DLC 428)
        "HARK! hear the Trumpet's pleasant Sound!"
        .....
        .....
        .....
        From the Pennsylvania Gazette.

323.   Sept. 11, 1779, #48, p. 4, col. 1.   (DLC 428)
        "LET venal poets praise a King"
        .....
        [An Officer in the American Army]
        .....
        From the NEW-JERSEY GAZETTE.

Massachusetts, Boston; The Evening Post; and the General
Advertiser, 1778-1780

324. Sept. 25, 1779, #50, p. 4, col. 1. (DLC 428)
      "JULY they say, the fifteenth day,"
      A NEW SONG.
      .....
      One Night as Ned stept into bed.
      The NEW-YORK PACKET.

325. Nov. 20, 1779, #58, p. 4, col. 1. (DLC 428)
      "THE god descends my soul is fir'd,"
      .....
      [Belinda]
      .....
      .....

326. Jan. 5, 1782, #12, p. 3, col. 2. (DLC 278)
      "CROWN'd be the man with lasting praise,"
      AMERICA.
      Soame Jenyns
      . . . . .
      . . . . .

327. Jan. 5, 1782, #12, p. 3, col. 2. (DLC 278)
      "TIS past; --Ah! calm thy cares to rest!"
      The DEATH of ALICO, An AFRICAN SLAVE.
      Bryant Edwards, Esq; of Jamaica.
      . . . . .
      . . . . .

328. Jan. 5, 1782, #12, p. 4, col. 3. (DLC 278)
      "'TWAS for the conquest nobly won"
      An ODE [in imitation of Dryden's Alexander's Feast.]
      [A SOUTHERN EXILE.]
      . . . . .
      PENNSYLVANIA PACKET.

329. Jan. 19, 1782, #14, p. 1, cols. 1-2. (DLC 278)
      "ARISE! arise! your voices raise,"
      The TEMPLE of MINERVA.
      [Francis Hopkinson] [a gentleman whose taste in the polite
         arts is well known]
      [The Temple of Minerva; Francis Hopkinson, arr.]
      From the FREEMAN's JOURNAL.

330. Feb. 16, 1782, #18, p. 2, col. 3. (DLC 278)
      "SHALL private cares torment the breast,"
      ON GENERAL WASHINGTON's Coming to take the Command at
         CAMBRIDGE: At which Time there was a fine Rain after
         a dry Season.
      Composed by a LADY, just after the cruel burning of
         CHARLESTOWN, by which she lost most of her Property.
      . . . . .
      . . . . .

Massachusetts, Boston; The Boston Evening Post and General
Advertiser, 1781-1784

331.   Feb. 16, 1782, #18, p. 3, col. 3.   (DLC 278)
        "PRINCE William of the Brunswick race"
        The ROYAL ADVENTURER.
        .....
        .....
        .....

332.   March 9, 1782, #21, p. 3, col. 1.   (DLC 278)
        "MY lords, I can hardly from weeping refrain,"
        [A SPEECH that should have been spoken by the king of the
          island of Britain to his parliament.]
        .....
        .....
        PHILADELPHIA.

333.   March 23, 1782, #23, p. 3, cols. 1-2.   (DLC 278)
        "SINCE life is uncertain, and no one can say,"
        RIVINGTON's LAST WILL and TESTAMENT.
        JAMES RIVINGTON, (L.S.), New-York, February 20, 1782.
        .....
        (A true copy from the Records.)

334.   April 20, 1782, #27, p. 4, cols. 2-3.   (DLC 278)
        "QUIDNUNC, my cronie, thou dost look"
        STANZAS for the Antigua Gazette.
        TRUTH. Old-Road, Jan. 28th.
        .....
        From the ANTIGUA GAZETTE.

335.   May 25, 1782, #32, p. 3, col. 1.   (DLC 278)
        "OE'R (sic) the waste of waters cruising,"
        .....
        RUSTICUS.
        The Tempest; or, Hosier's Ghost.
        FREEMAN's JOURNAL, May 8, 1782.

336.   June 29, 1782, #37, p. 2, col. 1.   (DLC 278)
        "FROM Britain's fam'd island once more I come over,"
        Sir Guy Carleton's ADDRESS to the Americans.
        G.C., May 30, 1782.
        .....
        .....

Massachusetts, Boston; The Boston Evening Post and General
Advertiser, 1781-1784

337.   June 29, 1782, #37, p. 4, col. 1. (DLC 278)
       "YE sons of Mars attend"
       SONG On the celebration of the birth of the DAUPHIN.
       .....
       To the restoration march.
       .....

338.   Aug. 24, 1782, #45, p. 4, cols. 1-2. (DLC 278)
       "CRIMSON slaughter! pallid care!"
       ODE on the Birth of the DAUPHIN.
       .....
       .....
       .....

339.   Jan. 4, 1783, #64, p. 3, col. 3. (RMEAN, Card #5)
       "D---l array'd in scarlet cloak,"
       To ------- -------, Cloak-Man.
       SPLINTER.
       .....
       .....

340.   March 22, 1783, #75, p. 3, col. 2. (RMEAN, Card #6)
       "In a chariot of light from the regions above,"
       .....
       By an American
       [Once the Gods of the Greeks].
       Philadelphia, March 4, Extract of a letter from Talbot
          Court-House, dated Feb. 12.

341.   May 3, 1783, #81, p. 3, col. 3. (DLC 279)
       "FROM Heaven descends sweet smiling Peace,"
       .....
       W.A., March 31, 1783.
       .....
       From the CHRONICLE of FREEDOM.

342.   Dec. 6, 1783, #112, p. 4, col. 1. (DLC 279)
       "COME rouse, brother Tories, the loyalists cry,"
       The Port-Roseway Garland.
       .....
       [Ye Medley of Mortals]
       From the NEW-JERSEY JOURNAL.

343. Jan. 18, 1773, #928, p. 3, col. 1. (DLC 301)
      "AMERICANS attend to Freedom's Cry!"
      The VOICE of FREEDOM.
      [THE IMMORTAL FARMER.]
      .....
      .....

344. Nov. 14, 1774, #1022, p. 3, col. 2. (DLC 302)
      "SINCE an Assembly most unlawful,"
      A PROCLAMATION.
      .....
      .....
      .....

345. July 24, 1775, #1052, p. 3, col. 3. (DLC 303)
      "WHEREAS the Rebels hereabout,"
      Thomas Gage's Proclamation versified.
      .....
      .....
      .....

346. Nov. 27, 1775, #1071, p. 4, cols. 1-2. (RMEAN, Card #152)
      "SINCE you all will have singing, and won't be said, nay,"
      The King's own REGULARS; And their Triumphs over the
         Irregulars, A New Song.
      .....
      An old Courtier of the Queen's and the Queen's old Courtier.
      .....

347. Feb. 12, 1776, #1082, p. 1, col. 3. (DLC 304)
      "LET little Tyrants, conscience gor'd"
      WARREN's GHOST, A PROPHETIC ELEGY. Found in a CAVE near
         LUTON HOO.
      .....
      .....
      From the PUBLIC LEDGER, Nov. 1.

348. April 15, 1776, #1091, p. 1, col. 2. (DLC 304)
      "AS near Boston's Township lying"
      WOLFE's GHOST.
      .....
      [Hosier's Ghost.]
      .....

349.   Sept. 1, 1777, #1200, p. 4, col. 1.   (DLC 305)
       "HAIL! Patriot hail! Brave Columbian,"
       A POEM. On the worthy Commander in Chief of the Army of
          the United States.
       Friend to his Country.
       .....
       .....

350.   Dec. 1, 1777, #1213, p. 2, col. 1.   (RMEAN, Card #159)
       "AS Jack the King's Commander,"
       Song.
       CANDIDUS
       "Lexington March"
       .....

351.   Dec. 8, 1777, #1214, p. 2, col. 2.   (DLC 305)
       "HAIL! glorious chief, whom destiny has chose"
       On General GATES.
       Libertas.
       .....
       .....

352.   March 23, 1778, #1229, p. 1, col. 3.   (DLC 306)
       "HOW comes it valiant John,"
       TITLED JOHN. A new SONG.
       .....
       [Gossip Joan]
       .....

353.   June 8, 1778, #1241, p. 4, col. 1.   (DLC 306)
       "AS late I travell'd o'er the plain,"
       DATE OBOLUM BELISARIO.
       .....
       .....
       .....

354.   Aug. 17, 1778, #1251, p. 4, col. 1.   (RMEAN, Card #161)
       "HOW comes all this! these pickets high,"
       .....
       A soldier, upon seeing the British prisoners within the
          stockade in Rutland. B. July 19, 1778.
       .....
       .....

Massachusetts, Boston; Boston Gazette and Country Journal, 1719-1798

355.   June 21, 1779, #1295, p. 4, col. 1.   (DLC 307)
       "THE Fates have past a firm Decree,"
       THE TORY's DOOM.
       .....
       .....
       .....

356.   May 8, 1780, #1341, p. 1, cols. 2-3.   (DLC 308)
       "HARK, Rebels hark! Sir Harry comes,"
       [PARODY on Sir Harry's Proclamation.]
       [A Constant Reader.]
       .....
       .....

357.   Aug. 14, 1780, #1355, p. 2, cols. 2-3.   (RMEAN, Card #169)
       "WHEN our m[a]s[te]r, God bless him, ascended the throne,"
       R[o]y[a]l Resolutions, imitation of Andrew Marvel's
          celebrated ballad.
       X.Y.Z.
       .....
       .....

358.   Nov. 26, 1781, #1422, p. 1, cols. 1-2.   (DLC 309)
       "YE loyalists all, within the town,"
       A NEW-YORK ADDRESS.   "To all honest hearts and sound
          bottoms."
       .....
       [Yankee Doodle]
       .....

359.   Dec. 31, 1781, #1427, p. 4, col. 1.   (RMEAN, Card #174)
       "I'M griev'd to see in this free LAND,"
       .....
       Jochelid, The Mother of Muses
       .....
       .....

360.   Feb. 11, 1782, #1433, p. 4, col. 1. (DLC 310)
        "AND shall we pause in freedom's cause,"
        Song.
        Written by an American Soldier, while he was a Prisoner
          with the Enemy.
        . . . . .
        . . . . .

361.   Feb. 18, 1782, #1434, p. 2, col. 1. (DLC 310)
        "PRINCE William of the Brunswick race,"
        The ROYAL ADVENTURER.
        . . . . .
        . . . . .
        . . . . .

362.   July 1, 1782, #1453, p. 3, col. 3 (DLC 310)
        "WHEN George in Madness gave command,"
        On the Birth of the DAUPHIN.
        . . . . .
        . . . . .
        . . . . .

363.   Sept. 16, 1782, #1464, p. 4, col. 1. (DLC 310)
        "THE old Tory rout"
        The REVERSE.
        . . . . .
        . . . . .
        . . . . .

364.   Jan. 27, 1783, #1483, p. 1, col. 3. (DLC 311)
        "BRIGHT flakes of snow compose the storm,"
        On the late Snow-Storm.
        PAUPER MULIER.
        . . . . .
        . . . . .

365.   June 9, 1783, #1502, p. 4, col. 1. (DLC 311)
        "AT length WAR's sanguine scenes are o'er;"
        On the PEACE: An ODE. Designed for Music.
        . . . . .
        . . . . .
        . . . . .

Massachusetts, Boston; Boston Gazette and Country Journal,
1719-1798

366.   Dec. 22, 1783, #1530, p. 4, col. 1.   (DLC 311)
        "THEY come! they come! the Heroes come!"
        ODE.-on the Arrival of their Excellencies General Washing-
           ton and Governor Clinton in New York, on the 25th of
           November 1783.
        .....
        He comes! He comes!
        .....

367.   Oct. 31, 1776, #428, p. 2, cols. 1-2. (DLC Box 11, folder
            17)
        "ALL hail G[e]rm[ai]ne, G[e]rm[ai]ne, all hail!"
        ODE to Lord G[eorge] G[e]rm[ai]ne.
        .....
        .....
        London.

368.   March 13, 1777, #447, p. 4, col. 1. (DLC 442)
        "BLUSH, Britains, blush! at thine inglorious war,"
        On BRITAIN.
        .....
        .....
        From the [British] Craftsman, or Say's Journal.

369.   April 24, 1777, #453, p. 2, cols. 1-2. (DLC 442)
        "WHEN Heaven for hidden causes shakes the rod,"
        The TIMES. An ELEGY.
        [a Friend to the Freedom of the Press.]
        .....
        .....

370.   May 2, 1777, #454, p. 4, col. 1. (DLC 442)
        "THE Stygian God, Great Belzebub"
        The FIREY DEVIL.
        .....
        WATRY GOD.
        .....

371.   June 12, 1777, #460, p. 4, cols. 1-2. (DLC 442)
        "WITHOUT wit, without wisdom, half stupid and drunk,"
        The EXPEDITION to DANBURY, under the command of General
            Tryon, to destroy the stores of Beef, Pork and Rum.
            SCENE, New-York.
        COMUS, Philadelphia, May 12, 1777.
        .....
        From the Pennsylvania Gazette.

Massachusetts, Boston; The Independent Chronicle; and the
Universal Advertiser, 1776-1820+

372.   Aug. 14, 1777, #468, p. 1, cols. 2-3.   (DLC 442)
       "COME soldiers all in chorus join,"
       On the Death of General MONTGOMERY.
       . . . . .
       Hark! Hark! the joy inspiring Horn.   A FAVORITE HUNTING
          SONG sung by Mr. Taylor.
       . . . . .

373.   Aug. 21, 1777, #470 (sic), p. 4, col. 1.   (DLC 442)
       "WHEN the great hero in arms himself array'd,"
       An ODE.
       . . . . .
       [Bunker-Hill?]
       . . . . .

374.   Oct. 9, 1777, #477, p. 4, col. 1.   (DLC 442)
       "IN a mouldring Cave, where th' oppressed retreat,"
       PARODY.
       . . . . .
       [Britannia or the Death of Wolfe].
       . . . . .

375.   Dec. 4, 1777, #485, p. 4, col. 1.   (DLC 442)
       "FAME, let thy Trumpet sound,"
       A NEW SONG.
       . . . . .
       God save the King.
       . . . . .

376.   Jan. 15, 1778, #491, p. 4, col. 1.   (DLC 443)
       "BY John Burgoyne, of noble line,"
       [New edition of Burgoyne's matchless proclamation.]
       [C.D.]
       . . . . .
       . . . . .

377.   Aug. 13, 1778, #521, p. 4, col. 1.   (DLC 443)
       "WHEN Satan first from Heaven's bright region fell,"
       . . . . .
       COMMONSENSE, Philadelphia, July 27, 1778.
       . . . . .
       . . . . .

Massachusetts, Boston; The Independent Chronicle; and the
Universal Advertiser, 1776-1820+

378.   Nov. 12, 1778, #534, p. 4, col. 3.   (DLC 443)
       "IN Newport there's been found of late,"
       [The Cushion Battle]
       . . . . .
       . . . . .
       . . . . .

379.   July 13, 1780, #620, p. 1, col. 1.   (DLC 445)
       "'TIS FREEDOM's Voice we hear!"
       The Triumph of AMERICAN FREEDOM, for New-Year, 1781.
       A SOLDIER.
       . . . . .
       . . . . .

380.   Oct. 26, 1780, #635, p. 3, cols. 1-2.   (DLC 445)
       "COLUMBIA! Columbia! to glory arise,"
       HAIL AMERICANS:
       A young gentleman in Connecticut.
       [Hail Americans, Music by Dr. Dwight]
       . . . . .

381.   Dec. 8, 1780, #641, p. 1, col. 2.   (DLC 445)
       "WEEP, British Muse, o'er Andre's grave!"
       . . . . .
       Tristi-Laetus.
       . . . . .
       . . . . .

382.   Sept. 20, 1781, #682, p. 4, col. 1.   (DLC 446)
       "IN the regions of light, at a banquet conven'd,"
       . . . . .
       NOVA-SCOTIA REFUGEE. Marlborough, 1781.
       The gods of the Greeks.
       . . . . .

383.   Nov. 8, 1781, #689, p. 1, col. 2.   (DLC 446)
       "WHEN southward Cornwallis first enter'd the land"
       NEW SONG. Occasioned by the surrender of Earl Cornwallis
          and his whole army, to General Washington.
       . . . . .
       Derry Down &c.
       . . . . .

Massachusetts, Boston; The Independent Chronicle; and the
Universal Advertiser, 1776-1820+

384.   Nov. 8, 1781, #689, p. 1, cols. 2-3.   (DLC 446)
       "SWEET Billy, precious royal boy,"
       General ROBERTSON's address to Prince WILLIAM
         HENRY.
       .....
       .....
       From Rivington's Gazette.

385.   June 15, 1778, #1, p. 4, cols. 1-2. (DLC 473)
        "SOON as the lark observes the morning's grey,"
        The Future GLORY of AMERICA.
        ADOLPHUS.
        .....
        .....

386.   Aug. 31, 1778, #12, p. 4, col. 1. (DLC 473)
        "SAMSON, before his head was shorn,"
        POOR Samson.
        .....
        .....
        Danish Gazette, July 8, 1778.

387.   Oct. 12, 1778, #18, p. 4, col. 1. (DLC 473)
        "COME and listen my lads to sweet Liberty's lay,"
        LIBERTY's CALL.
        .....
        The BLACK-Sloven.
        Camp, White Plains, Sept. 1, 1778.

388.   Oct. 19, 1778, #19, p. 4, cols. 1-2. (DLC 473)
        "IS there a word of magic found,"
        DISSIPATION.
        .....
        .....
        London Evening-Post.

389.   Nov. 2, 1778, #21, p. 4, col. 1. (DLC 473)
        "AWAKE my muse, from social scenes arise,"
        .....
        Amelia.
        .....
        .....

390.   Nov. 2, 1778, #21, p. 4, col. 1. (DLC 473)
        "TRUE Britons give o'er,"
        LABOUR in VAIN; OR, the Inefficacy of Truth.
        .....
        .....
        From the London Evening Post.

Massachusetts, Boston; The Independent Ledger, and the American
Advertiser, 1778-1786

391. Nov. 23, 1778, #24, p. 4, col. 1. (DLC 473)
      "'TIS past: --ah! calm thy* cares to rest!" (*He is
         supposed to address to his wife at the place of execu-
         tion.)
      The NEGRO's Dying Speech on his being executed for Re-
         bellion in the island of Jamaica.
      B.E. Esquire.
      . . . . .
      . . . . .

392. Jan. 11, 1779, #31, p. 4, col. 1. (RMEAN, Card #3)
      "YE Farmers all, with one accord,"
      The Devil and the Farmer. A Tale.
      . . . . .
      . . . . .
      . . . . .

393. Feb. 1, 1779, #34, p. 2, cols. 1-3. (DLC 474)
      "'TWAS at the royal show, and grand display"
      ALEXANDER's FEAST, PARODIED: Or, the Grand Portsmouth
         Puppet-Shew.
      By W[illiam] W[hitehead], Esq., Poet L[aurea]t.
      [George Friedrich Haendel, Alexander's Feast]
      From the London General Advertiser, &c.

394. April 5, 1779, #43, p. 4, col. 2. (DLC 474)
      "LET us take the road*!" (*Road of Spithead.)
      March in Rinaldo. On their Majesties Approach to Ports-
         mouth.
      JEMMY TWICHER and his Boat's Crew.
      March in Rinaldo.
      From a late London Paper.

395. April 5, 1779, #43, p. 4, col. 2. (DLC 474)
      "He comes! he comes! the Monarch comes!"
      Iö Triumphe.
      . . . . .
      [He Comes! He Comes!]
      . . . . .

Massachusetts, Boston; The Independent Ledger, and the American
Advertiser, 1778-1786

396. Aug. 9, 1779, #61, p. 4, col. 1. (RMEAN, Card #5)
     "ENGLAND, I feel for what I'm sure you must,"
     A contrast between Sir William Howe and Sir Henry
        Clinton, dedicated to Lord North.
     .....
     .....
     From the New-Jersey Journal.

397. Jan. 17, 1780, #84, p. 1, cols. 1-3. (DLC 475)
     "IN times of yore, there was a time;"
     .....
     [Constant Customer.]
     .....
     .....

398. March 13, 1780, #92, p. 4, col. 1. (DLC 475)
     "WHILE Nature reclin'd on the bosom of May,"
     The FLIGHT of the MUSES.
     ADOLPHUS.
     .....
     .....

399. May 22, 1780, #102, p. 4, col. 1. (DLC 475)
     "THERE was, and a very great fool,"
     A merry Song about MURDER.
     .....
     .....
     From the WESTMINSTER COURANT.

400. June 5, 1780, #104, p. 4, col. 1. (DLC 475)
     "HENCE with the lover who sighs o'er his wine,"
     The VOLUNTEER BOYS.
     .....
     Let the Toast Pass.
     From the DUBLIN EVENING POST.

401. Sept. 4, 1780, #117, p. 4, col. 1. (DLC 475)
     "THE Ministers bad,"
     The TIMES.
     .....
     .....
     A late London News-Paper.

Massachusetts, Boston; The Independent Ledger, and the American
Advertiser, 1778-1786

402. Oct. 23, 1780, #124, p. 2, cols. 1-2. (RMEAN, Card #9)
      "YE Patriots, go on,"
      The PATRIOTS.
      (Written about 1700)
      .....
      From the London Gazette.

403. Jan. 8, 1781, #136, p. 4, col. 1. (DLC 476)
      "THOU who in glory's shining track,"
      To General WASHINGTON, on the late Conspiracy.
      .....
      .....
      From the VIRGINIA GAZETTE.

404. Nov. 5, 1781, #180, p. 1, col. 2. (RMEAN, Card #13)
      "You know there goes a tale,"
      Copy of a Pasquinade stuck up in the city of N.Y.,
        August 12, 1780.
      .....
      .....
      From the Political Magazine for May, 1781.

405. Dec. 3, 1781, #184, p. 2, col. 3. (DLC 476)
      "WHEN British troops first landed here,"
      CORNWALLIS Burgoyn'd: A SONG.
      .....
      Maggie Lauder.
      .....

406. Dec. 24, 1781, #188, p. 3, col. 2. (DLC 476)
      "COME all Continentals, who WASHINGTON love,"
      .....
      TACITUS.
      .....
      .....

407. Dec. 31, 1781, #189, p. 4, col. 1. (DLC 476)
      "CORWALLIS (sic) led a country dance,"
      The DANCE, A Ballad.
      .....
      Yankey Doodle.
      .....

Massachusetts, Boston; The Independent Ledger, and the American
Advertiser, 1778-1786

408.   March 11, 1782, #201, p. 4, col. 1. (DLC 477)
        "MY lords, I can hardly from weeping refrain,"
        A SPEECH that should have been spoken by the king of the
           island of Britain to his parliament.
        .....
        .....
        .....

409.   March 18, 1782, #202, p. 2, col. 3. (RMEAN, Card #15)
        "FEW are content with what they've got,"
        .....
        Written by a Gentleman, on a Lady's saying she wished
           for Nothing more than SHE POSSESS'd.
        .....
        .....

410.   April 29, 1782, #208, p. 4, col. 3. (DLC 477)
        "STILL, tost tempestious on the sea of life,"
        Asent---(?)   [A SENTIMENTAL-----?]
        By a SAILOR.
        .....
        .....

411.   May 27, 1782, #212, p. 4, col. 1. (DLC 477)
        "OF great and glorious names to speak,"
        The GEORGES, a Song. On Lord Germain's Promotion.
        .....
        Push about the Forum.
        LONDON COURANT.

412.   June 17, 1782, #215, p. 4, col. 1. (DLC 477)
        "THE dog that is beat has a right to complain,--"
        On Sir Henry Clinton's recall.
        .....
        .....
        From the FREEMAN's JOURNAL.

413.   July 1, 1782, #217, p. 4, col. 1. (RMEAN, Card #16)
        "FAREWEL my Lord, may zephyrs waft you o'er,"
        An Address to Lord Cornwallis.
        .....
        .....
        .....

Massachusetts, Boston; The Independent Ledger, and the American
Advertiser, 1778-1786

414.   Sept. 2, 1782, #226, p. 4, col. 1.   (DLC 477)
        "YOUR golden dreams, your flattering schemes,"
        SATAN's REMONSTRANCE.
        .....
        .....
        From the (Pennsylvania) FREEMAN's JOURNAL.

415.   Sept. 30, 1782, #230, p. 4, col. 1.   (DLC 477)
        "I Sing of George's golden days,"
        WHO's the NOODLE.   A NEW SONG.
        .....
        Od's Blood Who's the NOODLE.
        From the London General Advertiser.

416.   June 9, 1783, #266, p. 1, col. 1.   (RMEAN, Card #19)
        "AT length WAR's sanguine scenes are o'er;"
        On the PEACE.   An ODE.   Designed for Music.
        .....
        .....
        From the New-Jersey Journal.

417.   Dec. 22, 1783, #309,(sic), p. 4, col. 1.   (RMEAN, Card #21)
        "THEY come! they come! the Heroes come!"
        ODE, On the Arrival of their Excellencies General
          WASHINGTON and Gov. CLINTON in New-York, on the 25th
          of Nov., 1783.
        .....
        "He comes! he comes!"
        .....

418. May 20, 1773, #120, p. 1, col. 2. (DLC 535)
      "WITH minds eclips'd and eke deprav'd,"
      Advice to the Tory inhabitants of the town of P----M.
      [Q.P.]
      .....
      .....

419. Jan. 27, 1774, #156, p. 3, col. 2. (DLC 536)
      "E'ER since the day that Adam fell,"
      .....
      JOE IRONY.
      .....
      .....

420. Jan. 27, 1774, #156, p. 4, col. 1. (DLC 536)
      "I Lately past a thirsty willow tree,"
      ......
      A----O.
      .....
      .....

421. Jan. 27, 1774, #156, p. 4, col. 1. (DLC 536)
      "AS near beauteous Boston lying"
      A NEW SONG.
      Brittanno-Americanus.
      Hosier's Ghost.
      From the Pennsylvania Packet.

422. Feb. 3, 1774, #157, p. 4, col. 1. (DLC 536)
      "NEW-England's annoyances you that would know them"
      New-England's annoyances.
      .....
      ["Old ballad composed and sung by some of the first
        settlers of New-England."]
      .....

423. Feb. 17, 1774, #159, p. 4, col. 1. (DLC 536)
      "FArewel the tea board with its equipage,"
      A Lady's Adieu to her TEA-TABLE.
      .....
      .....
      .....

Massachusetts, Boston; The Massachusetts Spy, or Thomas's Boston
Journal, 1770-1775

424.   March 10, 1774, #162, p. 4, col. 1.   (DLC 536)
        "WHEN the Foes of the Land, our destruction had plan'd"
        A SONG for the 5th of MARCH.
        .....
        Once the Gods of the Greeks.
        .....

425.   March 17, 1774, #163, p. 4, col. 1.   (DLC 536)
        "I HOPE there's no soul,"
        TRUE BLUE.
        .....
        From the East breaks the Morn.
        .....

426.   March 31, 1774, #165, p. 4, col. 1.   (DLC 536)
        "SWEEP all! Sweep all!"
        An ODE Sung at the opening of the Grand-India OPERA,
            performed at Boston, 16th of Dec., 1773. By Signiora
            Boheti.
        [By Signiora Boheti.]
        .....
        From the NEW-YORK JOURNAL, &c.

427.   April 28, 1774, #169, p. 4, col. 1.   (DLC 536)
        "WHO'EER (sic) with curious eye has rang'd,"
        The Origin of MACARONIES
        .....
        .....
        .....

428.   June 2, 1774, #174, p. 2, col. 4.   (RMEAN, Card: May 26-
            July 28)
        "O 'twas a joyful sound to hear,"
        .....
        .....
        .....
        The Massachusetts Spy.

429.   June 30, 1774, #178, p. 4, col. 1.   (DLC 536)
        "LORD, save us from our cruel Foes,"
        .....
        .....
        .....
        .....

Massachusetts, Boston; The Massachusetts Spy, or Thomas's Boston
Journal, 1770-1775

430.   Aug. 18, 1774, #185, p. 4, col. 1. (DLC 536)
       "HAIL LIBERTY! A glorious word,"
       .....
       .....
       .....
       From the NEW-YORK JOURNAL.

431.   Sept. 1, 1774, #187, p. 4, col. 1. (DLC 536)
       "COME, come, my brave boys, from my song you shall hear,"
       The glorious SEVENTY FOUR. A NEW SONG.
       .....
       Hearts of Oak.
       From the NEW-YORK JOURNAL.

432.   Sept. 8, 1774, #188, p. 4, col. 1. (DLC 536)
       "WITH graceful air and virtuous mein,"
       .....
       Tom Gingle.
       .....
       The Pennsylvania Packet.

433.   Sept. 15, 1774, #189, p. 4, col. 1. (DLC 536)
       "IN ancient times--tyranny and civil wars"
       .....
       .....
       .....
       .....

434.   Sept. 22, 1774, #190, #190, p. 4, col. 1. (DLC 536)
       "OH Boston! late with the ev'ry pleasure crown'd,"
       An ELEGY on the TIMES.
       .....
       .....
       .....

435.   Nov. 3, 1774, #196, p. 4, col. 1. (DLC 536)
       "YE Sons of Freedom smile!"
       LIBERTY SONG.
       .....
       Smile Britannia.
       .....

436. Nov. 10, 1774, #197, p. 4, col. 1. (DLC 536)
      "WHEN Britons first, by Heaven's command,"
      An AMERICAN PARODY, on the old song, of "RULE BRITANNIA."
      . . . . .
      Rule Britannia.
      . . . . .

437. Dec. 16, 1774, #202, p. 4, col. 1. (DLC 536)
      "WHEN mighty Roast beef was the Englishman's food,"
      The Roast Beef of OLD ENGLAND.
      . . . . .
      [Roast Beef of Old England.]
      . . . . .

438. Jan. 5, 1775, #205, p. 4, col. 1. (DLC 537)
      "In George the second's golden days,"
      ["parody on the Ballad of the Vicar of Bray."]
      A CANTAB., Dec. 15, 1774.
      [Vicar of Bray]
      . . . . .

439. Jan. 12, 1775, #206, p. 4, col. 1. (DLC 537)
      "OH heav'nly born! in deepest cells"
      An ode on SCIENCE.
      Dr. Swift.
      . . . . .
      . . . . .

440. Jan. 12, 1775, #206, p. 4, col. 1. (DLC 537)
      "WHEN Britain first her wars to wage,"
      An Heroical Panegyric on the valourous atchievements of
         G[eneral] G[age], in the Paper war in America, A.D. 1774.
         Occasioned by some late Proclamations.
      ...., Connecticut, December 18, 1774.
      . . . . .
      . . . . .

441. Jan. 26, 1775, #208, p. 4, col. 1. (DLC 537)
      "A Wond'rous Beast of late appears,"
      On the late Unconstitutional Acts. Monstrum, Horrendum,
         Animalum.
      AMOR, Rei, Publicae.
      . . . . .
      . . . . .

Massachusetts, Boston; The Massachusetts Spy, or Thomas's Boston
Journal, 1770-1775

442. Jan. 26, 1775, #208, p. 4, col. 1. (DLC 537)
      "WHOM virtue's native heav'nly force"
      [Horace Od. 5. Lib. 2.] IMITATED.
      .....
      .....
      .....

443. Feb. 16, 1775, #211, p. 4, col. 1. (DLC 537)
      "O MY baby, my baby,"
      A NEW SONG. Supposed to have been sung by Goody N[ort]h,
        by way of Lulla-by to the foundling Popish Quebec-Bill.
      .....
      O my Kitten, my Kitten.
      .....

444. March 2, 1775, #213, p. 4, col. 1. (DLC 537)
      "WHAT's the spring, or the sweet smelling rose?"
      On the LIBERTIES of the NATION.
      Ejus Sydney.
      .....
      .....

445. March 9, 1775, #214, p. 4, col. 1. (DLC 537)
      "HARK! or does the indignant ear"
      AN ODE. Humbly inscribed to William Whitehead, Esq; Poet
        Laureat to George, King of Great-Britain and America.
      .....
      .....
      From the LONDON MAGAZINE.

446. March 23, 1775, #216, p. 4, col. 1. (DLC 537)
      "HAPPY's the man, who unconstrain'd"
      An ODE on LIBERTY.
      Z.Y.
      .....
      .....

447. April 6, 1775, #218, p. 4, col. 1. (DLC 537)
      "BRITONS, if you pant for glory,"
      ODE to INDEPENDENCE.
      .....
      .....
      .....

448.   Oct. 6, 1774, #3706, p. 1, col. 3.   (DLC 521)
       "MOURN, hapless CALEDONIA, mourn"
       The TEARS of SCOTLAND.   Written in the Year 1746.
       A NEW-YORK FREEHOLDER.
       [The Tears of Scotland]
       . . . . .

449.   Broadside, 1775.   (DLC 523)
       "BEHOLD! poor Boston sore distrest,"
       ODE on the New-Year.
       [Carrier of Mass. Gazette and Boston Weekly News-
          Letter]
       . . . . .
       . . . . .

Massachusetts, Boston
The Massachusetts Gazette, and Boston Post-Boy and Advertiser,
1734-1775

450.   Feb. 8, 1773, #807, p. 4, col. 1. (DLC 509)
       "YE Cliffs, where wide-resounding o'er the main,"
       .....
       T.D.
       .....
       From the MORNING CHRONICLE.

451.   June 7, 1773, #824, p. 4, col. 1. (RMEAN, Card #94)
       "Twelve struck the clock, Sedition's trump blew high"
       THE PATRIOTIC PROCESSION.
       .....
       .....
       A London Paper.

452.   July 12, 1773, #829, p. 4, col. 1. (DLC 509)
       "OH! Why the complaints of poor mortals so grievous?"
       .....
       .....
       .....
       .....

453.   Aug. 30, 1773, #856, p. 2, col. 3. (RMEAN, Card #95)
       "HOWL, Stygian Muse, the Noise and Discord dire,"
       THE FESTIVAL: An Epic POEM, in twelve Books. Written
          with great Temperance.
       .....
       .....
       .....

454.   Jan. 24, 1774, #857, p. 4, col. 1. (RMEAN, Card #96)
       "AS near beauteous Boston Lying."
       A NEW SONG.
       Brittanno-Americanus
       Hosier's Mill.
       From the Pennsylvania Packet.

Massachusetts, Boston; The Massachusetts Gazette, and Boston
Post-Boy and Advertiser, 1734-1775

455.   March 7, 1774, #863, p. 2, col. 2.   (DLC 510)
       "WHEN the Foes of the Land, our Destruction had plan'd"
       A SONG for the 5th of MARCH.
       .....
       Once the Gods of the Greeks, &c.
       .....

456.   Dec. 12, 1774, #903, p. 4, col. 1.   (DLC 510)
       "THE expences of war, and corruptions of peace,"
       SONG.
       .....
       Derry Down.
       A Late London Paper.

457.   May 18, 1775, #355, p. 3, col. 1.   (DLC 555)
       "HARK! 'tis Freedom that calls, come Patriots awake!"
       A Song.
       .....
       "The echoing Horn."
       .....

458.   June 8, 1775, #358, p. 2, col. 2.   (DLC 555)
       "YE Heirs of Freedom! glorious is your Cause,"
       To the AMERICANS.
       CATO, April 18, 1775.
       .....
       .....

459.   Aug. 31, 1775, #370, p. 2, col. 3.   (DLC 555)
       "PALMIRA's Prospect, with her tumbling Walls,"
       .....
       .....
       .....
       .....

460.   Dec. 14, 1775, #385, p. 4, col. 1.   (DLC 555)
       "THO' some folks may tell us, it is not so clever"
       A SONG.
       Soldier in the Continental Army.
       Black Sloven.
       .....

461.   Jan. 12, 1774, #4, p. 4, col. 1.   (RMEAN, Card #1)
       "HAIL welcome dawn, Aurora doth appear,"
       .....
       .....
       .....
       .....

462.   Feb. 2, 1774, #7, p. 3, col. 2.   (RMEAN, Card #1)
       "AS near beauteous BOSTON lying"
       A NEW SONG.
       Brittanno-Americanus.
       Hosier's Ghost.
       The Pennsylvania Packet.

463.   March 2, 1774, #11, p. 2, col. 1.   (RMEAN, Card #1)
       "FAREWELL the Tea-board with your gaudy attire,"
       A lady's adieu to her Tea-Table.
       .....
       .....
       .....

464.   April 27, 1774, #19, p. 4, col. 1.   (RMEAN Card #2)
       "PERMIT a giddy trifling girl,"
       .....
       .....
       .....
       .....

465.   June 22, 1774, #27, p. 4, col. 1.   (RMEAN, Card #3)
       "O! TWAS a joyful sound to hear,"
       .....
       .....
       .....
       The Massachusetts Spy of June 2.

466.   Nov. 16, 1774, #48, p. 4, col. 1.   (RMEAN, Card #4)
       "WHEN Britons first, by heaven's command,"
       An AMERICAN PARODY on the old Song of "RULE BRITANNIA."
       .....
       Rule Britannia.
       .....

467. Dec. 7, 1774, #51, p. 4, col. 1.   (RMEAN, Card #4)
"BRAVE sons of peace, who live at ease,"
["on the gloomy aspect of affairs in both Englands"]
Youth who lives in New-Hampshire.
.....
.....

468. Dec. 28, 1774, #54, p. 4, col. 1.   (RMEAN, Card #4)
"COME come, my friends, let's drink about,"
SONG, for the benefit of the Social SONS of LIBERTY.
.....
.....
.....

469. Jan. 19, 1775, #57, p. 4, col. 1.   (DLC Box 13, folder 15)
"I AM an old Farmer, was born in the woods,"
A DREAM.
.....
.....
.....

470. Jan. 25, 1775, #58, p. 4, col. 1.   (DLC Box 13, folder 15)
"WHEN Britain first at Heaven's command,"
An ODE.
[Scholasticus]
[Rule Britannia]
.....

471. Feb. 15, 1775, #61, p. 4, col. 1.   (DLC Box 13, folder 15)
"BRITONS, if you pant for glory,"
ODE to INDEPENDENCE.
.....
.....
The London Magazine, Oct., 1774.

472. March 8, 1775, #64, p. 4, col. 1.   (DLC Box 13, folder 15)
"GREAT BRITAIN in her haughty pride,"
.....
.....
.....
.....

473. April 19, 1775, #70, p. 4, col. 1. (DLC Box 13, folder 15)
     "WHEN wicked men, with foul intent,"
     An ODE.
     .....
     .....
     .....

474. June 3, 1775, #75, p. 4, col. 1. (RMEAN, Card #6)
     "AWHILE fond Damon prithee tarry,"
     .....
     .....
     .....
     .....

475. Sept. 5, 1775, #87, p. 4, col. 1. (DLC Box 13, folder 15)
     "IN a chariot of light from the regions of day,"
     LIBERTY-TREE. A New Song.
     .....
     The Gods of the Greeks.
     .....

476. Nov. 3, 1775, #96, p. 2, col. 2. (RMEAN, Card #8)
     "O GREAT reverse of Tully's coward heart!"
     Ode to the Memory of Dr. Warren.
     LUCIUS
     .....
     The Morning Chronicle, Aug. 3.

477. Dec. 8, 1775, #101, p. 4, col. 1. (RMEAN, Card #8)
     "BY my faith, but I think you're all makers of Bulls,"
     The IRISHMAN's Epistle to the Officer's and Troops at
        BOSTON.
     .....
     .....
     .....

478. Dec. 15, 1775, #102, p. 4, col. 1. (RMEAN, Card #8)
     "OUR Vows thus chearfully we sing,"
     .....
     .....
     .....
     .....

479. Dec. 22, 1775, #103, p. 4, col. 1.   (RMEAN, Card #8)
     "THO' some folks may tell us, it is not so clever"
     A NEW SONG.
     A Soldier in the Continental Army.
     Tune of the Black-Sloven.
     . . . . .

480. Feb. 9, 1776, #110, p. 4, col. 1.   (DLC 559)
     "COME hither, brother Tradesmen,"
     A DOSE for the TORIES, A New SONG, much in Vogue in
        ENGLAND.
     . . . . .
     [A begging we will go, we'll go]
     . . . . .

481. Feb. 23, 1776, #112, p. 4, col. 1.   (DLC 559)
     "LET little tyrants, conscience gor'd,"
     WARREN's GHOST. A PROPHETIC ELEGY. Found in a CAVE
        near LUTON HOO.
     . . . . .
     . . . . .
     Public Ledger, Nov. 1.

482. March 15, 1776, #115, p. 2, col. 1.   (DLC 559)
     "HARK! hark! the solemn knell from yon tall spire"
     On hearing the Bells toll, in commemoration of the bloody
        Massacre in Boston, March 5th 1770.
     [Y.]
     . . . . .
     . . . . .

483. March 29, 1776, #117, p. 4, col. 1.   (DLC 559)
     "WHY should vain mortals tremble at the sight of"
     The AMERICAN HERO.--A Sapphic Ode.
     . . . . .
     [Bunker Hill; Music by Andrew Law].
     . . . . .

484. July 5, 1776, #131, p. 4, col. 1.   (DLC 559)
     "COME ye valiant sons of thunder,"
     The Soldier's Sentimental Toast.
     . . . . .
     . . . . .
     . . . . .

485. Aug. 2, 1776, #135, p. 4, col. 1. (DLC 559)
"HAPPY's the man, who unconstrain'd"
ODE on LIBERTY.
. . . . .
. . . . .
. . . . .

486. Sept. 6, 1776, #140, p. 4, col. 1. (DLC 559)
"GREAT ruler of the earth and skies,"
HYMN for NATIONAL PEACE.
. . . . .
. . . . .
. . . . .

487. Sept. 20, 1776, #142, p. 4, col. 1. (DLC 559)
"HAIL! Patriots, hail! by me inspired be!"
The GODDESS of LIBERTY.
. . . . .
. . . . .
. . . . .

488. Oct. 4, 1776, #144, p. 4, col. 1. (DLC 559)
"THE world's a bubble and the life of man"
. . . . .
. . . . .
[The world is a bubble]
. . . . .

489. Nov. 8, 1776, #149, p. 4, col. 1. (DLC 559)
"WHEN moral tale let ancient wisdom move,"
The Horse and the Olive, or War and Peace.
. . . . .
. . . . .
. . . . .

490.   June 25, 1776, #2, p. 4, col. 1.   (DLC 573)
       "FREEMEN, if you pant for glory,"
       ODE on INDEPENDENCE.
       . . . . .
       . . . . .
       . . . . .

491.   July 9, 1776, #4, p. 4, col. 1.   (MSaE)
       "AT length -- with generous indignation fir'd,"
       . . . . .
       PENNSYLVANIENSIS.
       . . . . .
       Pennsylvania Journal.

492.   July 30, 1776, #7, p. 4, col. 1.   (MSaE)
       "A WHILE, fond Damon, prithee tarry,"
       The STIPULATION.
       . . . . .
       . . . . .
       . . . . .

493. Jan. 25, 1774, #287, p. 3, col. 1. (DLC 580)
      "AS near beauteous Boston lying"
      A NEW SONG.
      BRITTANNO AMERICANUS.
      Hosier's Ghost.
      Pennsylvania Packet, Jan. 3, 1774.

494. June 7, 1774, #306, p. 3, col. 3. (DLC 580)
      "O! 'twas a joyful Sound to hear"
      .....
      .....
      .....
      Massachusetts Spy, June 2.

495. Oct. 25, 1774, #326, p. 4, col. 1. (DLC 580)
      "YE Sons of Freedom smile!"
      LIBERTY SONG.
      .....
      "Smile Britannia."
      .....

496.   Sept. 16, 1774, #12, p. 4, col. 1. (MWA)
        "Ye Princes of the earth, ye mighty few,"
        ON TYRANNICAL GOVERNMENT.
        . . . . .
        . . . . .
        . . . . .

497.   Feb. 17, 1775, #34, p. 140, cols. 1-2. (DLC Box 14,
            folder 14)
        "THERE is a Nation on the Earth,"
        . . . . .
        By a Countryman.
        . . . . .
        Boston Evening Post, Feb. 13.

498.   Feb. 17, 1775, #34, p. 140, col 2. (DLC Box 14, folder
            14)
        "SEE the poor native quit the Lybian shores,"
        To the Dealers in Slaves.
        . . . . .
        . . . . .
        . . . . .

499.   March 3, 1775, #36, p. 148, col. 1. (DLC Box 14, folder
            14)
        "FAIR Ladies, 'tis not very arch,"
        ADVERTISEMENT, Addressed to the LADIES.
        William Beadle, Wethersfield, Jan. 28, 1775.
        . . . . .
        Connecticut Courant, Feb. 13.

500.   Jan. 2, 1781, #1, p. 4, cols. 2-3.   (DLC 601)
       "GOD save the Thirteen States!"
       ["A SONG..for the Americans at Amsterdam, July 4, 1779."]
       Dutch Lady at the Hague.
       [God save the King]
       .....

501.   Jan. 2, 1781, #1, p. 4, col. 3.   (DLC 601)
       "GOD bless the Thirteen States!"
       [Song "written...at Amsterdam, July 4, 1779."]
       A Dutch Gentleman.
       [God save the King]
       .....

502.   Feb. 6, 1781, #6, p. 3, col. 1.   (DLC 601)
       "THOU who in glory's shining track,"
       To General WASHINGTON, on the late Conspiracy.
       .....
       .....
       Virginia Gazette.

503. Nov. 8, 1781, #4, p. 4, col. 2. (DLC 582)
"While scenes of transport, ev'ry breast inspire,"
.....
.....
.....
Camp, Peck's-Kill, Oct. 18, 1781.

504. Jan. 24, 1782, #15, p. 4, cols. 1-2. (DLC 583)
"ARISE! arise! your voices raise,"
The TEMPLE of MINERVA, An Oratorial ENTERTAINMENT.
[Francis Hopkinson]
[The Temple of Minerva; Francis Hopkinson, Arr.]
Philadelphia, From Freeman's Journal.

505. Oct. 17, 1782, #53, p. 4, col. 1. (DLC 583)
"WELCOME, one ARNOLD, to our shore;"
ODE, addressed to GENERAL ARNOLD.
LADY CRAVEN.
.....
Late British Publication.

506. Aug. 13, 1782, #14, p. 4, col. 1. (DLC 608)
      "GOOD People, I am come to let you know"
      CARLETON's Message to the United States of America.
      .....
      .....
      .....

507. Feb. 11, 1783, #40, p. 4, col. 1. (DLC 609)
      "THE world's a bubble: and the life of man"
      THE WORLD.
      .....
      .....
      .....

508. March 4, 1783, #43, p. 4, col. 1. (DLC 609)
      "HOW happy is he born or taught,"
      THE HAPPY LIFE. ["An excellent old ballad written...in
         the year, 1659"]
      Sir Henry Wotton. ["Provost of Eaton College"]
      [The Happy Life]
      .....

509. May 6, 1783, #52, p. 4, col. 1. (DLC 609)
      "FROM heaven descends sweet smiling peace,"
      .....
      W.A., March 31, 1783.
      .....
      The Independent Gazetter.

510. June 10, 1783, #57, p. 4, col. 1. (MWA)
      "No more my friends of vain applause,"
      A SKETCH OF THE TIMES.
      .....
      .....
      .....

511. July 22, 1783, #63, p. 4, col. 1. (MWA)
      "Your grand, fine piece, so laboured,"
      An ODE to be sung by the xxxxx xxx and xxxxx on all public
         occasions (if they please)
      Z.X.
      Low Dutch
      .....

Massachusetts, Worcester
The Massachusetts Spy Or, American Oracle of Liberty,
1775-1820+

512.　May 24, 1775, #222, p. 4, col. 1.　(DLC 611)
"HARK! 'tis Freedom that calls, come Patriots awake!"
A NEW SONG.
. . . . .
"The ecchoing Horn."
. . . . .

513.　June 28, 1775, #227, p. 3, col. 3.　(DLC 611)
"COME listen my cocks, to a brother and friend,"
The Sailors Address.　A NEW SONG.
. . . . .
[Hearts of Oak]
a London Paper.

514.　Aug. 23, 1775, #235, p. 4, col. 1.　(DLC 612)
"WE are the troops that ne'er will stoop"
The PENNSYLVANIA MARCH.
. . . . .
Scots SONG - I winna Marry ony Lad, but Sandy o'er the Lee.
The Pennsylvania Packet.

515.　Sept. 6, 1775, #237, p. 4, col. 1.　(DLC 612)
"IN a chariot of light from the regions of day,"
LIBERTY TREE.
. . . . .
The Gods of the Greeks.
. . . . .

516.　April 26, 1776, #263, p. 3, col. 1.　(DLC Box 15, folder 2)
"WHY should vain mortals tremble at the sight of"
The AMERICAN HERO.　A Sapphic Ode.
. . . . .
[Bunker Hill;　Music by Andrew Law].
. . . . .

517.　May 3, 1776, #264, p. 3, col. 2.　(DLC Box 15, folder 2)
"THE watry God, great Neptune, lay"
THE WATRY GOD.　A New Song.
. . . . .
[Watry God.]
From the Connecticut Courant.

Massachusetts, Worcester; The Massachusetts Spy Or, American
Oracle of Liberty, 1775-1820+

518.   May 31, 1776, #268, p. 3, col. 1.   (DLC Box 15, folder 2)
        "COME, ye valiant sons of thunder,"
        The Soldier's Sentimental Toast.
        .....
        .....
        New-York Journal.

519.   Nov. 13, 1776, #289, p. 4, col. 1.   (MWA)
        "The blue-faced boys, with eager haste,"
        THE SNOW-BALL. A Poem.
        .....
        .....
        .....

520.   Nov. 27, 1776, #291, p. 4, col. 1.   (MWA)
        "Let pa ta(?) Spirits still aloud complain,"
        ON THE UNITED STATES OF AMERICA.
        .....
        .....
        .....

521. Dec. 19, 1776, #294, p. 4, col. 1. (MWA)
"With Christmas Mirth, and Christmas Cheer,"
THE MEETING AFTER the RECESS. A Poem.
. . . . .
. . . . .
Extract from a London Paper.

522. March 27, 1777, #308, p. 4, col. 1. (MWA)
"My Lords with your leave,"
A New WAR Song.
Sir Peter Parker.
Well met Brother Tar.
. . . . .

523. April 17, 1777, #311, p. 3, col. 2. (MWA)
"Ye wrong heads and strong heads attend to my song,"
A New POLITICAL SONG.
. . . . .
[Derry Down]
. . . . .

524. July 3, 1777, #322, p. 4, cols. 1-2. (MWA)
"There was once it was said,"
Vicar and Moses.
GEORGE ALEXANDER STEVENS. (?)
[Vicar & Moses]
. . . . .

525. Aug. 14, 1777, #328, p. 4, col. 1. (MWA)
"Come soldiers all in chorus join,"
On the death of GENERAL MONTGOMERY.
. . . . .
HARK! HARK! the joy inspiring Horn.
. . . . .

526. Dec. 11, 1777, #345, p. 4, col. 1. (MWA)
"As Jack the King's Commander,"
A NEW SONG.
. . . . .
Lexington MARCH.
. . . . .

Massachusetts, Worcester; The Massachusetts Spy Or, American
Oracle of Liberty, 1775-1820+

527.   Dec. 25, 1777, #347, p. 4, col. 1.   (RMEAN, Card #9)
       "WHEN the great hero in arms himself array'd,"
       An ODE.
       . . . . .
       [Bunker-Hill?]
       . . . . .

528.   Jan. 1, 1778, #348, p. 4, col. 1.   (RMEAN, Card #9)
       "AGAIN returns the circling Year!"
       ODE, for the NEW YEAR, 1778.
       . . . . .
       [Ode for the NEW YEAR, 1778; Music by William Boyce.]
       . . . . .

529.   June 18, 1778, #372, p. 4, col. 1.   (RMEAN, Card #10)
       "GIVE ear to my song, I'll not tell you a story,"
       The HALCYON DAYS of OLD England: Or the Wisdom of Adminis-
           tration demonstrated: A Ballad.
       . . . . .
       Ye Medley of Mortals.
       London Evening Post.

530.   July 2, 1778, #374, p. 4, col. 1.   (RMEAN, Card #10)
       "WHEN Valor directed by motives sincere,"
       The TRUE SOLDIER. A New SONG.
       . . . . .
       BLACK SLOVEN.
       . . . . .

531.   Aug. 6, 1778, #379, p. 4, col. 1.   (DLC 613)
       "AS Collinet and Phebe sat"
       COLLINET and PHEBE. A New Song.
       Young Lady in Virginia.
       [As Collinet and Phebe sat]
       . . . . .

532.   Aug. 27, 1778, #382, p. 4, col. 1.   (DLC 613)
       "WEST of th' old Atlantic, firm liberty stands,"
       The GAMESTER. A New SONG.
       . . . . .
       A late worthy old Lion, &c.
       . . . . .

Massachusetts, Worcester; The Massachusetts Spy Or, American
Oracle of Liberty, 1775-1820+

533. Oct. 15, 1778, #389, p. 4, col. 1. (DLC 613)
      "LET croaker's croak, for croak they will,"
      On the Queen's Pregnancy of her Thirteenth Child.
      .....
      .....
      London Evening Post.

534. Oct. 15, 1778, #389, p. 4, col. 1. (DLC 613)
      "COME and listen my lads to sweet Liberty's lay,"
      LIBERTY's CALL. A new and original CAMP SONG.
      .....
      BLACK-SLOVEN.
      .....

535. Nov. 26, 1778, #395, p. 3, col. 3. (RMEAN, Card #12)
      "WITH humble gratitude to heav'n,"
      A THANKSGIVING ODE.
      .....
      .....
      .....

536. Dec. 24, 1778, #399, p. 4, col. 1. (RMEAN, Card #12)
      "BRITANNIA was sick, for a doctor they sent,"
      The STATE QUACKS.
      .....
      .....
      A late London Magazine.

537. Dec. 31, 1778, #400, p. 4, col. 1. (DLC 613)
      "'TIS past: --ah! calm thy* cares to rest!"
      The NEGRO's DYING SPEECH on his being executed for rebellion
         in the island of Jamaica.
      B.E. Esquire.
      .....
      .....

538. Jan. 7, 1779, #401, p. 3, col. 1. (DLC 614)
      "THO' Bute o'er earth and seas, or Kings had Power,"
      POLITICAL EPIGRAMS.
      .....
      .....
      .....

Massachusetts, Worcester; The Massachusetts Spy Or, American
Oracle of Liberty, 1775-1820+

539. Jan. 7, 1779, #401, p. 3, col. 1. (DLC 614)
      "TWO parties slay whole hecatombs to Jove,"
      POLITICAL EPIGRAMS.
      .....
      .....
      .....

540. Jan. 7, 1779, #401, p. 3, col. 1. (DLC 614)
      "WHAT makes the Yankees such enthusiasts hot?"
      POLITICAL EPIGRAMS.
      .....
      .....
      .....

541. Jan. 7, 1779, #401, p. 3, col. 1. (DLC 614)
      "THE Howes would root up every freedom's fence"
      POLITICAL EPIGRAMS.
      .....
      .....
      .....

542. Jan. 28, 1779, #404, p. 1, col. 1.   (RMEAN, Card #12)
      "BEHOLD how good and joyful a Thing it is, Brethren
        [to dwell together in UNITY,]"
      ANTHEM.
      .....
      .....
      .....

543. Feb. 10, 1780, #458, p. 3, col. 2. (DLC Box 15, folder 3)
      "HAIL! great CALASH! o'erwhelming veil,"
      The CALASH, favorite Song at all the Watering Places, Camps,
        &c. in the British service.
      .....
      .....
      .....

544. March 30, 1780, #464, p. 4, col. 1. (RMEAN, Card #16)
      "WHILE Nature reclin'd on the bosom of May,"
      The FLIGHT of the MUSES.
      ADOLPHUS.
      .....
      The Pennsylvania Journal.

Massachusetts, Worcester; The Massachusetts Spy Or, American
Oracle of Liberty, 1775-1820+

545.   July 6, 1780, #478, p. 2, col. 2.   (RMEAN, Card #17)
       "I AM glad my dear John, now to find that some laws,"
       PADDY Speaking to English JOHN.
       . . . . .
       Balanamona   oro.
       The Maryland Journal.

546.   Aug. 17, 1780, #484, p. 2, col. 3.   (RMEAN, Card #17)
       "KNOW all men, who may be concerned,"
       . . . . .
       Jesse Amble, ?
       . . . . .
       . . . . .

547.   Nov. 2, 1780, #495, p. 3, cols. 2-3.   (RMEAN, Card #18)
       "COLUMBIA! Columbia! to glory arise,"
       HAIL AMERICANS.   A NEW SONG.
       . . . . .
       [Hail Americans, Music by Dr. Dwight]
       . . . . .

548.   Jan. 25, 1781, #507, p. 3, col. 1.   (RMEAN, Card #19)
       "THOU who in glory's shining track,"
       To GENERAL WASHINGTON on the late conspiracy.
       . . . . .
       . . . . .
       By the Hartford Post.   From the Virginia Gazette.

549.   April 26, 1781, #520, p. 3, col. 3.   (RMEAN, Card #20)
       "POOR fellow, what hast thou to do,"
       A reflection on seeing a man loaded with two Sacks at
          one time, and an Oaken-Bough in his hat on the 29th
          of May.
       . . . . .
       . . . . .
       . . . . .

550.   May 4, 1781, #521, p. 4, col. 1.   (RMEAN, Card #20)
       "I'LL tell you what I have to do"
       . . . . .
       POOR FELLOW, Pequaig, May 1781.
       . . . . .
       . . . . .

Massachusetts, Worcester; The Massachusetts Spy Or, American
Oracle of Liberty, 1775-1820+

551.   May 4, 1781, #521, p. 4, col. 2.   (RMEAN, Card #20)
       "POOR Fellow - surely thou'rt an Ass,"
       . . . . .
       No Tory.
       . . . . .
       . . . . .

552.   Aug. 23, 1781, #537, p. 3, cols. 2-3.   (RMEAN, Card #21)
       "AS the papers inform us, a person of note,"
       EPIGRAM-Upon reading in the papers that the King's
          body coachman had killed himself.
       . . . . .
       . . . . .
       A late London Paper.

553.   Nov. 8, 1781, #548, p. 4, cols. 1-2.   (RMEAN, Card #2)
       "While scenes of transport, every breast inspire,"
       ODE.
       . . . . .
       . . . . .
       . . . . .

554.   Jan. 10, 1782, #557, p. 3, col. 3.   (DLC 615)
       "TO Thee great sov'reign of the skies!"
       Address of Praise to the Deity, (adapted to the occasion)
          was sung on the day of the late General Thanksgiving in
          several of the churches in New-Jersey.
       . . . . .
       . . . . .
       . . . . .

555.   Jan. 17, 1782, #558, p. 2, col. 2.   (DLC 615)
       "CORNWALLIS led a country dance,"
       The DANCE. A Ballad.
       . . . . .
       "Yankey Doodle"
       . . . . .

Massachusetts, Worcester; The Massachusetts Spy Or, American
Oracle of Liberty, 1775-1820+

556.   Jan. 17, 1782, #558, p. 4, cols. 1-2.   (DLC 615)
        "'TWAS for the conquest nobly won,"
        An ODE. An humble imitation of Dryden's Alexander's
            feast.
        A Southern Exile.
        .....
        PENNSYLVANIA PACKET.

557.   Feb. 28, 1782, #564, p. 4, cols. 1-2.   (DLC 615)
        ARISE! Arise! your voices raise,"
        The TEMPLE of MINERVA.
        ["a gentleman whose taste in the polite arts is well
            known"] [Francis Hopkinson]
        [The Temple of Minerva; Francis Hopkinson, arr.]
        PHILADELPHIA

558.   March 28, 1782, #568, p. 4, cols. 1-2.   (DLC 615)
        "SINCE life is uncertain, and no one can say,"
        RIVINGTON's (alias PORTABLE SOUP) LAST WILL and TESTAMENT.
        JAMES RIVINGTON, (L.S.) New-York, February 20, 1782.
        .....
        (A true copy from the Records.)

559.   May 2, 1782, #574, p. 4, col. 1.   (DLC 615)
        "THAT a silly old fellow much noted of yore,"
        Lord DUNMORE's PETITION to the Legislature of Virginia,
            Humbly Sheweth.
        Dunmore, Charlestown, Jan. 6, 1782.
        .....
        .....

560.   May 16, 1782, #576, p. 4, col. 1.   (DLC 615)
        "LET those who will, be proud and sneer,"
        A DIALOGUE at Hyde-Park Corner. [between Burgoyne and
            Cornwallis]
        .....
        .....
        .....

561.   June 6, 1782, #579, p. 4, col. 1.   (RMEAN, Card #24)
        "To years far distant, and to scenes more bright,"
        A prophecy of the future glory of AMERICA.
        Young Lady, in 1777.
        . . . . .
        The INDEPENDENT GAZETTER.

562.   June 27, 1782, #582, p. 4, col. 1.   (DLC 615)
        "YE sons of Mars attend,"
        A NEW SONG. Written on the celebration of the Birth of
          the Dauphin, at West-Point.
        . . . . .
        [Restoration March]
        . . . . .

563.   July 11, 1782, #584, p. 4, col. 1.   (DLC 615)
        "WELCOME one Arnold to our shore,"
        ODE addressed to General Arnold.
        LADY CRAVEN.
        . . . . .
        Late London Paper.

564.   Aug. 29, 1782, #591, p. 3, col. 3.   (DLC 615)
        "YOUR golden dreams, your flattering schemes,"
        SATAN's REMONSTRANCE.
        . . . . .
        . . . . .
        Freeman's Journal.

565.   Sept. 19, 1782, #594, p. 4, col. 1.   (DLC 615)
        "[Humbly Sheweth,] THAT your honour's petitioners, tories
          by trade,"
        The REFUGEES PETITION to Sir Guy Carleton. [and "SIR
          GUY's ANSWER"]
        . . . . .
        . . . . .
        . . . . .

Massachusetts, Worcester; The Massachusetts Spy Or, American
Oracle of Liberty, 1775-1820+

566.   Dec. 12, 1782, #606, p. 4, col. 1.   (RMEAN, Card #25)
       "TO thee, fair freedom, I retire"
       Written at an Inn, on a particular Occasion.
       . . . . .
       [The Inn. Music by Mr. Bates.]
       . . . . .

567.   Jan. 9, 1783, #610, p. 3, col. 4.   (RMEAN, Card #26)
       "LET the voice of musick breathe,"
       An ODE for the NEW-YEAR, January 1, 1783.
       . . . . .
       [ODE for the New-Year, 176-; Music by William Boyce].
       . . . . .

568.   Jan. 9, 1783, #610, p. 4, col. 1.   (RMEAN, Card #26)
       "THE Indian Chief who, fam'd of yore,"
       The PROPHECY of King TAMANY.
       . . . . .
       . . . . .
       Freeman's Journal.

569.   May 16, 1783, #629, p. 4, col. 1.   (DLC 616)
       "AT length War's sanguine scenes are o'er:"
       On PEACE: An ODE. Designed for Musick.
       . . . . .
       . . . . .
       New-Jersey Journal.

570.   May 16, 1783, #629, p. 4, col. 1.   (DLC 616)
       "FROM Heaven descends sweet smiling Peace,"
       On PEACE.
       . . . . .
       . . . . .
       Late Philadelphia Paper.

571.   June 5, 1783, #632, p. 4, col. 1.   (DLC 616)
       "LET ev'ry age due honours pay,"
       On PEACE.
       . . . . .
       . . . . .
       . . . . .

NEW HAMPSHIRE

572. June 16, 1778, #18, p. 4, col. 3.   (MWA)
      "Give ear to my song, I'll not tell you a story,"
      THE HALYCON DAYS of OLD ENGLAND.
      . . . . .
      Ye Medley of Mortals.
      London Evening Post.

573. Sept. 29, 1778, #32, p. 2, col. 3.   (MWA)
      "As Collinet and Phebe sat,"
      Collinet and Phebe.   A NEW SONG.
      . . . . .
      [As Collinet and Phebe sat]
      . . . . .

574. Sept. 29, 1778, #32, p. 3, col. 1.   (MWA)
      "When North first began,"
      On Lord North's Recantation.
      . . . . .
      . . . . .
      The London Evening Post.

575. June 1, 1779, #67, p. 1, col. 3.   (MWA)
      "War how I hate thy horrid Name,"
      War.
      . . . . .
      . . . . .
      . . . . .

576. Sept. 21, 1779, #83, p. 3, col. 2.   (MWA)
      "Hark! hear the Trumpet's pleasing Sound,"
      . . . . .
      . . . . .
      . . . . .
      The Pennsylvania Gazette.

577. Oct. 12, 1779, # , p. 4, col. 2.   (MWA)
      "Let venal poets praise a king,"
      . . . . .
      . . . . .
      . . . . .
      The New-Jersey Gazette.

578. Nov. 12, 1776, #26, p. 4, col. 1. (MWA)
      "What discontents, what dire events"
      A SONG.
      J.S.
      .....
      From a late London Paper.

579. Dec. 24, 1776, p. 4, col. 1. (MWA)
      "Hail! O America!"
      .....
      .....
      [God Save the King]
      .....

580. Feb. 11, 1777, p. 4, col. 1. (MWA)
      "As Mars, great God of Battles! lay,"
      A Parody on the "The Watry God"--occasioned by General
        Washington's late Successes in the Jersies.
      .....
      Watry God.
      .....

581. March 11, 1777, #43, p. 3, col. 3. (MWA)
      "The Stygian God, great Beelzebub."
      The Fiery Devil.
      .....
      Watry God.
      .....

582. April 29, 1777, #50, p. 4, col. 3. (MWA)
      "My Lords, with your leave,"
      A NEW WAR SONG.
      Sir Peter Parker.
      Well met Brother Tar.
      .....

583. June 24, 1777, #58, p. 2, cols. 1-2. (MWA)
      "Without wit, without wisdom, half stupid and drunk,"
      The Expedition to Danbury.
      .....
      .....
      .....

584. July 13, 1779, #11, p. 4, col. 1.   (MWA)
      "As Collinet and Phebe sat,"
      Song sung before his Excellency General Washington,
         appointed Grand Master of Free and Accepted Masons
         throughout the United States of America after the
         Procession St. John's Day, the 24th
      .....
      [As Collinet and Phebe sat]
      .....

585. Aug. 9, 1779, #15, p. 4, cols. 1-2.   (NN)
      "By Collier George, Sir Commodore,"
      Version of a late gasconnading and insidious address to
         the inhabitants of Connecticut.
      OBSTINATE, UNPARDONABLE REBEL, July 24th, 1779.
      .....
      The Connecticut Courant.

586. May 25, 1776, #1, p. 4, col. 1. (DLC Early State Records
         Supplement, Microfilm 1551, N.H. Na. Reel 1, Unit 3)
      "WHILST happy in my native land,"
      A SONG. From a new musical interlude called the
         ELECTION.
      . . . . .
      [WHILST happy in my native land]
      . . . . .

587. June 1, 1776, #2, p. 4, col. 1. (DLC Early State Records
         Supplement, Microfilm 1551, N.H. Na. Reel 1, Unit 3)
      "FREEMEN, if you pant for glory,"
      ODE to INDEPENDENCE. ["with a few alterations"]
      . . . . .
      . . . . .
      Town and Country Magazine for Oct. 1774.

588. June 8, 1776, #3, p. 4, col. 1. (DLC Early State Records
         Supplement, Microfilm 1551, N.H. Na. Reel 1, Unit 3)
      "FROM North, tho' stormy winds may blow"
      . . . . .
      . . . . .
      . . . . .
      . . . . .

589. June 29, 1776, #6, p. 4, col. 1. (DLC Early State Records
         Supplement, Microfilm 1551, N.H. Na. Reel 1, Unit 3)
      "YE Yankies who Mole-like still throw up the Earth,"
      ["incomparable Production from a Halifax Paper."]
      . . . . .
      . . . . .
      From a Halifax Paper.

590. July 6, 1776, #7, p. 4, col. 1. (DLC Early State Records
         Supplement, Microfilm 1551, N.H. Na. Reel 1, Unit 3)
      "A HOUND, the fleetest of the breed,"
      . . . . .
      . . . . .
      . . . . .
      . . . . .

New Hampshire, Portsmouth; The Freeman's Journal, or New-Hampshire Gazette, 1776-1778

591.   July 27, 1776, #10, p. 4, col. 1. (DLC Early State
            Records Supplement, Microfilm 1551, N.H. Na. Reel 1,
            Unit 3)
        "AT length, with generous indignation fir'd"
        . . . . .
        Pennsylvaniensis.
        . . . . .
        . . . . .

592.   Aug. 10, 1776, #12, p. 4, col. 1. (DLC Early State
            Records Supplement, Microfilm 1551, N.H. Na. Reel 1,
            Unit 3)
        "AMERICA no longer bears the cause"
        . . . . .
        . . . . .
        . . . . .
        . . . . .

593.   Aug. 17, 1776, #13, p. 4, col. 1. (DLC Early State
            Records Supplement, Microfilm 1551, N.H. Na. Reel 1,
            Unit 3)
        "COME all you brave soldiers, both valiant & free."
        ON INDEPENDENCE.
        . . . . .
        . . . . .
        . . . . .

594.   Sept. 21, 1776, #18, p. 4, col. 1. (DLC Early State
            Records Supplement, Microfilm 1551, N.H. Na. Reel 1,
            Unit 3)
        "NOT all the threats, or favours of a crown,"
        On HONOUR.
        . . . . .
        . . . . .
        . . . . .

595.   Oct. 5, 1776, #20, p. 4, col. 1. (DLC Early State
            Records Supplement, Microfilm 1551, N.H. Na. Reel 1,
            Unit 3)
        "O Despicable state of all that groan"
        ON Liberty.
        . . . . .
        . . . . .
        . . . . .

New Hampshire, Portsmouth; The Freeman's Journal, or New-Hampshire Gazette, 1776-1778

596. Oct. 22, 1776, #22, p. 4, col. 1.   (DLC Box 16, folder
          15)
      "RISE, rise, bright genius rise,"
      .....
      ...., Bordeaux, July 1, 1776.
      "Smile Britannia"
      .....

597. Nov. 5, 1776, #24, p. 4, col. 1.   (DLC Early State Records
          Supplement, Microfilm 1551, N.H. Na. Reel 1, Unit 3)
      "SINCE we are taught, in scripture-word,"
      A Common Prayer for the Present Times.
      .....
      .....
      .....

598. Nov. 19, 1776, #26, p. 4, col. 1.   (DLC Early State Records
          Supplement, Microfilm 1551, N.H. Na. Reel 1, Unit 3)
      "WHEN moral tale let ancient wisdom move,"
      The Horse and the Olive, or War and Peace.
      .....
      .....
      .....

599. Feb. 11, 1777, #38, p. 3, col. 2.   (DLC Early State Records
          Supplement, Microfilm 1551, N.H. Na. Reel 1, Unit 3)
      "AS Mars, Great God of battles! lay,"
      A PARODY on "The Watry God"--occasioned by General
          WASHINGTON's late successes in the Jersies.
      .....
      Watry God.
      .....

600. March 15, 1777, #43, p. 3, col. 3.   (DLC Early State Records
          Supplement, Microfilm 1551, N.H. Na. Reel 1, Unit 3)
      "GALL'WAY has fled, and join'd the venal Howe,"
      .....
      Print 'em egad, New-Town, Bucks County, Feb. 3, 1777.
      .....
      .....

New Hampshire, Portsmouth; The Freeman's Journal, or New-Hampshire Gazette, 1776-1778

601.   March 22, 1777, #44, p. 4, col. 1. (DLC Early State
          Records Supplement, Microfilm 1551, N.H. Na. Reel 1,
          Unit 3)
       "BLUSH, Britain's, blush! at thine inglorious War,"
       On BRITAIN.
       .....
       .....
       The Craftsman, or Say's (British) Journal.

602.   April 12, 1777, #47, p. 4, col. 1. (DLC Early State
          Records Supplement, Microfilm 1551, N.H. Na. Reel 1,
          Unit 3)
       "HARK, the loud Drums, hark, the shrill Trumpet call to
          Arms,"
       A SONG, just come to Hand, which was sung before General
          SULLIVAN, and a Number of respectable Inhabitants of
          Portsmouth, New-Hampshire, March 26th, 1777.
       .....
       The Eugeane's March (sic)
       .....

603.   April 19, 1777, #48, p. 4, col. 1. (DLC Early State
          Records Supplement, Microfilm 1551, N.H. Na. Reel 1,
          Unit 3)
       "MY Lords, with your leave,"
       A NEW WAR SONG.
       Sir Peter Parker.
       "Well met Brother Tar."
       .....

604.   April 26, 1777, #49, p. 4, col. 1. (DLC Early State
          Records Supplement, Microfilm 1551, N.H. Na. Reel 1,
          Unit 3)
       "YE wrong heads, and strong heads, attend to my strains;"
       .....
       .....
       [Derry Down]
       The (LONDON) PUBLIC LEDGER.

605.   Aug. 1, 1777, #8, p. 1, col. 1. (RMEAN Card #68)
       "MY Lord,/Thus the fierce North Wind,"
       A LETTER from Dr. WATTS to Lord Boreas.
       I.W.
       .....
       .....

New Hampshire, Portsmouth; The Freeman's Journal, or New-Hampshire Gazette, 1776-1778

606.   Aug. 16, 1777, #10, p. 3, cols. 1-2.   (DLC Box 16, folder
          15)
        "COME Soldiers all in Chorus join,"
        On the Death of Gen. MONTGOMERY.
        .....
        Hark! Hark! the joy inspiring Horn.   Favorite Hunting
          Song.   [sung by Mr. Taylor]
        .....

607.   Sept. 6, 1777, #13, p. 3, col. 2.   (RMEAN, Card #68)
        "Hail! Patriot Hail! Brave Columbian,"
        A POEM. On that worthy Commander in Cheif of the Army
          of the United States.
        A Friend to his country.
        .....
        .....

608.   Oct. 18, 1777, #19, p. 3, cols. 1-2.   (RMEAN, Card #69)
        "In a mouldering Cave, where th' oppressed retreat,"
        PARODY.
        .....
        [Britannia or the Death of Wolfe]
        Boston.

609.   March 10, 1778, #39, p. 4, col. 1.   (DLC Box 16, folder
          15)
        "HAIL! glorious chief, whom distiny has chose"
        On General GATES.
        .....
        .....
        .....

610.   June 9, 1778, #52, p. 1, cols. 1-2.   (RMEAN, Card #70)
        "As late I travell'd o'er the plain,"
        DATE OBOLUM BELISARIO.
        .....
        .....
        .....

New Hampshire, Portsmouth; The Freeman's Journal, or New-
Hampshire Gazette, 1776-1778

611. June 16, 1778, # , p. 4, col. 3. (RMEAN, Card #71)
      "Give ear to my song, I'll not tell you a story,"
      The Halcyon Days of Old England. Or the Wisdom of
        Adminstration, demonstrated.
      . . . . .
      Ye Medley of Mortals.
      The London Evening Post.

612. Sept. 29, 1778, # , p. 2, col. 3. (RMEAN, Card #72)
      "As Collinet and Phebe Sat,"
      Collinet and Phebe. A New Song.
      A Young Lady in Virginia.
      [As Collinet and Phebe sat].
      . . . . .

613.   1778, # , p. 4, col. 1. (RMEAN, Card #71
        or #72)
      "When North first began."
      On Lord North's Recantation.
      . . . . .
      . . . . .
      The London Evening Post.

614.   Feb. 5, 1773, #851, p. 3, col. 2.   (DLC 657)
       "DAME Liberty's breaking up House,"
       A SALE.
       R.D. C[ar]lington
       [A Sale, Music by Thomas D'Urfey?]
       .....

615.   Feb. 12, 1773, #852, p. 3, col. 1.   (DLC 657)
       "AS BRITANNIA set a wailing"
       ODE.
       .....
       .....
       .....

616.   Jan. 28, 1774, #901, p. 2, col. 3.   (RMEAN, Card #57)
       "As Near Beauteous Boston lying,"
       A New Song.
       .....
       Hosier's Ghost.
       From the Pennsylvania Packet.

617.   June 17, 1774, #921, p. 4, col. 1.   (DLC 658)
       "O! twas a joyful sound to hear"
       .....
       .....
       .....
       Massachusetts Spy, June 2, 1774.

618.   July 22, 1774, #926, p. 4, col. 1.   (RMEAN, Card #59)
       "Rouse ev'ry generous thoughtful Mind,"
       .....
       .....
       .....
       .....

619.   Dec. 23, 1774, #948, p. 3, col. 3.   (RMEAN, Card #61)
       "When Mighty Roast Beef was the Englishman's Food,"
       The Roast Beef of Old-England.
       .....
       [Roast Beef of Old-England]
       .....

New Hampshire, Portsmouth; (Portsmouth) New-Hampshire Gazette,
1756-1820+

620. Dec. 5, 1775, #996, p. 2, col. 2. (DLC Box 17, folder 4)
      "BY my Faith, but I think you're all Makers of Bulls,"
      The Irishman's Epistle to the Officers and Troops at
         Boston.
      .....
      .....
      .....

621. June 16, 1778, #   , p. 4, col. 3. (DLC Early State
         Records Supplement, Microfilm 1551, N.H. Na. Reel 1,
         Unit 4)
      "GIVE ear to my song, I'll not tell you a story,"
      The Halcyon Days of Old England; Or the Wisdom of Ad-
         ministration, demonstrated: A Ballad.
      .....
      Ye Medley of Mortals.
      From the London Evening Post.

622. Sept. 29, 1778, #32, p. 2, col. 3. (DLC Early State
         Records Supplement, Microfilm 1551, N.H. Na. Reel 1,
         Unit 4)
      "AS Collinet and Phebe sat,"
      COLLINET and PHEBE. A NEW SONG.
      By a Young Lady in Virginia.
      [As Collinet and Phebe sat]
      .....

623. Sept. 29, 1778, #32, p. 3, col. 1. (DLC Early State
         Records Supplement, Microfilm 1551, N.H. Na. Reel 1,
         Unit 4)
      "WHEN North first began,"
      On Lord NORTH's Recantation.
      FACT
      .....
      From the London Evening Post.

624. Dec. 1, 1778, #41, p. 3, col. 3. (DLC Early State
         Records Supplement, Microfilm 1551, N.H. Na. Reel 1,
         Unit 4.)
      "WEST of the old Atlantic, firm Liberty stands!"
      The GAMESTER. A New SONG.
      .....
      A late worthy Old LION.
      .....

New Hampshire, Portsmouth; (Portsmouth) New-Hampshire Gazette, 1756-1820+

625. May 11, 1779, #64, p. 3, col. 2. (DLC Early State Records
        Supplement, Microfilm 1551, N.H. Na. Reel 1, Unit 4)
      "OF all the ages ever known"
      The PRESENT AGE.
      .....
      .....
      .....

626. June 1, 1779, #67, p. 1, col. 3. (DLC Early State Records
        Supplement, Microfilm 1551, N.H. Na. Reel 1, Unit 4)
      "WAR! how I hate thy horrid Name,"
      WAR.
      .....
      .....
      .....

627. Sept. 21, 1779, #83, p. 3, col. 2. (DLC Early State
        Records Supplement, Microfilm 1551, N.H. Na. Reel 1,
        Unit 4)
      "HARK! hear the Trumpet's pleasant Sound,"
      .....
      .....
      .....
      From the Pennsylvania (sic) Gazette.

628. Oct. 12, 1779, #2197, p. 4, col. 2. (DLC Early State
        Records Supplement, Microfilm 1551, N.H. Na. Reel 1,
        Unit 4.)
      "LET venal poets praise a King,"
      .....
      An Officer in the American Army.
      .....
      From the NEW JERSEY GAZETTE.

629. Nov. 23, 1779, #2203, p. 1, col. 1. (DLC Box 16, folder 16)
      "POrtsmouth, behold with humble Dread,"
      On the Times.
      .....
      .....
      .....

New Hampshire, Portsmouth; (Portsmouth) New-Hampshire Gazette,
1756-1820+

630.   April 16, 1781, #1276, p. 2, col. 1. (DLC 639)
        "WHEN Alcides, the Son of Olympian Jove,"
        On General WASHINGTON.
        A Soldier, Feb. 11, 1781.
        The Highland March.
        Maryland Journal.

631.   Nov. 17, 1781, #1307, p. 4, col. 3. (DLC 639)
        "WHen southward Cornwallis first enter'd the land"
        NEW SONG. Occasioned by the surrender of Earl Cornwallis
          and his whole army, to General Washington.
        . . . . .
        Derry down.
        . . . . .

632.   Jan. 26, 1782, #1317, p. 2, col. 2. (DLC 640)
        "TO Thee great sov'reign of the skies!"
        Address of Praise to the Diety, (adapted to the occasion)
        . . . . .
        . . . . .
        . . . . .

633.   Feb. 16, 1782, #1320, p. 4, col. 1. (DLC 640)
        "BY your leave, gossip John?"
        PADDY's ADDRESS to JOHN BULL. A NEW BALLAD.
        . . . . .
        Larry Crogan.
        From a late Irish Paper.

634.   May 17, 1783, #1385, p. 1, cols. 2-3. (DLC 641)
        "CEASE that strepent trumpet's sound!--"
        ODE to PEACE.
        . . . . .
        . . . . .
        . . . . .

NEW JERSEY

635. June 3, 1778, #27, p. 2, col. 2. (DLC 674)
      "FROM Parliaments venal, who barter our laws,"
      The Englishman's Litany.
      ANGLICANUS. Cheapside, Feb. 9.
      .....
      London Evening Post of February 12.

636. Nov. 18, 1778, #50, p. 2, col. 1. (DLC 674)
      "TRUE Britons give o'er,"
      LABOUR in VAIN: Or, the Inefficacy of Truth.
      .....
      .....
      London Evening Post.

637.   Feb. 23, 1779, #2, p. 4, col. 1. (NJHi)
        "Gallants attend and hear a friend,"
        The Battle of the Kegs, fought on the river Delaware,
          opposite the city of Philadelphia, Jan. 5, 1778.
        .....
        [Battle of the Kegs]
        .....

638.   Feb. 2, 1780, #51, p. 3, col. 2. (NJHi)
        "With flames they threaten to destroy"
        .....
        ....., Rahway, N.J.
        [Psalm]
        .....

639.   Feb. 9, 1780, #52, p. 4, col. 1. (NJHi)
        "Let worth arise! and ev'ry name be hurl'd"
        The TEMPLE of FAME.
        A Soldier.
        .....
        .....

640.   Feb. 16, 1780, #53, p. 4, col. 1. (NJHi)
        "Heroes of modern or of ancient time"
        The Anticipation for the 99th year of American Independence.
        .....
        .....
        .....

641.   June 21, 1780, #71, p. 4, col. 1. (NJHi)
        "Hail Corsica! than whose recorded name"
        .....
        .....
        .....
        .....

642.   July 19, 1780, #74, p. 4, col. 1. (NJHi)
        "No more, my friends, of vain applause,"
        The TIMES.
        .....
        .....
        .....

643.   Aug. 2, 1780, #76, p. 4, col. 1. (NJHi)
        "All hail superior Sex, exalted fair"
        LINES addressed to the FEMALES of Pennsylvania and
          New Jersey, who have illustrated the nobility of
          their sentiment and the virtue of their patriotism,
          by the late generous subscriptions to the soldiery.
        ......
        ......
        ......

644.   Sept. 27, 1780, #84, p. 4, col. 1. (NJHi)
        "I'll tell you a tale, it's as strange as 'tis true"
        The DOCTOR and the ALDERMAN. Over head and Ears in the Hyp.
        ......
        ......
        ......

645.   Oct. 18, 1780, #87, p. 4, col. 1. (NJHi)
        "Good People we are come to let you know,"
        A POEM on the King's Commissioners offering Terms of
          Peace to AMERICA, July 1778.
        ......
        ......
        ......

646.   Oct. 25, 1780, #88, p. 4, col. 1. (NJHi)
        "When virtue calls, enraptur'd we obey,"
        ......
        ......
        ......
        Pennsylvania Packet.

647.   Dec. 27, 1780, #97, p. 2, col. 1. (NJHi)
        "Thou who in glory's shining track,"
        To General WASHINGTON, on the late conspiracy.
        ......
        ......
        ......

648.   April 4, 1781, #111, p. 2, cols. 1-2.   (NJHi)
        "From noise of camps once more I come"
        An ODE, Upon an Officer's going home on furlough.
        ......
        ......
        ......

649.   June 20, 1781, #122, p. 4, col. 1.   (MWA)
        "An Orphan's woes I sing, ye Great, attend;"
        The ORPHAN.
        Misericors.
        ......
        ......

650.   Aug. 8, 1781, #129, p. 4, col. 1.   (NJHi)
        "Of late the urchin God of love"
        VENUS and CUPID.   An EPIGRAM.
        ......
        ......
        Westminister Magazine.

651.   Aug. 22, 1781, #131, p. 4, col. 1.   (NJHi)
        "Our troops by Arnold thoroughly were bang'd"
        ARNOLD; or a QUESTION ANSWERED.
        ......
        ......
        Late London Paper.

652.   Sept. 19, 1781, #134, p. 4, col. 1.   (NJHi)
        "Accept, great chief, that share of honest praise"
        To his Excellency GENERAL WASHINGTON.
        ......
        ......
        Freeman's Journal.

653.   Sept. 26, 1781, #136, p. 4, col. 1.   (MWA)
        "From a poet that's proud of his wit and his pen,"
        A NEW LITANY.
        ......
        ......
        ......

New Jersey, Chatham; The New-Jersey Journal, 1779-1783

654. Nov. 7, 1781, #142, p. 2, cols. 2-3. (NJHi)
      "Ye loyalists all, within the town"
      Another NEW-YORK ADDRESS. To all honest hearts and sound
        bottoms.
      . . . . .
      [Yankee Doodle]
      . . . . .

655. Nov. 21, 1781, #144, p. 3, col. 1. (MWA)
      "You know there goes a tale,"
      Copy of a Pasquinade stuck up in the city of New-York,
        August 12, 1780.
      . . . . .
      . . . . .
      Political Magazine of May 1780.

656. Nov. 21, 1781, #144, p. 4, col. 1. (MWA)
      "Fame let thy trumpet sound,"
      A NEW SONG.
      . . . . .
      [God Save the King]
      . . . . .

657. Dec. 5, 1781, #146, p. 4, col. 1. (NJHi)
      "Says Richard to Thomas and seem'd half afraid"
      The PROGRESS of ADVICE. A Common Case.
      . . . . .
      . . . . .
      . . . . .

658. Dec. 12, 1781, #147, p. 4, col. 1. (NJHi)
      "I do not know a cheerless hour,"
      CONTENT.
      . . . . .
      . . . . .
      . . . . .

659. Dec. 19, 1781, #148, p. 3, col. 1. (MWA)
      "To Thee, great sov'reign of the skies!"
      ADDRESS of PRAISE to the DEITY, (adapted for the occasion)
      was sung on the day of the late GENERAL THANKSGIVING in
        several of the neighboring churches.
      . . . . .
      . . . . .
      . . . . .

660.   Dec. 26, 1781, #149, p. 2, col. 3. (MWA)
       "From the Americ shore,"
       A New Song.
       .....
       [God Save the King]
       .....

661.   Feb. 6, 1782, #155, p. 4, col. 1. (MWA)
       "Prince William of the Brunswick race,"
       The Royal Adventurer.
       .....
       .....
       .....

662.   April 24, 1782, #167, p. 4, col. 1. (MWA)
       "While free from force the Press remains,"
       On the Freedom of the Press.
       .....
       .....
       .....

663.   June 5, 1782, #173, p. 3, col. 3. (MWA)
       "Ye sons of Mars attend," (Chorus: A Dauphin born, let
         Cannon loud,")
       A NEW SONG. Written on the Celebration of the Birth of
         the Dauphin at West Point.
       .....
       [Restoration March]
       .....

664.   June 12, 1782, #174, p. 4, col. 1. (MWA)
       "From Britain's fam'd island once more I come over,"
       Sir Guy Carlton's ADDRESS to the Americans.
       .....
       .....
       .....

665.   June 19, 1782, #175, p. 4, col. 1. (MWA)
       "Farewell! my Lord, my Zephrys waft you o'er"
       An Address to Lord Cornwallis.
       .....
       .....
       .....

New Jersey, Chatham; The New-Jersey Journal, 1779-1783

666. Aug. 7, 1782, #182, p. 4, col. 1. (MWA)
      "Of great and glorious names to speak,"
      The GEORGES, A NEW SONG.
      .....
      Push about the Jorum.
      .....

667. Aug. 14, 1782, #183, p. 4, col. 1. (MWA)
      "Your golden dreams, your flattering schemes,"
      SATAN'S REMONSTRANCE.
      .....
      .....
      .....

668. Aug. 28, 1782, #185, p. 4, col. 1. (DLC Box 18, folder 1)
      "THE old tory rout"
      THE REVERSE.
      .....
      .....
      .....

669. Feb. 26, 1783, #211, p. 4, col. 1. (MWA)
      "When pregnant Nature strove relief to gain,"
      On American Independency.
      .....
      .....
      .....

670. May 7, 1783, #221, p. 4, col. 1. (MWA)
      "Old Homer--but what have we with him to do,"
      New Liberty-Hall. A SONG.
      .....
      [Liberty Hall, Music by Charles Dibdin?]
      .....

671. Oct. 22, 1783, #245, p. 4, col. 1. (MWA)
      "Ye blood thirsty TORIES, of every degree,"
      A NEW SONG.
      .....
      Derry Down.
      .....

672.   Oct. 21, 1783, #2, p. 4, col. 1.   (MWA)
         "Welcome! thrice welcome, to a rescu'd land,"
         To the AMERICAN ARMY.
         .....
         .....
         .....

673.   Aug. 18, 1779, #86, p. 1, col. 1. (DLC 687)
       "LET venal poets praise a King"
       .....
       An Officer of the American Army, July 20, 1779.
       .....
       .....

674.   Dec. 20, 1780, #156, p. 3, col. 2. (DLC 687)
       "THOU who in glory's shining track,"
       To General WASHINGTON, on the late Conspiracy.
       .....
       .....
       Virginia Gazette.

675.   Jan. 24, 1781, #161, p. 3, col. 2. (DLC 688)
       "HOW hard the lot of human kind --"
       ODE.
       JUVENIS, New-Brunswick, Jan. 20, 1781.
       .....
       .....

676.   Dec. 26, 1781, #209, p. 3, col. 3. (DLC 688)
       "TO Thee, great sov'reign of the skies!"
       Hymn ("..sung in several Churches on the Day of our
          publick Thanksgiving.")
       .....
       .....
       .....

677.   Feb. 6, 1782, #215, p. 3, cols. 1-2. (DLC 689)
       "PRINCE William, of the Brunswick race,"
       The ROYAL ADVENTURER.
       .....
       .....
       Freeman's Journal.

678.   May 21, 1783, #282, p. 3, cols. 2-3. (DLC Early State
          Records Supplement, Microfilm 1551, N.J.N.X., Reel 1,
          Unit 2.)
       "LET ev'ry age due honours pay,
       .....
       .....
       .....
       .....

New Jersey, Trenton; The New-Jersey Gazette, 1778-1786

679. Dec. 23, 1783, #293, p. 4, col. 1. (DLC 690)
      "THE great unequal conflict past,"
      VERSES occasioned by General Washington's arrival in
        this city, on his way to his seat in Virginia.
      . . . . .
      . . . . .
      Freeman's Journal.

NEW YORK

680. July 15, 1782, #7, p. 4, col. 1.   (MWA)
      "Of great and glorious names to speak,"
      The Georges, A New Song.
      .....
      Push about the Jorum.
      .....

681. Sept. 23, 1782, #17, p. 4, col. 1.   (MWA)
      "I sing of George's golden days,"
      Who's the Noodle, A NEW SONG.
      .....
      Od's Blood Who's the NOODLE.
      .....

682. June 9, 1783, #54, p. 4, col. 1.   (MWA)
      "SHall joy not put her Lute in tune,"
      On PEACE.
      A Lady.
      .....
      .....

683. Sept. 24, 1778, #114, p. 4, col. 1.   (MWA)
"Come and listen my lads to sweet Liberty's lay,"
LIBERTY's CALL.
.....
Black-Sloven
.....

684. Aug. 12, 1779, #138, p. 4, col. 1.   (NNHi)
"Hark! hear the Trumpet's pleasing sound!"
.....
.....
.....
Pennsylvania Gazette

685. Sept. 16, 1779, #143, p. 3, cols. 1-2.   (NNHi)
"July they say, the fifteenth day,"
A New Song.
.....
"One night as Ned stept into bed,"
.....

686. Jan. 11, 1781, #197, p. 3, col. 3.   (DLC 699)
"THOU who in glory's shining track,"
To General WASHINGTON, on the late conspiracy.
.....
.....
The Virginia Gazette.

687. Oct. 25, 1781, #235, p. 3, col. 2.   (DLC 699)
"While scenes of transport, every breast inspire,"
.....
.....
.....
.....

688. Jan. 10, 1782, #246, p. 1, col. 1.   (DLC 700)
"THE circling sun, bright monarch of the day,"
For the 1st of January, 1782.
N.W.
.....
.....

New York, Fishkill; (Fishkill) New-York Packet, 1777-1783

689.   June 13, 1782, #268, p. 1, col. 3.   (DLC 700)
       "YE SONS of Mars attend"
       SONG on the celebration of the Birth of the DAUPHIN.
       . . . . .
       Restoration March
       . . . . .

690.   Oct. 10, 1782, #285, p. 1, col. 3.   (DLC 700)
       "NO more my friends, of vain applause,"
       The PRESENT AGE.
       . . . . .
       . . . . .
       The Freeman's Journal.

691.   Oct. 31, 1782, #288, p. 1, col. 2.   (DLC 700)
       "GRAVE Autumn clad in hazy-tinctur'd hue,"
       . . . . .
       . . . . .
       . . . . .
       . . . . .

692.   July 17, 1783, #325, p. 1, cols. 2-3.   (NNHi)
       "Columbia, Columbia, to glory arise"
       The Song.
       . . . . .
       [Hail Americans, Music by Dr. Dwight]
       . . . . .

693.   Nov. 24, 1783, #335, p. 3, col. 2.   (NNHi)
       "Ye Nations Hear th' immortal tale"
       Britain on the Stool of Repentence; An Ode for the New
          Year, Jan. 1st, 1783.
       William Whitehead, Poet Laureat.
       . . . . .
       A London Magazine of January, 1783.

144

694.   July 7, 1777, #1757, p.   , col.   .   (NN)
       "To raise the soul above each base desire,"
       On the setting up the Press at Kingston, in the State
         of New-York.
       .....
       .....
       .....

695. Sept. 27, 1775, #17, p. 3, col. 2, p. 4, col. 1.   (MWA)
      "Americans beware! lest ministerial pow'r,"
      America to her Sons.
      .....
      .....
      .....

696. Oct. 4, 1775, #19, p. 2, col. 1.   (NNHi)
      "In ev'ry Civil War this hazard's run:"
      The DILEMMA.
      .....
      .....
      .....

697. Oct. 14, 1775, #22, p. 1, col. 2, p. 2, col. 1.   (NNHi)
      "While pleasure reigns unrivall'd on this shore"
      .....
      .....
      .....
      .....

698. Oct. 14, 1775, #22, p. 1, col. 2, p. 2, col. 1.   (NNHi)
      "A Stands for Americans -- who scorn to be slaves;"
      An Alphabet for little Masters and Misses.
      .....
      .....
      .....

699. Nov. 25, 1775, #34, p. 3, col. 2.   (NNHi)
      "Rudely forc'd to drink tea, Massachuset (sic) in anger"
      The Quarrel with America familiarly stated.
      .....
      .....
      .....

700. Jan. 3, 1776, #45, p. 3, cols. 1-2.   (NNHi)
      "Ah! yet shall we with horror hear,"
      An ODE for the New-Year.
      .....
      .....
      .....

New York, New York; (New York) Constitutional Gazette, 1775-1776

701. Jan. 6, 1776, #46, p. 3, col. 1. (NNHi)
     "Tho' some folks may tell us, it is not so clever,"
     A Song
     A soldier in the Continental Army.
     Black Sloven
     .....

702. Feb. 7, 1776, #55, p. 3, col. 2. (NNHi)
     "Ye ministers. Who every hour,"
     .....
     .....
     .....
     .....

703. March 2, 1776, #62, p. 1, cols. 1-2. (NNHi)
     "Let little Tyrants, conscience gor'd"
     Warren's Ghost. A Prophetic Elegy
     .....
     .....
     Public Ledger, found in a cave near Luton-Hoo.

704. April 6, 1776, #72, p. 2, cols. 1-2. (MWA)
     "Since you all will have singing, and wont be said nay,"
     The King's own Regulars and their Triumph over the
        Irregulars. A New Song.
     .....
     An old Courtier of the Queen's and the Queen's old
        Courtier...
     .....

705. April 13, 1776, #74, p. 1, cols. 1-2. (NNHi)
     "I WILLIAM TRYON on board the Dutchess"
     The last most excellent Address of William Tryon, Esq;
        to the people of this colony.
     .....
     .....
     .....

706. April 11, 1774, #1172, p. 2, col. 3. (DLC 853)
      "WHILST All with duteous zeal contend,"
      Ode to the MERCURY PACKET-BOAT occasioned by the embarka-
         tion of his Excellency Governor TRYON, for ENGLAND.
      King's-College, New-York, April 6, 1774.
      . . . . .
      . . . . .

707. Oct. 14, 1776, #1303, p. 4, col. 1. (DLC 857)
      "YE Western Gales, whose genial Breath,"
      ODE for His Majesty's Birth-Day, performed June 4, 1776
      Written by William Whitehead, Esq; Poet Laureat, and set
         to music by Dr. Boyce, Master of his Majesty's Band of
         Musicians.
      [Ode for his Majesty's Birthday, performed June 4, 1776]
      . . . . .

708. Oct. 14, 1776, #1303, p. 4, col. 1. (DLC 857)
      "WHO's there? who's there? what horrid din!"
      The RAP at the DOOR, A CATCH, In Four Parts.
      . . . . .
      [A Catch in 4 parts].
      . . . . .

709. Oct. 28, 1776, #1305, p. 4, col. 1. (DLC 857)
      "YET Goddess, sure thou must agree,"
      EXTRACT from Bedlam. A BALLAD.
      Dr. Price.
      . . . . .
      (Lately Published in London).

710. Nov. 25, 1776, #1309, p. 3, col. 3. (DLC 857)
      "THE watry God, great Neptune, lay"
      A Favourite SONG of the REBELS.
      . . . . .
      The Watry God.
      . . . . .

711. Dec. 23, 1776, #1313, p. 4, col. 1. (DLC 857)
      "FAIR Liberty came o'er,"
      . . . . .
      . . . . .
      . . . . .
      . . . . .

New York, New York; New-York Gazette, and Weekly Mercury,
1768-1783

712. April 7, 1777, #1328, p. 2, col. 2. (DLC 858)
      "AGAIN imperial Winter's Sway"
      Ode for the New Year, as performed before their Majesties
        and the Royal Family at St. James's.
      William Whitehead, Esq; Poet Laureat.
      .....
      .....

713. July 2, 1781, #1550, p. 3, col. 1. (DLC 867)
      "By sacred Influence hurl'd,"
      Song.
      .....
      God save the King.
      .....

714.   Dec. 24, 1783, #4, p. 4, col. 1.   (MWA)
        "The great unequal conflict past,"
        Verses occasioned by General WASHINGTON's arrival in
          this city on his way to his seat in Virginia.
        .....
        .....
        Freeman's Journal.

New York, New York
(New York) Independent Journal, 1783-1788

715. Nov. 17, 1783, #1, p. 2, col. 1. (NNHi)
     "Tell me my love, what means that downcast eye,"
     . . . . .
     British Officer.
     . . . . .
     . . . . .

716. Nov. 24, 1783, #2, p. 4, col. 1. (NNHi)
     "A Soldier, a Soldier, a Soldier for me!"
     A favourite song in the new Farce called the Best Bidder.
     . . . . .
     [A Soldier, a Soldier, a Soldier for me!]
     . . . . .

717.   Sept. 9, 1773, #1601, p. 4, col. 1. (DLC 898)
       "HAIL Parent of each manly Joy,"
       ODE to LIBERTY.
       .....
       .....
       .....

718.   Nov. 18, 1773, #1611, p. 4, col. 1. (DLC 898)
       "Permit a giddy trifling Girl"
       .....
       MARCIA
       .....
       .....

719.   Dec. 2, 1773, #1613, p. 4, col. 1. (DLC 898)
       "FAIR Liberty! celestial Goddess, hail!"
       ODE.
       [PHILO-PATRIA]
       .....
       .....

720.   Dec. 23, 1773, #1616, p. 4, col. 1. (PHi)
       "O Liberty! thou Goddess heavenly bright;"
       [On Freedom and Liberty]
       .....
       .....
       .....

721.   Jan. 6, 1774, #1618, p. 4, col. 1. (DLC 900)
       "OH despicable state of all that groan"
       [On Liberty]
       [EMILIA]
       .....
       .....

722.   Jan. 27, 1774, #1621, p. 4, col. 1. (PHi)
       "As near beauteous Boston lying,"
       A New Song
       .....
       Hosier's Ghost
       Pennsylvania Packet

New York, New York; (New-York) Journal, 1766-1776

723. March 10, 1774, #1627, p. 4, col. 1. (DLC 900)
"SWEEP all! sweep all!"
ODE. Sung at the Opening of the Grand India Opera,
   performed at Boston, 16th Dec., 1773. By Signiora Boheti.
[By Signiora Boheti]
. . . . .
. . . . .

724. April 28, 1774, #1634, p. 4, col. 1. (PHi)
"That seat of science, Athens, and earth's proud mistress,
   Rome,"
A Song on LIBERTY.
. . . . .
British Grenadiers.
. . . . .

725. May 12, 1774, #1636, p. 4, col. 1. (PHi)
"While fawning sycophants the nine implore,"
To the glorious Defender of LIBERTY.
. . . . .
. . . . .
. . . . .

726. May 19, 1774, #1637, p. 4, col. 1. (DLC 900)
"FREEDOM's Charms alike engage"
A Favourite Air.
. . . . .
. . . . .
. . . . .

727. June 9, 1774, #1640, p. 4, col. 1. (PHi)
"But should corruption, with despotick rage,"
. . . . .
. . . . .
. . . . .
. . . . .

728. June 16, 1774, #1641, p. 4, col. 1. (PHi)
"Lord, save us from our cruel Fate,"
. . . . .
. . . . .
. . . . .
. . . . .

New York, New York; (New-York) Journal, 1766-1776

729.   July 21, 1774, #1646, p. 4, col. 1. (PHi)
        "Peace to thy royal shade, illustrious [KING]!"
        An ELEGY to the Memory of the late [KING]
        .....
        .....
        London Mercury.

730.   July 28, 1774, #1647, p. 4, col. 1. (PHi)
        "Hail Liberty! A glorious word,"
        .....
        .....
        .....
        .....

731.   Aug. 18, 1774, #1650, p. 4, col. 1. (DLC 900)
        "COME, come, my brave boys, from my song you shall hear,"
        The Glorious SEVENTY FOUR. A NEW SONG.
        .....
        Hearts of Oak.
        .....

732.   Aug. 25, 1774, #1651, p. 4, col. 1. (DLC 900)
        "JOHN HOLT, thou daring treason hinter!"
        .....
        [the humble imitator, of the renown'd polite Mercator]
        .....
        .....

733.   Sept. 1, 1774, #1652, p. 4, col. 1. (PHi)
        "And whither then is British freedom fled,"
        .....
        .....
        .....
        London Evening Post.

734.   Sept. 15, 1774, #1654, p. 4, col. 1. (PHi)
        "To all the pretty girls and boys,"
        A Proclamation.
        .....
        .....
        .....

735.   Sept. 15, 1774, #1654, p. 4, col. 1.   (PHi)
        "Without one grain of honest sense,"
        A MIRROR for a PRINTER.
        .....
        .....
        .....

736.   Sept. 22, 1774, #1655, p. 4, col. 1.   (DLC 900)
        "HARK! --- or does the Muse's ear."
        For his Majesty's Birth-Day, June 4, 1774.
        William Whitehead, Esq; Poet Laureat.
        [Ode for his Majesty's Birth-Day, June 4, 1774]
        .....

737.   Sept. 22, 1774, #1655, p. 4, col. 1.   (DLC 900)
        "HARK! Or does the indignant ear"
        An ODE, humbly inscribed to William Whitehead, Esq; Poet
           Laureat to George, King of Great Britain, and America.
        .....
        .....
        The London Evening Post.

738.   Oct. 6, 1774, #1657, p. 4, col. 1.   (DLC 900)
        "GOD prosper long our liberty,"
        A PARODY on the Song of Chevy Chace.
        .....
        Chevy Chace.
        The London Evening Post.

739.   Oct. 13, 1774, #1658, p. 4, col. 1.   (PHi)
        "O My baby, my baby,"
        A New Song. Supposed to have been sung by Goody N[ort]h,
           by way of lullaby to the foundling brat, the Popish Quebec
           bill.
        .....
        O my kitten, my kitten.
        St. James's Chronicle.

740.   Oct. 27, 1774, #1660, p. 4, col. 1. (DLC 900)
        "LET others strive by servile arts to gain,"
        To GENERAL L---
        AMERICA.
        .....
        .....

741.   Nov. 17, 1774, #1663, p. 4, col. 1., continued in 1665,
            1666, 1667 (PHi)
        "Oh Boston! late with ev'ry pleasure crown'd,"
        .....
        .....
        .....

742.   Dec. 22, 1774, #1668, p. 4, col. 1. (DLC 900)
        "WHEN Britons first, by Heav'ns command,"
        An AMERICAN PARODY on the old song, of "RULE BRITANNIA."
        .....
        Rule Britannia.
        .....

743.   Feb. 16, 1775, #1676, p. 4, col. 1. (DLC 902)
        "LOST is our old simplicity of times,"
        On the Proceedings against America.
        .....
        .....
        A late London Magazine.

744.   March 2, 1775, #1678, p. 4, col. 1. (DLC 902)
        "HAIL to the man whose gen'rous soul disdains"
        Address to the Friends of Messrs. Cruger and Burke, on
            their election as Representatives in Parliament for the
            City of Bristol, in opposition to the ministerial
            interest.
        .....
        .....
        .....

745.   April 6, 1775, #1683, p. 4, col. 1. (DLC 902)
        "WHEN wicked men, with foul intent,"
        An Ode, a little altered.
        .....
        .....
        .....

New York, New York; (New-York) Journal, 1766-1776

746. April 13, 1775, #1684, p. 4, col. 1. (DLC 902)
"TO thee fair Freedom, I retire,"
Written at an Inn, on a particular Occasion.
.....
[The Inn. Music by Mr. Bates.]
.....

747. May 4, 1775, #1687, p. 4, col. 1. (DLC 902)
"LET Britons, now sunk into Tyrants and Slaves!"
.....
.....
.....
.....

748. May 11, 1775, #1688, p. 4, col. 1. (DLC 902)
"PRESERVE us Lord, from wicked hands,"
.....
.....
.....
.....

749. June 8, 1775, #1692, p. 4, col. 1. (DLC 902)
"COME listen my cocks, to a brother and friend,"
The SAILOR's ADDRESS.
.....
[Hearts of Oak]
A London Paper.

750. June 22, 1775, #1694, p. 4, col. 1. (DLC 902)
"BY my faith but I think ye're all makers of bulls,"
The Irishman's Epistle to the Officers and Troops of
    Boston.
PADDY.
.....
The Pennsylvania Magazine for May 1775.

751. July 6, 1775, #1696, p. 4, col. 1. (DLC 902)
"YE sons of true freedom and spirit,"
An EXTEMPORE SONG, Composed in a Jovial Company.
.....
A light heart and a thin pair of breeches goes through
    the world, brave boys.
.....

752. Aug. 3, 1775, #1700, p. 4, col. 1.   (DLC 902)
      "YE heirs of freedom! glorious is your cause,"
      To the AMERICANS.
      CATO, April 16, 1775.
      .....
      .....

753. Aug. 10, 1775, #1701, p. 4, col. 1.   (DLC 902)
      "AT length the Action is commenc'd,"
      .....
      .....
      .....
      .....

754. Aug. 17, 1775, #1702, p. 4, col. 1.   (DLC 902)
      "IN a chariot of light from the regions of day,"
      LIBERTY TREE. A new Song.
      .....
      The Gods of the Greeks.
      .....

755. Aug. 24, 1775, #1703, p. 4, col. 1.   (DLC 902)
      "WE are the troops that ne'er will stoop"
      The Pennsylnania March. (sic)
      .....
      The Scotch Song I winna Marry Ony Lad, but Sandy o'er
         the Lee.
      .....

756. Aug. 31, 1775, #1704, p. 4, col. 1.   (DLC 902)
      "FROM native skies, when Angels fell"
      .....
      .....
      .....
      .....

757. Sept. 7, 1775, #1705, p. 4, col. 1.   (DLC 902)
      "'TIS money makes the member vote,"
      A JUNTO SONG.
      .....
      A begging we will go, we'll go, &c.
      .....

758.   Oct. 5, 1775, #1709, p. 4, col. 1.   (DLC 902)
        "OUR political wrong heads, to shew themselves frantic,"
        On the American Expedition.
        The National Wish.
        .....
        The London Evening Post.

759.   Oct. 19, 1775, #1711, p. 4, col. 1.   (DLC 902)
        "WHENCE this wild uproar, Oh ye muses tell?"
        .....
        .....
        .....
        .....

760.   Oct. 26, 1775, #1712, p. 4, col. 1.   (DLC 902)
        "HOW sleep the brave, who sink to rest,"
        On the American Heroes who bravely fell in Defence of the
            dearest Rights and Freedom of their Country, in the late
            Battles at Lexington and Charles-Town.
        .....
        .....
        .....

761.   Nov. 2, 1775, #1713, p. 4, col. 1.   (DLC 902)
        "HIGH on the banks of Delaware,"
        .....
        ...., September 1775.
        .....
        .....

762.   Nov. 16, 1775, #1715, p. 4, col. 1.   (DLC 902)
        "WHOM should we fear, since God to us,"
        .....
        .....
        .....
        .....

763.   Nov. 23, 1775, #1716, p. 4, col. 1.   (DLC 902)
        "REBELS! Americans disclaim"
        On a late Proclamation.
        .....
        .....
        .....

764. Dec. 14, 1775, #1719, p. 4, col. 1. (DLC 902)
      "WHILE selfish knaves, to virtue's dictates blind,"
      To Col. A--- M---.
      PHILO PATRIOTA.
      .....
      .....

765. Jan. 4, 1776, #1722, p. 4, col. 1. (DLC Box 22, 15)
      "FAIR Liberty, celestial maid,"
      An Ode to LIBERTY.
      ....., New-York, December 27, 1775.
      .....
      .....

766. Feb. 15, 1776, #1728, p. 4, col. 1. (PHi)
      "Parent of all, omnipotent,"
      The Patriot's Prayer.
      .....
      .....
      .....

767. Feb. 22, 1776, #1729, p. 4, col. 1. (PHi)
      "He whose heart with social fire,"
      .....
      .....
      .....
      .....

768. Feb. 29, 1776, #1730, p. 4, col. 1. (PHi)
      "Why should vain mortals, tremble at the sight of"
      The American Hero. A Saphic Ode.
      .....
      [Bunker Hill, Music by Andrew Law]
      .....

769. March 14, 1776, #1732, p. 4, col. 1. (DLC Box 22, 15)
      "WHEN haughty monarchs quit this chequer'd scene,"
      .....
      .....
      .....
      .....

New York, New York; (New-York) Journal, 1766-1776

770.   April 11, 1776, #1736, p. 4, col. 1. (PHi)
       "As Collinet and Phebe sat"
       A New Song
       .....
       [As Collinet and Phebe sat]
       .....

771.   May 16, 1776, #1741, p. 4, col. 1. (DLC Box 22, 15)
       "LORD, save us, for thy glorious name,"
       .....
       .....
       .....
       .....

772.   May 30, 1776, #1743, p. 4, col. 1. (PHi)
       "No muse I ask to aid my lays,"
       .....
       .....
       .....
       .....

773.   July 11, 1776, #1749, p. 4, col. 1. (DLC Box 22, 15)
       "FREEMEN, if you paint (sic) for glory,"
       .....
       .....
       .....
       .....

774.   July 18, 1776, #1750, p. 4, col. 1. (DLC Box 22, 15)
       "IF that my foes did seek my shame,"
       Psalm IV. Verses 13-26.
       Sternhold and Hopkins's Translation
       .....
       An old prayer Book. (IV Psalm. Verses 13-26)

775. April 28, 1780, #35, p. 2, col. 2.   (NN)
      "Now, my jolly boys, attack 'em,"
      The SPANISH WAR. Addressed to the TARS of OLD-ENGLAND
      ......
      ......
      ......

776. Aug. 15, 1783, #211, p. 4, col. 1.   (MWA)
      "At length the troubled waters rest,"
      ODE for his MAJESTY's BIRTH-DAY, June 4, 1783.
      ......
      ......
      ......

New York, New York
New-York Morning Post, 1783-1792

777.   July 25, 1783, #125, p. 3, col. 2.   (MWA)
       "At length War's sanguine scenes are o'er,"
       On the Peace, An Ode. Designed for Music.
       .....
       .....
       Maryland Gazette, July 4.

778.   Jan. 18, 1776, #3, p. 4, col. 1. (DLC 931)
        "WHILE tyrants lift their impious hands,"
        An ODE: Suitable to the Times
        .....
        .....
        .....

779.   Feb. 1, 1776, #5, p. 4, col. 1. (DLC 931)
        "WHILE base, ambitious minds contend"
        An ODE.
        .....
        .....
        .....

780.   Feb. 22, 1776, #8, p. 4, col. 1. (DLC 931)
        "AMERICA lift up thy head,"
        The Rising Glories of AMERICA.
        .....
        .....
        .....

781.   June 13, 1776, #24, p. 4, col. 1. (DLC 931)
        "WHEN virtuous ardour, from motives sincere,"
        A NEW SONG.
        .....
        [Black Sloven]
        .....

782.   June 27, 1776, #26, p. 4, col. 1. (DLC 931)
        "AT length--with generous indignation fir'd,"
        .....
        P.
        .....
        .....

783.   July 11, 1776, #28, p. 4, col. 1. (DLC 931)
        "FROM North, tho' stormy winds may blow,"
        .....
        .....
        .....
        .....

New York, New York; New York Packet, 1776

784.   July 18, 1776, #29, p. 4, col. 1. (DLC 931)
        "HAPPY's the man, who unconstrain'd"
        ODE on LIBERTY.
        . . . . .
        . . . . .
        . . . . .

785.   July 25, 1776, #30, p. 4, col. 1. (NN)
        "Come ye valiant sons of thunder"
        The Soldier's Sentimental Toast.
        . . . . .
        . . . . .
        . . . . .

786.   Aug. 1, 1776, #31, p. 4, col. 1. (NN)
        "Hail! O America!"
        . . . . .
        . . . . .
        [God save the King]
        . . . . .

787.   Aug. 15, 1776, #33, p. 4, col. 1. (DLC 931)
        "AUSPICIOUS hour! again the fav'ring muse"
        . . . . .
        . . . ., Cow-Neck, Aug. 2, 1776.
        . . . . .
        . . . . .

New York, New York
New York Packet, 1783

788. Dec. 18, 1783, #342, p. 1, col. 4. (MWA)
      "COME! to Columbia's God your voices raise,"
      An ODE. Written on the late THANKSGIVING DAY.
      .....
      .....
      .....

New York, New York
Rivington's New-York Gazette, 1783

789. Dec. 24, 1783, #756, p. 2, col. 4, p. 3, col. 1-2.   (NNHi)
      "Life of the Hero, as well as of the Sage"
      Feste Champestre
      Madame La Countesse de Houdetot
      . . . . .
      . . . . .

790. Dec. 24, 1783, #756, p. 2, col. 4, p. 3, col. 1-2.   (NNHi)
      "Ame du Héros, it du Sâge"
      Feste Champestre
      Madame La Countesse de Houdetot
      . . . . .
      . . . . .

791.   Nov. 25, 1773, #32, p. 2, col. 4. (DLC 949)
        "There's Pop--li--cola, that Lags of a Tory,"
        To the Sons of Liberty in New York; A Hint, as a Song,
           to be improved, as the Tea Occasion may require.
        .....
        .....
        .....

792.   Dec. 2, 1773, #33, p. 3, col. 1. (DLC 949)
        "There's GIN and there's BRAN-DY, and heigh doodle-dandy,"
        CONTINUATION of the Song in our Last; (the chorus being
           adapted to the present mode.)
        .....
        .....
        .....

793.   Dec. 23, 1773, #36, p. 1, col. 3. (DLC 949)
        "Troddle, troddle, 'tis got in my noddle,"
        A Second Continuation of the Liberty Song.
        .....
        .....
        .....

794.   Feb. 3, 1774, #42, p. 1, col. 2. (DLC 950)
        "HUZZA! HUZZA! then cry'd a Skinner,"
        The Hottentot Chief presents the following to publick view,
           which he found in the Kraal of one of his subjects.
        X., New-York, 28th January, 1774.
        .....
        .....

795.   Feb. 3, 1774, #42, p. 1, col. 2. (DLC 950)
        "An INDEPENDENT and a PAGE,"
        The Hottentot Chief presents the following to publick view,
           which he found in the Kraal of one of his subjects.
        ....., N.Y., Jan. 28, 1774
        .....
        .....

New York, New York; Rivington's New-York Gazetteer, 1773-1775

796. Feb. 17, 1774, #44, p. 1, col. 1.   (DLC 950)
     "WHAT did my Phlogy, my Phlogy,"
     A NEW SONG on Doctor Lucas.
     Mary the Nurse, [Philadelphia, Feb. 14, 1774]
     Hey! my Kitten, my Kitten, &c.
     Philadelphia, Feb. 14, 1774.

797. Feb. 17, 1774, #44, p. 2, col. 3, part of cols. 2-3.
        (DLC 950)
     "A PIGEON* who'd think it, alas! a fine trinket,"
     Hickup-Ho, Ho, Ho,---Halloo.--Halloo.---......
     An Hottentot Priest
     .....
     .....

798. March 17, 1774, #48, p. 3, col. 1. (DLC 950)
     "IF Fortune would smile, and I cannot complain"
     A MORAL SONG, Music by Dr. Arne.
     K.C., New York, March 14, 1774.
     [If Fortune would smile, and I cannot complain]
     .....

799. April 7, 1774, #51, p. 2, col. 2. (DLC 950)
     "WHILST ALL with duteous zeal contend,"
     Ode to the MERCURY PACKET-BOAT; occasioned by the em-
        barkation of his Excellency Governor TRYON, for England.
     Kings-College, New-York, April 6, 1774.
     .....
     .....

800. July 21, 1774, #66, p. 1, col. 4.   (DLC 950)
     "SOME Muse assist me to relate,"
     A NEW SONG
     .....
     Blubber-Hall, alias Kitty Fell
     .....

801. Aug. 4, 1774, #68, p. 4, col. 1. (DLC 950)
     "WHAT a hubbub is here, my dear father, of late,"
     ADVICE from a young Lady to her Father.
     .....
     .....
     .....

New York, New York; Rivington's New-York Gazetteer, 1773-1775

802.   Dec. 22, 1774, #88, p. 2, col. 2.   (DLC 950)
       "UPON my word it's very hard"
       On hearing that the Poor Man was tarred and feathered.
       A Poor Man, New-York, Dec. 19, 1774
       . . . . .
       . . . . .

803.   Jan. 5, 1775, #90, p. 2, col. 2.   (DLC 951)
       "ON Calvert's plains new faction reigns,"
       . . . . .
       Agricola, Baltimore, Dec. 19, (1774)
       Abbot of Canterbury, or Wilkes's Wriggle
       . . . . .

804.   Jan. 12, 1775, #91, p. 2, col. 3.   (DLC 951)
       "COULD I the Abundance of my Sorrow show,"
       O Tempora! O Mores!
       No Yankee (one of the People called FRIENDS.)
       . . . . .
       . . . . .

805.   Jan. 26, 1775, #93, p. 2, col. 3.   (DLC 951)
       "WOULD you know what a Whig is, and always was,"
       The Whig: A Song.
       . . . . .
       "Would you have a young virgin of fifteen years."
       . . . . .

806. Jan. 16, 1777, #1, p. 4, col. 1. (PHi)
      "AMERICANS swarming by thousands on shore,"
      A new SONG
      A Prisoner in Boston Goal
      BLACK SLOVEN
      .....

807. March 6, 1777, #8, p. 4, col. 1. (PHi)
      "Ye critics, who wait for an end of the scene,"
      A VAUDEVIL. Sung by the characters at the conclusion
        of a new Farce called the BOSTON BLOCKADE.
      .....
      .....
      .:...

808. March 20, 1777, #10, p. 1, col. 2. (PHi)
      "GODDESS! or MUSE! --whate'er thy name,"
      The SEIGE OF QUEBEC.
      .....
      .....
      .....

809. June 5, 1777, #21, p. 3, col. 2. (PHi)
      "Blest cause of genial life, arise,"
      SONG
      A loyal subject, for the 4th day of June, 1777
      Rule Britannia
      .....

810. Sept. 17, 1778, #106, p. 3, col. 1. (PHi)
      "There was a time, when Britan's (sic) daring sons"
      The past, present, and future.
      BELLARIO
      .....
      From a late English MAGAZINE.

811. Jan. 1, 1779, Broadside (PHi)
      "BREATHING Sedition a rash fiery Band,"
      A HAPPY NEW YEAR to the LOYAL CUSTOMERS of the ROYAL
        AMERICAN GAZETTE
      .....
      .....
      .....

New York, New York; N.Y. Royal American Gazette, 1777-1783

812.   March 11, 1779, #156, p. 3, col. 1.   (PHi)
        "RESTOR'D Britannia views her long lost son,"
        On hearing of Lieutenant Colonel CAMPBELL's success in
            GEORGIA
        I.C.
        .....
        .....

813.   May 18, 1779, #175, p. 3, col. 1.   (PHi)
        "WITHOUT complaisance I appeal,"
        To STANDFAST
        .....
        .....
        See Mr. Rivington's paper of 15th May, 1779

814.   May 20, 1779, p. 3, col. 3.   (PHi)
        "Thy Spirit Standfast, let me share,"
        To STANDFAST
        EDGAR, N.Y., May 19, 1779
        .....
        .....

815.   May 25, 1779, #177, p. 3, cols. 1-2.   (PHi)
        "ANTIQUITY exults no more,"
        A SONG
        .....
        First of August
        .....

816.   June 6, 1779, #189, p. 3, cols. 1-2.   (PHi)
        "When faction brandishing her horrid sting"
        The TIMES.   A POEM (Part I)
        Michael Querno, Poet Laureat to the Congress.
        .....
        .....

817.   June 8, 1779, #190, p. 3, col. 1.   (PHi)
        "WHIGS of all denominations"
        .....
        .....
        .....
        .....

New York, New York; N.Y. Royal American Gazette, 1777-1783

818.   July 13, 1779, #191, p. 2, cols. 1-3. (PHi)
       "Why hast thou soar'd so high, ambitious muse?"
       The TIMES. (Part II)
       Camillo Querno, Poet Laureat to the Congress
       .....
       .....

819.   Aug. 10, 1779, #199, p. 2, cols. 1-3. (PHi)
       "When the wise ruler of Clubdubdrib's isle,"
       The TIMES. (Part III)
       Camillo Querno, Poet Laureat to the Congress
       .....
       .....

820.   Sept. 2, 1779, #206, p. 3, col. 1. (PHi)
       "Let Gallia mourn! th'insulting foe,"
       ODE for HIS MAJESTY's BIRTH-DAY June 4, 1779
       .....
       .....
       .....

821.   March 30, 1780, #266, p. 2, cols. 1-2. (PHi)
       "SLUGGARDS from my soul I scorn"
       The BRITISH SOLDIER. An ODE.
       .....
       .....
       .....

822.   March 30, 1780, #266, p. 2, col. 2. (PHi)
       "I'm sure that, like Boteler, I am not afraid"
       The BRITISH SAILOR. An ODE.
       .....
       .....
       .....

823.   April 4, 1780, #267, p. 3, col. 1. (PHi)
       "When heroes seek the realms above,"
       On the Death of Captain FARMER.
       .....
       .....
       .....

New York, New York; N.Y. Royal American Gazette, 1777-1783

824.   May 18, 1780, #280, p. 3, col. 3. (PHi)
        "By various means the tuneful choir"
        AN ODE.
        .....
        .....
        .....

825.   May 30, 1780, #283, p. 2, col. 3. (PHi)
        "YE Hearts of Oak, who wish to try"
        A new Song
        .....
        Ye Hearts of Oak, who wish to try.
        A late London Paper.

826.   June 15, 1780, #287, p. 2, col. 3. (PHi)
        "With party away,"
        The BRITISH FLAG TRIUMPHANT, A SONG, On the defeat of the
          Spanish Fleet.
        .....
        [The British Flag Triumphant]
        .....

827.   June 22, 1780, #289, p. 3, col. 2. (PHi)
        "Heard ye the welcome sound of joy?"
        ODE for HIS MAJESTY's Birth-Day.
        J.W.H.
        .....
        .....

828.   July 4, 1780, #292, p. 2, col. 3. (PHi)
        "Now the British Boys with spirit"
        The ENCAMPMENTS.
        .....
        .....
        .....

829.   July 6, 1780, #293, p. 3, col. 1. (PHi)
        "WEEP! Gallia, weep! thy crested flow'rs"
        To GALLIA.
        .....
        .....
        From WHITEHALL EVENING POST

New York, New York; N.Y. Royal American Gazette, 1777-1783

830.   July 25, 1780, #298, p. 1, col. 3.   (PHi)
       "Now vernal gales refresh the cheerful sky,"
       On the British Fleet rendezvousing at Spithead for Channel
         Service.
       .....
       .....
       From the MORNING CHRONICLE

831.   July 27, 1780, #291, p. 1, col. 3.   (PHi)
       "ADORN'D by sun-beams from the skies,"
       An ODE for the BIRTH-DAY of her MAJESTY.   May 19, 1780.
       .....
       .....
       From the MORNING CHRONICLE.

832.   Dec. 12, 1780, #330, p. 2, col. 3.   (PHi)
       "While faction lifts her impious hand,"
       .....
       .....
       .....
       From the MORNING CHRONICLE.

833.   Dec. 19, 1780, #332, p. 2, col. 3.   (PHi)
       "Oppress'd and struggling with a weight of woe,"
       STANZAS on the late dreadful insurrections in the cities
         of London and Westminster, and the irrepairable NATIONAL
         loss in the consumption of Lord MANSFIELD's MANU-
         SCRIPTS.
       .....
       .....
       From the MORNING CHRONICLE.

834.   March 6, 1781, #   , p. 3, col. 3.   (PHi)
       "Freedom, Peace, Plenty, all in advance,"
       .....
       .....
       .....
       Universal Magazine.

New York, New York; N.Y. Royal American Gazette, 1777-1783

835.   Aug. 14, 1781, #399, p. 3, cols. 1-2.   (MWA)
       "Still does the rage of war prevail!"
       ODE for his Majesty's Birth-Day, June 4, 1781.
       .....
       [Ode for his Majesty's Birth-day, June 4, 1781. Music by
         Mr. Stanley]
       .....

836. June 6, 1778, #176, p. 3, col. 3. (RMEAN, Card 14)
      "THE trembling Muse her grateful lays"
      On His MAJESTY's BIRTH-DAY
      .....
      .....
      .....

837. Sept. 19, 1778, #206, p. 2, col. 1. (DLC 952)
      "IN Esop's days, when all things spoke,"
      The Dog and the Shadow, A Modern Apologue.
      .....
      .....
      .....

838. Oct. 3, 1778, #210, p. 3, col. 2. (DLC 952)
      "From Lewis, Monsieur Gerard came"
      Yankee Doodle's Expedition to Rhode-Island.
      Written at Philadelphia
      [Yankee Doodle]
      .....

839. Oct. 24, 1778, #216, p. 3, col. 1. (RMEAN, Card 16)
      "Our farce is now finish'd, your sport's at an end,"
      SONG. (Chorus sung in "an admirable Farce called
         INDEPENDENCE")
      .....
      [Derry Down]
      .....

840. Nov. 11, 1778, #221, p. 3, cols. 1-2. (DLC 952)
      "It was on Mr. Peroy's land,"
      ["Authentic account of the affair of honour which happened
         on the 13th ultimo."]
      ...., Charles-Town, S.C., Sept. 1.
      [Yankee Doodle]
      .....

841. Dec. 5, 1778, #228, p. 3, col. 2. (DLC 952)
      "REJOICE, Americans, rejoice!"
      A FABLE. Addressed to the Americans, upon their Treaty
         with France.
      .....
      .....
      .....

New York, New York; Royal Gazette, 1777-1783

842. Dec. 23, 1778, #233, p. 3, cols. 1-2. (DLC 952)
      "Hark! hark! the bugle's lofty sound"
      SONG
      Soldier, N.Y., Dec. 18, 1778.
      Hark! Hark! the joy-inspiring Horn
      . . . . .

843. Dec. 30, 1778, #235, p. 3, col. 4. (DLC 952)
      "FOR Battle prepar'd in their country's just cause,"
      BRITISH LIGHT INFANTRY.
      Loyal American Refugee, N.Y., Dec. 29, 1778.
      Black Sloven
      . . . . .

844. Jan. 2, 1779, #236, p. 3, col. 1. (DLC 953)
      "WHAT though last year be past and gone,"
      The Old Year and the New. A Prophecy.
      . . . . .
      'Tis not yet Day
      . . . . .

845. Jan. 2, 1779, #236, p. 3, col. 2. (DLC 953)
      "The Prophet, as became a Reverend Seer,"
      THE SACRIFICE [Recitative]
      . . . . .
      . . . . .
      . . . . .

846. Jan. 2, 1779, #236, p. 3, col. 2. (DLC 953)
      "As tyrant power and slavish fear"
      THE SACRIFICE [Air]
      . . . . .
      How much superior beauty awes
      . . . . .

847. Jan. 2, 1779, #236, p. 3, col. 2. (DLC 953)
      "Thus, having buried the daemon of enmity,"
      THE SACRIFICE [Alegro]
      . . . . .
      If you can caper as well as you modulate, &c., Daphne in
        Midas.
      . . . . .

New York, New York; Royal Gazette, 1777-1783

848.   Jan. 2, 1779, #236, p. 3, col. 3. (DLC 953)
        "AND so, you've been courting the Muses, my boy;"
        To the Loyal American Refugee who made the Musical
            Offering to the British Light Infantry in the last
            Gazette.
        SQUIB.
        . . . . .
        . . . . .

849.   Jan. 2, 1779, #236, p. 3, col. 3. (DLC 953)
        "YOUR boy, my good master, is happy to find,"
        To Mr. SQUIB.
        SIMPLE FLASH.
        . . . . .
        . . . . .

850.   Jan. 23, 1779, #242, p. 3, col. 3.   (DLC 953)
        "SOLDIER whilst the flowing bowl"
        A MEDLEY for the LIGHT INFANTRY.
        A Soldier, N.Y., Jan. 20, 1779.
        Over the Hills and far away
        . . . . .

851.   Jan. 23, 1779, #242, p. 3, col. 3.   (DLC 953)
        "Listen to that swelling noise!"
        A MEDLEY for the LIGHT INFANTRY.
        A Soldier
        By the gayly circling Glass
        . . . . .

852.   Jan. 23, 1779, #242, p. 3, col. 3.   (DLC 953)
        "Behold with what ardor to action they press,"
        A MEDLEY for the LIGHT INFANTRY.
        A Soldier
        Away to the Copse.
        . . . . .

853.   Jan. 23, 1779, #242, p. 3, col. 3.   (DLC 953)
        "Mark yon wretch submissive bending,"
         A MEDLEY for the LIGHT INFANTRY.
         A Soldier
        Hosier's Ghost.
        . . . . .

New York, New York; Royal Gazette, 1777-1783

854. Jan. 23, 1779, #242, p. 3, col. 3. (DLC 953)
      "We've shewn them full oft' of what stuff we are made,"
      A MEDLEY for the LIGHT INFANTRY.
      A Soldier
      Lumps of Pudding
      . . . . .

855. March 17, 1779, #257, p. 3, col. 1. (DLC 953)
      "BEHOLD this Badge the Female Test,"
      ["on Occasion of Mr. Gerard's Entertainment at the
        City Tavern."]
      ["a Lady of the first Fashion in Philadelphia"]
      . . . . .
      . . . . .

856. March 17, 1779, #257, p. 3, col. 1. (DLC 953)
      "HERE's a Bumper brave boys to the Health of our King,"
      A SONG.
      ["A Refugee on reading the King's Speech, and sung at
        the Refugee Club in this City"]
      Hearts of Oak
      . . . . .

857. June 26, 1779, #286, p. 1, cols. 2-4. (DLC 953)
      "'TWAS on the twenty fourth of May," (CANTO I)
      An Historical BALLAD of the Proceedings at Philadelphia
        24th and 25th May, 1779.
      Loyalist
      . . . . .
      . . . . .

858. June 26, 1779, #286, p. 1, cols. 2-4. (DLC 953)
      "Now Titan rais'd his flaming head" (CANTO II)
      An Historical BALLAD of the Proceedings at Philadelphia
        24th and 25th May, 1779.
      Loyalist
      . . . . .
      . . . . .

New York, New York; Royal Gazette, 1777-1783

859.   June 30, 1779, #287, p. 3, col. 3. (DLC 953)
        "WHEN Royal George rul'd o'er this land,"
        The American Vicar of Bray. 1779.
        .....
        Vicar of Bray
        .....

860.   Nov. 6, 1779, #324, p. 2, cols. 2-3. (DLC 954)
        "JOY to great Congress, joy an hundred fold,"
        The CONGRATULATION. A POEM.
        .....
        .....
        .....

861.   Nov. 24, 1779, #329, p. 2, cols. 2-3. (DLC 954)
        "LET Songs of triumph every voice employ,"
        The FEW DE JOIE: A POEM.
        .....
        .....
        .....

862.   Nov. 27, 1779, #330, p. 2, col. 2. (DLC 954)
        "ROUSE, Britons! at length,"
        A NEW BALLAD.
        .....
        [Derry Down]
        .....

863.   Nov. 27, 1779, #330, p. 3, col. 3. (DLC 954)
        "COME let us rejoice,"
        The Seige of SAVANNAH.
        .....
        The Free Mason's Song
        .....

864.   Nov. 27, 1779, #330, p. 3, cols. 3-4. (DLC 954)
        "THE Frenchmen came upon the coast,"
        A New Song to an Old Tune.
        A Yankee
        Doodle-doo
        .....

New York, New York; Royal Gazette, 1777-1783

865. Nov. 27, 1779, #330, Supplement, p. 1, col. 2. (DLC 954)
      "COME cheer up, my Lads, let us haste to the Main,"
      The JOLLY TARS of OLD ENGLAND. A NEW SONG.
      .....
      Hearts of Oak
      .....

866. Jan. 1, 1780, #340, p. 2, col. 3. (RMEAN, Card 26)
      "The World can bear Witness, that nothing cou'd ruffle,"
      OLD Mother Dover's Farewell Speech, Or, the Spanish
        Manifesto.
      .....
      .....
      .....

867. Jan. 1, 1780, #340, p. 3, col. 3. (RMEAN, Card 26)
      "OLD Time flew panting by, in full career,"
      ODE for the NEW-YEAR. (Recitative)
      .....
      .....
      .....

868. Jan. 1, 1780, #340, p. 3, col. 3. (RMEAN, Card 26)
      "When Britain, by Divine command,"
      ODE for the NEW-YEAR (Air)
      .....
      Rule Britannia
      .....

869. Jan. 5, 1780, #341, p. 2, col. 3. (RMEAN, Card 26)
      "SEE France and Spain to battle dare;"
      STANZAS on the present WAR.
      .....
      .....
      .....

870. Jan. 8, 1780, #342, p. 2, col. 2. (RMEAN, Card 26)
      "SURE never, my Lord, was a time more distressing,"
      The BRITISH MAIDEN's Remonstrance and Petition to Lord
        Sandwich.
      .....
      .....
      .....

New York, New York; Royal Gazette, 1777-1783

871.   Jan. 8, 1780, #342, p. 2, col. 2.   (RMEAN, Card 26)
       "HOW oft we've seen in every form"
       STANZAS to the BRITISH NAVY
       NAVALIS
       .....
       .....

872.   Jan. 22, 1780, #346, p. 3, cols. 3-4.   (DLC Box 23, folder
          15)
       "GOOD Neighbors, if you'll give me leave,"
       MARY CAY, or Miss in her Teens. An old Canterbury Tale,
          from Chaucer.
       .....
       [Yankee Doodle?]
       .....

873.   Jan. 29, 1780, #348, p. 3, col. 4.   (RMEAN, Card 26)
       "THE Old English cause knocks at every man's door,"
       .....
       "transposed by a Refugee"
       Cut-Purse
       .....

874.   Feb. 9, 1780, #351, p. 2, col. 1.   (RMEAN, Card 26)
       "With flames they threaten to destroy"
       [Psalm sung at loyalist church service in Chatham, N.J.]
       .....
       [Psalm]
       .....

875.   Feb. 12, 1780, #352, p. 2, col. 1.   (RMEAN, Card 27)
       "Come let us run at once they cry,"
       HYMN
       ....., Elizabeth-Town, Feb. 3, 1780
       O Mother dear Jerusalem
       .....

876.   Feb. 12, 1780, #352, p. 2, col. 1.   (RMEAN, Card 27)
       "WHEN at first this land I prest,"
       .....
       Supposed to be written by a Loyalist without the lines
       .....
       .....

New York, New York; Royal Gazette, 1777-1783

877.   Feb. 16, 1780, #353, p. 3, col. 2.   (RMEAN, Card 27)
        "WHEN faction, in league with the treacherous Gaul,"
        The LORDS of the MAIN
        .....
        Nottingham Ale
        .....

878.   March 11, 1780, #360, p. 3, cols. 2-3.   (RMEAN, Card 27)
        "OLD Time flew panting by, in full career,"
        ODE for the NEW-YEAR, 1780   (Recitative)
        .....
        .....
        .....

879.   March 11, 1780, #360, p. 3, cols. 2-3.   (RMEAN, Card 27)
        "When rival nations first descried,"
        ODE for the NEW-YEAR, 1780 (Air)
        .....
        Rule Britannia
        .....

880.   June 26, 1780, #391, p. 3, col. 3.   (DLC Box 23, folder
            15)
        "AS his worm eaten volumes old time tumbled o'er,"
        On the Defeat of the Rebels in South Carolina.
        .....
        .....
        .....

881.   July 8, 1780, #394, p. 2, col. 2.   (DLC Box 23, folder
            15)
        "WHEN Britain on her sea-girt shore,"
        The WOODEN WALLS of ENGLAND, An ODE.
        Henry Green and Dr. Arne
        [The Wooden Walls of England]
        Sung lately at Convent Garden Theatre.

882.   Aug. 16, 1780, #405, p. 3, col. 1.   (RMEAN, Card 30)
        "TO drive the Kine one summer's morn,"
        COW CHACE. Canto I.
        ...., Elizabeth-Town, Aug. 1, 1780
        .....
        .....

New York, New York; Royal Gazette, 1777-1783

883.   Aug. 30, 1780, #409, p. 3, cols. 1-2.   (RMEAN, Card 31)
        "NEAR his meridian pomp the Sun"
        COW CHACE. Canto II.
        .....
        .....
        .....

884.   Sept. 16, 1780, #414, p. 3, cols. 3-4.   (RMEAN, Card 31)
        "WHEN faction, in league with the treacherous Gaul,"
        The LORDS of the MAIN
        .....
        Nottingham Ale
        .....

885.   Sept. 23, 1780, #416, p. 2, cols. 1-2.   (RMEAN, Card 31)
        "NOT all delights the bloody spear,"
        COW CHACE. Canto III.
        .....
        .....
        .....

886.   Sept. 27, 1780, #417, p. 3, col. 1.   (RMEAN Card 31)
        "O wherefore, brother Jonathan,"
        A PASTORAL ELEGY
        .....
        Set to Music by Signora Carolina
        .....

887.   Oct. 4, 1780, #419, p. 3, col. 3.   (RMEAN, Card 31)
        "AS for his Religion he could mix,"
        .....
        J-B-y Clericus, Halifax, Nova-Scotia, May 13, 1780.
        .....
        Late London Paper

888.   Feb. 28, 1781, #461, p. 3, col. 3.   (DLC. 956)
        "SING to his Shade a solemn strain,"
        In Memory of Mr. JAMES BREMNER.
        F.H.
        [In Memory of Mr. James Bremner]
        .....

New York, New York; Royal Gazette, 1777-1783

889. May 2, 1781, #479, p. 2, col. 3. (DLC 956)
     "ALL hail! Britannia Hail!"
     At the Feast of St. GEORGE, New York 1781
     .....
     Smile Britannia
     .....

890. May 2, 1781, #479, p. 2, cols. 3-4. (DLC 956)
     "On this day our Countrymen, ages before ye,"
     Allegro. The Roast Beef of Old England
     .....
     Roast Beef of Old England
     .....

891. July 11, 1781, #499, p. 2, cols. 1-4, and p. 3, cols. 1-2.
        (DLC 957)
     "LOUD howls the storm! the vex'd Atlantic roars!"
     MONODY on MAJOR ANDRE.
     Miss Seward.
     .....
     .....

892. Aug. 1, 1781, #505, p. 2, col. 1. (DLC 957)
     "KING Hancock sat in regal state"
     On the Reduction of Charl'stown, by his Majesty's Forces.
        A Song.
     An Officer at Pensacola
     The Watry God
     .....

893. Sept. 1, 1781, #514, p. 3, cols. 2-3. (DLC 957)
     "THE third day of June in the year sixty-seven,"
     A Song.---The Xth Regiment's voyage to Quebec.
     A Gentleman in the Xth Regiment
     .....
     .....

894. Jan. 5, 1782, #550, p. 2, col. 1. (DLC 958)
     "ARISE! arise! your voices raise,"
     The TEMPLE of MINERVA: An Oratorial Entertainment.
     [Francis Hopkinson]
     [The Temple of Minerva: An Oratorial Entertainment.
        Francis Hopkinson, Arr.]
     .....

186

New York, New York; Royal Gazette, 1777-1783

895. Jan. 5, 1782, #550, p. 2, col. 2. (DLC 958)
      "STRAIN hard! strain hard! your voices raise,"
      The TEMPLE of CLOACINA: An Ora-whig-ial Entertainment.
      .....
      [The TEMPLE of MINERVA: An Oratorial Entertainment.
        Francis Hopkinson, Arr.]
      .....

896. March 2, 1782, #566, p. 3, col. 1. (DLC 958)
      "SAYS Satan to Jemmy, I hold you a Bet"
      EPIGRAM occasioned by the Title of Rivington's Royal
        Gazette being scarcely legible.
      M.
      .....
      Freeman's Journal, Philadelphia, Feb. 13, 1782.

897. March 23, 1782, #572, p. 3, cols. 1-2. (DLC 958)
      "MY Soldiers all,"
      General WATERBURY's FAREWELL To his SOLDIERS.
      A young Lady
      .....
      .....

898. May 11, 1782, #586, p. 3, col. 1. (DLC 958)
      "THE cloud is burst, behold a clearer sky!"
      Addressed to Lord SHELBURNE.
      CAUSIDICUS.
      .....
      .....

899. May 22, 1782, #589, p. 2, col. 4. (DLC 958)
      "SEE yon black cloud that big with tempest lows,"
      Serious Advice of BRITANNIA to her contentious Sons.
      Causidicus.
      .....
      .....

900. June 8, 1782, #594, p. 2, col. 4. (DLC 958)
      "FROM Heav'n behold a charming ray"
      AN ODE, On Sir GEORGE RODNEY's Victory over the COMTE
        De GRASSE.
      Peter Linsay, a common Seaman on Board his Majesty's Ship
        the Namur April 12, 1782.
      .....
      .....

New York, New York; Royal Gazette, 1777-1783

901. Oct. 16, 1782, #632, p. 3, col. 3. (RMEAN, Card 47)
      "AS bending o'er the azure tide,"
      Rodney's Victory: A New Song.
      .....
      The Watry God. Chorus: Rule Britannia
      .....

902. Nov. 2, 1782, #637, p. 3, col. 1. (RMEAN, Card 47)
      "WHO dares---tho' ev'n of patriot name---"
      ODE, For the BIRTH-DAY of his ROYAL HIGHNESS THE PRINCE
         OF WALES, August 12, 1782.
      .....
      .....
      .....

903. Nov. 23, 1782, #643, p. 3, col. 1. (DLC 959)
      "THO' the fate of battle on to-morrow wait,"
      The MUSICAL INTERLUDE of the TOBACCO-BOX: Or, The
         SOLDIER's PLEDGE of LOVE.
      Original Music French, accompaniment by Dr. Arnold
      [The Tobacco Box; or, the Soldiers Pledge of Love]
      as performed at the Hay Market Theatre

904. Dec. 4, 1782, #646, p. 3, col. 1. (RMEAN, Card 47)
      "AS Spain's proud Monarch sat in state,"
      On the Destruction of the SPANIARD's floating Batteries
         before GIBRALTAR
      By the Author of the ACQUISITION, or BRITANNIA TRIUMPHANT,
         an Heroick Poem, which was addressed to his Royal
         Highness Prince William Henry, and appeared in our
         Paper in October last. DIOMEDE, December 4, 1782 (?)
      .....
      .....

905. Dec. 28, 1782, #653, p. 2, col. 3. (RMEAN, Card 47)
      "MY dear Brother Ned,we are knock'd o' the head,"
      From dejected JONATHAN, a Prisoner taken in the South
         Carolina, to his Brother NED at Philadelphia.
      DIOMEDE, off New-York, 25th December 1782
      .....
      .....

New York, New York; Royal Gazette, 1777-1783

906.   Feb. 12, 1783, #666, p. 2, col. 4.   (DLC 960)
       "WHICH of my sons, proclaim'd War's God,"
       ELLIOTT TRIUMPHANT.
       W.A.
       . . . . .
       . . . . .

907.   Feb. 12, 1783, #666, p. 2, col. 4.   (DLC 960)
       "WHEN Hawke, the British Neptune, reign'd,"
       HE DON'T FIGHT FAIR.   An IMPROMPTU.
       . . . . .
       . . . . .
       . . . . .

908.   Feb. 12, 1783, #666, p. 2, col. 4.   (DLC 960)
       "WHEN ancient Rome, the Empress of the World,"
       Lines on the Return of Admiral RODNEY from the West-
          Indies.
       E.M.
       . . . . .
       . . . . .

909.   July 23, 1783, #712, p. 2, col. 1.   (DLC 961)
       "COME, my boys, in jovial strain,"
       SONG, sung by one of the Young Gentlemen of the
          Maritime School.
       . . . . .
       . . . . .
       . . . . .

910. Dec. 11, 1783, #   , p. 4, col. 1.   (NNHi)
      "Some long to range (?), so fond of change,"
      .....
      .....
      .....
      .....

NORTH CAROLINA

911. July 7, 1775, #331, p. 4, col. 3. (DLC 1023)
      "HARK! 'tis Freedom that calls, come Patriots awake;"
      AMERICAN FREEDOM. A New SONG.
      . . . . .
      . . . . .
      . . . . .

912. Nov. 14, 1778, #454, p. 4, col. 1. (DLC 1025)
      "FREE States attend my Song,"
      A New SONG.
      . . . . .
      [God save the King]
      . . . . .

PENNSYLVANIA

913. Dec. 10, 1777, #   , p. 4, col. 3.   (DLC 1067)
      "TAX'D as we are beyond our strength,"
      A certain Speech versified.
      .....
      .....
      The London Public Advertiser, May 21.

914. Jan. 7, 1778, #   , p. 3, col. 3.   (DLC 1067)
      "AS Jack, the King's commander,"
      A SONG On the Surrender of Lieutenant-General Burgoyne
        and his Army, to Major-General Gates.
      .....
      My Daddy was in the Rebellion.
      .....

915. Jan. 21, 1778, #   , p. 4, col. 1.   (DLC 1067)
      "VAIN Britons boast no longer with proud indignity,"
      A New Liberty SONG.
      .....
      British Grenadiers
      .....

916. March 4, 1778, #   , p. 4, col. 1.   (DLC 1067)
      "GALLANTS attend, and hear a friend,"
      BRITISH VALOUR DISPLAYED: Or, The BATTLE of the KEGS.
      [Francis Hopkinson]
      [Battle of the Kegs]
      .....

917. April 8, 1778, #   , p. 3, col. 2.   (DLC 1067)
      "COME on my hearts of temper'd steel,"
      The NEW RECRUIT, or the GALLANT VOLUNTEER, A New Song.
      P., Lancaster, April 5, 1778.
      [A begging we will go, we'll go]
      .....

918. April 8, 1778, #   , p. 4, col. 1.   (DLC 1067)
      "MAKE room O ye Kingdoms in hist'ry renowned,"
      .....
      [Bob Jingle]
      [Pepperell and Pumpkinshire People]
      .....

Pennsylvania, Lancaster; Pennsylvania Packet, 1777-1778

919. April 8, 1778, #   , p. 4, col. 1. (DLC 1067)
      "'Tis Washington's Health; fill a bumper all round,"
      The TOAST.
      [Bob Jingle]
      ['Tis Washington's Health; fill a bumper all round, Music
        by Francis Hopkinson]
      .....

920. April 22, 1778, #   , p. 3, col. 1. (DLC 1067)
      "AS late I travell'd o'er the plain,"
      DATE OBOLUM RELESARIO.
      .....
      .....
      .....

921.   Aug. 8, 1781, #16, p. 2, cols. 2-3. (DLC 1161)
        "O'ER the rough main with flowing sheet"
        A Poem on the memorable victory obtained by the gallant
           capt. Paul Jones, of the Good Man Richard, over the
           Seraphis, &c. under the Command of capt. Pearson.
        .....
        .....
        .....

922.   Oct. 3, 1781, #24, p. 2, col. 3. (DLC 1161)
        "WE lose him, my Daphnis! and where shall we find"
        An EXTEMPORE.
        Juvenis
        .....
        .....

923.   Oct. 17, 1781, #26, p. 2, col. 3. (DLC 1161)
        "YOU know there goes a tale,"
        Copy of a Pasquinade stuck up in the city of New-York,
           August 12, 1780.
        .....
        .....
        The Political Magazine for May, 1781

924.   Dec. 19, 1781, #35, p. 3, cols. 1-2. (DLC 1161)
        "ARISE! arise! your voices raise,"
        The TEMPLE of MINERVA: An Oratorial Entertainment.
        [Francis Hopkinson]
        [The Temple of Minerva. Francis Hopkinson, Arr.]
        .....

925.   Dec. 26, 1781, #36, p. 4, col. 1. (DLC 1161)
        "BY your leave, gossip John;"
        PADDY's ADDRESS to JOHN BULL, A new Ballad.
        .....
        Larry Grogan
        From a late Irish Paper

926.   Jan. 2, 1782, #37, p. 4, col. 1. (DLC 1162)
        "WHY Theon wouldst thou longer groan"
        PLATO the philosopher to his friend THEON.
        .....
        .....
        .....

Pennsylvania, Philadelphia; Freeman's Journal, 1781-1792

927. Jan. 2, 1782, #37, p. 4, col. 1. (DLC 1162)
      "IN days of yore, as sages tell,"
      . . . . .
      . . . . .
      . . . . .
      . . . . .

928. Jan. 30, 1782, #41, p. 3, col. 2. (DLC 1162)
      "PRINCE William of the Brunswick race"
      The ROYAL ADVENTURER.
      . . . . .
      . . . . .
      . . . . .

929. April 3, 1782, #50, p. 1, cols. 1-3. (DLC 1162)
      "AS Jove the Olympian who, both I and you know,"
      The POLITICAL BALANCE; or, The Fates of Britain and
         America compared. A Tale.
      . . . . .
      . . . . .
      . . . . .

930. April 10, 1782, #51, p. 3, col. 1. (DLC 1162)
      "There was a little judge,"
      . . . . .
      CALUMNIATOR.
      [there was a little man/and he woo'd a little maid]
      . . . . .

931. April 17, 1782, #52, p. 2, col. 2. (DLC 1162)
      "COME gentlemen Tories, firm, loyal and true,"
      SIR HARRY's CALL.
      . . . . .
      . . . . .
      . . . . .

932. April 24, 1782, #53, p. 2, col. 2. (DLC 1162)
      "LET those who will, be proud and sneer,"
      A DIALOGUE at Hyde-Park Corner.
      . . . . .
      . . . . .
      . . . . .

933.   May 8, 1782, #55, p. 2, cols. 1-2.   (DLC 1162)
        "OE'R (sic) the waste of water cruising,"
        [relative to capt. Barney's late gallant exploit]
        Rusticus, Dover, April 26, 1782.
        The Tempest; or, Hosier's Ghost
        .....

934.   May 22, 1782, #57, p. 2, col. 2.   (DLC 1162)
        "THE dog that is beat has a right to complain,--"
        On Sir Henry Clinton's recall.
        .....
        .....
        .....

935.   May 29, 1782, #58, p. 2, cols. 2-3.   (DLC 1162)
        "WELCOME one Arnold to our Shore,"
        ODE Addressed to General ARNOLD.
        Lady CRAVEN
        .....
        A late London Paper

936.   June 5, 1782, #59, p. 4, col. 1.   (DLC 1162)
        "FROM Britain's fam'd island once more I come over,"
        Sir Guy Carleton's ADDRESS to the Americans.
        G.C., May 30, 1782
        .....
        .....

937.   June 19, 1782, #61, p. 4, col. 1.   (DLC 1162)
        "OF great and glorious names to speak,"
        The GEORGES, a New Song. On Lord George Germaine's
          Promotion.
        .....
        Push about the Jorum.
        London Courant

938.   June 26, #62, p. 4, col. 1.   (DLC 1162)
        "MY native shades delight no more,"
        The English Quixote of 1778; or, Modern Idolatry.
        .....
        .....
        .....

939.   July 10, 1782, #64, p. 3, col. 1. (DLC 1162)
        "OLD Judas the traitor (nor need we much wonder)"
        .....
        .....
        .....
        .....

940.   Oct. 2, 1782, #76, p. 3, col. 1. (DLC 1162)
        "NO more my friends, of vain applause,"
        The PRESENT AGE.
        .....
        .....
        .....

941.   Feb. 19, 1783, #96, p. 4, col. 1. (DLC 1163)
        "HIS triumphs of a moment done,"
        STANZAS, occasioned by the departure of the British from
          CHARLESTOWN, Dec. 14, 1782.
        .....
        .....
        .....

942.   June 18, 1783, #113, p. 1, cols. 1-2. (DLC 1163)
        "TAKE, O Muse! the breathing lyre,"
        LIBERTY: A PINDARIC ODE.
        .....
        .....
        .....

943.   June 25, 1783, #114, p. 1, cols. 1-2. (DLC 1163)
        "COLD blew the blast with hollow shrieks,"
        The DYING PROSTITUTE.
        CLASSICUS.
        .....
        (Written in London.)

944.   Sept. 10, 1783, #125, p. 1, col. 3. (DLC 1163)
        "THOU mistress of a warlike state,"
        NEW-YORK.
        .....
        .....
        .....

Pennsylvania, Philadelphia; Freeman's Journal, 1781-1792

945.   Nov. 19, 1783, #135, p. 2, cols. 2-3.   (DLC 1163)
        "YE nations hear th'immortal tale---"
        BRITAIN on the STOOL of REPENTANCE; Or, an ODE for the
          NEW YEAR, Jan. 1st, 1783.
        William Whitehead, esq. Poet Laureat.
        .....
        London Magazine, Jan. 1783.

946.   Dec. 10, 1783, #138, p. 2, col. 1.   (DLC 1163)
        "THE great unequal conflict past,"
        VERSES occasioned by General WASHINGTON's arrival in this
          city, on his way to his Seat in Virginia.
        .....
        .....
        .....

947.   Dec. 31, 1783, #141, p. 2, cols. 2-3.   (DLC 1163)
        "LONG life and low spirits were never my choice,"
        Rivington's Confessions. Addressed to the Whigs of New-
          York.
        .....
        .....
        .....

200

948. June 1, 1782, #8, p. 4, col. 1. (DLC 1218)
      "FAREWEL (sic) my Lord, my Zephyrs waft you o'er,"
      An Address to Lord Cornwallis.
      .....
      .....
      .....

949. June 22, 1782, #11, p. 4, col. 1. (DLC 1218)
      "YE sons of Mars attend,"
      SONG on the Celebration of the Birth of the Dauphin.
      .....
      Restoration March
      Loudon's NEW-YORK PACKET, printed at Fishkill

950. July 20, 1782, #15, p. 4, col. 1. (DLC 1218)
      "CRIMSON slaughter! pallid care!"
      ODE on the BIRTH of the DAUPHIN.
      .....
      .....
      .....

951. Aug. 17, 1782, #19, p. 4, col. 1. (DLC 1218)
      "THE old Tory rout"
      THE REVERSE.
      .....
      .....
      .....

952. Aug. 31, 1782, #21, p. 4, col. 1. (DLC 1218)
      "SOUND, sound the music, sound it,"
      General Gate's March, on the memorable Event of the Re-
         duction of General Burgoyne and his Army.
      A Philanthorpist, Philadelphia, Oct. 20, 1777.
      [General Gate's March]
      .....

953.   Oct. 15, 1782, #32, p. 2, col. 3.   (DLC 1218)
        "FR-N-U, great man! 'tis thee I sing,"
        STANZAS addressed to little FR-N-U, Poetaster to the
          Skunk-scented association, and successful imitator of
          STERNHOLD and HOPKINS, of poetical memory; in humble
          imitation of his own doggrel.
        .....
        .....
        .....

954.   Oct. 19, 1782, #33, p. 4, col. 1.   (DLC 1218)
        "WHO'D know the sweets of liberty?"
        The Genius of America to her Sons.
        .....
        [Sweets of Liberty]
        .....

955.   Nov. 26, 1782, #44, p. 4, col. 1.   (DLC 1218)
        "MAY Peace her olive wand extend,"
        A Wish from CLARINDA to ---
        .....
        .....
        .....

956.   Dec. 28, 1782, #52, p. 4, col. 1.   (DLC 1218)
        "ON the banks of the fam'd Delaware,"
        A NEW SONG on the present arbitrary attempt to subvert
          the Freedom of the Press.
        A Volunteer
        My fond Shepherds of late were so bless'd, &c.
        .....

957.   Jan. 4, 1783, #53, p. 4, col. 1.   (DLC 1219)
        "WHILE free from force the Press remains,"
        On the FREEDOM of the PRESS
        .....
        .....
        .....

958.   Feb. 15, 1783, #63, p. 4, col. 1.   (DLC 1219)
        "DEAR Doctor, 'tis somewhat mysterious"
        To DOCTOR SLOP.
        . . . . .
        . . . . .
        . . . . .

959.   Feb. 18, 1783, #64, p. 4, col. 1.   (DLC 1219)
        "WHEN pregnant Nature strove relief to gain,"
        On AMERICAN INDEPENDENCY.
        . . . . .
        . . . . .
        . . . . .

960.   March 1, 1783, #67, p. 4, col. 1.   (DLC 1219)
        "'TIS strange to think, so many men"
        VERSES on a late COMBINATION.
        Exeunt Omnes
        . . . . .
        . . . . .

961.   March 4, 1783, #68, p. 3, cols. 1-2.   (DLC 1219)
        "In a chariot of light from the regions above,"
        . . . . .
        An American
        [Once the Gods of the Greeks]
        Extract of a letter from Talbot Court-House, dated
          Feb. 11.

962.   March 4, 1783, #68, p. 4, col. 1.   (DLC 1219)
        "TO blast thy fame though pining envy tries,"
        To JOHN DICKINSON, Esquire.
        . . . . .
        . . . . .
        . . . . .

963.   March 11, 1783, #70, p. 4, col. 1.   (DLC 1219)
        "TO many till now it was truly mysterious,"
        EPIGRAM.
        . . . . .
        . . . . .
        . . . . .

964. March 22, 1783, #73, p. 4, col. 1.   (DLC 1219)
      "THE Muse in winter's hoary reign,"
      On SPRING.--To a Lady.
      .....
      .....
      .....

965. April 5, 1783, #75, p. 4, col. 1.   (DLC 1219)
      "GREAT ruler of the earth and skies,"
      HYMN for NATIONAL PEACE.
      .....
      .....
      .....

966. April 12, 1783, #76, p. 4, col. 1.   (DLC 1219)
      "FROM Heaven descends sweet smiling Peace,"
      .....
      W.A., March 31, 1783
      .....
      .....

967. May 3, 1783, #79, p. 4, col. 1.   (DLC 1219)
      "BEHOLD, array'd in light"
      A HYMN on PEACE.
      .....
      [Worcester]
      .....

968. May 10, 1783, #80, p. 4, col. 1.   (DLC 1219)
      "DECK'D be his tomb with ever verdant bays!"
      On the Death of General MONTGOMERY.
      .....
      .....
      ["published in the English news-papers"]

969. May 17, 1783, #81, p. 4, col. 1.   (DLC 1219)
      "OLD Homer---but what have we with him to do,"
      New LIBERTY-HALL; A SONG.
      .....
      [Liberty Hall]
      .....

Pennsylvania, Philadelphia; Independent Gazetteer, 1782-1796

970.   May 24, 1783, #82, p. 4, col. 1.   (DLC 1219)
       "'TIS now the horrid din of arms shall cease,"
       On PEACE.
       .....
       .....
       .....

971.   Aug. 16, 1783, #94, p. 4, col. 1.   (DLC 1219)
       "OF all the leaders in the state"
       A SONG.   On the wise Coalition compleated the 1st of
         April, 1783.
       .....
       Nancy Dawson
       .....

972.   Sept. 27, 1783, #100, p. 4, col. 1.   (DLC 1219)
       "MONARCHS, 'tis true, should calm the storms of war,"
       THOUGHTS on PEACE.
       .....
       .....
       .....

973.   Dec. 20, 1783, #112, p. 4, col. 1.   (DLC 1219)
       "HAIL to the blest return of peace,"
       On the Return of PEACE.
       .....
       .....
       .....

974.   March 8, 1773, #321, p. 3, col. 2.   (RMEAN, Card 31)
        "Behold the SOCIAL BAND appears!"
        ODE for the Festival of St. JOHN EVANGELIST in South
          Carolina.
        Sir EGERTON LEIGH, Baronet, GRAND-MASTER; music by
          Brother Peter Valton
        . . . . .
        SOUTH CAROLINA and AMERICAN GENERAL GAZETTE

975.   March 8, 1773, #321, p. 3, col. 2.   (RMEAN, Card 31)
        "Boast not, Mortals, human Skill,"
        ODE for the Festival of St. JOHN EVANGELIST in South
          Carolina.
        Sir EGERTON LEIGH, & BROTHER Peter Valton
        . . . . .
        SOUTH CAROLINA and AMERICAN GENERAL GAZETTE

976.   May 17, 1773, #331, p. 4, col. 1.   (RMEAN, Card 32)
        "With vulgar minds, which judge from what they see,"
        THE MOON.
        . . . . .
        . . . . .
        . . . . .

977.   June 7, 1773, #334, p. 4, col. 1.   (RMEAN, Card 32)
        "You love my dearest life"
        PROTESTATION.
        . . . . .
        . . . . .
        . . . . .

978.   June 21, 1773, #336, p. 4, col. 1.   (RMEAN, Card 32)
        "Now the leaden year is gone,"
        FAREWELL to 1772.
        . . . . .
        . . . . .
        . . . . .

Pennsylvania, Philadelphia; Pennsylvania Chronicle, 1767-1774

979. Aug. 30, 1773, #346, p. 4, col. 1.   (RMEAN, Card 33)
      "Born for millions are the Kings"
      ODE for his MAJESTY's Birth-day JUNE 4, 1773.
      WILLIAM WHITEHEAD, Esq; POET LAUREAT
      [Ode for his Majesty's Birth-day, June 4, 1773, Music
        by Dr. Boyce]
      .....

980. Nov. 29, 1773, #359, p. 4, col. 1.   (RMEAN, Card 34)
      "Whilst others court the honours of the bench"
      The MAN of HONOUR.
      .....
      .....
      .....

981.   March 30, 1775, #29, p. 2, (p. 114), cols. 1-2.   (DLC 1255)
        "WHEN wicked men, with foul intent,"
        Irregular ODE from Boston
        [Thalestris?, Philadelphia, March 29, 1775]
        .....
        .....

982.   May 27, 1775, #54, p. 4, col. 2.   (RMEAN, Card 4)
        "Hark! 'tis freedom that calls, come patriots, awake!"
        A SONG.
        .....
        The Echoing Horn
        .....

983.   June 3, 1775, #59, p. 4, col. 1.   (RMEAN, Card 4)
        "Come listen, my cocks, to a brother and friend,"
        The SAILOR's ADDRESS.
        .....
        [Hearts of Oak]
        LONDON EVENING POST of March 14

984.   Sept. 12, 1775, #102, p. 3, col. 1.   (RMEAN, Card 6)
        "In a chariot of light from the regions of day,"
        LIBERTY TREE.   A New Song.
        .....
        The Gods of the Greeks
        .....

985.   Nov. 16, 1775, #128, p. 4, (p. 528), col. 2.   (DLC 1256)
        "REBELS--avaunt th' inglorious name,"
        On the late most extraordinary proclamation
        .....
        .....
        .....

986.   Feb. 17, 1776, #168, p. 4, col. 1.   (RMEAN, Card 10)
        "Some mice deep intrench'd in a rich Cheshire cheese,"
        .....
        R.R.
        .....
        .....

Pennsylvania, Philadelphia; Pennsylvania Evening Post; 1775-
1784

987.   March 30, 1776, #186, p. 1, (p. 161), col. 2, and p. 2,
          (p. 162), col. 1.   (DLC 1257)
       "Since you all will have singing, and won't be said nay,"
       The KING's own REGULARS, and their TRIUMPH over the
          IRREGULARS.   A new SONG.
       .....
       An old Courtier of the Queen's, and the Queen's Old
          Courtier
       .....

988.   April 13, 1776, #192, p. 4, (p. 188), col. 1.   (DLC 1257)
       "YE poor silly people, who foolishly think,"
       On the Promotion of Lord GEORGE SACKVILLE GERMAIN, to
          be Secretary of the American Department.
       .....
       A Cobler there was
       Late London Paper

989.   April 30, 1776, #199, p. 3, (p. 215), cols. 1-2.   (DLC
          1257)
       "OF St. George, or St. Bute, let the poet laureat sing,"
       The First of MAY.   A NEW SONG, in praise of St. TAMMANY,
          The American Saint.
       .....
       The hounds are all out, &c.
       American Tragi-comedy, THE FALL of BRITISH TYRANNY, or
          AMERICAN LIBERTY TRIUMPHANT

990.   Nov. 30, 1776, #291, p. 4, (p. 600), col. 1.   (DLC 1258)
       "HARK! the Goddess of fame,"
       An ODE addressed to the FREEMEN of America, and of Penn-
          sylvania in particular, on this dreadful crisis of
          affairs.
       .....
       .....
       .....

Pennsylvania, Philadelphia; Pennsylvania Evening Post, 1775-
1784

991.   Jan. 1, 1777, Broadside, p. 4, col. 1.   (RMEAN, Card 18)
       "Hail! O America!"
       New Year's Verses, Addressed to the CUSTOMERS, of The
          PENNSYLVANIA Evening Post.
       The PRINTER's LADS who carry it
       [God save the King]
       . . . . .

992.   Feb. 1, 1777, #309, p. 1, cols. 1-2.   (RMEAN, Card 19)
       "Another Patriot claims the votive strain,"
       An original ELEGY on the death of Brigadier General
          MERCER of Virginia, slain in the action near Princeton,
          January 1, 1777, glorious fighting the cause of Heaven
          and mankind.
       . . . . .
       . . . . .
       . . . . .

993.   Feb. 13, 1777, #314, p. 3, (p. 77), col. 2.   (DLC 1259)
       "ALAS, poor Joe's great soul's on float;"
       The Tories Lamentation on the death of their friend
          Drunken Joe, the Wooden Leg Beggar.
       . . . . .
       . . . . .
       . . . . .

994.   Feb. 25, 1777, #319, p. 7, (p. 105), col. 1.   (DLC 1259)
       "JOE's wonderful deeds far surpasses all story,"
       The TORY's consolation On Cornwallis's preservation,
          Through Joe's negotiation.
       . . . . .
       . . . . .
       . . . . .

995.   Feb. 27, 1777, #320, p. 3, (p. 109), col. 2.   (DLC 1259)
       "HOW blest is he, who unconstrain'd"
       The SWEETS of LIBERTY. An Ode.
       P.J.
       [The Sweets of Liberty]
       . . . . .

Pennsylvania, Philadelphia; Pennsylvania Evening Post, 1775-
1784

996. April 17, 1777, #340, p. 8, (p. 216), col. 1. (DLC 1259)
      "YE wrong heads, and strong heads, attend to my strains;"
      The HEADS, or The Year 1776.
      .....
      [Derry Down]
      The Public Ledger

997. April 26, 1777, #344, p. 2, (p. 234), col. 2. (DLC 1259)
      "A Bard, when warm'd with rage poetic,"
      .....
      COR.
      .....
      .....

998. May 22, 1777, #355, p. 1, (p. 277), cols. 1-2, and p. 2,
         (p. 278), col. 1. (DLC 1259)
      "WITHOUT wit, without wisdom, half stupid and drunk,"
      The EXPEDITION to DANBURY, under the command of General
         Tryon, to destroy the stores of beef, pork and rum.
      .....
      .....
      From Pennsylvania Gazette of May 14, 1777

999. June 14, 1777, #365, p. 4, (p. 320), cols. 1-2. (DLC 1259)
      "TO praise true merit is no easy art,"
      To a Renegade Member of C-----. WOOLSEY. A SATIRE.
      Serjeant KITE, Philadelphia June 14.
      .....
      .....

1000. June 28, 1777, #371, p. 3, (p. 343), col. 2. (DLC 1259)
      "TORIES, pray what will ye do,"
      A CORDIAL for the disconsolate, low spirited friends of
         government.
      LENITY
      .....
      .....

Pennsylvania, Philadelphia; Pennsylvania Evening Post, 1775-
1784

1001.   Nov. 25, 1777, #424, p. 4, (p. 550), col. 1.   (DLC 1260)
        "For neither pedant nor for prude,"
        SONGS, comic, satyrical, and sentimental, Prologue.
        George Alexander Stevens
        [Sing-Song]
        .....

1002.   Nov. 29, 1777, #426, p. 4, (p. 558), col. 1.   (DLC 1260)
        "LIKE a Newton sublimely he soar'd"
        Inscription on a curious chamber stove, in the form of
           an urn, contrived in such a manner as to make the
           flame descend instead of rise from the fire, in-
           vented by the celebrated Dr. Franklin.
        An Episcopal clergyman, at Brunswick, in New-Jersey
        .....
        Gentleman's Magazine for April last

1003.   Dec. 2, 1777, #427, p.3, (p. 561), cols. 1-2.   (DLC 1260)
        "COME all ye good people attend,"
        A NEW SONG.
        Flirtilla, Philadelphia, Dec. 1, 1777
        Come, my kitten, my kitten, & c.
        .....

1004.   Dec. 2, 1777, #427, p. 4, (p. 562), col. 1.   (DLC 1260)
        "MEDDLE not with state affairs,"
        To DAVID RITTENHOUSE.
        .....
        .....
        .....

1005.   Dec. 4, 1777, #428, p. 4, (p. 566), col. 1.   (DLC 1260)
        AMericans swarming by thousands on shore,"
        A new SONG
        A prisoner in Boston jail
        Black Sloven
        .....

Pennsylvania, Philadelphia; Pennsylvania Evening Post, 1775-
1784

1006.   Dec. 11, 1777, #431, p. 4, (p. 574), col. 1. (DLC 1260)
        "WHILE rebel sons with ruffian hand"
        A New SONG
        A loyalist while in confinement at Sleepy Hole on
            Nansemond, Va.
        Rule Britannia, &c.
        .....

1007.   Dec. 20, 1777, #435, p. 4, (p. 594), cols. 1-2. (DLC
            1260)
        "YE Tories all rejoice and sing"
        A SONG, wrote in the spring of the year 1776
        .....
        Nancy Dawson
        .....

1008.   June 20, 1778, #496, p. 3, (p. 209), col. 2. (DLC 1261)
        "WHEN North first began,"
        On Lord North's Recantation.
        FACT., Chester, March 1.
        .....
        London Evening Post

1009.   June 30, 1778, #498, p. 2, (p. 216), col. 1. (DLC 1261)
        "MAKE room, O ye kingdoms, in hist'ry renowned,"
        A SONG.
        [Bob Jingle]
        Pepperell and Pumpkinshire people.
        Pennsylvania Gazette, April 4, 1778

1010.   June 30, 1778, #498, p. 2, (p. 216), col. 1. (DLC 1261)
        "'Tis Washington's health---Fill a bumper all round,"
        The TOAST.
        .....
        ['Tis Washington's health---Fill a bumper all round, Music
            by Francis Hopkinson]
        .....

Pennsylvania, Philadelphia; Pennsylvania Evening Post, 1775-
1784

1011.   July 6, 1778, #501, p. 4, (p. 224), cols. 1-2.   (DLC 1262)
         "AS late I travell'd o'er the plain,"
         DATE OBOLUM BELISARIO.
         .....
         .....
         From the Pennsylvania Packet.   April 24, 1778.

1012.   July 16, 1778, #505, p. 4, (p. 242), cols. 1&2.   (DLC
            1262)
         "WEST of the' old Atlantic, firm Liberty stands!"
         The GAMESTER.   A new song.
         .....
         A Late worthy old lion, &c."
         .....

1013.   July 18, 1778, #506, p. 2, (p. 244), cols. 1-2.   (DLC
            1262)
         "GALLANTS attend, and hear a friend"
         BRITISH VALOUR DISPLAYED, or the BATTLE of the KEGS.
         .....
         [Battle of the Kegs].
         Pennsylvania Packet

1014.   Oct. 23, 1778, #544, p. 4, (p. 394), cols. 1-2.   (DLC
            1262)
         "SINCE all must die as well as I,"
         The SAILOR's WILL.
         .....
         .....
         Town and Country Magazine

1015.   Nov. 13, 1778, #549, p. 2, (p. 412), col. 1.   (DLC 1262)
         "BRITANNIA was sick, for a doctor they sent,"
         The STATE QUACKS.
         .....
         .....
         Late LONDON MAGAZINE

1016.   March 26, 1779, #585, p. 2, col. 2.   (MWA)
         "Come ye valiant sons of thunder,"
         The Soldier's HEALTH
         .....
         .....
         .....

Pennsylvania, Philadelphia; Pennsylvania Evening Post, 1775-
1784

1017.   July 16, 1779, #614, p. 3, (p. 183), cols. 1-2.   (DLC Box
            25, folder 13)
         "HAIL mighty Thomas! In whose works are seen"
         An EPISTLE.
         .....
         .....
         .....

1018.   Sept. 11, 1779, #628, p. 4, cols. 1-2.   (RMEAN, Card 36)
         "When our master, God bless him, ascended the throne,"
         ROYAL RESOLUTIONS. Imitation of Andrew Marvel's Ballad
            called Royal Resolutions
         .....
         .....
         London Packet, or New Lloyd's Evening Post, of March 3,
            1779

1019.   1781, Broadside.   (RMEAN, Card 39)
         "Oh, pardon the faults I've committed before;"
         New Year's Verses, For the printer's lads who carry the
            Evening Post To the customers
         .....
         .....
         .....

1020. April 20, 1774, #2365, p. 3, col. 1.   (DLC 1294)
       "BLUSH! Albion, blush! at the unmanly Rage"
       (Occasioned by reading the Ill-usage of the worthy Dr.
         Franklin in the Packet of this Day)
       An Englishman, Philadelphia, April 18, 1774.
       .....
       .....

1021. Oct. 19, 1774, #2391, p. 3, col. 1.   (DLC 1294)
       "WHEN Britons first, by Heaven's Command,"
       An AMERICAN PARODY on the old Song of "RULE BRITANNIA."
       .....
       Rule Britannia
       .....

1022. Feb. 8, 1775, #2407, p. 1, col. 2.   (DLC 1295)
       "LOST is our old simplicity of times,"
       On the Proceedings against America.
       .....
       .....
       Late London Magazine

1023. May 14, 1777, #2516, p. 3, cols. 2-3.   (DLC 1297)
       "WITHOUT wit, without wisdom, half stupid and drunk,"
       The EXPEDITION to DANBURY, under the command of General
         Tryon, to destroy the stores of Beef, Pork and Rum.
       COMUS, Philadelphia, May 12.
       .....
       .....

1024. Jan. 17, 1778, #   , p. 4, col. 2.   (DLC Box 27,
         folder 13)
       "AS Jack, the King's commander,"
       A SONG, On the Surrender of Lieutenant-General Burgoyne
         and his Army, to Major-General Gates.
       .....
       As Jack the brisk young Drummer
       .....

1025. Feb. 28, 1778, #   , p. 3, col. 1.   (DLC 1447, Film 2502-
         2659, Reel 18)
       "TAX'D as we are, beyond our strength,"
       .....
       .....
       .....
       .....

Pennsylvania, Philadelphia; Pennsylvania Gazette, 1728-1815

1026.   April 4, 1778, #   , p. 2, col. 2.   (DLC 1447, Film
          2502-2659, Reel 18)
        "MAKE room, O ye kingdoms, in hist'ry renowned,"
        A SONG
        . . . . .
        Pepperell and Pumpkinshire People
        . . . . .

1027.   April 4, 1778, #   , p. 2, col. 2.   (DLC 1447, Film
          2502-2659, Reel 18)
        "'Tis Washington's Health, fill a Bumper all round,"
        The Toast
        . . . . .
        [Tis Washington's Health, fill a bumper all round, Music
          by Francis Hopkinson]
        . . . . .

1028.   April 18, 1778, #   , p. 3, col. 2.   (DLC 1447, Film
          2502-2659, Reel 18)
        "GAGE nothing did; and went to pot,"
        On the BRITISH COMMANDERS.
        . . . . .
        . . . . .
        London Paper of December 2, 1777

1029.   May 9, 1778, #   , p. 4, col. 1.   (DLC 1447, Film
          2502-2659, Reel 18)
        "GIVE ear to my song, I'll not tell you a story,"
        The Halcyon Days of Old England; Or The Wisdom of Ad-
          ministration demonstrated: A Ballad.
        . . . . .
        Ye Medley of Mortals
        London Evening Post

1030.   May 9, 1778, #   , p. 4, col. 2.   (DLC 1447, Film
          2502-2659, Reel 18)
        "AS late I travell'd o'er the Plain;"
        DATE OBOLUM [BELISARIO]
        . . . . .
        . . . . .
        . . . . .

1031. May 16, 1778, #   , p. 4, col. 1. (DLC 1447, Film 2502-
          2659, Reel 18)
       "WHY towards two Georges good, humane and great,"
       . . . . .
       OMICRON.
       . . . . .
       London General Advertiser of Jan. 6, 1778

1032. May 30, 1778, #   , p. 2, cols. 1-2. (DLC 1447, Film
          2502-2659, Reel 18)
       "FROM fair America's insulted coast,"
       The MUSE of AMERICA: AN ODE:
       Gentleman in France
       . . . . .
       . . . . .

1033. May 30, 1778, #   , p. 2, cols. 1-2. (DLC 1447, Film
          2502-2659, Reel 18)
       "Why flings the Muse (he cry'd) her art away,"
       The MUSE of AMERICA: AN ODE:
       Gentleman in France
       . . . . .
       . . . . .

1034. July 28, 1779, #2563, p. 3, col. 1. (DLC 1298)
       "HARK! hear the Trumpet's pleasant Sound!"
       . . . . .
       . . . . .
       . . . . .
       . . . . .

1035. May 14, 1783, #2761, p. 1, col. 2. (DLC 1302)
       "LET ev'ry age due honors pay,"
       . . . . .
       . . . . .
       . . . . .
       Roads-Town, Cumberland Country, N.J., April 24

1036.   March 30, 1774, #1634, p. 3, col. 1. (DLC 1320)
        "WHEN Heaven, indulgent, bless'd this land,"
        .....
        Correspondent in St. Croix
        .....
        .....

1037.   Aug. 31, 1774, #1656, p. 3, col. 2. (DLC 1320)
        "THAT New-England's abus'd, and by sons of sedition,"
        To the Author of the lines, in Mr. Rivington's Paper, on
            the Snake depicted in some of the American News-Papers.
        NEW-JERSEY.
        .....
        .....

1038.   Sept. 7, 1774, #1657, p. 2, col. 2. (DLC 1320)
        "AMERICA! thou fractious nation,"
        A PROCLAMATION.
        .....
        .....
        The VIRGINIA GAZETTE

1039.   Sept. 7, 1774, #1657, p. 3, col. 2. (DLC 1320)
        "WHEN mighty Shakespeare summoned each sp'rit,"
        On the passing of the BILL for the more effectual provision
            for Government of the Province of QUEBEC.
        C---.
        .....
        .....

1040.   Sept. 16, 1774, PS to #1658, p. 2, col. 2. (DLC 1320)
        "YOUR Colonel H[ancoc]k by neglect,"
        A General sample of Gubernatorial Eloquence, as lately
            exhibited to the Company of C[adet]s.
        .....
        .....
        MASSACHUSETTS SPY

1041.   Sept. 21, 1774, #1659, PS, p. 2, col. 1.   (DLC 1320)
        "BEGON pernicious baneful Tea,"
        VIRGINIA BANISHING TEA.
        A LADY.
        .....
        .....

1042.   Oct. 19, 1774, #1663, p. 3, col. 1.   (DLC 1320)
        "ATTEND your country's call, ye lovely fair,"
        To the WOMEN of PENNSYLVANIA.
        .....
        .....
        .....

1043.   Oct. 19, 1774, #1663, p. 4, col. 1.   (DLC 1320)
        "LET others strive by servile arts to gain,"
        To GENERAL L--.
        AMERICA.
        .....
        .....

1044.   May 31, 1775, #1695, p. 2, col. 2.   (DLC 1321)
        "HARK! 'tis Freedom that calls, come Patriots awake!"
        A SONG
        .....
        The echoing Horn
        .....

1045.   Aug. 2, 1775, #1704, p. 4, col. 1.   (PPL)
        "While civil wars distract this happy Land,"
        The PRESENT TIMES. Addressed to a Young Lady
        .....
        .....
        .....

1046.   June 19, 1776, #1750, p. 4, col. 1.   (DLC 1322)
        "AT length---with generous indignation fir'd,"
        .....
        PENNSYLVANIENSIS.
        .....
        .....

1047. Feb. 26, 1777, #1778, p. 3, col. 1. (PPL)
       "My Lords, with your leave,"
       A NEW WAR SONG
       Sir PETER PARKER
       Well met, Brother Tar
       London (written and printed)

1048. Jan. 13, 1779, #1811, p. 2, col. 1. (PPL)
       "Our order, ancient as the world's first date,"
       On Free-MASONRY
       GAVEL, Philadelphia, Jan. 4, 1779
       .....
       .....

1049. March 24, 1779, #1821, p. 4, col. 1. (PPL)
       "Proud Buckingham for law too mighty grown,"
       A HINT for Modern TYRANTS
       .....
       .....
       .....

1050. March 24, 1779, #1821, p. 4, col. 1. (PPL)
       "The common soldier who has broke"
       EPIGRAM
       .....
       .....
       LONDON PACKET

1051. April 7, 1779, #1283 (sic), p. 4, col. 1. (DLC 1324)
       "I TIM GAFF, literary vain,"
       .....
       T.G.
       .....
       .....

1052. May 19, 1779, #1288, p. 4, col. 1. (PHi)
       "From sea to sea we scan the endless main,"
       The PATRIOT
       W., Philad., May 24, 1779.
       .....
       .....

1053.   May 26, 1779, #1289, p. 4, col. 1.   (DLC 1324)
        "'TIS true, some seem devout in ev'ry deed;"
        THE PATRIOT.
        W., Philad. May 24, 1779.
        ......
        (cont. from last Paper)

1054.   Feb. 16, 1780, #1327, p. 4, col. 1.   (DLC 1325)
        "WHILE Nature reclin'd on the bosom of May,"
        The FLIGHT of the MUSES.
        ADOLPHUS, Philadelphia, Feb. 10, 1780.
        ......
        ......

1055.   May 3, 1780, #1338, p. 4, col. 1.   (DLC 1325)
        "WHEN Israel's chiefs were captives led,"
        ......
        [ZACH. vii. 8th, 9th and 10th verses.]
        ......
        ......

1056.   May 10, 1780, #1339, p. 4, col. 1.   (DLC 1325)
        "AID me, ye Nine, my Muse assist,"
        On GENERAL WASHINGTON.
        ......
        ......
        ......

1057.   May 17, 1780, #1340, p. 4, col. 1.   (DLC 1325)
        "ADIEU ye tow'ring spires, no more"
        ......
        A Gentleman lately gone into the country
        ......
        ......

1058.   July 19, 1780, #1349, p. 4, col. 1.   (DLC 1325)
        "SAY Lovely Fair One's that thus greatly vie"
        To the LADIES who subscribed to the RELIEF of their
          VIRTUOUS COUNTRYMEN, now employed in their DEFENCE.
        JUVENIS.
        ......
        ......

1059.   Nov. 3, 1781, #1436, p. 3, cols. 1-2.   (DLC 1326)
        "While scenes of transport, every breast inspire,"
        .....
        .....
        .....
        Camp, Peeks-Kill, Oct. 18, 1781.

1060.   Nov. 21, 1781, #1441, p. 3, cols. 2-3.   (DLC 1326)
        "SWEET Billy, precious, royal boy,"
        General ROBERTSON's Address to Prince WILLIAM HENRY, from
           Rivington's Gazette.   (Paraphras'd.)
        .....
        .....
        BOSTON INDEPENDENT CHRONICLE

1061.   Jan. 30, 1782, #1461, p. 3, cols. 2-3.   (DLC 1327)
        "GOD save the thirteen states,"
        For the ANNIVERSARY of the 4th of July, An ODE.
        An American prisoner, during his captivity at St. Augustine,
           in East Florida, beginning of 1781.
        God save the King
        .....

1062.   Feb. 27, 1782, #1469, p. 3, cols. 1-2.   (DLC 1327)
        "GALLIA's increasing fame"
        .....
        Mr. Walter Davids(?)
        [God save the King?]
        .....

1063.   March 5, 1783, #1571, p. 2, col. 3, and p. 3, col. 1.
           (DLC 1328)
        "In a chariot of light from the regions above,"
        .....
        an American.
        [Once the God of the Greeks]
        Extract of a letter from Talbot Court-House, dated
           Feb. 11.

1064.   Jan. 28, 1775, #1, p. 4, col. 1. (DLC 1341)
        "SEE the poor native quit the Lybian shores,"
        .....
        .....
        .....
        .....

1065.   Feb. 11, 1775, #3, p. 4, col. 1. (DLC 1341)
        "FROM NORTH, tho' stormy winds may blow"
        .....
        .....
        .....
        .....

1066.   April 8, 1775, #11, p. 4, col. 1. (DLC 1341)
        "FROM orchards of ample extent,"
        POMONA: A Pastoral.
        .....
        .....
        .....

1067.   May 6, 1775, #15, p. 4, col. 1. (DLC 1341)
        "IN days of Yore, as sages tell,"
        .....
        .....
        .....
        From the LYON's MOUTH.

1068.   May 20, 1775, #17, p. 4, col. 1. (DLC 1341)
        "'TIS money makes the Member vote,"
        A JUNTO SONG.
        .....
        A begging we will go, we'll go, &c.
        .....

1069.   May 27, 1775, #18, p. 4, col. 1. (DLC 1341)
        "COME join hand in hand all ye true, loyal souls,"
        A SONG, composed at a Town-Meeting in Chester, Burling-
          ton county, July, 1774.
        .....
        [Hearts of Oak]
        .....

1070. June 17, 1775, #21, p. 4, col. 1. (DLC 1341)
       "MEN of every size and station,"
       LIBERTY.
       [C.]
       . . . . .
       . . . . .

1071. June 24, 1775, #22, p. 4, col. 1. (DLC 1341)
       "THE Coward, when his country claims his aid,"
       . . . . .
       . . . . .
       . . . . .
       . . . . .

1072. July 22, 1775, #26, p. 4, col. 1. (DLC 1341)
       "WHILST happy in my native land,"
       A SONG. From a new musical interlude called the ELECTION.
       . . . . .
       [WHILST happy in my native land]
       . . . . .

1073. Aug. 5, 1775, #28, p. 4, col. 1. (DLC 1341)
       "O LIBERTY! thou Goddess heavenly bright,"
       LIBERTY.
       . . . . .
       . . . . .
       . . . . .

1074. Aug. 12, 1775, #29, p. 4, col. 1. (DLC 1341)
       "IN a chariot of light from the regions of day,"
       LIBERTY TREE. A new Song.
       ATLANTICUS.
       The Gods of the Greeks
       . . . . .

1075. Aug. 26, 1775, #31, p. 3, col. 1. (DLC 1341)
       "YE Powers, who rule o'er states and kings,"
       ODE for his MAJESTY'S BIRTH-DAY.
       . . . . .
       [ODE for his Majesty's Birth-Day, 1775]
       . . . . .

1076.   Sept. 30, 1775, #36, p. 4, col. 1.   (DLC 1341)
        "WHY shou'd we of our lot complain,"
        SONG.
        POLYDORE
        The Bird
        From the LYON's MOUTH.

1077.   Oct. 21, 1775, #39, p. 4, col. 1.   (DLC 1341)
        "PROPITIOUS us'd to rise the morn"
        .....
        .....
        .....
        .....

1078.   Oct. 28, 1775, #40, p. 4, col. 1.   (DLC 1341)
        "IN ev'ry civil war this hazard's run:"
        The DILEMMA.
        .....
        .....
        .....

1079.   Nov. 4, 1775, #41, p. 4, col. 1.   (DLC 1341)
        "AS soldiers now, we do surmise,"
        EPIGRAMS.
        .....
        .....
        From the LYON's MOUTH.

1080.   Nov. 25, 1775, #44, p. 4, col. 1.   (DLC 1341)
        "I THINK, indeed, 'tis very odd,"
        A Quiet MAN's Opinion of the TIMES.
        T.C.
        .....
        .....

1081.   Dec. 16, 1775, #47, p. 4, col. 1.   (DLC 1341)
        "O THOU whom next to Heav'n we most revere,"
        LIBERTY.
        .....
        .....

1082.   Dec. 23, 1775, #48, p. 4, col. 1. (DLC 1341)
         "PARENT of all, Omnipotent"
         The PATRIOT's Prayer.
         .....
         .....
         .....

1083.   Feb. 17, 1776, #56, p. 4, col. 1. (DLC 1341)
         "WHEN haughty monarchs quit this chequer'd scene,"
         On the Death of Gen. Montgomery.
         .....
         .....
         From the Lyon's Mouth.

1084.   March 16, 1776, #60, p. 4, col. 1. (DLC 1341)
         "MOURN,mourn, my lyre, in each string,"
         On the Death of Capt. HENDRICK's.
         .....
         .....
         .....

1085.   March 16, 1776, #60, p. 4, col. 1. (DLC 1341)
         "Strong as the oak upon the plain,"
         On the Death of Capt. HENDRICK's. [Air.]
         .....
         .....
         .....

1086.   March 16, 1776, #60, p. 4, col. 1. (DLC 1341)
         "I'll seek out the cave of despair,"
         On the Death of Capt. HENDRICK's. [Air]
         .....
         .....
         .....

1087.   April 27, 1776, #66, p. 4, col. 1. (DLC 1341)
         "SAINT George for their Patron our ancestors chose,"
         A SONG.
         .....
         Derry down.
         .....

1088.   May 4, 1776, #67, p. 4, col. 1.   (DLC 1341)
        "LORD NORTH has sent over an Army and Fleet,"
        A SONG.
        AMERICANUS
        Derry Down
        From the Lyon's Mouth.

1089.   June 15, 1776, #73, p. 4, col. 1.   (DLC 1341)
        "ON all these dreary plains,"
        WAR An ODE.
        . . . . .
        . . . . .
        From the Lyon's Mouth.

1090.   June 29, 1776, #75, p. 4, col. 1.   (DLC 1341)
        "HOW wise are our Rulers? Our Nobles, how good?"
        . . . . .
        . . . . .
        . . . . .
        From the Lyon's Mouth.

1091.   Aug. 10, 1776, #81, p. 4, col. 1.   (DLC 1341)
        "GREAT ruler of the earth and skies,"
        HYMN for NATIONAL PEACE.
        . . . . .
        . . . . .
        From the Lyon's Mouth.

1092.   Aug. 31, 1776, #84, p. 4, col. 1.   (DLC 1341)
        "THE world's a bubble, and the life of man"
        . . . . .
        . . . . .
        . . . . .
        From the Lyon's Mouth.

1093.   Sept. 14, 1776, #86, p. 4, col. 1.   (DLC 1341)
        "THE life of man to represent,"
        The PUPPET-SHEW.
        . . . . .
        . . . . .
        From the Lyon's Mouth.

Pennsylvania, Philadelphia; Pennsylvania Ledger, 1775-1778

1094.   Oct. 22, 1777, #100, p. 4, col. 1.   (DLC 1342)
        "AGAIN, my social Friends, we meet"
        Tradesmens' SONG for his MAJESTY's BIRTH-DAY, 1777.
        .....
        When Britain first at Heaven's Command
        .....

1095.   Nov. 12, 1777, #103, p. 4, col. 1.   (DLC 1342)
        "AND are you sure the news is true?"
        A Scotch Ballad, sung by Miss Sharpe, at Ranelagh
        .....
        [A Scotch Ballad]; Music composed by Mr. Bates.
        .....

1096.   Dec. 10, 1777, #108, p. 4, col. 1.   (DLC 1342)
        "WHAT times are these?---a perfect riddle!"
        In commemoration of the glorious action on the evening
            of the 4th of July last
        MANY
        .....
        .....

1097.   Jan. 31, 1778, #123, p. 3, col. 3.   (DLC 1342)
        "TO thee, O God! by whom I live,"
        Stanzas written the 10th of May, 1776
        An Exile from America
        .....
        .....

1098.   Feb. 7, 1778, #125, p. 1, col. 3.   (DLC 1342)
        "WHEN the sheep were in the fauld, and the ky were a' at
            hame,"
        An Old Scotch SONG revived.
        .....
        [When the sheep were in the fauld, and the ky were a' at
            hame].
        .....

Pennsylvania, Philadelphia; Pennsylvania Ledger, 1775-1778

1099.   Feb. 11, 1778, #126, p. 2, cols. 2-3.   (DLC 1342)
        "A little farm was my paternal lot,"
        .....
        ....., Lancaster, Jan. 21
        .....
        .....

1100.   Feb. 18, 1778, #128, p. 3, col. 3.   (DLC 1342)
        "Exalted on her ebon throne,"
        ENTHUSIASM.
        .....
        .....
        .....

1101.   Feb. 18, 1778, #128, p. 3, col. 3.   (DLC 1342)
        "THE fields, disconsolate and sad,"
        Stanzas on the present dreary season
        [An officer]
        .....
        .....

1102.   Feb. 21, 1778, #129, p. 3, col. 3.   (DLC 1342)
        "CROWN'D be the man with lasting praise,"
        AMERICA. Addressed to the Rev. Dean TUCKER
        Said to be written by Soame Jennyns, Esq;
        .....
        .....

1103.   March 14, 1778, #135, p. 4, col. 1.   (DLC 1342)
        "O Thou! who smil'st no more"
        An irregular ODE to PEACE,
        J.C., 42nd reg.
        .....
        .....

1104.   March 25, 1778, #138, p. 3, col. 3.   (DLC 1342)
        "GREAT Washington, thou mighty son of Mars,"
        .....
        M'L----n, a private soldier in the British light infantry
        .....
        .....

Pennsylvania, Philadelphia; Pennsylvania Ledger, 1775-1778

1105.   April 11, 1778, #143, p. 4, col. 1.   (DLC 1342)
        "WHEN rival nations, great in arms,"
        ODE for the NEW-YEAR, January 1, 1778.
        Wm. Whitehead, Esq. and Dr. Boyce
        [Ode for the New-Year, Jan. 1, 1778, Music by Dr.
          Boyce.]
        .....

1106.   Feb. 22, 1773, #70, Supplement, p. 1, col. 3.   (DLC 1387)
        "COME, youthful Muse, my breast inspire"
        HOPE.   An ODE.
        .. ....
        .. ....
        .. ....

1107.   Jan. 3, 1774, #115, p. 1, col. 1.   (DLC 1143)
        "AS near beauteous Boston lying"
        A New SONG.
        Brittanno-Americanus, Philadelphia, January 1st, 1774.
        Hosier's Ghost
        .. ....

1108.   Aug. 15, 1774, #147, p. 3, cols. 2-3.   (DLC 1143)
        "WITH graceful air and virtuous mein,"
        .. ....
        Tom Gingle
        .. ....
        .. ....

1109.   Aug. 29, 1774, #149, p. 3, col. 1.   (DLC 1143)
        "O MY baby, my baby,"
        A New SONG.   Supposed to have been sung by Goody N[ort]h,
        By way of lullaby to the foundling brat, the Popish
        Quebec bill.
        .. ....
        O my Kitten, my Kitten
        St. James's Chronicle

1110.   Aug. 7, 1775, #198, p. 3, col. 3.   (DLC 1144)
        "WE are the troops that ne'er will stoop"
        The PENNSYLVANIA MARCH
        .. ....
        Scots Song, I winna Marry ony Lad, but Sandy o'er the
        Lee
        .. ....

1111.   Oct. 9, 1775, #207, p. 2, col. 2.   (DLC 1144)
        "YE stately Sisters!"
        To the Queen...[A dialogue between an oracle and Britannia
          pleading for the continuation of Industry]
        IMPARTIAL.
        .....
        MORNING CHRONICLE

1112.   Oct. 16, 1775, #208, p. 3, col. 3.   (DLC 1144)
        "O GREAT reverse of Tully's coward heart!"
        ODE to the memory of Dr. WARREN, celebrated orator, who
          was slain upon the Heights of Charlestown, fighting for
          the Liberties of America, on June 17, 1775.
        .....
        .....
        MORNING CHRONICLE, August 3.

1113.   Oct. 23, 1775, #209, p. 4, col. 1.   (DLC 1144)
        "HIGH on the banks of Delaware,"
        .....
        ...., September 1775.
        .....
        .....

1114.   March 18, 1776, #230, p. 4, col. 1.   (RMEAN, Card 26)
        "In Abram's plains there lies interr'd"
        .....
        ...., Philadelphia, February 1776
        .....
        .....

1115.   May 13, 1776, #238, p. 3, col. 2.   (DLC 1146)
        "AMERICANS! awake, awake!"
        .....
        A VIRGINIAN
        .....
        .....

1116.   Feb. 25, 1777, #276, p. 3, col. 2.   (DLC 1147)
        "BEHOLD the valiant and the great,"
        .....
        .....
        .....
        .....

1117.   May 27, 1777, #289, p. 3, cols. 2-3.   (DLC 1147)
        "WITHOUT wit, without wisdom, half stupid and drunk,"
        The EXPEDITION to DANBURY, under the command of General
            Tryon, to destroy the stores of beef, pork and rum.
        COMUS, Philadelphia, May 12.
        .....
        Pennsylvania Gazette of May 14, 1777

1118.   July 4, 1778, #   , p. 1, col. 3.   (DLC 1347)
        "Behold! the Cerberus the Atlantic plough,"
        .....
        .....
        .....
        A London Paper

1119.   July 14, 1778, #   , p. 4, col. 1.   (DLC 1347)
        "WELL I remember on that crouded day,"
        Upon the largest Jewel's dropping out of his Majesty's
            Crown on his Coration. (sic)
        N.
        .....
        .....

1120.   Aug. 6, 1778, #   , p. 2, col. 2.   (DLC 1347)
        "WHEN the white horse doth over the lion rule,"
        MERLIN's PROPHECY, Anno 1715.
        .....
        .....
        New-London, July 17.

1121.   Aug. 8, 1778, #   , p. 3, col. 1.   (DLC 1347)
        "WHEN North first began,"
        On Lord NORTH's Recantation.
        FACT.
        .....
        London Evening Post

1122.   Aug. 11, 1778, #   , p. 4, col. 1.   (DLC 1347)
        "YE poor simple people, who foolishly think,"
        .....
        TOMAHAWK
        A Cobler there was, &c.
        London Evening Post

1123.   Oct. 10, 1778, #   , p. 3, col. 1.   (DLC 1347)
        "IN Virtue's cause the honest man is bold,"
        .....
        SOCRATES
        .....
        .....

1124.   Nov. 7, 1778, #   , p. 3, col. 1.   (DLC 1347)
        "'TIS past:--Ah! calm thy cares to rest!"
        The NEGRO's Dying Speech on his being executed for
            rebellion in the Island of Jamaica
        B.E. Esquire
        .....
        .....

1125.   Dec. 24, 1778, #   , p. 3, col. 1.   (DLC 1347)
        "LET me too see the great, good man!"
        Lines spoken extempore by a friend as he rushed to his
            front door to gratify himself with a sight of our
            great Deliverer General Washington.
        .....
        .....
        .....

1126.   Dec. 24, 1778, #   , p. 3, col. 1.   (DLC 1347)
        "WHEN God to punish reigning crimes,"
        The AMERICAN HERO.
        .....
        .....
        .....

1127.   Sept. 4, 1779, #   , p. 1, col. 1.   (DLC 1349)
        "LET others toil, their empire to extend"
        .....
        .....
        .....
        .....

1128.   Sept. 4, 1779, #   , p. 1, col. 1.   (DLC 1349)
        "UPON the tressel pig was laid;"
        Piece of Oxford Wit
        .....
        .....
        .....

1129.   Sept. 21, 1779, #   , p. 3, col. 1.   (DLC 1349)
        "WHEN Sc-dd-r, in bombastic strain,"
        The Eloquent and Political DOCTOR.   An Epigram.
        . . . . .
        . . . . .
        . . . . .

1130.   Sept. 21, 1779, #   , p. 3, col. 1.   (DLC 1349)
        "WHEN Cyclops rough or Polypheme"
        The CONTRAST.
        Justus, Philadelphia, August 13, 1779.
        . . . . .
        . . . . .

1131.   Jan. 1, 1780, #   , p. 4, col. 1.   (DLC 1350)
        "GOD save the Thirteen States!"
        A SONG for the Sailors of the five American vessels at
            Amsterdam.   June 1779.
        A Dutch Lady at the Hague.
        [God Save the King]
        . . . . .

1132.   Jan. 1, 1780, #   , p. 4, cols. 1-2.   (DLC 1350)
        "GOD bless the Thirteen States,"
        Another song to be sung on the 4th of July.
        A Dutch Gentleman at Amsterdam.
        [God Save the King]
        . . . . .

1133.   Jan. 8, 1780, #   , p. 3, col. 1.   (DLC 1350)
        "LOUD rumour speaks, "The French and Spaniards steer" "
        On the reported invasion of the British Islands by the
            French and Spaniards.
        U., Springhill, Aug. 31, 1779.
        . . . . .
        LONDON EVENING POST.

1134.   Jan. 13, 1780, #   , p. 3, col. 1.   (DLC 1350)
        "IN good King George's golden days,"
        A NEW SONG, occasioned by the...illiberal, and un-
          warrantable aspersion thrown out by Dr. TUCKER, DEAN of
          GLOUCESTER......
        .....
        The Vicar of Bray.
        The LONDON EVENING POST.

1135.   Jan. 18, 1780, #   , p. 4, col. 1.   (DLC 1350)
        "TO all our countrymen at land,"
        SONG.
        An Officer on board Sir Charles Hardy's Fleet.
        To all you ladies now at land.
        LONDON EVENING POST.

1136.   April 25, 1780, #   , p. 3, col. 1.   (DLC 1350)
        "HENCE with the Lover who sighs o'er his wine,"
        The VOLUNTEER BOYS.
        .....
        Let the Toast Pass.
        .....

1137.   May 2, 1780, #   , p. 2, cols. 2-3.   (DLC 1350)
        "THERE was, and a very great fool,"
        A merry Song about MURDER.
        .....
        .....
        The WESTMINSTER COURANT, 25th January, 1780.

1138.   July 15, 1780, #   , p. 1, cols. 1-3, p. 2, col. 1.   (DLC
          1351)
        "[FELIX,] good morn. 'Tis now five irksome years"
        Dialogue composed for...the Public Commencement at the
          University in the City.
        .....
        .....
        .....

1139.   July 15, 1780, #   , p. 1, cols. 1-3, p. 2, col. 1.
            (DLC 1351)
         "May ev'ry blessing on their arms attend," [Recitative]
         Dialogue composed for...the Public Commencement at the
            University in the City.
            .....
            .....
            .....

1140.   July 15, 1780, #   , p. 1, cols. 1-3, p. 2, col. 1.
            (DLC 1351)
         "Rise! O rise! ye pow'rs supreme," [Air]
         Dialogue composed for...the Public Commencement at the
            University in the City.
            .....
            .....
            .....

1141.   July 15, 1780, #   , p. 1, cols. 1-3, p. 2, col. 1.
            (DLC 1351)
         "Wide as the ocean rolls her flowing tide" [Recitative]
         Dialogue composed for...the Public Commencement at the
            University in the City.
            .....
            .....
            .....

1142.   July 15, 1780, #   , p. 1, cols. 1-3, p.2, col. 1.
            (DLC 1351)
         "Welcome all ye friendly pow'rs" [Air]
         Dialogue composed for...the Public Commencement at the
            University in the City.
            .....
            .....
            .....

1143.   Aug. 1, 1780, #   , p. 4, col. 1. (DLC 1351)
         "THO' age at my elbow has taken his stand,"
         An Old Man's SONG on the public spirit of our Women.
            .....
            .....
            .....

1144.   Oct. 7, 1780, #   , p. 2, col. 2.   (DLC 1351)
        "WHEN virtue calls, enraptur'd we obey,"
        .....
        SOCRATES
        .....
        .....

1145.   Jan. 20, 1781, #   , p. 3, col. 2.   (DLC 1352)
        "ALL hail! Superiour Sex, exalted fair,"
        To those AMERICAN LADIES who have lately distinguished
           their patriotism, in generously contributing to the
           relief of the Soldiery.
        A SOLDIER.
        .....
        .....

1146.   July 10, 1781, #753, p. 1, col. 3.   (DLC 1353)
        "OH! Old England, Old England;"
        New-Year's Day, 1781.
        .....
        Get you gone, Raw-head and Bloody-bones.
        Late LONDON PAPER.

1147.   Oct. 18, 1781, #795, p. 1, col. 3.   (DLC 1353)
        "THEY, who content on earth to stay,"
        CASTLES in the AIR.
        ANONYMOUS.
        .....
        The LONDON EVENING POST of July.

1148.   Nov. 10, 1781, #805, p. 3, cols. 1-2.   (DLC 1353)
        "WHEN British troops first landed here,"
        CORNWALLIS Burgoyne'd: A SONG.
        .....
        Maggie Lauder.
        .....

1149.   Nov. 20, 1781, #809, p. 1, cols. 2-3.   (DLC 1353)
        "YE loyalists all, within the town,"
        Another NEW-YORK ADDRESS, "To all honest hearts and sound
           bottoms."
        .....
        [Yankee Doodle]
        .....

1150.   Nov. 27, 1781, #812, p. 1, col. 1.   (DLC 1353)
        "CORNWALLIS led a country dance,"
        The DANCE, A Ballad.
        .....
        Yankey Doodle.
        .....

1151.   Dec. 11, 1781, #818, p. 3, col. 2.   (DLC 1353)
        "'TWAS for the conquest nobly won"
        An ODE,...imitation of Dryden's Alexander's Feast
        A SOUTHERN EXILE.
        .....
        .....

1152.   March 2, 1782, #853, p. 3, col. 3.   (DLC 1354)
        "THERE was--and a very great Fool,"
        A Merry SONG about MURDER.
        .....
        .....
        London, for the Anniversary of the GENERAL FAST, the
          21st. of February 1781.

1153.   March 23, 1782, #862, p. 1, col. 1.   (DLC 1354)
        "QUIDNUNC, my cronie, thou dost look"
        STANZAS for the Antigua Gazette.
        TRUTH, old-Road, Jan. 28th
        .....
        Antigua Gazette.

1154.   May 25, 1782, #889, p. 3, col. 3.   (DLC 1354)
        "Oh how merry how merry,"
        An ODE to the New Year, 1782, which ought to be perform-
          ed at the Commandant's.
        .....
        Hey my Kitten
        .....

1155.   June 25, 1782, #902, p. 3, col. 2.   (DLC 1354)
        "YE belles, and ye flirts and ye pert little things,"
        .....
        JUVENIS.
        [A Song for Ranelagh?]
        .....

1156.   Aug. 31, 1782, #931, p. 2, col. 3.   (DLC 1355)
        "I sing of George's golden days,"
        WHO's the NOODLE, A NEW SONG.
        .....
        [Ods' Blood Who's the Noodle]
        The London General Advertiser

1157.   Dec. 21, 1782, #979, p. 3, cols. 1-2.   (DLC 1355)
        "SWEET Poll of Plymouth was my dear,"
        POLL of Plymouth: A Ballad.
        .....
        [Poll of Plymouth]
        .....

1158.   Jan. 7, 1783, #986, p. 3, cols. 1-2.   (DLC 1356)
        "YE maidens all who would be married,"
        A NEW BALLAD.
        .....
        .....
        .....

1159.   June 21, 1783, #1057, p. 2, col. 1.   (DLC 1356)
        "WHAT constitutes a State?"
        An ODE in imitation of ALCAEUS. To the PROPRIETORS of
           LAND in SCOTLAND, whether holding of the CROWN, of the
           Prince, or of a Subject superior,...
        SINCERE FRIEND TO HIS COUNTRY
        .....
        Edinburgh Evening Post, dated Sept. 4,(?), 1782.

1160.   July 19, 1783, #1069, p. 3, col. 2.   (DLC 1356)
        "AT length WAR'S sanguine scenes are o'er;"
        On the PEACE: An ODE. Designed for Music.
        .....
        .....
        MARYLAND GAZETTE, July 4.

Pennsylvania, Philadelphia; Pennsylvania Packet, 1771-1790

1161.   Oct. 14 (sic for 16), 1783, #1608, p. 2, col. 3.   (DLC 1357)
         "WHEN rous'd by the trumpet's loud clangor to arms,"
         Favourite BALLAD, sung by Mr. ARROWSMITH, at Vauxhall
         Mr. Arne.
         [When rous'd by the trumpet's loud clangor to arms]
         . . . . .

1162.   Dec. 4, 1783, #1629, p. 3, col. 3.   (DLC 1357)
         "IN our dependent golden days,"
         . . . . .
         . . . . .
         [Vicar of Bray]
         . . . . .

Pennsylvania, Philadelphia
Pennsylvania Staats-Courier, 1777-1778

1163.   May 6, 1778, #745, p. 263-264.   (DLC Box 26, folder 18)
        "Was neues gibt es wohl, was sagen die Rebellen?"
        Gespraech zweyer Bauern in Tolpehacken, des Abends bey
          einem Glass Wisky und gutem Hickory Feuer, am Iten
          May, 1778.
        .....
        .....
        .....

Pennsylvania, Lancaster
Pennsylvanische Zeitungs-Blat, 1778

1164.   June 10, 1778, #19, p. 3, col. 1.   (PHi)
        "PreisS und Danck sey Vievlamor (?)"
        Ein Vortrag an unsere junge Landes-Mitbrueder
        .....
        .....
        .....

Pennsylvania, Philadelphia
Wochentliche Philadelphische Staatsbote, 1762-1779

1165.   5 Jenner, 1773, #572, p. 1, col. 1.   (DLC 1412)
        "Von Ihm, dem Ursprung aller Dinge,"
        Zum Anfange des Jahres 1773.
        . . . . .
        . . . . .
        . . . . .

1166.   Aug. 9, 1774, #655, p. 1, col. 2.   (DLC 1412)
        "Wofern ihr Obern Maechte"
        . . . . .
        Ein Soldat
        . . . . .
        Londoner Morgen-Zeitung, vom 14ten May

RHODE ISLAND

1167. March 6, 1777, #8, p. 2, col. 3, & p. 3, col. 1.   (DLC
     1415)
     "WHile you, my Lord! with wealth and tides (titles?)
     blest,"
     An ELEGY, ADDDRESSED TO LORD PERCY.
     A Youth of Twenty.
     . . . . .
     . . . . .

1168. March 20, 1777, #10, p. 4, col. 1.   (DLC 1415)
     "CONFINEMENT, hail! in Honour's justest cause,"
     . . . . .
     A Gentleman confined in Philadelphia Goal.
     . . . . .
     Royal American Gazette.

1169. April 3, 1777, #12, p. 4, col. 1.   (DLC 1415)
     "OF all the gifts by God on man bestow'd,"
     . . . . .
     . . . . .
     . . . . .
     . . . . .

1170. April 17, 1777, 14, p. 4, col. 1.   (DLC 1415)
     "AGAIN imperial Winter's Sway"
     ODE for the NEW-YEAR, as performed before their MAJESTIES,
        and the Royal Family at St. James's.
     William Whitehead, Esq; Poet-Laureat.
     . . . . .
     . . . . .

1171. April 17, 1777, #14, p. 4, cols. 1-2.   (DLC 1415)
     "YE gentle Nymphs! whose matchless Charms,"
     To the LADIES of RHODE-ISLAND
     . . . . .
     . . . . .
     . . . . .

Rhode Island, Newport; The Newport Gazette, 1777-1779

1172.   April 24, 1777, #15, p. 4, col. 1.   (DLC 1415)
        "WHEN Sons ungrateful to kind Parents prove,"
        SOLILOQUY.
        BRITANNIA, on recovering from her Despondency.
        .....
        .....

1173.   Oct. 16, 1777, #39, p. 4, col. 1.   (DLC 1415)
        "AGAIN, my social Friends, we meet"
        Tradesmen's SONG for his MAJESTY's BIRTH-DAY, 1777.
        .....
        "When Britain first, at Heaven's Command."
        Lloyd's Evening-Post.

1174.   May 21, 1778, #70, p. 4, col. 1.   (DLC 1416)
        "WHEN rival nations, great in arms,"
        ODE for the NEW-YEAR, January 1, 1778.
        William Whitehead, Esq; Poet Laureat.
        Set to music by Dr. Boyce. [Ode for the New-Year, Jan.
           1, 1778]
        .....

1175. Jan. 25, 1773, #751, p. 2, col. 3. (DLC 1433)
       "AMERICANS attend to Freedom's Cry!"
       The VOICE of FREEDOM. By uniting we Stand, by dividing
          we Fall.
       THE IMMORTAL FARMER.
       .....
       .....

1176. Sept. 6, 1773, #783, p. 2, col. 2. (DLC 1433)
       "Who has e'er been at Versailles must needs know the King;"
       MUSICAL INTELLIGENCE EXTRAORDINARY. (A Song in Praise of
          the King of France.)
       .....
       "Who has e'er been at Baldock must needs know the Mill."
       London, June 24.

1177. Sept. 6, 1773, #783, p. 2, col. 2. (DLC 1433)
       "Hanover, thou Land of Pleasure,"
       MUSICAL INTELLIGENCE EXTRAORDINARY. (AIR in PRAISE of
          HANOVER)
       .....
       Air in Praise of Hanover.
       London, June 24.

1178. Sept. 6, 1773, #783, p. 2, col. 2. (DLC 1433)
       "Then here's to thee my Boy Jack,"
       MUSICAL INTELLIGENCE EXTRAORDINARY. ("a grand chorus")
       .....
       .....
       London, June 24.

1179. Sept. 13, 1773, #784, p. 4, col. 1. (DLC 1433)
       "A Monarch in my rustic bower,"
       The HERMIT's EMPIRE.
       .....
       .....

Rhode Island, Newport; The Newport Mercury, 1758-1820+

1180.   Dec. 13, 1773, #797, p. 2, col. 3.   (DLC 1433)
         "PARLIAMENT an act has made,"
         .....
         Mrs. M-----s, a Taylor.
         .....
         .....

1181.   Feb. 7, 1774, #805, p. 3, col. 2.   (DLC 1434)
         "WHEN first the grand constructor form'd this ball,"
         .....
         ["composed by the ladies on the occasion" of the "meeting
             of the daughters of liberty in Bedford"]
         .....
         .....

1182.   Feb. 7, 1774, #805, p. 3, col. 2.   (DLC 1434)
         "WE chose a day, for to survey"
         .....
         ["composed by the ladies on the occasion" of the "meeting
             of the daughters of liberty in Bedford"]
         .....
         .....

1183.   Feb. 14, 1774, #806, p. 4, col. 1.   (DLC 1434)
         "WHAT you can raise upon your farms"
         .....
         Some of the ladies at their meeting to resolve against
             TEA.
         .....
         Sent from Bedford

1184.   March 14, 1774, #810, p. 4, col. 1.   (DLC 1434)
         "WHEN the Foes of the Land, our Destruction had plan'd,"
         A SONG for the 5th of MARCH.
         .....
         Once the Gods of the Greeks.
         .....

1185.   Sept. 12, 1774, #836, p. 4, col. 1. (DLC 1434)
        "YOUR Colonel H[ancoc]k by neglect,"
        A General sample of Gubernatorial Eloquence, as lately
          exhibited to the Company of C[adet]s.
        .....
        .....
        Massachusetts Spy.

1186.   Dec. 19, 1774, #850, p. 4, col. 1. (DLC 1434)
        "THE expences of war, and corruptions of peace,"
        SONG.
        .....
        Derry Down.
        late London Paper.

1187.   Feb. 13, 1775, #858, p. 4, col. 1. (DLC 1435)
        "I AM an old farmer, was born in the woods,"
        A DREAM.
        .....
        .....
        .....

1188.   March 15, 1775, [#862], extra, p. 2, col. 2. (DLC 1435)
        "O MY baby, my baby,"
        A NEW SONG. Supposed to have been sung by Goody N[ort]h,
          by Way of Lulla-by, to the foundling Popish Quebec Bill.
        .....
        O my Kitten, my Kitten.
        .....

1189.   May 29, 1775, #873, p. 4, col. 1. (DLC 1435)
        "HARK! 'tis Freedom that calls, come Patriots awake!"
        A SONG.
        .....
        "The echoing Horn."
        .....

1190.   July 3, 1775, #878, p. 4, col. 1. (DLC 1435)
        "COME listen my cocks, to a brother and friend,"
        The SAILOR's ADDRESS.
        .....
        [Hearts of Oak]
        London Paper.

Rhode Island, Newport; The Newport Mercury, 1758-1820+

1191.   July 3, 1775, #878, p. 4, col. 1.   (DLC 1435)
        "HAPPY's the man, who unconstrain'd"
        An ODE on LIBERTY.
        .....
        .....
        .....

1192.   July 10, 1775, #879, p. 4, col. 1.   (DLC 1435)
        "BY my faith but I think ye're all makers of bulls,"
        The IRISHMAN's Epistle to the Officers and Troops of
           Boston.
        PADDY
        .....
        Pennsylvania Magazine for May 1775.

1193.   Sept. 4, 1775, #887, p. 4, col. 1.   (DLC 1435)
        "COME, Sisters come, your injur'd Country calls,"
        An Invitation to the FAIR-SEX, to assist in supporting
           their country's freedom.
        .....
        .....
        .....

1194.   Sept. 11, 1775, #888, p. 4, col. 1.   (DLC 1435)
        "IN a chariot of light from the regions of day,"
        LIBERTY TREE. A new Song.
        ATLANTICUS
        The Gods of the Greeks.
        .....

1195.   Oct. 2, 1775, #891, p. 3, col. 1.   (DLC 1435)
        "WHen late the hero* of our land took flight," *Dr. Warren.
        Inscribed to the Hon. James Warren, Esq; Speaker of the
           House of Representatives, and Pay-Master General of the
           Continental Army.
        EUGENIO, Province Massachusetts-Bay.
        .....
        .....

Rhode Island, Newport; The Newport Mercury, 1758-1820+

1196.   July 11, 1776, Extra, p. 4, col. 1. (DLC 1436)
         "AT length--with generous indignation fir'd,"
         .....
         Pennsylvaniensis.
         .....
         .....

1197.   Jan. 20, 1781, #1008, p. 4, col. 2. (DLC 1438)
         "THOU who in glory's shining track,"
         To General WASHINGTON, on the late Conspiracy.
         .....
         .....
         Virginia Gazette.

1198.   Feb. 23, 1782, #1065, p. 3, cols. 1-2. (DLC 1439)
         "PRINCE William of the Brunswick race"
         The ROYAL ADVENTURER.
         .....
         .....
         late Pennsylvania Paper.

1199.   Aug. 30, 1782, #1092, p. 4, col. 1. (DLC 1439)
         "AGAIN the auspicious day returns,"
         An ODE On the anniversary of the birth of the King of
            France, Navarre, &c.
         CRITO, Newport, August 26, 1782.
         .....
         .....

1200.   Oct. 26, 1782, #1100, p. 4, col. 1. (DLC 1439)
         "WELCOME, one Arnold, to our shore;"
         ODE addressed to GENERAL ARNOLD.
         LADY CRAVEN.
         .....
         late British Publication.

1201.   Aug. 30, 1783, #1144, p. 4, col. 1. (DLC 1440)
         "ALAS! brother Tories, now what shall we do,"
         The penetential TORY's Lamentation.
         .....
         .....
         .....

Rhode Island, Newport; The Newport Mercury, 1758-1820+

1202.   Sept. 13, 1783, #1146, p. 4, col. 1.   (DLC 1440)
        "OF all the leaders in the state"
        A SONG. On the wise Coalition compleated the 1st of
        April, 1783.
        .....
        Nancy Dawson.
        .....

1203.   March 18, 1779, #1, p. 4, cols. 1-2.   (RPB)
        "Soon as the lark observes the morning's grey,"
        The Future Glory of America.
        . . . . .
        . . . . .
        . . . . .

1204.   April 15, 1779, #5, p. 4, col. 1.   (DLC Box 28, folder 3)
        "OF all the ages ever known"
        The PRESENT AGE.
        ["one of your Country Subscribers"]
        . . . . .
        . . . . .

1205.   April 29, 1779, #7, p. 4, col. 1.   (MWA)
        "Descend my muse, on airy wings sublime,"
        On MUSIC.
        YORICK (?)
        . . . . .
        . . . . .

1206.   May 13, 1779, #9, p. 3, col. 1.   (DLC Box 28, folder 3)
        "WAR! how I hate they horrid name,"
        WAR!
        . . . . .
        . . . . .
        . . . . .

1207.   June 10, 1779, #13, p. 4, col. 1.   (MWA)
        "Come and listen my lads to sweet liberty's lay,"
        LIBERTY's CALL.
        . . . . .
        Black Sloven.
        . . . . .

1208.   Jan. 20, 1780, #45, p. 4, col. 1.   (DLC Box 28, folder 4)
        "YE tuneful nine, my artless lay inspire,"
        The Duty of a WIFE.
        a Lady.
        . . . . .
        from a novel, entitled a Description of Modern Life, said
          to have been written by a Lady.

Rhode Island, Providence; American Journal, 1779-1781

1209.   Jan. 20, 1780, #45, p. 4, col. 2.   (DLC Box 28, folder 4)
        "THrice hallowed grace! that keep'st   thy pow'r,"
        ODE to CHARITY. Occasioned by the Subscription for the
          American Prisoners.
        ......
        ......
        (London) Gentleman's Magazine, June, 1778.

1210.   April 19, 1780, #58, p. 4, col. 1.   (DLC Box 28, folder 4)
        "I'M not high church nor low church, nor tory, nor whig,"
        ......
        J.R., Newport, April 13, 1780.
        [Derry Down]
        ......

1211.   May 24, 1780, #63, p. 4, col. 1.   (DLC Box 28, folder 4)
        "PITY the sorrows of a poor old man,"
        The BEGGAR.
        ......
        ......
        American Magazine.

1212.   Nov. 18, 1780, #86, p. 4, col. 1.   (RHi)
        "Quoth Satan to Arnold, my worthy good fellow,"
        A DIALOGUE between SATAN and ARNOLD.
        ......
        ......
        ......

1213.   Jan. 20, 1781, #95, p. 4, col. 1.   (DLC Box 28, folder 5)
        "THOU who in glory's shining track,"
        To General WASHINGTON, on the late conspiracy.
        ......
        ......
        Virginia Gazette.

1214.   May 2, 1781, #123, p. 4, col. 1.   (MWA)
        "This is the FAST which I will choose,"
        HYMN.
        A.B.?, Providence, May 1, 1781.
        ......
        ......

Rhode Island, Providence; American Journal, 1779-1781.

1215.   Aug. 15, 1781, #153, p. 2, col. 3.   (RHi)
         "Our troops by Arnold thoroughly were bang'd,"
         ARNOLD; or a Question answered.
         .....
         .....
         late London Paper.

1216. Jan. 2, 1773, #469, p. 4, col. 1.   (RMEAN, Card #36)
       "Lo! mantled in a show'ry cloud,"
       JANUARY, AN ODE.
       .. . . . .
       .. . . . .
       .. . . . .

1217. June 5, 1773, #491, p. 4, col. 1.   (RMEAN, Card #37)
       "Sov'reign of All, whose Will ordains"
       On His Majesty's Birthday, June 4, 1773.
       .. . . . .
       .. . . . .
       .. . . . .

1218. Aug. 28, 1773, #503, p. 2, col. 1.   (DLC Box 28, folder
          7)
       "WHO has e'er been at Versailles must needs know the
          King;"
       MUSICAL INTELLIGENCE EXTRAORDINARY.   (Song in Praise of
          the King of France)
       .. . . . .
       Who has e'er been at Baldock must needs know the Mill
       London, June 24.

1219. Aug. 28, 1773, #503, p. 2, col. 1.   (DLC Box 28, folder
          7)
       "Hanover, thou Land of Pleasure,"
       MUSICAL INTELLIGENCE EXTRAORDINARY (AIR IN PRAISE of
          HANOVER)
       .. . . .
       AIR IN PRAISE of HANOVER.
       London, June 24.

1220. Aug. 28, 1773, #503, p. 2, col. 1.   (DLC Box 28, folder
          7)
       "Then here's to thee my Boy Jack,"
       MUSICAL INTELLIGENCE EXTRAORDINARY (grand Chorus)
       .. . . .
       .. . . . .
       London, June 24.

Rhode Island, Providence; Providence Gazette, 1762-1820+

1221.   Jan. 22, 1774, #524, p. 4, col. 1.   (RMEAN, Card #40)
        "A Game Cock once, of English breed,"
        Aesop at Guild hall, an imperfect Fable; or Tale of a
           Cock and a Bull.
        . . . . .
        . . . . .
        The Morning Chronicle.

1222.   Jan. 28, 1775, #577, p. 4, col. 1   (RMEAN, Card #43)
        "See the poor native quit the Lybian Shore"
        To the Dealers in Slaves.
        . . . . .
        . . . . .
        . . . . .

1223.   March 4, 1775, #582, p. 4, col. 1.   (RMEAN, Card #44)
        "O my baby, my baby,"
        A NEW SONG. Supposed to have been sung by Goody N[ort]h,
           by way of Lullaby to the foundling Popish Quebec Bill.
        . . . . .
        O my Kitten, my Kitten.
        . . . . .

1224.   May 27, 1775, #595, p. 4, col. 1.   (RMEAN, Card #45)
        "Brother Soldiers, all fight on,
        The Christian SOLDIER.
        . . . . .
        . . . . .
        . . . . .

1225.   June 17, 1775, #598, p. 4, col. 1.   (RMEAN, Card #45)
        "Come join hand in hand all ye true loyal souls,"
        A SONG.
        . . . . .
        [Hearts of Oak]
        . . . . .

1226.   July 1, 1775, #600, p. 4, col. 1.   (RMEAN, Card 45)
        "Come listen my cocks, to a brother and friend;"
        The SAILOR's ADDRESS
        . . . . .
        [Hearts of Oak]
        A late London Paper

Rhode Island, Providence; Providence Gazette, 1762-1820+

1227. Oct. 28, 1775, #617, p. 4, col. 1. (RMEAN, Card 46)
       "While pleasure reigns unrival'd on this shore,"
       .....
       .....
       .....
       .....

1228. Nov. 4, 1775, #618, p. 4, col. 1. (RMEAN, Card 46)
       "O Great reverse of Tully's coward heart,"
       .....
       .....
       .....
       The Morning Chronicle, Aug. 3.

1229. Nov. 25, 1775, #621, p. 4, col. 1. (RMEAN, Card 47)
       "Have we not seen, at Pleasure's lordly call,"
       TYRANNY TRIUMPHING
       .....
       .....
       .....

1230. Dec. 23, 1775, #625, p. 3, col. 2. (RMEAN, Card 47)
       "Tho' some folks may tell us, it is not so clever,"
       A SONG
       A Soldier in the Continental Army
       Black Sloven
       .....

1231. Dec. 23, 1775, #625, p. 4, col. 1. (RMEAN, Card 47)
       "Hark the Herald-Angels sing,"
       On the Birth of Christ
       .....
       .....
       .....

1232. Nov. 8, 1776, #671, p. 1, col. 3, p. 2, col. 1. (RMEAN,
       Card 50)
       "All hail G[e]rm[ai]ne, G[e]rm[ai]ne, all hail!"
       Ode to Lord G[ermaine]
       .....
       .....
       .....

Rhode Island, Providence; Providence Gazette, 1762-1820+

1233.   Jan. 11, 1777, #680, p. 4, col. 1.   (RMEAN, Card 51)
         "While Britain's arms triumphant trophies boast,"
         .....
         .....
         .....
         .....

1234.   March 15, 1777, #689, p. 4, col. 1.   (RMEAN, Card 51)
         "My Lords, with your leave,"
         A NEW WAR Song
         Sir Peter Parker
         "Well met Brother Tar"
         .....

1235.   May 17, 1777, #698, p. 4, col. 1.   (DLC 1461)
         "YE wrong heads, and strong heads, attend to my strains;"
         The HEADS, or the Year 1776.
         .....
         [Derry Down]
         London Public Ledger

1236.   July 12, 1777, #706, p. 4, col. 1.   (DLC 1461)
         "BY the Red Sea the Hebrew host detain'd,"
         The Miracle near Sullivan's Island.
         .....
         .....
         The St. James's Chronicle

1237.   May 30, 1778, #752, p. 4, col. 1.   (DLC 1462)
         "GIVE ear to my song, I'll not tell you a story,"
         The Halcyon Days of Old England: Or the Wisdom of Ad-
             ministration demonstrated: A Ballad.
         .....
         Ye Medley of Mortals
         London Evening Post

1238.   Aug. 8, 1778, #762, p. 4, col. 1.   (DLC 1462)
         "WEST of th' old Atlantic, firm Liberty stands!"
         The GAMESTER. A new Song.
         .....
         A late worthy old lion, &c.
         .....

Rhode Island, Providence; Providence Gazette, 1762-1820+

1239.   Aug. 29, 1778, #765, p. 4, col. 1.   (DLC 1462)
        "WHEN North first began"
        On Lord NORTH's Recantation.
        FACT
        .....
        London Evening Post

1240.   Dec. 12, 1778, #780, p. 4, col. 1.   (DLC 1462)
        "WIthin these Walls fair Freedom's Sons immur'd,"
        .....
        A Prisoner in the Provost at Newport
        .....
        .....

1241.   Dec. 26, 1778, #782, p. 3, col. 2.   (DLC 1462)
        "BEhold that splendor! Hear the shout!"
        A CHRISTMAS CAROL.
        .....
        .....
        .....

1242.   Jan. 23, 1779, #786, p. 4, col. 1.   (DLC 1463)
        "Attend, Brittannia's sons, attend to Heaven's decree,"
        .....
        ["written by as brave, humane, and sensible an officer as
        any in the English army"]
        .....
        Extract of letter from New-York, June 8.

1243.   June 19, 1779, #807, p. 4, col. 1.   (DLC 1463)
        "GOD save America,"
        A New SONG.
        .....
        [God save the King]
        .....

1244.   Jan. 1, 1780, #835, p. 4, col. 1.   (DLC 1464)
        "GOD save the Thirteen States!"
        A SONG. for the Americans at Amsterdam, July 4, 1779.
        A Dutch Lady at the Hague
        [God Save the King]
        .....

Rhode Island, Providence; Providence Gazette, 1762-1820+

1245.   Jan. 1, 1780, #835, p. 4, cols. 1-2.   (DLC 1464)
        "GOD bless the Thirteen States!"
        .....
        A Dutch Gentleman at Amsterdam, July 4, 1779
        [God Save the King]
        .....

1246.   Feb. 12, 1780, #841, p. 4, col. 1.   (DLC 1464)
        "TO all our countrymen at land,"
        SONG
        An Officer on board Sir Charles Hardy's fleet
        To all you ladies now at land
        The London Evening Post

1247.   Dec. 8, 1781, #936, p. 4, col. 1.   (DLC Box 28, folder 8)
        "WHEN British troops first landed here,"
        CORNWALLIS Burgoyn'd. A SONG.
        .....
        Maggie Lauder
        .....

1248.   Jan. 12, 1782, #941, p. 3, col. 2.   (DLC 1465)
        "HARK! whence that charming Sound! that joyful Shout!"
        .....
        A.Z.
        .....
        .....

1249.   Jan. 19, 1782, #942, p. 4, col. 1.   (DLC 1465)
        "BY your leave, gossip John;"
        PADDY's ADDRESS to JOHN BULL. A new Ballad.
        .....
        Larry Crogan
        A late Irish Paper

1250.   Feb. 2, 1782, #944, p. 2, cols. 1-2.   (DLC 1465)
        "ARISE! arise! your voices raise,"
        The TEMPLE of MINERVA, An Oratorial Entertainment.
        [F.H.]
        [The Temple of Minerva; Francis Hopkinson, Arr.]
        Philadelphia.

Rhode Island, Providence; Providence Gazette, 1762-1820+

1251.　June 22, 1782, #964, p. 3, col. 3.　(DLC 1465)
　　　　"YE sons of Mars, attend,"
　　　　A new SONG. Written on the Celebration of the Birth of
　　　　　the Dauphin, at West-Point.
　　　　. . . . .
　　　　[Restoration March]
　　　　. . . . .

1252.　April 19, 1783, #1007, p. 4, col. 1.　(DLC 1466)
　　　　"LO Peace refulgent, with her olive wand,"
　　　　On PEACE.
　　　　Academicus.
　　　　. . . . .
　　　　. . . . .

1253.　May 17, 1783, #1011, p. 4, col. 1.　(DLC 1466)
　　　　"BEHOLD, array'd in Light,"
　　　　A HYMN on PEACE.
　　　　. . . . .
　　　　[Worcester]
　　　　Philadelphia.

1254.　May 24, 1783, #1012, p. 4, col. 1.　(DLC 1466)
　　　　"LONG now has the God of Arms"
　　　　ODE to PEACE.
　　　　. . . . .
　　　　. . . . .
　　　　The London General Advertiser

1255.　May 31, 1783, #1013, p. 4, col. 1.　(DLC 1466)
　　　　"AT length War's sanguine scenes are o'er:"
　　　　On PEACE.--An Ode.　Designed for Music.
　　　　. . . . .
　　　　. . . . .
　　　　The New-Jersey Journal

SOUTH CAROLINA

South Carolina, Charlestown
Charlestown Gazette, 1778-1780

1256.   Jan. 18, 1780, #68, p. 2, cols. 1-2.   (DLC Microfilm
         1468, Reel 9).
         "There's scarce a Gazette now, you'll see,"
         THE REDUCTION OF FORT SAND. ("A fearful battle rendered
         you in music")
         .. ...
         .. ...
         .. ...

South Carolina, Charleston
(Charleston) Gazette of the State of South-Carolina,
1777-1780, 1783-1785

1257.   June 23, 1777, #2066, p. 2, cols. 1-2.   (DLC Microfilm
        1468, Reel 7).
     "WIthout wit, without wisdom, half stupid and drunk,"
     The Expdition (sic) to Danbury, Under the Command of
        General Tryon, to destroy the stores of Beef, Pork,
        and Rum.
     COMUS, Philadelphia, May 12.
     . . . . .
     . . . . .

1258.   June 27, 1781, #34, p. 2, col. 3.   (DLC 1508)
        "WHILE Peers and Commons head the riot,"
        VERSES written on the great rejoicings and illuminations
           at the acquittal of Admiral Keppel.
        a very gallant SEAMAN
        .....
        .....

1259.   Aug. 1, 1781, #44, p. 2, col. 3.   (DLC 1508)
        "STILL does the Rage of War prevail,"
        ODE for his MAJESTY's BIRTH-DAY, June 4, 1781.
        William Whitehead, Esq; Poet-Laureat, set to Musick by
           Mr. Stanley.
        [Ode for his Majesty's Birthday, June 4, 1781]
        .....

1260.   Jan. 1, 1782, Broadside.   (DLC Microfilm 1468, Reel 12).
        "THE News-Paper Lads, vows and wishes sincere"
        TO the CUSTOMERS of the ROYAL GAZETTE.
        ...., Charlestown, January 1st, 1782.
        .....
        .....

1261.   May 18, 1782, #127, p. 3, col. 2.   (DLC 1508)
        "ONCE more, Britannia, rears her drooping head,"
        VERSES occasioned by the late Victory obtained by Sir
           George Brydges Rodney, over the Count de Grasse.
        Rusticus
        .....
        .....

1262.   June 12, 1782, #134, p. 2, col. 1.   (DLC 1508)
        "'Twas at the Birth-night ball, Sir,"
        .....
        .....
        [The Royal Disaster]
        .....

South Carolina, Charleston; (Charleston) Royal Gazette, 1781-
1782

1263.   June 12, 1782, #134, p. 2, col. 1.   (DLC 1508)
        "YE Lads of true Spirit,"
        MORRIS's VOLUNTEERS. A New Song.
        C.
        [Ye lads of true Spirit]
        .....

1264.   July 6, 1782, #141, p. 2, col. 2.   (DLC 1508)
        "'TWAS at th'imperial throne below,"
        Tribute to the splendid and important victory of the 12th
          of April last.
        J.J., Spanish-Town, May 16, 1782.
        .....
        .....

1265.   July 27, 1782, #147, p. 3, col. 3.   (DLC 1508)
        "HARK! hear Apollo strikes his lyre!"
        An ODE, For his Majesty's Birth-day, 1782.
        J.M., Prince George, Port-Royal-Harbour, June 4, 1782.
        .....
        The Jamaica Gazette

South Carolina, Charleston
(Charleston) Royal South-Carolina Gazette, 1780-1782

1266. Sept. 12, 1782, #339, p. 3, cols. 1-2. (DLC Microfilm
       1468, Reel 11).
       "COME, meek-ey'd Maid, long banish'd hence,"
       An irregular ODE to PEACE.
       .....
       .....
       .....

1267. Aug. 12, 1774, #830, p. 2, col. 2. (DLC Microfilm 1468,
          Reel 10).
       "HARK! -- or does the Muse's ear"
       ODE For His MAJESTY's BIRTH-DAY, June 4, 1774.
       By William Whitehead, Esq; Poet Laureat, Set to Musick
          by Dr. Boyce
       [Ode for his Majesty's Birth-day, June 4, 1774]
       . . . . .

1268. Aug. 4, 1775, #882, p. 4, col. 1. (DLC Microfilm 1468,
          Reel 10)
       "PROPITIOUS us'd to rise the morn"
       . . . . .
       . . . ., Written June 4, 1775.
       . . . . .
       . . . . .

1269. Aug. 25, 1775, #885, p. 2, col. 2. (DLC Microfilm 1468,
          Reel 10)
       "YE Powers, who rule o'er States and Kings,"
       ODE for his Majesty's Birth-Day, 1775.
       . . . . .
       [ODE for his Majesty's Birth-Day, 1775]
       . . . . .

1270. May 8, 1777, #956, p. 1, col. 1. (DLC Microfilm 1468,
          Reel 11)
       "BY the Red Sea the Hebrew host detain'd,"
       The Miracle near Sullivan's Island.
       . . . . .
       . . . . .
       St. James's CHRONICLE

1271. July 10, 1777, #966, p. 4, col. 1. (DLC Microfilm 1468,
          Reel 11)
       "YE wrong heads, and strong heads, attend to my strains;"
       The HEADS, or the Year 1776.
       . . . . .
       [Derry Down]
       London Publick Ledger.

South Carolina, Charleston; (Charleston) South-Carolina and
American General Gazette, 1764-1781

1272. Nov. 20, 1777, #985, p. 2, col. 2. (DLC Microfilm 1468,
          Reel 11)
       "THAT Power who form'd the unmeasured Seas,"
       A SONG.
       Mr. SEWELL of Boston
       [That Power who form'd the unmeasured Seas]
       .....

1273. March 12, 1778, #999, p. 1, col. 1. (DLC Microfilm 1468,
          Reel 11)
       "GAGE nothing did, and went to pot,"
       On the BRITISH COMMANDERS.
       .....
       .....
       London Paper of December 2, 1777.

1274. Dec. 10, 1778, #1040, p. 4, col. 1. (DLC Microfilm 1468,
          Reel 11)
       "COME and listen my lads to sweet Liberty's lay,"
       LIBERTY's CALL. A New and Original CAMP SONG.
       .....
       BLACK SLOVEN
       .....

1275. Sept. 20, 1780, #1100, p. 3, col. 3. (DLC Microfilm 1468,
          Reel 11)
       "SINCE Discord still rages, we'll plough the Salt Main,"
       The new NAVAL ODE for 1780, sung at Vauxhall by Mr.
          Vernon, Mrs. Weichseil, Mrs. Wrighten, Miss Thorton,
          and others.
       .....
       [Music by Mr. Hook]
       .....

1276. Sept. 27, 1780, #1101, p. 4, col. 1. (DLC Microfilm 1468,
          Reel 11)
       "WHEN 'tis night, and the mid-watch is come,"
       SONG. Mr. Bannister (sung in HARLEQUIN FORTUNATUS)
       .....
       [When 'tis night, and the mid-watch is come]
       LONDON

South Carolina, Charleston; (Charleston) South-Carolina and
American General Gazette, 1764-1781

1277.   Sept. 27, 1780, #1101, p. 4, col. 1.   (DLC Microfilm
            1468, Reel 11)
        "CHEERLY my hearts, of courage true,"
        SONG. Mr. VERNON (sung in HARLEQUIN FORTUNATUS)
        .....
        [Cheerly my hearts, of courage true]
        LONDON

1278.   Nov. 15, 1780, #1114, p. 2, cols. 1-2.   (DLC Microfilm
            1468, Reel 11)
        ISAAC. (Allegro)   "O Wherefore, brother Jonathan,"
        A PASTORAL ELEGY, set to Musick by Signora Carolina
        .....
        Music by Signora Carolina
        New-York, September 27.

1279.   Nov. 15, 1780, #1114, p. 2, col. 2.   (DLC Microfilm
            1468, Reel 11)
        "A Refugee Captain lost two of his Men,"
        Written on a late Exchange of Prisoners.
        .....
        .....
        .....

1280. March 22, 1773, #1944 (Supplement) p. 3, col. 3. (DLC
        Microfilm 1468, Reel 6).
        "NOW the leaden year is done,"
        FAREWEL to 1772.
        CENSOR.
        ......
        ......

1281.   Aug. 17, 1773, #403, p. 1, col. 1. (DLC Microfilm 1468,
             Reel 8)
         "BORN for millions are the Kings"
         ODE for his MAJESTY's BIRTH-DAY, June 4, 1773.
         William Whitehead, Esq. and set to musick by Dr. Boyce
         [Ode for his Majesty's Birthday, June 4, 1773]
         London, June 5

1282.   Nov. 9, 1773, #415, p. 3, col. 1. (DLC Microfilm 1468,
             Reel 9)
         "OH Breth'ren from Play-Houses all,"
         Lines occasioned by a scandalous and abusive Sermon...
         A PLAIN DEALER
         .....
         .....

1283.   April 12, 1774, #437, p. 4, col. 1. (DLC Microfilm 1468,
             Reel 9)
         "SEE Spring once more erects each purple plume,"
         SPRING. AN ODE.
         .....
         .....
         .....

1284.   May 17, 1774, #442, p. 2, col. 3. (DLC Microfilm 1468,
             Reel 9)
         "WHEN heaven, indulgent, bless'd this land,"
         .....
         .....
         .....
         Basseterre (in St. Christophers) February 5.

1285.   Sept. 6, 1774, #458, p. 2, col. 3. (DLC Microfilm 1468,
             Reel 9)
         "CANST thou, Spectator, view this wicked Scene,"
         Lines occasioned by Sight of the AMERICAN having TEA
             poured down her Throat....
         .....
         .....
         .....

South Carolina, Charleston; (Charleston) South-Carolina Gazette; And Country Journal, 1765-1775

1286.   Oct. 25, 1774, #465, p. 2, col. 1.   (DLC Microfilm 1468, Reel 9)
        "In happier times if such should ever be,"
        Lines engraved on a tree in Easton.
        .....
        .....
        .....

1287.   Jan. 10, 1775, #476, p. 2, col. 2.   (DLC Microfilm 1468, Reel 9)
        "Behold the swift revolving Months disclose"
        .....
        Benjamin West(?)
        .....
        South Carolina Almanack

South Carolina, Charleston
(Charleston) South-Carolina Gazette and General Advertiser,
1783-1785

1288.   April 5, 1783, #8, p. 4, col. 1.   (DLC 1531)
        "WHEN pregnant Nature strove relief to gain,"
        American Independence.
        . . . . .
        . . . . .
        . . . . .

1289.   July 12, 1783, #40, p. 1, col. 3.   (DLC 1531)
        "SAYS F-----, if I ever my honour should place"
        A hasty Defence of a late Coalition.
        . . . . .
        . . . . .
        . . . . .

1290.   Dec. 2, 1783, #82, p. 3, col. 3, p. 4, col. 1.   (DLC 1531)
        "SEE, with stern eye, relenting Vengeance weeps!"
        [Mutilated] ELEGY To a Friend.
        . . . . .
        . . . . .
        . . . . .

1291.   April 23, 1783, #10, p. 4, col. 1.   (DLC Box 29, folder
        25)
        "FAIR Peace, how lovely, how delightful thou,"
        ON PEACE.
        . . . . .
        . . . . .
        . . . . .

VERMONT

Vermont, Bennington
Vermont Gazette, 1783-1796, 1797-1807, 1816-1820+

1292.   Dec. 18, 1783, #29, p. 4, col. 1.   (DLC Early State
        Records Supplement, Microfilm 1551, Vt. Na. Reel 1,
        Unit 1)
        "They come! they come! the Heroes come!"
        ODE. On the Arrival of their Excellencies Gen. Wash-
        ington and Gov. Clinton, in N.Y., on Nov. 25, 1783.
        . . . . .
        He comes! he comes!
        . . . . .

VIRGINIA

Virginia Gazette, or, The Norfolk Intelligencer, 1774-1775

1293.   Feb. 23, 1775, #38, p. 4, col. 1.   (DLC Box 30, folder 25)
         "WHETHER you lead the patriot band,"
         To any Minister or great Man.
         ....
         ....
         ....

1294.   Nov. 15, 1783, #14, p. 4, col. 1.   (Vi)
        "Hail Liberty! A glorious word,"
        .....
        .....
        .....
        .....

1295.   Nov. 22, 1783, #15, p. 4, col. 1.   (Vi)
        "In our dependent golden days,"
        .....
        ...., Nov. 9, 1783
        Vicar of Brae (sic)
        .....

1296.   Dec. 13, 1783, #18, p. 4, col. 1.   (ViW)
        "Return ye enraptur'd hearts"
        Medley.
        ELEUTHENIUS, Manchester, Dec. 8, 1783
        [Return ye enraptur'd hearts?]
        .....

1297.   Dec. 13, 1783, #18, p. 4, col. 1.   (ViW)
        "But since independence we lately have got"
        Medley.
        ELEUTHENIUS, Manchester, Dec. 8, 1783
        [Lilliburlerro]
        .....

1298.   Dec. 13, 1783, #18, p. 4, col. 1.   (ViW)
        "Cupid God of soft persuasion,"
        Medley.
        Eleuthenius, Manchester, Dec. 8, 1783
        [Cupid God of soft persuasion]
        .....

1299.   Dec. 13, 1783, #18, p. 4, col. 1.   (ViW)
        "Those daughters (most charming and young)"
        Medley.
        ELEUTHENIUS, Manchester, Dec. 8, 1783
        [Those daughters (most charming and young?)]
        .....

Virginia, Richmond; Virginia Gazette and Independent Chronicle,
1783-1789

1300.   Dec. 13, 1783, #18, p. 4, col. 1. (ViW)
        "Nor in summer, when softly the breezes are playing,"
        Medley.
        ELEUTHENIUS, Manchester, Dec. 8, 1783
        [Nor in summer, when softly the breezes are playing?]
        .....

1301.   Feb. 23, 1782, #9, p. 4, col. 1.   (ViW)
        "Young ladies in town, and those that live round,"
        ADDRESS TO THE LADIES
        . . . . .
        . . . . .
        . . . . .

1302.   March 2, 1782, #10, p. 4, col. 1.   (ViW)
        "Humbly shewest, That a silly old fellow much noted of
            yore,"
        Lord DUNMORE's petition to the legislature of Virginia
        . . . . .
        . . . . .
        . . . . .

1303.   April 6, 1782, #15, p. 4, col. 1.   (ViW)
        "While freedom's sons triumphant shine in arms,"
        The WISH
        A LADY in Richmond
        . . . . .
        . . . . .

1304.   May 5, 1782, #19, p. 4, col. 1.   (ViW)
        "Farewell my Lord, may Zephyr's waft you o'er"
        Address to LORD CORNWALLIS.
        . . . . .
        . . . . .
        . . . . .

1305.   July 5, 1782, #80, p. 4, col. 1.   (ViW)
        "Welcome one Arnold to our shore"
        Ode addressed to General Arnold.
        Lady Craven
        . . . . .
        . . . . .
        . . . . .

1306.   July 27, 1782, #31, p. 4, col. 1.   (DLC Box 31, folder 25)
        "TO hail the day that annual rolls,"
        A SONG. Composed and Sung on the ANNIVERSARY of AMERICAN
            INDEPENDENCE.
        . . . . .
        . . . . .
        . . . . .

1307.   Jan. 19, 1782, #5, p. 4, col. 1.   (ViW)
        "As the papers inform us, a person of note"
        Epigram upon reading in the London paper that the King's
          bodycoachman had hanged himself.
        .....
        .....
        .....

1308.   Feb. 2, 1782, #7, p. 3, col. 2.   (ViW)
        "YOU know there goes a tale,"
        Copy of a Pasquinade stuck up in the city of New-York
        .....
        .....
        .....

1309.   Feb. 2, 1782, #7, p. 3, col. 2. (ViW)
        "FROM Arb--h-t, my friend, pray tell me the news,"
        Copy of a second Pasquinade
        .....
        .....
        .....

1310.   Feb. 2, 1782, #7, p. 3, cols. 2-3.   (ViW)
        "HAS the Marquis la Fayette,"
        Copy of a third pasquinade, stuck up in New-York when the
          rebels were carrying off Forage and burning houses in
          the fight of General Clinton.
        .....
        .....
        .....

1311.   Aug. 17, 1782, #35, p. 1, cols 1-2.   (DLC 1592)
        "OLD Judas the traitor (nor need we much wonder)"
        .....
        .....
        Freeman's Journal, Philadelphia, July 10, 1782.

1312.   March 4, 1773, #1127, p. 4, col. 1.   (DLC 1613)
        "YE well array'd! ye Lillies of our Land!"
        Doctor YOUNG to the MACARONIES.
        .....
        .....
        .....

1313.   March 18, 1773, #1129, p. 3, col. 1.   (DLC 1613)
        "But honest Ardour conscious as I am"
        .....
        .....
        .....
        .....

1314.   March 18, 1773, #1129, p. 3, col. 1.   (DLC 1613)
        "REMEMBER when again you stride"
        Verses in Praise of Winter.
        .....
        .....
        .....

1315.   April 29, 1773, #1135, p. 4, col. 1.   (DLC 1613)
        "SEE where the Farmer, with a Master's Eye,"
        The INDEPENDENT FARMER.
        .....
        .....
        .....

1316.   May 6, 1773, #1136, p. 4, col. 1.   (DLC 1613)
        "YOU I love, my dearest Life,"
        A ROUNDELAY, addressed from the Author to his Mistress.
        .....
        .....
        .....

1317.   May 13, 1773, #1137, p. 3, col. 1.   (DLC 1613)
        "WHATE'ER we great or small conceive,"
        A COMPLIMENT. TO THE AUTHOR OF THE BALLAD.
        T.O., CHELLOW, April 5, 1773.
        .....
        .....

Virginia, Williamsburg; Virginia Gazette (Hunter, Royle, Purdie
& Dixon, Dixon & Hunter), 1751-1778

1318.   May 20, 1773, #1138, p. 4, col. 1.   (DLC 1613)
        "NOW the leaden Year is gone,"
        FAREWELL to 1772.
        .. ...
        .. ...
        .. ...

1319.   June 10, 1773, #1141, p. 2, col. 1.   (DLC 1613)
        "WHEN you your birchen Rod resign'd,"
        To Mr. A.B. who has distinguished himself lately as a
            Writer against the Author of a Poem called WINTER.
        .. ...
        .. ...
        .. ...

1320.   Aug. 5, 1773, #1149, p. 4, col. 1.   (DLC 1613)
        "THREE ravenous Creatures,"
        On the STATE of POLAND.   The CANNIBALS. A SONG.
        .. ...
        .. ...
        .. ...

1321.   Sept. 2, 1773, #1153, p. 4, col. 1.   (DLC 1613)
        "DAUGHTER of Heaven, whose magick call,"
        To HARMONY.
        .. ...
        .. ...
        .. ...

1322.   Sept. 16, 1773, #1155, p. 4, col. 1.   (DLC 1613)
        "TO thee, fair Freedom! I retire,"
        Written at an INN on a Particular Occasion.
        .. ...
        [The Inn. Music by Mr. Bates.]
        .. ...

1323.   Sept. 23, 1773, #1156, Supplement, p. 2, col. 1.   (DLC 161)
        "GEORGE on his Throne,"
        PARODY of the first Song in MIDAS.
        .. ...
        [Think not lewd Jove]
        .. ...

Virginia, Williamsburg; Virginia Gazette (Hunter, Royle, Purdie
& Dixon, Dixon & Hunter), 1751-1778

1324.   Oct. 21, 1773, #1160, p. 4, col. 1.   (DLC 1613)
        "NOT all who are accounted great"
        On True NOBILITY and False.
        . . . . .
        . . . . .
        . . . . .

1325.   Jan. 6, 1774, #1161 (sic), p. 4, col. 1.   (DLC 1614)
        "THAT Seat of Science, Athens, and Earth's proud Mistress,
            Rome,"
        A Song on LIBERTY
        A Bostonian
        The British Grenadiers
        . . . . .

1326.   Jan. 20, 1774, #1136, p. 3, col. 1.   (DLC 1614)
        "AS near beauteous Boston lying,"
        A new SONG
        . . . . .
        Hosier's Ghost
        . . . . .

1327.   Jan. 20, 1774, #1163, p. 4, col. 1.   (DLC 1614)
        "DAUGHTER of Heaven, whose magick call,"
        HYMN to HARMONY.
        . . . . .
        . . . . .
        . . . . .

1328.   March 3, 1774, #1169, p. 2, col. 2.   (DLC 1614)
        "WHILST the Virginians boast a grateful Claim,"
        To the Countess of DUNMORE.
        . . . . .
        . . . . .
        . . . . .

1329.   March 3, 1774, #1169, p. 2, col. 2.   (DLC 1614)
        "WHILE Cannon roar to hail thee, Bonfires blaze,"
        On the Arrival of Lady DUNMORE.
        . . . . .
        . . . . .
        . . . . .

Virginia, Williamsburg; Virginia Gazette (Hunter, Royle, Purdie
& Dixon, Dixon & Hunter), 1751-1778

1330.   March 17, 1774, #1171, p. 2, col. 2.   (DLC 1614)
        "WHAT you can raise upon your Farms"
        Verses addressed by the Ladies of Bedford at their Meeting
           to resolve against TEA, to the Gentleman of that Place.
        .. . ..
        .. . ..
        [NEWPORT (Rhode Island) February 14.]

1331.   March 24, 1774, #1172, p. 4, col. 1.   (DLC 1614)
        "TO Years far distant, and to Scenes more bright,"
        A PROPHECY of the future Glory of AMERICA.
        .. . ..
        .. . ..
        .. . ..

1332.   May 5, 1774, #1178, p. 4, col. 1.   (DLC 1614)
        "THE King (God bless him!) is an honest Man;"
        SIMPLICITY.
        .. . ..
        .. . ..
        .. . ..

1333.   May 19, 1774, #1180, p. 4, col. 2.   (DLC 1614)
        "But should Corruption, with despotick Rage,"
        .. . ..
        .. . ..
        .. . ..
        .. . ..

1334.   May 26, 1774, #1181, p. 4, col. 1.   (DLC 1614)
        "FREEDOM's Charms alike engage"
        SONGS.
        .. . ..
        .. . ..
        .. . ..

1335.   May 26, 1774, #1181, p. 4, col. 1.   (DLC 1614)
        "FRIENDSHIP is the Joy of Reason,
        SONGS.
        .. . ..
        .. . ..
        .. . ..

Virginia, Williamsburg; Virginia Gazette (Hunter, Royle, Purdie
& Dixon, Dixon & Hunter), 1751-1778

1336.   June 2, 1774, #1182, p. 4, col. 1.   (DLC 1614)
        "PERMIT a giddy trifling Girl,"
        .....
        .....
        .....
        .....

1337.   June 16, 1774, #1184, p. 4, col. 1.   (DLC 1614)
        "SPECIOUS Instrument of Ill,"
        On recieving a handsome Set of TEA CHINA
        A Lady
        .....
        .....

1338.   June 23, 1774, #1185, p. 4, col. 1.   (DLC 1614)
        "PEACE, heavenly Goddess! born on balmy Wings,"
        PEACE.
        .....
        .....
        .....

1339.   July 7, 1774, #7118 (sic), p. 4, col. 1.   (DLC 1614)
        "GAY Bacchus, one Evening, inviting his Friends"
        GAY BACCHUS.
        .....
        [Gay Bacchus]
        .....

1340.   July 28, 1774, #1190, p. 3, col. 2.   (DLC 1614)
        "REMONSTRANCE, Petition, and Address,"
        To the Author of Considerations on the present State
           of Virginia.
        .....
        .....
        .....

1341.   Aug. 11, 1774, #1192, p. 4, col. 1.   (DLC 1614)
        "COME join Hand in Hand, brave Americans all,"
        The LIBERTY SONG.
        .....
        [Hearts of Oak]
        .....

Virginia, Williamsburg; Virginia Gazette (Hunter, Royle, Purdie & Dixon, Dixon & Hunter), 1751-1778

1342.   Aug. 18, 1774, #1202 (sic), p. 4, col. 1.   (DLC 1614)
        "THY Spirit, Independence, let me share!"
        Extract from INDEPENDENCE.   An ODE (Strophe)
        The late Dr. Smollet
        .. ...
        .. ...

1343.   Aug. 18, 1774, #1202 (sic), p. 4, col. 1.   (DLC 1614)
        "The Saxon Prince in Horrour fled,"
        Extract from INDEPENDENCE. An ODE. (Antistrophe)
        The late Dr. Smollet
        .. ...
        .. ...

1344.   Aug. 25, 1774, #1203, p. 2, col. 2.   (DLC 1614)
        "HUMBLY to imitate our Lord the King"
        A PARODY on a late PROCLAMATION.
        .. ...
        .. ...
        .. ...

1345.   Sept. 1, 1774, #1204, p. 4, col. 1.   (DLC 1614)
        "BEHOLD! what martial Bands are those,"
        ODE for his MAJESTY's BIRTHDAY, June 4, 1774.
        .. ...
        .. ...
        .. ...

1346.   Sept. 8, 1774, #1205, p. 4, col. 1.   (DLC 1614)
        "SONS of social Mirth and Glee,"
        SOCIAL CONVERSE.
        .. ...
        .. ...
        .. ...

1347.   Sept. 15, 1774, #1206, p. 4, col. 1.   (DLC 1614)
        "AN Esquire born, a Templar bred;"
        The FREETHINKER's FAITH.
        .. ...
        .. ...
        .. ...

Virginia, Williamsburg; Virginia Gazette (Hunter, Royle, Purdie
& Dixon, Dixon & Hunter), 1751-1778

1348. Sept. 29, 1774, #1208, p. 4, col. 1. (DLC 1614)
       "TO all the pretty Girls and Boys,"
       A PROCLAMATION.
       .....
       .....
       .....

1349. Nov. 3, 1774, #1213, p. 4, col. 1. (DLC 1614)
       "YOU who can read no Doubt remember,"
       Hark! hark! you young Dogs, there's a Noise in the Nation
       .....
       .....
       .....

1350. Nov. 17, 1774, #1215, p.4, col. 1. (DLC 1614)
       "WHEN mighty Roast Beef was the Englishman's Food,"
       The Roast Beef of OLD ENGLAND.
       .....
       [The Roast Beef of Old England]
       .....

1351. Dec. 8, 1774, #1218, p. 4, col. 1. (DLC 1614)
       "BE gone! ye Vulgar and Profane,"
       HAPPINESS.
       .....
       .....

1352. Feb. 11, 1775, #1227, p. 4, col. 1. (DLC 1616)
       "TO the sage Smyrna, every day,"
       the POLITICIANS.
       .....
       .....
       .....

1353. March 4, 1775, #1230, p. 1, col. 2. (DLC 1616)
       "LOST is our old simplicity of times,"
       On the Proceedings against AMERICA.
       .....
       .....
       A late London Magazine

Virginia, Williamsburg; Virginia Gazette (Hunter, Royle, Purdie & Dixon, Dixon & Hunter), 1751-1778

1354. March 4, 1775, #1230, p. 4, col. 1. (DLC 1616)
      "TO years far distant, and to scenes more bright,"
      A PROPHECY of the Future Glory of AMERICA.
      .. ...
      .. ...
      .. ...

1355. March 18, 1775, #1232, p. 4, col. 1. (DLC 1616)
      "TO thee, fair FREEDOM, I retire,"
      Written at an INN, on a particular occasion
      .. ...
      [The Inn. Music by Mr. Bates.]
      .. ...

1356. April 22, 1775, #1237, p. 4, col. 1. (DLC 1616)
      "HAPPY's the man, who, unconstrain'd,"
      AN ODE on LIBERTY.
      .. ...
      .. ...
      .. ...

1357. May 20, 1775, #1241, p. 1, cols. 1-3 (DLC 1616)
      "BOLD is the hope, by virtuous deeds"
      ELEGY. That ignorance and envy restrain, and that letters
        and candour excite the efforts of virtue.
      D.C.
      .. ...
      .. ...

1358. May 27, 1775, #1242, p. 4, col. 1. (DLC 1616)
      "WELCOME! once more,"
      To the Friend of his Country, and of Mankind, Doctor
        Benjamin Franklin, On his arrival from England, May
        6th, 1775.
      ...., May 8, 1775, Philadelphia
      .. ...
      .. ...

Virginia, Williamsburg; Virginia Gazette (Hunter, Royle, Purdie
& Dixon, Dixon & Hunter), 1751-1778

1359. May 27, 1775, #1242, p. 4, col. 1. (DLC 1616)
       "LET Britons, now sunk into tyrants and slaves!"
       .....
       .....
       .....
       .....

1360. June 3, 1775, #1243, p. 4, col. 1. (DLC 1616)
       "AN unbelieving Jew one day"
       The Monk and Jew.
       .....
       .....
       .....

1361. July 1, 1775, #1247, p. 4, col. 1. (DLC 1616)
       "WHILST happy in my native land,"
       A SONG. From a new musical interlude called the ELECTION.
       .....
       [WHILST happy in my native land]
       .....

1362. July 15, 1775, #1249, p. 4, col. 1. (DLC 1616)
       "WHAT a Court hath Old England of folly and sin,"
       FISH and TEA. A New Song.--
       .....
       To an Old Tune [Derry Down?]
       .....

1363. July 29, 1775, #1251, p. 4, col. 1. (DLC 1616)
       "COME rouse up my lads, and join in this great cause,"
       A New SONG on the present critical times.
       J.W. Hewlings, Nansemond, July 8, 1775
       Hearts of Oak
       .....

1364. Aug. 19, 1775, #1254, p. 4, col. 1. (DLC 1616)
       "WHILE civil wars distract this happy land,"
       The PRESENT TIMES: Addressed to a young LADY.
       .....
       .....
       .....

Virginia, Williamsburg; Virginia Gazette (Hunter, Royle, Purdie
& Dixon, Dixon & Hunter), 1751-1778

1365. Sept. 23, 1775, #1259, p. 4, col. 1. (DLC 1616)
      "PROPITIOUS us'd to rise the morn"
      .....
      ....., June 4, 1775
      .....
      .....

1366. Sept. 30, 1775, #1260, p. 4, col. 1. (DLC 1616)
      "OH despicable state of all that groan"
      On LIBERTY.
      .....
      .....
      .....

1367. Oct. 28, 1775, #1264, p. 4, col. 1. (DLC 1616)
      "BRAVE race of men! that lately shew'd,"
      On Taking the Fort and Stores of Ticonderoga, by the
         Provincials.
      .....
      .....
      Morning Chronicle, July 14

1368. Nov. 11, 1775, #1266, p. 4, col. 1. (DLC 1616)
      "WE came, we saw, but could not beat,"
      The modern Veni, Vidi, Vici.
      .....
      .....
      A London paper

1369. Dec. 2, 1775, #1269, p. 4, col. 1. (DLC 1616)
      "JUSTICE, that heretofore was of such fame,"
      .....
      A Monitor
      .....
      .....

1370. Dec. 16, 1775, #1271, p. 4, col. 1. (DLC 1616)
      "WHOM should we fear, since God to us"
      .....
      .....
      .....
      .....

Virginia, Williamsburg; Virginia Gazette (Hunter, Royle, Purdie & Dixon, Dixon & Hunter), 1751-1778

1371. Dec. 23, 1775, #1272, p. 4, col. 1.   (DLC 1616)
      "FOREVER hail! auspicious morn,"
      On CHRISTMAS DAY.
      .....
      .....
      .....

1372. Jan. 13, 1776, #1275, p. 4, col. 1.   (DLC 1619)
      "PARENT of all, Omnipotent"
      The PATRIOT's PRAYER.
      .....
      .....
      .....

1373. Jan. 13, 1776, #1275, p. 4, col. 1.   (DLC 1619)
      "FREEDOM's charms alike engage"
      On FREEDOM.
      .....
      .....
      .....

1374. Jan. 13, 1776, #1275, p. 4, col. 1.   (DLC 1619)
      "FRIENDSHIP is the joy of reason,"
      On FRENDSHIP.
      .....
      .....
      .....

1375. Jan. 20, 1776, #1276, p. 4, col. 1.   (DLC 1619)
      "PRAY say what's that, which smirking trips this way?"
      The MODERN COURTIER.
      .....
      .....
      .....

1376. Feb. 24, 1776, #1281, p. 3, col. 1.   (DLC 1619)
      "VAIN BRITON's, boast no longer with proud indignity,"
      A New SONG.
      .....
      The British Grenadiers
      .....

Virginia, Williamsburg; Virginia Gazette (Hunter, Royle, Purdie
& Dixon, Dixon & Hunter), 1751-1778

1377.   May 25, 1776, #1294, p. 3, col. 3.   (DLC 1619)
        "AMERICANS! awake, awake!"
        .....
        A Virginian
        .....
        .....

1378.   June 15, 1776, #1297, p. 8, col. 1.   (DLC 1619)
        "WHEN good Queen BESSY rul'd the land"
        CHARACTERISTICS from Queen ELIZABETH's time to the present
          aera.
        Americanus, Buckingham, June 1, 1776.
        .....
        .....

1379.   July 13, 1776, #1301, p. 1, col. 2.   (DLC 1619)
        "AT length, with generous indignation fir'd,"
        .....
        Pennsylvaniensis
        .....
        .....

1380.   Aug. 24, 1776, #1307, p. 8, col. 1.   (DLC 1619)
        "FREE STATES, attend the song,"
        An ODE, In imitation of one written in the year 1759,
          by Alexander Martin, Esq; of North Carolina.
        W.P., Buckingham, August 1776.
        [God save the King]
        .....

1381.   Oct. 18, 1776, #1315, p. 2, col. 1.   (DLC 1619)
        "NOW LIBERTY is all the plan,"
        To the Honourable HOUSE of DELEGATES for the commonwealth
          of VIRGINIA, now sitting at Williamsburg
        A country poet
        .....
        .....

Virginia, Williamsburg; Virginia Gazette (Hunter, Royle, Purdie & Dixon, Dixon & Hunter), 1751-1778

1382.   Nov. 22, 1776, #1320, p. 3, col. 2.   (DLC 1619)
        "WHEN Britain first, without a cause,"
        An AMERICAN SONG
        .....
        The Watery God
        .....

1383.   March 14, 1777, #1335(sic), p. 3, col. 1.   (DLC 1621)
        "MY Lords, with your leave,"
        A NEW WAR SONG
        Sir Peter Parker
        Well met, Brother Tar
        Written, and printed in London

1384.   March 28, 1777, #1337, p. 7, col. 1.   (DLC 1621)
        "COLD winter's past, the icicles no more"
        .....
        ....., Port Royal, March 16, 1773.
        .....
        .....

1385. Jan. 21, 1773, #350, p. 2, cols. 1-2. (DLC 1625)
       "HERE, gen'rous Briton, drop the manly tear,"
       EPITAPHS on General WOLFE.
       .. .. ..
       .. .. ..
       .. .. ..

1386. March 25, 1773, #359, p. 1, col. 1. (DLC 1625)
       "BEHOLD the social Band appears,"
       ODE for the festival of St. John Evangelist, in South
         Carolina, 5772 (sic). (Recitative)
       Sir Egerton Leigh, Baronet, Grand Master and set to music
         by brother Peter Valton.
       .. .. ..
       .. .. ..

1387. March 25, 1773, #359, p. 1, col. 1. (DLC 1625)
       "Boast not, mortals, human skill,"
       Ode for the festival of St. John Evangelist... (song)
       Sir Egerton Leigh and brother Peter Valton
       .. .. ..
       .. .. ..

1388. March 25, 1773, #359, p. 1, col. 1. (DLC 1625)
       "'Tis from the watchful culture of the mind,"
       Ode for the festival of St. John Evangelist...(Recitative)
       Sir Egerton Leigh and brother Peter Valton
       .. .. ..
       .. .. ..

1389. March 25, 1773, #359, p. 1, col. 1. (DLC 1625)
       "Let the di'mond's lustre blaze,"
       Ode for the festival of St. John Evangelist...(Air)
       Sir Egerton Leigh and brother Peter Valton
       .. .. ..
       .. .. ..

1390. March 25, 1773, #359, p. 1, col. 1. (DLC 1625)
       "Ye blessed MINISTERS above,"
       Ode for the festival of St. John Evangelist...(Recitative)
       Sir Egerton Leigh and brother Peter Valton
       .. .. ..
       .. .. ..

Virginia, Williamsburg; Virginia Gazette, (Rind, Pinckney),
1766-1776

1391.   March 25, 1773, #359, p. 1, col. 1.   (DLC 1625)
        "Blessings await this western land,"
        Ode for the festival of St. John Evangelist...(Air)
        Sir Egerton Leigh and Peter Valton
        .....
        .....

1392.   March 25, 1773, #359, p. 1, col. 1.   (DLC 1625)
        "Our Social Band, by love and honour join'd,"
        Ode for the festival of St. John Evangelist...(Recitative)
        Sir Egerton Leigh and brother Peter Valton
        .....
        .....

1393.   March 25, 1773, #359, p. 1, col. 1.   (DLC 1625)
        "Let the day be ever prais'd"
        Ode for the festival of St. John Evangelist...(Duetto)
        Sir Egerton Leigh and brother Peter Valton
        .....
        .....

1394.   March 25, 1773, #359, p. 1, col. 1.   (DLC 1625)
        "Give the heroes all their due,"
        Ode for the festival of St. John Evangelist...(Chorus)
        Sir Egerton Leigh and brother Peter Valton
        .....
        .....

1395.   Sept. 2, 1773, #382, p. 2, col. 3.   (DLC 1625)
        "A NOISE was heard thro' all the land,"
        The CONSULTATION, a new Ballad
        D.C.
        Over the water, &c, Jenny Dang the weaver, and others of
          equal dignity with the metre.
        .....

Virginia, Williamsburg; Virginia Gazette (Rind, Pinckney),
1766-1776

1396.   Sept. 16, 1773, #384, p. 1, cols. 2-3.   (DLC 1625)
        "SOMETIMES the man who bears the breech,"
        VERSES relative to a certain notorious counterfeiter of
           Wit and Humour, with an humble remonstrance to the Right
           Honourable the E--- of D---.
        D.C.
        .....
        .....

1397.   Oct. 7, 1773, #387, p. 2, col. 3.   (DLC 1625)
        "WHEN I take an attentive survey of mankind,"
        The LAUGHING PHILOSOPHER.
        .....
        .....
        .....

1398.   Oct. 7, 1773, #387, p. 2, col. 3.   (DLC 1625)
        "HONOUR gone, and virtue fled,"
        .....
        O.Z.
        .....
        .....

1399.   Nov. 25, 1773, #394, p. 3, col. 1.   (DLC 1625)
        "IN the dry desart of a leathern pocket"
        SOLILOQUY on the LAST SHILLING.
        .....
        .....
        .....

1400.   Jan. 13, 1774, #401, p. 2, col. 2.   (DLC 1625)
        "When you censure the age"
        ANECDOTE of Sir ROBERT WALPOLE at Beggar's Opera
           performance
        .....
        ["When you censure the age"]
        .....

Virginia, Williamsburg; Virginia Gazette (Rind, Pinckney),
1766-1776

1401.   Jan. 20, 1774, #402, p. 1, col. 3.   (DLC Microfilm 1518,
           Reel #4)
         "PRETTY little charming thing,"
         A Gentleman's Address to his VIOLIN.
         .....
         .....
         .....

1402.   Feb. 10, 1774, #405, p. 2, col. 2.   (DLC Microfilm 1518,
           Reel #4)
         "DESCEND, my muse, on airy wings sublime,"
         On MUSIC.
         A youth.
         .....
         .....

1403.   March 3, 1774, #408, p. 3, col. 2.   (DLC Microfilm 1518,
           Reel #4)
         "HAIL, noble Charlotte! Welcome to the plain,"
         .....
         A Lady
         .....
         .....

1404.   May 19, 1774, #419, p. 4, col. 2.   (DLC 1625)
         "But should corruption, with despotic rage,"
         [On the Anniversary of Saint TAMMINY]
         A Customer
         .....
         .....

1405.   [June 16, 1774, #423,] p. 1, col. 3.   (DLC Microfilm 1518,
           Reel 4)
         "SPECIOUS instrument of ill,"
         On receiving a handsome set of TEA CHINA
         A Lady
         .....
         .....

Virginia, Williamsburg; Virginia Gazette (Rind, Pinckney),
1766-1776

1406.   Aug. 11, 1774, #431, p. 1, col. 2.   (DLC Microfilm 1518,
           Reel #5)
        "TO manhood he makes vain pretence"
        .....
        A Customer
        .....
        .....

1407.   Aug. 11, 1774, #431 (mutilated), p. 3, col. 2.   (DLC
           Microfilm 1518, Reel #5)
        "...............glasses"
        [Mutilated but about FANUEL HALL, Virginians standing with
           the Bostonians against Britain]
        .....
        .....
        .....

1408.   Aug. 25, 1774, #433, p. 1, col. 3.   (DLC 1625)
        "His royal majesty,"
        To general Gage
        .....
        .....
        The Pennsylvania Packet

1409.   Aug. 25, 1774, #433, p. 3, col. 2.   (DLC 1625)
        "THE man, whate'er be his pretence,"
        .....
        A SINCERE FRIEND
        .....
        .....

1410.   Aug. 25, 1774, #433, p. 3, col. 2.   (DLC 1625)
        "OUR Order, antient as the world's first date,"
        On FREE MASONRY.
        .....
        .....
        .....

Virginia, Williamsburg; Virginia Gazette (Rind, Pinckney) 1766-
1776

1411.   Sept. 1, 1774, #434, p. 3, col. 1.   (DLC 1625)
         "WITH graceful air and virtuous mien,"
         .....
         Tom Gingle
         .....
         The Pennsylvania Packet

1412.   Sept. 15, 1774, #436, p. 1, col. 2.   (DLC 1625)
         "O MY baby, my baby,"
         A new SONG, supposed to have been sung by Goody North,
            by way of lullaby to the foundling brat, the Popish
            Quebec Bill.
         .....
         O my Kitten, my Kitten, &c.
         The St. James Chronicle

1413.   Sept. 15, 1774, #436, p. 2, col. 3.   (DLC 1625)
         "IN spite of rice, in spite of wheat,"
         On the poor of Boston being employed in paving the streets.
         .....
         .....
         .....

1414.   Oct. 6, 1774, #439, p. 2, col. 2.   (DLC 1625)
         "COME, come, my brave boys, from my song you shall hear,"
         The Glorious SEVENTY FOUR (A New Song)
         .....
         Hearts of Oak
         .....

1415.   Dec. 1, 1774, #447, p. 3, col. 1.   (DLC 1625)
         "WHEN Britons first by Heaven's command,"
         An AMERICAN PARODY on the old song of "RULE BRITANNIA"
         .....
         Rule Britannia
         .....

Virginia, Williamsburg; Virginia Gazette (Rind, Pinckney),
1766-1776

1416. Dec. 15, 1774, #449, p. 1, col. 2. (DLC 1625)
       "WHAT cou'd possess you, effeminate Ben,"
       In answer to the Enemy to NONSENSE
       .....
       .....
       .....

1417. Dec. 29, 1774, #451, p. 3, col. 2. (DLC 1625)
       "OH! have pity on thy brother,"
       On the ANSWER to the Enemy to Nonsense
       Y.F.
       .....
       .....

1418. Dec. 29, 1774, #451, p. 3, col. 2. (DLC 1625)
       "YOUR charge to confute,"
       To the Rhyming L-NE
       A Correspondent
       .....
       .....

1419. Jan. 5, 1775, #452, p. 3, col. 2. (DLC 1627)
       "I THINK, Pro Bono Publico,"
       .....
       A Legislator
       .....
       .....

1420. Jan. 12, 1775, #453, p. 1, col. 2. (DLC 1627)
       "LORD SHIPLEY is a man of sense"
       A Song
       An Intended Customer
       Last Sunday morning we sail'd from Cork"
       .....

1421. Jan. 19, 1775, #454, p. 2, col. 3. (DLC 1627)
       "THE expences of war, and corruptions of peace,"
       Song
       .....
       Derry Down
       A Late London Paper

Virginia, Williamsburg; Virginia Gazette (Rind, Pinckney),
1766-1776

1422. Jan. 26, 1775, #455, p. 2, col. 2   (DLC 1627)
      "IF blood of ancestors of fame"
      EPITAPH of an HOTENTOT, translated by a gentleman from
         the Cape of Good Hope.
      . . . . .
      . . . . .
      . . . . .

1423. Feb. 23, 1775, #450, p. 2, cols. 2-3.   (DLC 1627)
      "WHAT canker'd pen of brass, what characters"
      On CALUMNY
      The Late Reverend Mr. Josiah Johnson
      . . . . .
      . . . . .

1424. Feb. 23, 1775, #459, p. 2, col. 3.   (DLC 1627)
      "PRAISE, praise, the mighty he,"
      A New Song
      . . . . .
      Prussian Hero
      . . . . .

1425. Feb. 23, 1775, #459, p. 3, col. 2.   (DLC 1627)
      "WHAT unrelenting hand from me has torn"
      The ELEGY of a Blackbird, on seeing a row of trees cut
         down.
      . . . . .
      . . . . .
      . . . . .

1426. March 2, 1775, #460, p. 2, cols. 1-2.   (DLC 1627)
      "COME, muses nine, come string my lyre,"
      To the COMPOSERS of the pieces signed A FRIEND to TRUTH,
         An ENEMY to NONSENSE, &c.
      G. Lyne
      . . . . .
      . . . . .

Virginia, Williamsburg; Virginia Gazette (Rind, Pinckney),
1766-1776

1427.   March 9, 1775, #461, p. 1, col. 2. (DLC 1627)
        "WHEN Querist writes, 'tis strange to tell,"
        .....
        .....
        .....
        .....

1428.   March 9, 1775, #461, p. 1, col. 2. (DLC 1627)
        "PEACE to thy royal shade, illustrious king,"
        ELEGY to the Memory of the late KING
        A Constant Reader
        .....
        .....

1429.   March 23, 1775, #463, p. 1, col. 2. (DLC 1627)
        "IF you wou'd aspire"
        Advice to Poets Guilty of Plagiarism
        A Correspondent
        .....
        .....

1430.   April 13, 1775, #466, p. 4, col. 2. (DLC 1627)
        "ONE bottom leaves the crew to dip,"
        The Provident Family, An Epigram.
        Constant   Readers. (The Double Associators)
        .....
        .....

1431.   April 20, 1775, #467, p. 1, col. 1. (DLC 1627)
        "'TIS true, two bottoms seamen chuse,"
        A reply to the PROVIDENT FAMILY, an EPIGRAM.
        H.S.
        .....
        .....

1432.   May 11, 1775, #470, p. 2, col. 3. (DLC 1627)
        "WE'VE said one bottom wou'd suffice"
        For Lo! He made Answer to Himself.
        D.A.
        .....
        .....

Virginia, Williamsburg; Virginia Gazette (Rind, Pinckney),
1766-1776

1433.   May 18, 1775, #471, p. 4, col. 1.   (DLC 1627)
        "TO years far distant, and to scenes more bright,"
        A PROPHECY of the future GLORY of AMERICA.
        .....
        .....
        .....

1434.   June 15, 1775, #475, p. 3, col. 1.   (DLC 1627)
        "HARK! 'tis Freedom that calls, come patriots awake!"
        A SONG
        .....
        The Ecchoing Horn
        .....

1435.   June 22, 1775, #476, p. 4, col. 1.   (DLC 1627)
        "COME join hand in hand, all ye true, loyal souls,"
        A SONG, composed at a town meeting in Chester, Burlington
           county, July, 1774.
        .....
        [Hearts of Oak]
        .....

1436.   June 29, 1775, #477, p. 4, col. 1.   (DLC 1627)
        "COME listen, my cocks, to a brother and friend,"
        The SAILOR's ADDRESS.
        .....
        [Hearts of Oak]
        A London Paper

1437.   July 6, 1775, #478, p. 4, col. 1.   (DLC 1627)
        "COME chear up, my lads, to our country be firm;"
        LIBERTY. A new SONG
        .....
        Hearts of Oak
        .....

1438.   July 27, 1775, #481, p. 4, col. 1.   (DLC 1627)
        "YE sons of true freedom and spirit"
        An extempore SONG
        A jovial company
        A light heart and a thin pair of breeches go through the
           world, brave boys
        .....

Virginia, Williamsburg; Virginia Gazette, (Rind, Pinckney),
1766-1776

1439.   Aug. 3, 1775, #482, p. 4, col. 1.   (DLC 1627)
        "THE coward, when his country claims his aid,"
        .....
        .....
        .....
        .....

1440.   Aug. 17, 1775, #484, p. 4, col. 1.   (DLC 1627)
        "'TIS money makes the member vote,"
        A JUNTO SONG
        .....
        A Begging we will go, we'll go, &c.
        .....

1441.   Sept. 14, 1775, #488, p. 3, col. 2.   (DLC 1627)
        "FAIR LIBERTY now each American charms,"
        A New SONG
        .....
        .....
        .....

1442.   Sept. 14, 1775, #488, p. 4, col. 1.   (DLC 1627)
        "YE powers who rule o'er states and kings,"
        ODE for his MAJESTY's BIRTH DAY, 1775.
        .....
        [ODE for his Majesty's Birth-Day, 1775]
        .....

1443.   Oct. 5, 1775, #491, p. 4, col. 1.   (DLC 1627)
        "WHO'D know the sweets of Liberty?"
        The GENIUS of AMERICA to her SONS.
        .....
        [Sweets of Liberty]
        .....

1444.   Oct. 5, 1775, #491, p. 4, col. 1.   (DLC 1627)
        "WHILST here I live,"
        The AUTHOR's PRAYER to the DEITY.
        .....
        .....
        .....

Virginia, Williamsburg; Virginia Gazette, (Rind, Pinckney),
1766-1776

1445.   Nov. 16, 1775, #497, p. 4, col. 1.   (DLC 1627)
        "WAR makes the vulgar multitude to drink"
        DIALOGUE betwixt PEACE and WAR.
        .....
        .....
        .....

1446.   Nov. 30, 1775, #499, p. 4, col. 1.   (DLC 1627)
        "O THOU whom next to Heav'n we most revere,"
        LIBERTY.
        .....
        .....
        .....

1447.   Dec. 13, 1775, #501, p. 2, col. 1.   (DLC 1627)
        "Indeed, master Gage,"
        Lines said to have been sent to General Gage some time
           before the action at Concord.
        .....
        .....
        .....

1448.   Feb. 17, 1775, #3, p. 2, col. 1.   (DLC 1629)
        "May each unkind report,"
        Stanza added to song God save the King
        .....
        .....
        God save the King
        London, Dec. 2.

1449.   May 12, 1775, #15, p. 1, col. 3.   (DLC 1629)
        "MAY all the evils of Pandora's box,"
        A CURSE.
        .....
        .....
        .....

1450.   Dec. 8, 1775, #45, p. 1, col. 2.   (DLC 1629)
        "FINDING Virginia stubborn still,"
        A PROCLAMATION. DESOLATION.
        .....
        .....
        .....

1451.   May 23, 1777, #121, p. 1, col. 1.   (DLC 1633)
        "YE wrong heads, and strong heads, attend to my strains;"
        The HEADS: Or, the Year 1776
        .....
        [Derry Down]
        [From the Publick Ledger]

1452.   Aug. 28, 1779, #228, p. 4, col. 1.   (DLC Box 32, folder
           6)
        "TO thee, brave WASHINGTON, these humble lays,"
        .....
        W.M., Amelia, Aug. 21, 1779.
        .....
        .....

1453.   March 4, 1780, #56, p. 2, cols. 2+3.   (DLC 1634)
        "STERN winter scowl'd along the plain,"
        .....
        .....
        .....
        .....

1454.   Dec. 2, 1780, #91, p. 2, col. 3.   (DLC 1634)
        "AT freedom's call see Arnold take the field,"
        On General Arnold.
        .....
        .....
        .....

1455.   Dec. 2, 1780, #91, p. 2, col. 3.   (DLC 1634)
        "THOU who in glory's shining track,"
        To General WASHINGTON, on the late conspiracy.
        .....
        .....
        .....

First Line Index
Numbers are main entry not page numbers.
Entry numbers are in chronological not numerical order.

698	"A Stands for Americans--who scorn to be slaves;"
652	"Accept, great chief, that share of honest praise"
157	"Adieu, adieu, to SANS SOUCIE,"
1	"Adieu New England's smiling Meads,"
1057; 209	"Adieu ye tow'ring spires, no more"
831	"ADORN'D by sun-beams from the skies,"
712; 1170	"Again imperial Winter's Sway"
1173; 1094	"Again, my social Friends, we meet"
528	"Again returns the circling year!"
1199	"Again the auspicious day returns,"
121	"Ah me! what means my rising Soul!"
700; 176	"Ah! yet shall we with horror hear," or "Ah! yet shall we wish horror hear,"
1056	"Aid me, ye Nine, my muse assist,"
236	"ALACK-a-day my muse has stray'd,"
1201	"ALAS! brother Tories, now what shall we do,"
993	"ALAS, poor Joe's great soul's on float;"
29	"Alas! (said Cynthia, as she pour'd the Tea)"
889	"All hail! Britannia hail!"
367; 1232; 184	"All hail G[e]rm[ai]ne, G[e]rm[ai]ne all hail!"
643; 241; 1145	"All hail superior Sex, exalted fair"
790	"Ame du Héros, it du Sâge"
780	"America lift up thy head,"
592	"America no longer bears the cause"

First Line Index

Entry No.

929   "AS Jove the Olympian who, both I and you know"

920; 1030; "AS late I travell'd o'er the plain,"
54; 353;
610; 1011

305; 580;   "AS Mars, great God of battles! lay,"
599

193   "AS mushrooms in a night are grown,"

1107; 1326; "AS near beauteous Boston lying" or, "AS near
309; 454;   bounteous BOSTON lying"
493; 421;
722; 616;
462; 81;
10

348   "AS near Boston's Township lying"

239   "AS round the globe I took my way,"

1079   "AS soldiers now, we do surmise,"

904   "AS Spain's proud Monarch sat in state,"

552; 1307   "AS the papers inform us, a person of note"

846   "As tyrant power and slavish fear"

222   "TH' Assembly call'd the first of May,"

1454   "AT freedom's call see Arnold take the field,"

119; 753;   "AT length the Action is commenc'd,"
174

776   "At length the troubled waters rest,"

569; 1255; "AT length War's sanguine scenes are o'er:"
416; 365;
269; 1160;
777

1046; 782; "AT length --- with generous indignation fir'd,"
491; 1196;
1379; 591

220   "AT this unwonted Hour, behold,"

First Line Index

First Line Index

Entry No.

First Line Index

Entry No.

368; 601	"BLUSH! Britains blush! at thine inglorious war,"
975; 1387	"Boast not, Mortals, human Skill,"
1357	"BOLD is the hope, by virtuous deeds"
1281; 979	"BORN for millions are the Kings"
1367	"BRAVE race of men! that lately shew'd,"
98	"BRAVE race of men, who boldly shew's,"
467	"BRAVE sons of peace, who live at ease,"
811	"BREATHING Sedition a rash fiery Band,"
364	"BRIGHT flakes of snow compose the storm,"
1015; 315; 536	"BRITANNIA was sick, for a doctor they sent," or: "BRITANNA (sic) was sick, for a doctor they sent,"
471; 106; 447; 34	"BRITONS, if you pant for glory,"
1224; 117	"Brother Soldiers, all fight on,"
1313	"But honest Ardour conscious as I am"
1333; 1404; 727	"But should Corruption, with despotic(k) Rage,"
1297	"But since independence we lately have got"
162; 103	"BY art and surprize, my Lord swears he'll succeed,"
60; 585	"BY Collier George, Sir Commodore,"
376	"BY John Burgoyne, of noble line,"
750; 115; 1192; 620; 477	"BY my faith but I think ye're all makers of bulls,"
713	"By sacred Influence hurl'd,"
1270; 1236	"BY the Red Sea the Hebrew host detain'd,"
824	"By various means the tuneful choir"

First Line Index

First Line Index

Entry No.

1285	"CANST thou, Spectator, view this wicked Scene,"
243; 634	"CEASE that strepent trumpet's sound!--"
1277	"CHEERLY my hearts, of courage true,"
688	"THE circling sun, bright monarch of the day,"
898	"THE cloud is burst, behold a clearer sky!"
943	"COLD blew the blast with hollow shrieks,"
1384	"COLD winter's past, the icicles no more"
380; 547; 692	"COLUMBIA! Columbia! to glory arise,"
406	"COME all Continentals, who WASHINGTON love,"
1003	"COME all ye good people attend,"
593; 180	"COME all you brave soldiers, both valiant & free."
683; 387; 534; 1274; 1207	"COME and listen my lads to sweet Liberty's lay,"
1437	"COME chear up, my lads, to our country be firm;"
865	"COME cheer up, my Lads, let us haste to the Main,"
731; 431; 1414	"COME, come, my brave boys, from my song you shall hear,"
468	"COME, come, my friends, let's drink about,"
931	"COME gentlemen Tories, firm, loyal and true,"
480	"COME hither, brother Tradesmen,"
1069; 1225; 1435	"COME join hand in hand all ye true, loyal souls,"
1341; 253	"COME join hand in hand, brave Americans all,"
230	"COME join, my brave lads, come all from afar,"
25	"COME let us join the glorious Train,"
863	"COME let us rejoice,"

322

First Line Index

Entry No.

875	"Come let us run at once they cry,"
983; 749; 36; 173; 513; 1436; 1226; 1190	"COME listen, my cocks, to a brother and friend,"
1266	"COME, meek-ey'd Maid, long banish'd hence,"
1426	"COME, muses nine, come string my lyre,"
909	"COME, my boys, in jovial strain,"
129	"COME, my boys, let us sing"
917	"COME on my hearts of temper'd steel,"
342	"COME rouse, brother Tories, the loyalists cry,"
1363	"COME rouse up my lads, and join in this great cause,"
1193	"COME, Sisters come, your injur'd Country calls,"
50; 372; 525; 606	"COME soldiers all in chorus join,"
788	"COME! to Columbia's God your voices raise,"
518; 303; 484; 785; 1016	"COME, ye valiant sons of thunder,"
311	"Come you my Subjects let me know,"
1106; 265	"COME, youthful Muse, my breast inspire"
1050; 295	"The common soldier who has broke"
1168	"CONFINEMENT, hail! in Honour's justest cause,"
1150; 407; 62; 555	"CORNWALLIS led a country dance,"
804	"COULD I the Abundance of my Sorrow show,"
1071; 1439	"THE Coward, when his country claims his aid,"
950; 338	"CRIMSON slaughter! pallid care!"

First Line Index

Entry no.

First Line Index

First Line Index

Entry No.

419; 82	"E'ER since the day that Adam fell,"
321; 396; 203	"ENGLAND, I feel for what I'm sure you must,"
1347	"AN Esquire born, a Templar bred;"
1100	"Exalted on her ebon throne,"
456; 1186; 159; 1421	"THE expences of war, and corruptions of peace,"

First Line Index

Entry No.

28; 499	"FAIR Ladies, 'tis not very arch,"
711	"FAIR Liberty came o'er,"
719	"FAIR Liberty! celestial Goddess, hail!"
765	"FAIR Liberty, celestial maid,"
1441	"FAIR LIBERTY now each American charms,"
1291	"FAIR Peace, how lovely, how delightful thou,"
375; 656	"FAME, let thy Trumpet sound,"
1304; 948; 665; 413	"FAREWELL my Lord, may Zephyr's waft you o'er,"
423; 11	"FArewel the tea board with its gaudy equipage,"
463; 94	"FAREWELL the Tea-board with your gaudy attire,"
355	"THE Fates have past a firm Decree,"
	[FELIX] "good morn. 'Tis now five irksome years" See: "good morn. 'Tis now five irksome years"
409	"FEW are content with what they've got,"
1101	"THE fields, disconsolate and sad,"
1450	"FINDING Virginia stubborn still,"
843	"FOR Battle prepar'd in their country's just cause,"
319	"FOR George the Third I turn'd my coat,"
1001	"For neither pedant nor for prude,"
1371	"FOREVER hail! auspicious morn,"
912	"FREE States attend my Song,"
1380	"FREE STATES, attend the song,"
147	"FREEDOM, Freedom, aloudly cries,"
834	"Freedom, Peace, Plenty, all in advance,"
726; 1334; 87; 13; 1373; 280	"FREEDOM's Charms alike engage"

First Line Index

Entry No.

587; 490; 773	"FREEMEN, if you pant for glory" or: "FREEMEN, if you paint for glory,"
864	"THE Frenchmen came upon the coast,"
953	"FR[E]N[EA]U, great man! 'tis thee I sing,"
1335; 1374	"FRIENDSHIP is the Joy of Reason,"
653	"From a poet that's proud of his wit and his pen,"
1309	"FROM Arb--h-t, my friend, pray tell me the news,"
936; 664; 336	"FROM Britain's fam'd island once more I come over,"
1032	"FROM fair America's insulted Coast,"
900	"FROM Heav'n behold a charming ray"
966; 341; 509; 570	"FROM Heaven descends sweet smiling Peace,"
838	"From Lewis, Monsieur Gerard came"
756	"FROM native skies, when Angels fell"
648	"FROM noise of camps once more I come"
1065; 588; 126; 783	"FROM North, tho' stormy winds may blow"
1066; 168	"FROM orchards of ample extent,"
635	"FROM Parliaments venal, who barter our laws,"
1052	"From sea to sea we scan the endless main,"
660	"From the Americ shore,"

328

First Line Index

Entry No.

1273; 1028	"GAGE nothing did, and went to pot,"
916; 195; 266; 308; 1013; 637	"GALLANTS attend, and hear a friend," or: "GALLANTS attends(sic), and hear a friend,"
1062	"GALLIA's increasing fame"
600; 188	"GALL'WAY has fled, and join'd the venal Howe,"
1221	"A Game Cock once, of English breed,"
1339	"GAY Bacchus, one Evening, inviting his Friends"
73	"Genius of Freedom! whether (sic) art thou fled?"
80	"GENTEEL is my Damon, engaging his air,"
1323	"GEORGE on his Throne,"
1029; 1237; 55; 572; 611; 621; 529	"GIVE ear to my song, I'll not tell you a story,"
1394	"Give the heroes all their due,"
1407	".........glasses"
1132; 1245; 501	"GOD bless the Thirteen States,"
325	"THE god descends my soul is fir'd,"
738; 155	"GOD prosper long our liberty,"
288; 1243	"GOD save America,"
1131; 1244; 500	"God save the Thirteen States!"
1061	"GOD save the thirteen states!"
808	"GODDESS! or MUSE! --whate'er thy name,"
1138	"good morn. 'Tis now five irksome years"
872	"GOOD Neighbors, if you'll give me leave,"
506	"GOOD People, I am come to let you know"

First Line Index

Entry No.

113	"HAIL America, Hail! Still unrival'd in Fame,"
641	"Hail Corsica! than whose recorded name"
351; 609	"HAIL! glorious chief, whom destiny has chose" or: "HAIL! glorious chief, whom distiny has chose"
543	"HAIL! great CALASH! o'verwhelming veil,"
314	"Hail happy Freedom, whose reviving Ray."
214	"HAIL, heav'n born muse! thy sire some godlike sage--"
132	"Hail joyful Day! which on our western Earth,"
730; 17; 430; 153; 89; 1294	"Hail Liberty! A glorious word,"
1017	"HAIL mighty Thomas! In whose works are seen"
1403	"HAIL, noble Charlotte! Welcome to the plain,"
786; 185; 579; 991	"HAIL! O America!"
717	"HAIL Parent of each manly Joy,"
349; 607	"HAIL! Patriot hail! Brave Columbian,"
487	"HAIL! Patriots, hail! by me inspired be!"
973	"HAIL to the blest return of peace,"
744	"HAIL to the man whose gen'rous soul disdains"
461	"HAIL welcome dawn, Aurora doth appear,"
313	"HAIL ye gallant sons of freedom,"
78; 1219; 1177	"Hanover, thou Land of Pleasure,"
446; 1356; 32; 114; 1191; 784; 485; 282	"HAPPY's the man, who unconstrain'd"

First Line Index

Entry No.

842	"Hark! hark! the bugle's lofty sound"
482	"HARK! hark! the solemn knell from yon tall spire"
1265	"HARK! hear Apollo strikes his lyre!"
1034; 627; 684; 322; 204; 576	"HARK! hear the Trumpet's pleasant Sound!"
737; 445	"HARK! Or does the indignant ear"
1267; 227; 736	"HARK! --or does the Muse's ear"
356	"HARK, Rebels hark! Sir Harry comes,"
264	"Hark! the drum beats To Arms--to your girls laid adieu,"
990; 257	"HARK! the Goddess of fame,"
1231	"Hark the Herald-Angels sing,"
602	"HARK! the loud Drums, hark, the shrill Trumpet call to Arms,"
457; 512; 111; 982; 1189; 1044; 1434; 911	"HARK! 'tis Freedom that calls, come Patriots awake!"
1248	"HARK! whence that charming Sound! that joyful Shout!"
1310	"HAS the Marquis la Fayette,"
1229	"Have we not seen, at Pleasure's lordly call,"
395	"He comes! he comes! the Monarch comes!"
767	"He whose heart with social fire,"
827	"Heard ye the welcome sound of joy?"
1136; 207; 400	"HENCE with the Lover who sighs o'er his wine,"
1385	"HERE, gen'rous Briton, drop the manly tear,"

332

First Line Index

333

First Line Index

First Line Index

Entry No.

822	"I'm sure that, like Boteler*, I am not afraid" *Cap't. of the Ardent.
961; 1063; 340	"In a chariot of light from the regions above,"
1074; 249; 754; 475; 515; 1194; 984; 275	"IN a chariot of light from the regions of day,"
374; 608	"IN a mouldring Cave, where th' oppressed retreat,"
1114	"In Abram's plains there lies interr'd"
6	"IN ancient times e'er frequent vice began,"
433	"IN ancient times--tyranny and civil wars"
1067; 927	"IN days of Yore, as sages tell,"
837	"IN Esop's days, when all things spoke,"
696; 1078	"IN ev'ry Civil War this hazard's run:"
69	"IN former days--no matter when--"
438; 101	"IN George the second's golden days,"
1134	"IN good King George's golden days,"
1286	"In happier times if such should ever be,"
194	"IN nature's works, we here behold"
378	"IN Newport there's been found of late,"
1295; 1162	"IN our dependent golden days,"
1413	"IN spite of rice, in spite of wheat,"
276	"In story, we're told,/That heroes of old,"
1399	"IN the dry desart of a leathern pocket"
382	"IN the regions of light, at a banquet conven'd,"
197	"IN this, dear George, we both agree,"

First Line Index

Entry No.

First Line Index

Entry No.

994	"JOE's wonderful deeds far surpasses all story,"
732	"JOHN HOLT, thou daring treason hinter!"
860	"JOY to great Congress, joy an hundred fold,"
	"Joyful days at length have come," See: ["Dearly beloved brethren"]
83	"JUBA! a Name that carries in the Sound"
685; 324; 205	"July they say, the fifteenth day,"
93	"JUST is the Strife, in thy devoted Land"
1369	"JUSTICE, that heretofore was of such fame,"

First Line Index

Entry No.

1332   "THE King (God bless him!) is an honest Man;"

892   "KING Hancock sat in regal state"

277   "A kingdom that's fam'd for politeness and dress,"

546   "KNOW all men, who may be concerned,"

First Line Index

Entry No.

747; 1359	"LET Britons, now sunk into Tyrants and Slaves!"
533; 291	"LET croaker's croak, for croak they will,"
1035; 678; 571; 267	"LET ev'ry age due honours pay,"
49	"LET freedom and love be the glee of our song,"
820	"Let Gallia mourn! th'insulting foe,"
347; 481; 703	"LET little Tyrants, conscience gor'd"
1125	"LET me too see the great, good man!"
1043; 740; 102	"LET others strive by servile arts to gain,"
1127	"LET others toil, their empire to extend"
520	"Let pa ta (?) Spirits still aloud complain,"
192	"LET poets sing, in raptures high,"
74	"LET Rome, the glories of her Pompey tell,"
861	"LET Songs of triumph every voice employ,"
1393	"Let the day be ever prais'd"
1389	"Let the di'mond's lustre blaze,"
567	"LET the voice of musick breathe,"
932; 560; 138	"LET those who will, be proud and sneer,"
104	"LET's look to Greece and Athens!"
394	"LET us take the road*!" (*Road of Spithead.)
673; 323; 577; 628	"LET venal poets praise a King"
639	"Let worth arise! and ev'ry name be hurl'd"
	"Let ye banjers play and bagpipes join." See: "Dearly beloved brethren, Let ye banjers play and bagpipes join."

First Line Index

Entry No.

255   "A Maid from affection free,"

     [Majesty] "Come you my Subjects let me know,"
     See: "Come you my Subjects let me know,"

1026; 918; "MAKE room, O ye kingdoms, in hist'ry renowned,"
1009

1409   "THE man, whate'er be his pretence,"

853   "Mark yon wretch submissive bending,"

1449   "MAY all the evils of Pandora's box,"

1448   "May each unkind report,"

1139   "May ev'ry blessing on their arms attend,"

955   "MAY Peace her olive wand extend,"

1004   "MEDDLE not with state affairs,"

1070; 116 "MEN of every size and station,"

401   "THE Ministers bad,"

5; 1179 "A Monarch in my rustic bower,"

972; 71 "MONARCHS, 'tis true, should calm the storms of war,"

260   "The Morning air, my senses chear,"

448   "MOURN, hapless CALEDONIA, mourn"

1084   "MOURN mourn, my lyre, in each string,"

16   "THE muse, disgusted at an age and clime"

964   "THE Muse in winter's hoary reign,"

905   "MY dear Brother Ned, we are knock'd o' the head,"

605   "My Lord,/Thus the fierce North Wind,"

65; 332; "MY lords, I can hardly from weeping refrain,"
408; 136

First Line Index

Entry No.

283; 46;   "MY Lords, with your leave,"
1047; 186;
258; 1383;
1234; 522;
603; 582

938   "MY native shades delight no more,"

897   "MY Soldiers all,"

First Line Index

Entry No.

First Line Index

Entry No.

434; 741	"Oh Boston! late with ev'ry pleasure crown'd,"
1282	"OH Breth'ren From Play-Houses all,"
721; 86; 1366; 251; 595	"OH despicable state of all that groan"
23	"O GOD of mercy bend thine ear,"
1112; 476; 1228	"O GREAT reverse of Tully's coward heart!"
1417	"OH! have pity on thy brother,"
439	"OH heav'nly born! in deepest cells"
1154	"Oh how merry how merry,"
720; 1073	"O Liberty! thou Goddess heavenly bright;"
1109; 1412; 739; 95; 443; 164; 1223; 1188	"O MY baby, my baby,"
1146	"OH! Old England, Old England;"
1019	"Oh, pardon the faults I've committed before;"
52	"O Spirit of the truly brave,"
24	"OH! Thou great Ruler of my Soul!"
1103	"O Thou! who smil'st no more"
1446; 1081	"O THOU whom next to Heav'n we most revere,"
428; 494; 617; 465	"O! 'twas a joyful sound to hear."
886; 1278	"O wherefore, brother Jonathan,"
452	"OH! Why the complaints of poor mortals so grievous?"
921	"O'ER the rough main with flowing sheet"
933; 216; 335	"O'ER the waste of waters cruising,"

First Line Index

Entry No.

1204; 625; 320	"OF all the ages ever known"
1169	"OF all the gifts by God on men bestow'd,"
971; 1202; 70	"OF all the leaders in the state"
318	"Of Bray the vicar long I've been"
411; 937; 680; 666	"OF great and glorious names to speak,"
650	"Of late the urchin God of love"
989	"OF St. George, or St. Bute, let the poet laureat sing,"
873	"THE Old English cause knocks at every man's door,"
670; 969	"Old Homer--but what have we with him to do,"
939; 1311	"OLD Judas the traitor (nor need we much wonder)"
867; 878	"OLD Time flew panting by, in full career,"
951; 668; 363; 221	"THE old Tory rout"
1089	"ON all these dreary plains,"
803	"ON Calvert's plains new faction reigns,"
956	"ON the banks of the fam'd Delaware,"
213	"ON the day set apart to be cheerful and gay,"
890	"On this day our Countrymen, ages before ye,"
1261	"ONCE more, Britannia, rears her drooping head,"
131; 196	"ONCE more our Rulers call a Fast,"
306	"ONCE the Court of Great-Britain in parliament sat(?),"
1430	"ONE bottom leaves the crew to dip,"
833	"Oppress'd and struggling with a weight of woe,"
2	"Ordain'd to tread the thorney Ground,"

First Line Index

First Line Index

Entry No.

232   "THE pains you've been at and the things you have
       wrote,"

459   "PALMIRA's Prospect, with her tumbling Walls,"

1082; 1372; "PARENT of all, Omnipotent"
279; 766

1180; 9   "PARLIAMENT an act has made,"

225   "PASS but a few short fleeting years,"

1338   "PEACE, heavenly Goddess! born on balmy Wings,"

729; 152; "Peace to thy royal shade, illustrious [KING]!"
1428; 223

718; 464; "Permit a giddy trifling Girl"
85; 1336

797   "A PIGEON* who'd think it, alas! a fine trinket,"

1211   "PITY the sorrows of a poor old man,"

551   "POOR Fellow - surely thou'rt an Ass,"

549   "POOR fellow, what hast thou to do,"

629   "POrtsmouth, behold with humble Dread,"

1424   "PRAISE, praise, the mighty he,"

43   "PRAISE to that God who arch'd the sky,"

1375   "PRAY say what's that, which smirking trips this
       way?"

1164   "PreisS und Danck sey Vievlamor(?)"

748   "PRESERVE us Lord, from wicked hands,"

1401   "PRETTY little charming thing,"

928; 661; "PRINCE William of the Brunswick race,"
677; 63;
331; 361;
1198

845   "The Prophet, as became a Reverend Seer,"

First Line Index

First Line Index

Entry No.

1153; 334   "QUIDNUNC, my cronie, thou dost look"

1212   "Quoth Satan to Arnold, my worthy good fellow,"

First Line Index

Entry No.

350

First Line Index

Entry No.

1087; 256	"SAINT George for their Patron our ancestors chose,"
386	"SAMSON, before his head was shorn,"
1343	"The Saxon Prince in Horrour fled,"
1058	"SAY Lovely Fair One's that thus greatly vie"
1289	"SAYS F-----, "if I ever my honour should place"
657	"Says Richard to Thomas and seem'd half afraid"
896	"SAYS Satan to Jemmy, I hold you a Bet"
127	"SCOTCH Machiavel, in Tory spleen grown old,"
869	"SEE France and Spain to battle dare;"
1283	"SEE Spring once more erects each purple plume,"
1064; 1222; 498	"SEE the poor native quit the Lybian shores,"
1315	"SEE where the Farmer, with a Master's Eye,"
1290	"SEE, with stern eye, relenting Vengeance weeps!"
899	"SEE yon black cloud that big with tempest lows,"
248	"Serene the Even, behold the PATRIOT TRAIN,"
202	"SEVEN marks the crisis of the rising states,"
133	"SEVEN marks the trifle of the rising States,"
107	"SHall George our King, misled by wicked Knaves,"
682	"SHall joy not put her Lute in tune,"
330	"SHALL private cares torment the breast,"
252	"Shall venal chains th'aspiring soul detain?"
59	"SHINE Phoebus, shine, to cheer the land,"
307	"SHOUT, shout America,"
1014	"SINCE all must die as well as I,"

First Line Index

First Line Index

Entry No.

895   "STRAIN hard! strain hard! your voices raise,"

293   "Strange paradox among the fowl;"

1085   "Strong as the oak upon the plain,"

581; 370   "THE Stygian God, great Beelzebub."

870   "SURE never, my Lord, was a time more distressing,"

723; 426   "SWEEP all! sweep all!

384; 1060   "SWEET Billy, precious royal boy,"

1157   "SWEET Poll of Plymouth was my dear,"

First Line Index

First Line Index

Entry No.

146; 1292; 366; 417	"THEY come! they come! the Heroes come!"
1147	"THEY, who content on earth to stay,"
67	"THE third and general State Convention,"
893	"THE third day of June in the year sixty-seven,"
1214	"This is the FAST which I will choose,"
1143	"THO' age at my elbow has taken his stand,"
538	"THO' Bute o'er earth and seas, or Kings had Power,"
460; 120; 479; 1230; 701	"THO' some folks may tell us, it is not so clever"
903; 300	"THO' the fate of battle on to-morrow wait;"
1299	"Those daughters (most charming and young)"
944	"THOU mistress of a warlike state,"
1455; 674; 647; 403; 686; 211; 1197; 1213; 548; 502	"THOU who in glory's shining track,"
1320	"THREE ravenous Creatures,"
1209	"THrice hallowed grace! that keep'st thy pow'r,"
7	"THUS fell barbarians: whose rapacious breast,"
847	"Thus, having buried the daemon of enmity,"
1342	"THY Spirit, Independence, let me share!"
814	"Thy Spirit Standfast, let me share,"
379	"'TIS FREEDOM's Voice we hear!"
1388	"'Tis from the watchful culture of the mind,"
1068; 171; 1440; 757	"'TIS money makes the Member vote,"

First Line Index

First Line Index

Entry No.

659; 676; 554; 632	"TO Thee, great sov'reign of the skies!"
1097	"TO thee, O God! by whom I live,"
12; 1331; 1354; 1433; 281; 561	"TO years far distant, and to Scenes more bright,"
247	"To you, Ye all enchanting Maids, belong,"
1000	"TORIES, pray what will ye do,"
14	"TRAITORS would fix Rebellion's odious Name"
836	"THE trembling Muse her grateful lays,"
793	"Troddle, troddle, 'tis got in my noddle,"
390; 636	"TRUE Britons give o'er,"
134	"TWAS Arnold's post, Sir Henry sought,"
1262	"'Twas at the Birth-night ball, Sir,"
1264	"'TWAS at th'imperial throne below,"
393	"'TWAS at the royal show, and grand display"
1151; 135; 328; 556	"'TWAS for the conquest nobly won"
857	"'TWAS on the twenty fourth of May,"
451	"Twelve struck the clock, Sedition's trump blew high"
539	"TWO parties slay whole hecatombs to Jove,"

First Line Index

Entry No.

First Line Index

First Line Index

First Line Index

Entry No.

First Line Index

Entry No.

1382	"WHEN Britain first, without a cause,"
881	"WHEN Britain on her sea-girt shore,"
1148; 405; 1247; 61	"WHEN British troops first landed here,"
1021; 156; 436; 466; 97; 1415; 742	"WHEN Britons first, by Heaven's Command,"
1130	"WHEN Cyclops rough or Polypheme"
30	"WHEN De La Manca's famous Knight,"
816	"When faction brandishing her horrid sting"
877; 884	"WHEN faction, in league with the treacherous Gaul,"
1181	"WHEN first the grand constructor form'd this ball,"
362	"WHEN George in Madness gave command,"
1126	"WHEN God to punish reigning crimes,"
1378	"WHEN good Queen BESSY rul'd the land"
1083; 769	"WHEN haughty monarchs quit this chequer'd scene,"
907	"WHEN Hawke, the British Neptune, reign'd,"
369; 189	"WHEN Heaven for hidden causes shakes the rod,"
1036; 1284	"WHEN Heaven, indulgent, bless'd this land,"
823	"When heroes seek the realms above,"
1397	"WHEN I take an attentive survey of mankind,"
1055	"WHEN Israel's chiefs were captives led,"
1195	"WHen late the hero* of our land took flight," *Dr. Warren.
1350; 437; 619; 100	"WHEN mighty Roast Beef was the Englishman's Food,"

362

First Line Index

Entry No.

1039	"WHEN mighty Shakespeare summoned each sp'rit,"
489; 598	"WHEN moral tale let ancient wisdom move,"
1008; 1121; 1239; 574; 623; 613	"WHEN North first began,"
1018; 357	"When our master, God bless him, ascended the throne,"
109	"WHEN party-spirit prevail's a pace,"
3	"WHEN Popery in Britain sway'd I've read,"
959; 669; 1288	"WHEN pregnant Nature strove relief to gain,"
1427	"WHEN Querist writes, 'tis strange to tell,"
879	"When rival nations first descried,"
1105; 1174	"WHEN rival nations, great in arms,"
1161	"WHEN rous'd by the trumpet's loud clangor to arms,"
859	"WHEN Royal George rul'd o'er this land,"
377; 57	"WHEN Satan first from Heaven's bright region fell"
1129	"WHEN Sc-dd-r, in bombastic strain,"
1172	"WHEN Sons ungrateful to kind Parents prove,"
383; 631	"WHEN southward Cornwallis first enter'd the land"
455; 424; 1184	"WHEN the Foes of the Land, our Destruction had plan'd"
51; 373; 527	"WHEN the great hero in arms himself array'd,"
1098	"WHEN the sheep were in the fauld, and the ky were a' at hame,"
1120	"WHEN the white horse doth over the lion rule,"
819	"When the wise ruler of Clubdubdrib's isle,"

First Line Index

Entry No.

First Line Index

Entry No.

77; 1218; 1176	"WHO has e'er been at Versailles must needs know the King;"
231	"WHO has not heard, what few have seen"
1443; 954	"WHO'D know the sweets of Liberty?"
427	"WHO'EVER (sic) with curious eye has rang'd,"
762; 1370; 278	"WHOM should we fear, since God to us,"
442	"WHOM virtue's native heav'nly force"
708	"WHO's there? who's there? what horrid din!"
237	"WHY did I leave my cheerful home,"
161	"WHY do we fast and hang the Head,"
1033	"Why flings the Muse (he cry'd) her art away,"
818	"Why hast thou soar'd so high, ambitious muse?"
122; 768; 42; 483; 516	"WHY should vain Mortals tremble at the sight of"
1076	"WHY shou'd we of our lot complain,"
926	"WHY Theon wouldst thou longer groan"
238	"WHY throbs my heart? ah! -- whence that sigh!"
183	"WHY toils the world so eager after fame?"
1031	"WHY towards two Georges good, humane and great,"
1141	"Wide as the ocean rolls her flowing tide"
521	"With Christmas Mirth, and Christmas Cheer,"
638; 874	"With flames they threaten to destroy"
1108; 1411; 432	"WITH graceful air and virtuous mein,"
285	"WITH hearts, at York, as light as cork,"

First Line Index

First Line Index

First Line Index

Entry No.

751; 1438   "YE sons of true freedom and spirit,"

1111   "YE stately Sisters!"

1007   "YE Tories all rejoice and sing" "

1208   "YE tuneful nine, my artless lay inspire,"

1312   "YE well array'd! ye Lillies of our Land!"

707   "YE Western Gales, whose genial Breath,"

47; 523;   "YE wrong heads, and strong heads, attend to my
996; 604;   strains;" Or: "YE wrong heads, and strong
1235; 1451;   heads, attend to my song,"
190; 1271

589   "YE Yankies who Mole-like still throw up the
       Earth,"

709   "YET Goddess, sure thou must agree,"

1316   "YOU I love, my dearest Life,"

923; 404;   "YOU know there goes a tale,"
655; 1308

977   "You love my dearest life"

1349   "YOU who can read no Doubt remember,"

250   "Young Florimel, of gentle race,"

1301   "Young ladies in town, and those that live round,"

849   "YOUR boy, my good master, is happy to find,"

1418   "YOUR charge to confute,"

91; 20;   "YOUR Colonel Hancock by neglect,"
1185; 1040

667; 564;   "Your golden dreams, your flattering schemes,"
414

511   "Your grand, fine piece, so laboured,"

301   "The youth, who's destin'd by the muse"

Title Index
Numbers are main entry not page numbers
Entry numbers are in chronological not numerical order.

Title Index

Entry No.

Title Index

Title Index

Entry No.

380; 547	HAIL AMERICANS: (A NEW SONG) See: The Song. ("COLUMBIA! Columbia! to glory arise")
1029; 1237; 55; 572; 611; 621; 529	The Halcyon Days of Old England; Or the Wisdom of Administration demonstrated: A BALLAD.
1351	HAPPINESS.
298; 508	The Happy Life, ["An excellent old Ballad written... in the year, 1659"]
811	A HAPPY NEW YEAR to the LOYAL CUSTOMERS of the ROYAL AMERICAN GAZETTE.
1349	Hark! hark! you young Dogs, there's a Noise in the Nation
1289	A hasty Defence of a late Coalition.
907	HE DON'T FIGHT FAIR. An IMPROMPTU.
47; 996; 604; 1235; 1451; 190; 1271	THE HEADS, Or, The Year 1776. See: A New POLITICAL SONG.
5; 1179	The HERMIT's EMPIRE.
440	An Heroical Panegyric on the valourous atchieve- ments of G---L G---, In the Paper war in America, A.D. 1774, Occasioned by some late Proclamations.
797	Hickup-Ho, Ho, Ho,---Halloo.---Halloo.---....
1049	A HINT for Modern TYRANTS.
857	An Historical BALLAD of the Proceedings at Phila- delphia 24th and 25th of May, 1779. CANTO I ("'TWAS on the 24th of May,")
858	An Historical Ballad of the Proceedings at Phila- delphia 24th and 25th May, 1779. CANTO II ("Now Titan rais'd his flaming head")

Title Index

Entry No.

Title Index

Entry No.

Title Index

Entry No.

Title Index

Entry No.

210	A NEW SONG. ("SINCE Heav'n has bless'd us with a soil,")
800	A NEW SONG. ("SOME Muse assist me to relate,")
479	A NEW SONG. ("THO' some folks may tell us, it is not so clever") See: A Song. ("THO' some folks may tell us, it is not so clever")
1376	A New SONG. ("VAIN BRITON's,boast no longer with proud indignity,") See: A New LIBERTY SONG.
781	A NEW SONG. ("WHEN virtuous ardour, from motives sincere,")
1006	A New SONG. ("WHILE rebel sons with ruffian hand")
286	A NEW SONG. ("WHILST the saucy Buckskins bluster,")
671	A NEW SONG. ("Ye blood-thirsty TORIES, of every degree,")
825	A new Song. ("YE Hearts of Oak, who wish to try")
1134	A NEW SONG, occasioned by the...illiberal, and unwarrantable aspersion thrown out by Dr. TUCKER, DEAN of GLOUCESTER......
383; 631	NEW SONG. Occasioned by the surrender of Earl Cornwallis and his whole army, to General Washington.
796	A NEW SONG on Doctor Lucas.
956	A NEW SONG on the present arbitrary attempt to subvert the Freedom of the Press.
1363	A New SONG on the present critical times.
1109; 1412; 739; 95; 443; 164; 1223; 1188	A New SONG. Supposed to have been sung by Goody N[ort]h, by way of a lulla-by to the foundling (brat, the) Popish Quebec Bill.
125; 44; 517	A New SONG. The Watry God. See: A Favorite SONG of the REBELS.

Title Index

Entry No.

Title Index

Entry No.

406

Title Index

Entry No.

33	A SONG compos'd by a SON of LIBERTY. See: A Song on LIBERTY.
288	Song composed extempore on receiving the Treaties from France. See: A New SONG. ("God Save America")
43	A SONG for BOSTON, Upon the preceipitate (sic) Flight of the King's Troops out of Town.

1244; 500	[A SONG...for the Americans at Amsterdam, July 4,
	    1779.]
	See: A SONG, for the Sailors of the five American
	    vessels at Amsterdam. June 1779.

468	SONG, for the benefit of the Social SONS of LIBERTY.
455; 424; 1184	A SONG for the 5th of MARCH.

1131	A SONG for the Sailors of the five American vessels
	    at Amsterdam. June 1779.
	See: [A SONG...for the Americans at Amsterdam,
	    July 4, 1779.]

1361; 1072; 586	A SONG. From a new musical interlude called the ELECTION.

602	A SONG, just come to Hand, which was sung before
	    General SULLIVAN, and a Number of respectable
	    Inhabitants of Portsmouth, New-Hampshire,
	    March 26th, 1777.

1276	SONG. Mr. Bannister (sung in HARLEQUIN FORTUNATUS).
1277	SONG: Mr. VERNON (sung in HARLEQUIN FORTUNATUS).
239	The SONG of the MAN in the MOON.
1325; 724	A Song on LIBERTY. See: A SONG compos'd by a SON of LIBERTY.
689; 949; 337	SONG on the celebration of the Birth of the DAUPHIN. See: A NEW SONG. Written on the Celebration of the Birth of the Dauphin at West Point.
285	A SONG. On the Grand AMERICAN EXPEDITION, in the Year 1777.

413

Title Index

Entry No.

415

Title Index

Entry No.

Title Index

Entry No.

764	To Col. A--- M---.
1004	To DAVID RITTENHOUSE.
958	To DOCTOR SLOP.
829	To GALLIA.
1408	To general Gage.
1043; 740; 102	To GENERAL L--.
1455; 674; 647; 403; 686; 211; 1213; 1197; 548; 502	To General WASHINGTON, on the late conspiracy
377; 57	To Governor Johnstone, one of the British Commissioners, on his late letters and offers to bribe certain eminent characters in America, and threatening afterwards to appeal to the public.
1321	To HARMONY. See: HYMN to HARMONY.
652	To his Excellency GENERAL WASHINGTON.
962	To JOHN DICKINSON, Esquire.
1319	To Mr. A. B. who had distinguished himself lately as a Writer against the Author of a Poem called WINTER.
235	To Mr. Charles Peale, on his exquisite and celebrated picture of beauty, addressing itself to insensibility.
849	To Mr. SQUIB.
814	To STANDFAST. ("Thy Spirit Standfast, let me share,")
813	To STANDFAST. ("WITHOUT complaisance I appeal,")
313	To the AMERICAN ARMY. ("HAIL ye gallant sons of freedom,"

Title Index

Title Index

Entry No.

290; 1206; 575; 626	WAR!
1089	WAR An ODE.
347; 481; 703	WARREN's GHOST, A PROPHETIC ELEGY.
197	WASHING WEEK.
125; 44; 517	The Watry God. A new SONG.
805	The Whig: A Song.
1156; 681; 415; 141	WHO's the NOODLE. A NEW SONG.
240	A WINTER PASTORAL, Addressed to Mrs. LIVINGSTON*, *Lady of Walter Livingston, Esq.; of the state of New-York.
1303	The WISH.
955	A Wish from CLARINDA to ---.
348	WOLFE's GHOST.
881	The WOODEN WALLS of ENGLAND, An ODE.
1092; 488; 507	THE WORLD.
1322; 1355; 746; 566	Written at an INN on a Particular Occasion.
1279	Written on a late Exchange of Prisoners.

Title Index

Title Index

Author Index
Numbers are main entry not page numbers.
Entry numbers are in chronological not numerical order.

A.B.?, Providence, May 1, 1781.
See: B., A. (?), Providence, May 1, 1781.

1432   A., D.

906   A., W. ("WHICH of my sons, proclaim'd War's God,")

966; 341; A., W., March 31, 1783. ("FROM Heaven descends
509; 560   sweet smiling Peace,")

       A.Z.
       See: Z., A.

420   A---O.

1252   Academicus.

385; 1203 ADOLPHUS. ("SOON as the lark observes the morning's
       grey,")

1054; 398; ADOLPHUS, Philadelphia, Feb. 10, 1780. ("WHILE
544   Nature reclin'd on the bosom of May,")

803   Agricola, Baltimore, Dec. 19, (1774).

546   Amble, Jessie

389   Amelia.

1043; 740; AMERICA.
102

961; 1063; An American.
340

1061   An American prisoner, during his captivity at St.
       Augustine, in East Florida, beginning of 1781.

210   An American Sailor, in a British Prison.

360   An American Soldier, while he was a Prisoner with
       the Enemy.

1088   AMERICANUS. ("LORD NORTH has sent over an Army and
       Fleet,")

1378   Americanus, Buckingham, June 1, 1776. ("WHEN good
       Queen BESSY rul'd the land")

1214   B., A. ?, Providence, May 1, 1781.

             B.H., Frederick Town, November 3, 1773.
             See: H., B., Frederick Town, November 3, 1773.

1095   Bates, Mr.

28; 499   Beadle, William, (Wethersfield, Jan. 28, 1775).

325   [Belinda.]

810   BELLARIO.

16   Berkeley, Dr. George.

723; 426   Boheti, Signiora.

1325; 724   A Bostonian.
             See: SON of LIBERTY.

             Boyce, Dr., master of the King's Musicians.   (musick)
             ("Born for millions are the Kings")
             ("HARK! -- or does the Muse's ear.")
             ("Pass but a few short fleeting years,")
             ("When rival nations, great in arms,")
             ("Ye Western Gales, whose genial Breath,")
             See: Whitehead, William, Esq.;   Poet Laureat.

1172   BRITANNIA, on recovering from her Despondency.

715   British Officer.

1107; 1326;   Brittanno-Americanus, Philadelphia, January 1, 1774.
309; 454;
493; 421;
722; 616;
462; 81;
10

232   Broomstick and Quoad.

1263   C. ("YE Lads of true Spirit,")

1070; 116   [C.] ("MEN of every size and station,")

1357   C., D. ("BOLD is the hope, by virtuous deeds")

1395   C., D. ("A NOISE was heard thro' all the land,")

1396   C., D. ("SOMETIMES the man who bears the breech,")

              [C.D.]
              See: [D., C.]

936; 664;   C., G., May 30, 1782.
336

812   C., I.

1103   C., J., 42nd reg.

798   C., K., New York, March 14, 1774.

1080   C., T.

1039   C---. ("WHEN mighty Shakespeare summoned each
                 spirit,")

930   CALUMNIATOR.

262; 350;   CANDIDUS.
526; 914;
1024; 53

438; 101   A CANTAB., Dec. 15, 1774.

614   C[ar]lington, R.D.

449   [Carrier of Mass. Gazette and Boston Weekly
                 News-Letter.]

458; 172;   CATO, April 18, 1775.
752

899   Causidicus. ("SEE yon black cloud that big with
                 tempest lows,")

898   CAUSIDICUS. ("THE cloud is burst, behold a clearer
                 sky!")

Author Index

Entry No.

1418	Correspondent. ("YOUR charge to confute,")
1036; 1284	Correspondent in St. Croix.
1381	A country poet.
311	A Countryman. ("COME you my Subjects let me know,")
310; 497; 166	A COUNTRYMAN. ("THERE is a Nation on the Earth,")
235	CRITO. ("GREAT nature, Peale! that bade thy genius rise,")
1199	CRITO, Newport, August 26, 1782. ("AGAIN the auspicious day returns,")
1333; 1404; 727	A Customer. ("But should corruption, with despotic rage,")
147	A Customer. ("FREEDOM, Freedom, aloudly cries,")
1406	A Customer. ("TO manhood he made vain pretence")

D.A.
See: A., D.

376   [D., C.]

D.C.
("Bold is the hope, by virtuous deeds")
(" A Noise was heard thro' all the land,")
("Sometimes, the man who bears the breech,")
See: C., D.

450   D., T.

260   D., W.C., Garrison Forest, April 24.

9   A Daughter of Liberty.
            See: M----s, Mrs., a Taylor.

1062   Davids(?), Mr. Walter.

790   de Houdetot, Madame La Countesse. ("Ame du Héros,
               it du Sage")

789   de Houdetot, Madame La Countesse. ("Life of the
               Hero, as well as of the Sage")

293   De La Cour, James. ("Strange paradox among the
               fowl;")

148; 84   de la Cour, Rev. James. ("WHAT mortal but Slander,
               that serpent, hath stung,")

119; 753;   [DIANA.]
174

905   DIOMEDE, off New York, 25th December, 1782. ("My
               dear Brother Ned, we are knock'd on the head,")

904   Diomedes, December 4, 1782 (?). ("As Spain proud
               Monarch sat in state.")

1302; 559   Dunmore, Charlestown, Jan. 6, 1782.

1132; 1245; A Dutch Gentleman (at Amsterdam, July 4, 1779).
501

1131; 1244; A Dutch Lady at the Hague.
500

	F.H. ("ARISE! arise! your voices raise,")
	See: H., F. ("ARISE! arise! your voices raise,")
	F.H. ("SING to his Shade a solemn strain,")
	See: H., F. ("Sing to his shade a solemn strain,")
1417	F., Y.
1008; 1121; 1239; 574; 623; 613	FACT., Chester, March 1.
110; 474	[Female Reader.]
1003	Flirtilla, Philadelphia, Dec. 1, 1777.
349; 607	A Friend to his Country.
93	A Friend to LIBERTY, Aug. 24, 1774.
369; 189	A Friend to the Freedom of the Press.

Author Index

Entry No.

I.C.
See: C., I.

I.W.
See: W., I.

343; 1175   [THE IMMORTAL FARMER.]

1111   IMPARTIAL.

1420   An Intended Customer.

419; 82   IRONY, JOE.

J.C., 42nd Reg.
See: C., J., 42nd reg.

1264   J., J., Spanish-Town, May 16, 1782.

J.M., Prince George, Port-Royal-Harbour, Issue 4,
    1782.
See: M., J., Prince George, Port-Royal-Harbour,
    Issue 4, 1782.

995   J., P.
See: P. ("HOW blest is he, who unconstrain'd,")

J.R. (?), Newport, April 13, 1780.
See: R., J.(?), Newport, April 13, 1780.

J.S.
See: S., J.

J.W.H.
See: H., J.W.

1102; 326   Jenyns, Soame.

1026; 918;   [Jingle, Bob.]   ("Make room, O ye Kingdoms, in hist'r
1009   renowned,")

1027; 919;   [Jingle, Bob.]   ("'TIS Washington's Health, fill a
75; 1010   bumper all round,")

359   Jochelid, The Mother of Muses.

1423   Johnson, Josiah, the Late Reverend.

["Joint Composition of three or four eminent Poets
    of this Province."]   ("Who has not heard, what few
    have seen")
See: three or four eminent Poets of this Province.

1438   A jovial company.

1130   Justus, Philadelphia, Aug. 13, 1779.

675   JUVENIS, New-Brunswick, Jan. 20, 1781.   ("HOW hard
                  the lot of human kind --")

1058   JUVENIS.   ("SAY Lovely Fair One's that thus greatly
                  vie")

922   Juvenis.   ("WE lose him, my Daphnis! and where shall
                  we find")

Author Index

Entry No.

1155   JUVENIS. ("YE belles, and ye flirts and ye pert
              little things,")

L.M.
See: M., L.

1104   L------n, M', a private soldier in the British
            light infantry.

            La Cour, Rev. James De, (D.D.)
            ("Strange paradox among the fowl;")
            ("What mortal but Slander, that serpent, hath stung,")
            See: de la Cour, Rev. James (D.D.)

1041   A LADY.   ("BEGON pernicious baneful Tea,")

1403   A Lady.   ("HAIL, noble Charlotte! Welcome to the
            plain,")

682   A Lady.   ("SHall joy not put her Lute in tune,")

1337; 1405 A Lady.   ("SPECIOUS Instrument of Ill,")

1208   A Lady.   ("Ye tuneful nine, my artless lay inspire,")

935; 217;   LADY CRAVEN.
1305; 563;
505; 1200

1303   A LADY in Richmond.

330   A LADY, just after the cruel burning of CHARLESTOWN,
            by which she lost most of her Property.

855   ["Lady of the first Fashion in Philadelphia."]

302   A LADY of this State.

1419   A Legislator.

974; 1386   LEIGH, Sir EGERTON, Baronet, GRAND-MASTER;
            music by Brother Peter Valton. ("Behold the
            SOCIAL BAND appears,")

1391   Leigh, Sir Egerton, and Peter Valton. ("Blessings
            await this western land,")

975; 1387   LEIGH, Sir EGERTON, and BROTHER Peter Valton.
            ("Boast not, Mortals, human Skill,")

Author Index

Entry No.

896	M. ("SAYS Satan to Jemmy, I hold you a Bet")
252	M. ("Shall venal chains th'aspiring soul detain?")
908	M., E.
1265	M., J., Prince George, Port-Royal-Harbour, June 4, 1782.
1452	N., W., Amelia, Aug. 21, 1779.
1180	M------s, Mrs., a Taylor.
1096	MANY.
83	MARCIA. ("Juba! a Name that carries in the Sound")
718; 464; 85; 1336	MARCIA. ("Permit a giddy trifling girl,")
796	Mary the Nurse, [Philadelphia, Feb. 14, 1774.]
271	A Marylander, Baltimore, May 17.
194	A MECHANICK.
751; 1438	[Member of] a jovial company.
649	Misericors.
1369	A Monitor.

917   P., Lancaster, April 5, 1778. ("COME on my hearts
     of temper'd steel,")

259   P. ("How blest is he, who unconstrain'd,")
     See: J., P.

     P.J.
     See: J., P.

418   P., Q.

1380   P., W., Buckingham, August, 1776.

     P.Z., Norwich, January 25, 1775.
     See: Z., P., Norwich, January 25, 1775.

750; 115; PADDY.
1192; 620;
477

283; 46;   PARKER, Sir PETER.
1047; 186;
258; 1383;
1234; 522;
603; 582

364   PAUPER MULIER.

1046; 782; PENNSYLVANIENSIS.
491; 1196;
1379; 591

952   A Philanthorpist, Philadelphia, Oct. 20, 1777.

140   PHILANTHROPOS.

121   PHILO-MUSICUS.

719   [PHILO-PATRIA.]

764   PHILO PATRIOTA.

15   Philo Sappho. ("BEneath fair FREEDOM's banner, wa-
     ving high,")

25   PHILO SAPPHO, Oct. 12, 1774. ("COME let us join the
     glorious Train,")

214   PHILOMEIDES.

Author Index

Entry No.

Q.P.
See: P., Q.

T.C.
See: C., T.

T.D.
See: D., T.

T.G.
See: G., T.

T.H.
See: H., T.

T.O., CHELLOW, April 5, 1773.
See: O., T., CHELLOW, April 5, 1773.

[T.Z.]
See: [Z., T.]

406	TACITUS.
981; 745; 473	[Thalestris(?), Philadelphia, March 29, 1775.]
231	Three or four eminent Poets of this Province, joint Composition of.
1122; 199	TOMAHAWK.
381	Tristi-Laetus.
729; 152; 1428; 223	A TRUE BRITON.
1153; 334	TRUTH, Old-Road, Jan. 28th.
394	TWICHER, JEMMY and his Boat's Crew.

Author Index

Entry No.

1133   U., Springhill, Aug. 31, 1779.

1259; 835;   Whitehead, William, Esq., Poet Laureat, set to
229   Musick by Mr. Stanley. ("STILL does the Rage of
                    War prevail,")

393   W[hitehead], W[illiam], Esq.; Poet L[aurea]t.
                    ("'TWAS at the Royal Show, and grand display,")

1105; 1174   Whitehead, William, Esq., Poet Laureat. ("WHEN
                    rival nations, great in arms")

945; 693   Whitehead, William, Esq., Poet Laureat. ("Ye
                    Nations hear th' immortal tale---")

707   Whitehead, William, Esq., Poet Laureat, and Dr.
                    Boyce, Master of his Majesty's Band of Musicians.
                    ("YE Western Gales, whose genial Breath.")

107   WISHWELL, TOM.

298; 508   Watton, Sir Henry, (1639). ["Provost of Eaton
                    College"]

Author Index

Entry No.

482	[Y.]
	Y.F. See: F., Y.
7	Y., X.
446; 1356; 32; 114; 1191; 784; 485; 282	Y., Z.
864	A Yankee.
1205	YORICK (?). See: A Youth. ("Descend, my muse, on airy wings sublime,")
380; 547; 692	A young gentleman in Connecticut.
143	Young LADY. ("LONG has Columbia's crimson'd shore,")
897	A young Lady. ("MY Soldiers all,")
12; 1331; 1354; 1433; 281; 561	Young Lady, in 1777. ("To years far distant, and to scenes more bright,")
313	Young Lady in the country.
770; 531; 573; 612; 622; 584	A Young Lady in Virginia.
45	A young Lady of Fifteen.
264	Young Lady - PORTIA.
1402	A youth. ("DESCEND, my muse, on airy wings sublime,") See: YORICK (?).
1167	A Youth of Twenty.
467	Youth who lives in New-Hampshire.

Place of Composition (?)
Numbers are main entry not page numbers.
Entry numbers are in chronological not numerical order.

1452	Amelia, Aug. 21, 1779. See: M., W.
1245; 501	Amsterdam, July 4, 1779. See: A Dutch Gentleman.
240	Annapolis, January 21, 1780.
803	Baltimore, Dec. 19, [1774]. See: Agricola.
246	Baltimore, May 1st, 1775.
271	Baltimore, May 17. See: A Marylander.
596	Bordeaux, July 1, 1776.
1272	Boston. See: SEWELL, Mr.
1002	Brunswick, in New-Jersey. See: An Episcopal clergyman.
1378	Buckingham, June 1, 1776. See: Americanus.
1380	Buckingham, August, 1776. See: P., W.
840	Charles-Town, S.C., Sept. 1.
1260	Charlestown, Jan. 1st, 1782.
559	Charlestown, Jan. 6, 1782. See: DUNMORE.
222	Charlestown, 20th May, 1783. See: HERRIOT, JAS.
635	Cheapside, Feb. 9. See: ANGLICANUS.
1317	CHELLOW, April 5, 1773. See: O., T.
1069	Chester, Burlington county, July 1774 (town meeting).

Place of Composition (?)

Entry No.

1008   Chester, March 1.
                See: FACT.

163   Colchester, February 10, 1775.

380   [Connecticut.]
                See: [young gentleman].

440   Connecticut, Dec. 18, 1774.

787; 179   Cow-Neck, Aug. 2, 1776.

933   Dover, April 26, 1782.
                See: RUSTICUS.

243; 634   Eastern Shore, Maryland, March 30, 1783.

875   Elizabeth-Town, Feb. 3, 1780.

882   Elizabeth-Town, Aug. 1, 1780.

237   Frederick Town, November 3, 1773.
                See: H., B.

260   Garrison Forest, April 24.
                See: D., W.C.

887   Halifax, Nova-Scotia, May 13, 1780.
                See: Clericus, J--B--y.

799; 706   King's-College, New York, April 6, 1774.

1099   Lancaster, Jan. 21.

917   Lancaster, April 5, 1778.
                See: P.

157   Lisbon, 10th March, 1789 (sic).

1297   Manchester, Dec. 8, 1783.
                See: ELEUTHENIUS. ("But since independence we
                   lately have got,")

1298   Manchester, Dec. 8, 1783.
                See: ELEUTHENIUS. ("Cupid God of soft persuasion,")

1300   Manchester, Dec. 8, 1783.
                See: ELEUTHENIUS. ("Nor in summer, when softly
                   the breezes are playing,")

Place of Composition (?)

Entry No.

1296   Manchester, Dec. 8, 1783.
         See: ELEUTHENIUS. ("Return ye enraptur'd hearts")

1299   Manchester, Dec. 8, 1783.
         See: ELEUTHENIUS. ("Those daughters (most charming
           and young)")

382   [MARLBOROUGH, 1781.]
         See: [NOVA-SCOTIA REFUGEE.]

231   [Maryland.]
         See: ["Joint composition of three or four eminent
           Poets of this Province"]

302   [Maryland.]
         See: A LADY of this State.

1195   Massachusetts-Bay Province.
         See: EUGENIO. ("WHen late the hero* of our Land
           took flight,") *Dr. Warren.

1363   Nausemond, July 8, 1775.
         See: Hewlings, J.W.

675   New-Brunswick, Jan. 20, 1781.
         See: JUVENIS.

1037   NEW-JERSEY.

1210   Newport, April 13, 1780.
         See: R., J.

1199   Newport, Aug. 26, 1782.
         See: CRITO.

600   New-Town, Bucks County, Feb. 3, 1777.
         See: Print 'em egad.

794   New-York, 28th January, 1774.
         See: X.

795   N.Y., Jan. 28, 1774.

798   New York, March 14, 1774.
         See: C., K.

802   New-York, Dec. 19, 1774.
         See: A Poor Man.

Place of Composition (?)

Entry No.

765   New-York, December 27, 1775.

842   N.Y., Dec. 18, 1778
            See: Soldier.

843   N.Y., Dec. 29, 1778
            See: Loyal American Refugee

850   N.Y. Jan. 20, 1779.
            See: Soldier.

333; 558   New-York, February 20, 1782.
            See: RIVINGTON, JAMES.

905   New York, 25th Dec. 1782
            See: DIOMEDE.

161   Norwich, January 25, 1775.
            See: Z.,P.

1153; 334 Old-Road, Jan. 28th.
            See: TRUTH.

838   Philadelphia. ("From Lewis, Monsieur Gerard came")

855   [Philadelphia] ("BEHOLD this Badge the Female
            Test,")
            See: ["Lady of the first Fashion in Philadelphis"]

1107   Philadelphia, Jan. 1st, 1774.
            See: BRITTANNO-AMERICANUS.

796   Philadelphia, Feb. 14, 1774.
            See: Mary the Nurse.

1020   Philadelphia, April 18, 1774.
            See: An Englishman.

981   [Philadelphia, March 29, 1775.]
            See: [Thalestria?]

1358; 35   Philadelphia, May 8, 1775.

1114   Philadelphia, February, 1776.

1023; 1117; Philadelphia, May 12.
371; 1257 See: COMUS.

Place of Composition (?)

Entry No.

999   Philadelphia June 14.
               See: KITE, Sergeant.

952   Philadelphia, Oct. 20, 1777.
               See: A PHILANTHROPIST.

1003   Philadelphia, Dec. 1, 1777.
               See: Flirtilla.

377; 57   Philadelphia, July 27, 1778.
               See: COMMON SENSE.

1048   Philadelphia, Jan. 4, 1779.
               See: GAVEL.

1052   Phila., May 24, 1779. ("From sea to sea we scan
               the endless main,")
               See: W.

1053   Philad., May 24, 1779. ("'TIS true, some seem
               devout in ev'ry deed;")
               See: W.

1130   Philadelphia, Aug. 13, 1779.
               See: Justus.

1054   Philadelphia, Feb. 10, 1780.
               See: ADOLPHUS.

1384   Port Royal, March 16, 1773.

               Port-Royal-Harbour, June 4, 1782.
               See: Prince George, June 4, 1782.

1265   Prince George, Port-Royal-Harbour, June 4, 1782.
               See: M.,J.

1214   Providence, May 1, 1781.
               See: B.,A.?

638; 874   Rahway, N.J.

1303   Richmond.
               See: A LADY in Richmond.

1061   Saint Augustine, East Florida, beginning of 1781.
               See: American prisoner, during the captivity at
                  St. Augustine, in East Florida, beginning of 1781.

Place of Composition (?)

Entry No.

1036   Saint Croix.
          See: Correspondent in St. Croix.

1264   Spanish-Town, May 16, 1782.
          See: J.J.

1133   Springhill, Aug. 31, 1779
          See: U.

531   Virginia
          See: Young Lady in Virginia.

499   Wethersfield, Jan. 28, 1775.
          See: Beadle, William.

Date of Composition (?)

Entry No.

33   Feb. 13, 1770.
          See: SON OF LIBERTY; A BOSTONIAN.

1384   March 16, 1773.

1317   April 5, 1773.
          See: O., T., CHELLOW.

123   Sept. 21, 1773 (?)

237   Nov. 3, 1773.
          See: H., B., Frederick Town.

1107   January 1, 1774.
          See: BRITTANO-AMERICANUS, Philadelphia.

794   28th January, 1774.
          See: X., N.Y., 28th January, 1774.

795   Jan. 28, 1774.
          See: New-York.

796   [Feb. 14, 1774.]
          See: Mary the Nurse, [Philadelphia, Feb. 14, 1774]

798   March 14, 1774.
          See: C., K.

799; 706 April 6, 1774.
          See: King's-College, New York.

1020   April 18, 1774.
          See: An Englishmen, Philadelphia.

1069   July, 1774.
          See: Chester, Burlington County, (town meeting).

93   August 24, 1774.
          See: A Friend TO LIBERTY.

25   Oct. 12, 1774.
          See: PHILO SAPPHO, Oct. 12, 1774. ("COME let us
            join the glorious Train,")

438   Dec. 15, 1774.
          See: A CANTAB.

440   Dec. 18, [1774.]
          See: Connecticut.

466

Date of Composition (?)

Entry No.

802   Dec. 19, 1774.
    See: A Poor Man, New-York, Dec. 19, 1774.

803   Dec. 19, 1774.
    See: Agricola, Baltimore.

161   Jan. 25, 1775.
    See: Z., P., Norwich, January 25, 1775.

499   Jan. 28, 1775.
    See: Beadle, William, Weathersfield.

163   Feb. 10, 1775.
    See: Colchester.

981   [March 29, 1775.]
    See: [Thalestria(?), Philadelphia, March 29,
     1775.]

752   April 16, 1775.
    See: CATO.

458   April 18, 1775.
    See: CATO.

246   May 1st, 1775.
    See: Baltimore.

1358; 35 May 8, 1775.
    See: Philadelphia.

271   May 17.
    See: A Marylander, Baltimore, May 17.

112   May 27, 1775.
    See: W---, May 27, 1775.

1268; 1365; June 4, 1775.
1077

1363   July 8, 1775.
    See: Hewlings, J.W., Nansemond.

1113; 761 September, 1775.

765   December 27, 1775.
    See: New-York.

1114   February, 1776.
    See: Philadelphia.

Date of Composition (?)

Entry No.

1378
June 1, 1776.
See: Americanus, Buckingham.

596
July 1, 1776.
See: Bordeaux.

1380
August, 1776.
See: P., W., Buckingham, August, 1776.

787
Aug. 2, 1776.
See: Cow-Neck, Aug. 2, 1776.

561
1777.
See: Young Lady, in 1777.

600
Feb. 3, 1777.
See: Print 'em egad, New-Town, Bucks County, Feb. 3, 1777.

260
April 24.
See: D., W.C., Garrison Forest.

1117; 371; 1257
May 12.
See: COMUS; Philadelphia, May 12.

999
June 14.
See: KITE, Serjeant, Philadelphia.

952
Oct. 20, 1777.
See: A PHILANTHROPIST, Philadelphia, Oct. 20, 1777.

1003
Dec. 1, 1777.
See: Flirtilla, Philadelphia, Dec. 1, 1777.

1099
Jan. 21, [1778.]
See: Lancaster.

131
Feb. 7, 1778.
See: Sternford, Bishop, Feb. 7.

635
Feb. 9.
See: ANGLICANUS, Cheapside.

1008
March 1.
See: FACT, Chester, March 1.

917
April 5, 1778.
See: P., Lancaster, April 5, 1778. ("COME on my hearts of temper'd steel,")

Date of Composition (?)

Entry No.

354   July 19, 1778.
               See: A soldier, upon seeing the British prisoners
                     within the stockade in Rutland.

377; 57   July 27, 1778.
               See: COMMON SENSE; Philadelphia, July 27, 1778.
                     ("WHEN Satan first from Heaven's bright region
                     fell,")

840   Sept. 1, [1778.]
               See: Charles-Town, S.C.

842   Dec. 18, 1778.
               See: A Soldier, New-York, Dec. 18, 1778.

843   Dec. 29, 1778.
               See: Loyal American Refugee, New York.

1048   Jan. 4, 1779.
               See: GAVEL, Philadelphia, Jan. 4, 1779.

850   Jan. 20, 1779.
               See: A Soldier, New-York, Jan. 20, 1779.

1052   May 24, 1779.
               See: W., Philadelphia, May 24, 1779. ("From sea
                     to sea we scan the endless main,")

1053   May 24, 1779.
               See: W., Philadelphia, 1779. ("'TIS true, some
                     seem devout in ev'ry deed;")

1245; 501   July 4, 1779.
               See: A Dutch Gentleman, Amsterdam, July 4, 1779.

673   July 20, 1779.
               See: An Officer of (in) the American Army.

60; 585   July 24, 1779.
               See: Obstinate, Unpardonable Rebel.

1130   Aug. 13, 1779.
               See: Justus, Philadelphia.

1452   Aug. 21, 1779.
               See: M., W., Amelia.

1133   Aug. 31, 1779.
               See: U., Springhill, Aug. 31, 1779.

Date of Composition (?)

Entry No.

240   Jan. 21, 1780.
    See: Annapolis.

875   Feb. 3, 1780.
    See: Elizabeth-Town.

1054   Feb. 10, 1780.
    See: ADOLPHUS, Philadelphia.

1210   April 13, 1780.
    See: R., J., Newport, April 13, 1780.

887   May 13, 1780.
    See: Clericus, J--B--y, Halifax, Nova-Scotia, May
     13, 1780.

882   Aug. 1, 1780.
    See: Elizabeth-Town.

382   1781.
    See: [NOVA-SCOTIA REFUGEE.] [MARLBOROUGH.]

675   Jan. 20, 1781.
    See: JUVENIS, New-Brunswick.

297; 630 Feb. 11, 1781.
    See: A SOLDIER, Feb. 11, 1781.

1214   May 1, 1781.
    See: B., A.?, Providence.

1260   January 1, 1782.
    See: CHARLESTON, Jan. 1st, 1782.

559   Jan. 6, 1782.
    See: Dunmore, Charlestown, Jan. 6, 1782.

1153; 334 Jan. 28, 1782.
    See: TRUTH, Old-Road, Jan. 28th.

333; 558 February 20, 1782.
    See: RIVINGTON, JAMES, (L.S.) New-York, Feb. 20,
     1782.

900   April 12, 1782.
    See: LINDSAY, PETER, a common Seaman on Board his
     Majesty's Ship the Namur.

Date of Composition (?)

Entry No.

933   April 26, 1782.
               See: RUSTICUS, Dover, April 26, 1782. ("O'ER the
                  waste of water cruising,")

1264   May 16, 1782.
               See: J., J., Spanish-Town, May 16, 1782.

936; 336   May 30, 1782.
               See: C., G.

1265   June 4, 1782.
               See: M., J., Prince George, Port-Royal-Harbour.

1199   Aug. 26, 1782.
               See: CRITO, Newport.

904   December 4, 1782.
               See: DIOMEDES, Dec. 4, 1782.

905   25th December 1782
               See: DIOMEDE, of New York, 25th Dec. 1782.

243   March 30, 1783.
               See: Eastern Shore, Maryland.

966; 341;   March 31, 1783.
509   See: A., W.

244; 144;   April 10, 1783.
224

245   April 17, 1783.

222   May 20, 1783.
               See: HERRIOT, JAS., Charlestown.

1295; 1162   Nov. 9, 1783.

1297   Dec. 8, 1783.
               See: ELEUTHENIUS, ("But since independence we
                  lately have got,")

1298   Dec. 8, 1783.
               See: ELEUTHENIUS, ("Cupid God of soft persuasion,")

1300   Dec. 8, 1783.
               See: ELEUTHENIUS, ("Nor in summer, when softly the
                  breezes are playing,")

Date of Composition (?)

Entry No.

1296   Dec. 8, 1783.
            See: ELEUTHENIUS, ("Return ye enraptur'd hearts")

1299   Dec. 8, 1783.
            See: ELEUTHENIUS, ("Those daughters (most charming
              and young)")

157   March 10th, 1789 (sic)
            See: Lisbon.

Numbers are main entry not page numbers.
Entry numbers are in chronological not numerical order.

ABBOT OF CANTERBURY or WILKES'S WRIGGLE: or,
Archbishop of Canterbury; or, A Cobler There
Was; or, Cobler's End; or, Derry Down.

803 Abbot of Canterbury or Wilkes's Wriggle.
<u>IN</u>:
James Aird, ed., <u>A Selection of Scotch, English,
Irish and Foreign Airs</u>..., Vol. I (Glascow:
n.p., 1782?), p. 51. #145. Wilkes's Wrigle.
(GB/Lbm, a.27.)

78; 1219; Air in Praise of Hanover.
1177 <u>IN</u>:

393 [Alexander's Feast.]
<u>IN</u>:
George Friedrich Handel, <u>Alexander's feast: an
oratorio</u> (London: n.p., 1785?). (PU,
fAC7.H7777.A837c.Vol. 10.)
George Friedrich Handel, <u>Alexander's Feast or
the Power of Musick</u> (London: J. Walsh, 1738).
(DLC, M3.3.H13A46.)

214 All cry and no wool.
<u>IN</u>:

ANDRE'S LAMENT.
See: Medley [Return enraptur'd Hours]

ARCHBISHOP OF CANTERBURY: or, The Abbot of Canterbury; or, A Cobler There Was; or, Cobler's
End; or, Derry Down.

236 Archbishop of Canterbury.
<u>IN</u>:
The Cobler in A.   (GB/Lbm, Add. Ms. 34126,f.59v.)
(cont.)

The Coblers End. Sung by Mr. Leveridge. (n.p.:
Cross, n.d.). [A Collection of Old English
Ballads, p. 109.] (DLC, M1740.A2C69.)
Thomas D'Urfey, ed., Wit and Mirth: or, Pills to
Purge Melancholy, Vol. IV (London: n.p. 1719-20),
p. 28. The Ballad of King John and the Abbot of
Canterbury. (DLC, M1740.W78.1876a.)
See: A Cobler There Was; and, Derry Down.

770; 531;   [As Collinet and Phebe Sat.]
573; 612;   IN:
622; 584

AS JACK THE BRISK YOUNG DRUMMER.
   See: Lexington March; and, Yankee Doodle.

ASK IF YON DAMASK ROSE.
   See: The Temple of Minerva.

AWAY TO THE COPSE.
   See: A MEDLEY for the LIGHT INFANTRY.

296; 545   Ballanamonaoro.
               IN:
            Rev. Wilkes Allen, Manuscript Tune and Song
               Book, p. 24. Cap. O Blunder. "Where ever I'm
               going & all the day long." (DLC, M1.A1A.)

BATTLE OF THE KEGS: or, British Valour Displayed.

916; 195;   Battle of the Kegs.
266; 308;   IN:
1013; 637   Whittier Perkins, Collection of Dancing Tunes,
               Marches and Song Tunes (1790), p. 45. Battle
               of the Kegs. (NNC, Hunt/Berol Music.)

            A BEGGING WE WILL GO, WE'LL GO

480   [A Begging we will go, we'll go.] ("COME hither,
               brother Tradesmen")

917   [A begging we will go, we'll go.] ("COME on my
               hearts of temper'd steel")

474

1068; 171;   A begging we will go, we'll go.   ("'TIS money
1440; 757   makes the Member vote,")

                  IN:
                  Thomas D'Urfey, ed., Wit and Mirth: or, Pills to
                    Purge Melancholy, Vol. III (London: n.p.,
                    1719-20), p. 265-6. A SONG.   "There was a
                    Jovial Beggar."   (DLC, M1740.W78.1876a.)
                  John Frederick Lampe, ed., British Melody; Or,
                    the Musical Magazine (London: Benjamin Cole,
                    1739), p. 43.   The Stag Chace...by Mr. Lampe.
                    "I am a jolly Huntsman,"   (DLC, M1619.L25.Case.)
                  The Musical Miscellany..., Vol. V (London: John
                    Watts, 1731), p. 63-65. The JOVIAL BEGGARS.
                    Sung in the Beggar's Wedding. "Whilst Discord
                    and Envy In Mighty Kingdoms dwell,"   (DLC,
                    M1738.A2.M81.)

1076   The Bird.
                  IN:
                  Clio and Euterpe, or, British Harmony, Vol. IV
                    (London: John Welcker, n.d.), p. 6-7. The
                    Bird. "The Bird that hears her nestlings cry,"
                    (DLC, M1619.A2C6.)
                  The Musical Miscellany..., Vol. III (London:
                    John Watts, 1730), p. 134-7. The FOND LOVER.
                    [To the tune of To a LADY more Cruel than
                    Fair..Set by Mr. Leveridge.]   "The Bird, that
                    hears her Nestlings cry"   (DLC, M1738.A2.M81.)

                          BLACK SLOVEN

806; 1005   Black Sloven.   ("AMERICANS swarming by thousands
                  on shore,")

683; 387;   Black Sloven.   ("Come and listen my lads to sweet
534; 1274;   Liberty's lay,")
1207

843   Black Sloven.   ("FOR Battle prepar'd in their
                  country's just cause,")

460; 120;   Black Sloven.   ("THO' some folks may tell us,
479; 1230;   it is not so clever")
701

56; 530   Black Sloven.   ("WHEN valor directed by motives
                  sincere")

781   [Black Sloven.] ("WHEN virtuous ardour, from motives sincere,")

        IN:
        Rev. Wilkes Allen, Manuscript Tune and Songbook, p. 68-69. Black Sloven. "As I was a walking to take the fresh air." (DLC, Ml.AlA.)
        A Choice Collection of Favorite Hunting Songs set for the Voice...Book 1 (London: C. & S. Thompson, 1770?), p. 10. Black Sloven. (GB/Lbm, G.302.)
        Edward Murphy, Manuscript (Newport, October 26, 1790), p. 9. Black Sloven. [Bound with Entire new and compleat Instructions for the Fife (London: Longman & Broderip, n.d.).] (DLC, MT356.062.)
        Whittier Perkins, Collection of Dancing Tunes, Marches and Song Tunes (1790), p. 28. Black Sloven. (NNC, Hunt/Berol Music.)

        BLUBBER HALL.
        See: Kitty Fell. ("Some muse assist me to relate")

        BRITANNIA OR THE DEATH OF WOLFE: or, The Death of Wolfe.

374; 608   [Britannia or the Death of Wolfe.]
        IN:
        Britannia or the Death of Wolfe (Edinburg: N. Steward, n.d.). "In a moudering(sic) Cave a wretched retreat," (DLC, Ml621.B.)
        Henry Brown, Manuscript Book of Poetry and Songs (1789), p. 40-1. The Death of General Wolfe. "In a mouldering cave, where the wretched retreat," (NHi.)
        The Pennsylvania Magazine or American Monthly Museum, March, 1775. General Wolfe. A New Song Engrav'd for The Pennsylvania Magazine. "In a mould'ring cave where the wretched retreat."

826   [The British Flag Triumphant.]
        IN:
        The English Flag Triumphant (London: n.p., 1782). "By the blessing of God we have conquered at last" (GB/Lbm, G.306.(190).)

        BRITISH GRANADIER.
        See: British Grenadier.

A CATCH IN 4 PARTS: or, The RAP at the DOOR.

708   [A CATCH in 4 parts.] ("WHO's there? who's there?
what horrid din!")
IN:

CEASE RUDE. BOREAS.
    See: Hosier's Ghost; and, The Tempest.

1277   [Cheerly my hearts, of courage true,]
    IN:
    [T. Linley, the elder] The Favourite Songs sung...
    in the revived Pantomime of Fortunatus...(London:
    A. Portal, 1780?). (GB/Lbm, H.1648.a.(2.).)

738; 155   Chevy Chace.
    IN:
    Robert Bremner, arr., A Second Set of Scots
      Songs...(London: Preston & Son, n.d.), p.
      28-29. Chevy Chase. "God prosper long our
      noble King," (DLC, M1746.B833T53. Vol. 2.)
    Chevy Chace. (GB/Lbm, Add. Ms. 21763, f. 18v.)
    Thomas D'Urfey, ed., Wit and Mirth: or, Pills
      to Purge Melancholy, Vol. IV (London: n.p.,
      1719-20), p. 289. An Unhappy memorable SONG,
      of the Hunting IN CHEVY-CHASE... "God prosper
      long our Noble King," (DLC, M1740.W78.1876a.)
    The Musical Miscellany...Vol. III (London:
      John Watts, 1730), p. 50-55. A True and
      Lamentable BALLAD; call'd the EARL's Defeat.
      "God prosper long from being broke." (DLC,
      M1738.A2M81.)
    Whittier Perkins, Collection of Dancing Tunes,
      Marches, & Song Tunes (1790), p. 50. A Tune
      to Chevy-Chase, &c. (NNC, Hunt/Berol Music.)

COBLER'S END.
  See: The Abbot of Canterbury; Archbishop of
    Canterbury; A Cobler There Was; and, Derry
    Down.

A COBLER THERE WAS: or, Abbott of Canterbury; or,
  Archbishop of Canterbury; or, Cobler's End; or,
  Derry Down.

          A COBLER THERE WAS

988   A Cobler there was.   ("YE poor silly people,
          who foolishly think")

1122; 199 A Cobler there was.   ("YE poor simple people,
          who foolishly think")

          IN:
          The Cobler in A.   (GB/Lbm, Add. Ms. 34126,f. 59v.)
          The Coblers End.   Sung by Mr. Leveridge (n.p.:
            Cross, n.d.). [A Collection of Old English
            Ballads, p. 109.]   (DLC, M1740.A2C69.)
          Thomas D'Urfey, ed., Wit and Mirth: or, Pills
            to Purge Melancholy, Vol. IV (London: n.p.,
            1719-20), p. 28. The Ballad of King John and
            the Abbot of Canterbury. (DLC, M1740.W78.1876a.)
          See: The Archbishop of Canterbury; and, Derry Down.

COLUMBIA.
  See: Hail Americans.

COME, JOLLY BACCHUS.
  See: First of August.

COME MY KITTEN, MY KITTEN: or, Hey my kitten, my
  kitten; or, O my kitten, my kitten.

1003   Come My Kitten, my Kitten.
          IN:
          Convivial Songster...(London: John Fielding,
            1782), p. 26-7. Song XII. "Hey my kitten, my
            kitten," (DLC, M1738.A2C76.)
          James Johnson, ed., The Scots Musical Museum,
            Vol. 6 (Edinburgh: J. Johnson, 1803), p. 577.
            Hey my Kitten my kitten. (DLC, M1746.A2J67.)
                                        (cont.)

A New Song. For Young Mother's, & Nurses. (n.p.:
n.p., n.d.). "Oh my Kitten, a Kitten," [A
Collection of Old English Ballads, p. 100.]
(DLC, M1740.A2.C69.)
See: Hey my kitten my kitten; and, O my kitten,
my kitten.

CUPID GOD OF SOFT PERSUASION.
See: Medley.

271   [Curs'd be the Wretch, that's bought and sold.]
IN:
The Merry Musician: Or, a Cure for the Spleen...,
Vol. II (London: I. Walsh, n.d.), p. 148-9.
Carey's Wish. A Catch for Three Voices.
Curst be the Wretch that's bought & Sold,"
(DLC, M1740.M62.Case.)
The Universal Musician (London: n.p., n.d.),
p.? The Englishman's Wish. "Curst be the
Wretch that's bought & sold" (DLC, M1619.
A2.U58.)

873   Cut-Purse.
IN:
Thomas D'Urfey, ed., Wit and Mirth: or, Pills
to Purge Melancholy, Vol. IV (London: n.p.,
1719-20), p. 20. The CUT-PURSE. By B. Johnson.
"My Masters and Friends, and good People draw
near," (DLC, M1740.W78.1876a.)

DAPHNE IN MIDAS. ("If you can caper as well as you
modulate etc.")
See: The Sacrifice.

THE DEATH OF WOLFE.
See: Britannia or the Death of Wolfe.

DERRY DOWN: or, Abbot of Canterbury; or,
Archbishop of Canterbury; or, A Cobler There
Was; or, Cobler's End.

DERRY DOWN

456; 1186;   Derry Down. ("THE expences of war, and corrup-
159; 1421   tions of peace,")

457; 512;   The echoing Horn.
111; 982;   IN:
1189; 1044;   Thomas Augustine Arne, Thomas and Sally (London:
1434; 911   Harrison & Co., n.d.), p. 5. "The Echoing
           Horn calls the Sportsmen abroad" (DLC, M1543.
           A74.)
       A Choice Collection of Favorite Hunting Songs,
         Book I (London: n.p., 1770?), p. 24. The
         Ecchoing Horn. In Thomas and Sally Set by
         Dr. Arne. (GB/Lbm, G.302.)

       EUGEANE'S MARCH: or Eugene's March; or, Prince
         Eugene's March.

602   Eugeane's March
         IN:
       Thomas Walter, ed., The Grounds and Rules of
         Musick Explained (Boston: Barry Mecom, 1760),
         p. 54. Prince Eugene's March. (MB, M2116.W23.)
       WARLIKE MUSICK, Book I (London: I. Walsh, [1760?]),
         p. 13. Prince Eugene's March. (DLC, M63.W28.
         Case.)

       FIRST OF AUGUST: or, Come, jolly Bacchus; or,
         Glorious First of August.

815   First of August.
         IN:
       Twenty Four NEW COUNTRY DANCES for the year
         1719...(London: Daniel Wright, 1719), #4.
         First of August. (DLC, M1450.T92.1718.Case.)

863   The Free Mason's Song.
         IN:
       Whittier Perkins, Collection of Dancing Tunes,
         Marches and Song Tunes (1790), p. 14, 26.
         Free Masons Health, Free Masons March.
         (NNC, Hunt/Berol Music.)

       FRIEND AND PITCHER
         See: 'Tis not yet day.

425   From the East Breaks the Morn.
         IN:
       Clio and Euterpe, or, British Harmony, Vol. III,
                              (cont.)

        (London: John Welcker, n.d.), p. 174-5.
        A Favourite Hunting Song. Set to Musick by Mr.
        Joseph Baildon. "Hark the Horn calls come the
        grave"   (DLC, M1619.A2C6.)
          See: [True Blue.]

952   [General Gate's March.]
            IN:
            [GEN. GATES' MARCH (BALTIMORE: G. Willig, [18--]).
             (DLC, M1.A131.Case. On the same page as The
             Indian Chief's March.)]

1146   Get you gone, Raw-head and Bloody-bones.
            IN:

        GLORIOUS FIRST OF AUGUST.
            See: First of August.

                     GOD SAVE THE KING

713   God Save the King.   ("By Sacred Influence hurl'd,")

375; 656 [God Save the King.]   ("FAME, let thy Trumpet sound,")

912   [God Save the King.]   ("FREE States attend my
            Song,")

1380   [God Save the King.]   ("FREE STATES, attend the song,")

660   [God Save the King.]   ("From the Americ shore,")

1062   [God Save the King?]   ("GALLIA's increasing fame")

1132; 1245; [God Save the King.[("GOD bless the Thirteen States,")
501

288; 1243 [God Save the King.]   ("God save America.")

1131; 1244; [God Save the King.]   ("GOD save the Thirteen States,")
500

1061   God Save the King. ("GOD save the thirteen states!")

786; 185;   [God Save the King.] ("Hail! O America")
579; 991

1448   God Save the King. ("May each unkind report,")

                    IN:
                    The Muses Delight (Liverpool: John Sadler, 1754),
                        p. 152-3. A Loyal Song, for Two Voices.
                        "God save great George ye King." (DLC,
                        M1619.A2.M9.)

                 THE GODS OF THE GREEKS: or, Once the Gods of the
                    Greeks.

                        THE GODS OF THE GREEKS

1074; 249;   The Gods of the Greeks. ("IN a chariot of light
754; 475;   from the regions of day,")
515; 1194;
984; 275

382   The Gods of the Greeks. ("IN the regions of light,
                    at a banquet conven'd,")

                    IN:
                    The Origin of English Liberty. The Words by
                        G. A. Stevens. Sung by Mr. Hudson (n.p.: n.p.,
                        n.d.). "Once the Gods of the Greeks, at
                        Ambrosial feast." (GB/Lbm, H.1994.a.(189).)
                        See: Once the Gods of the Greeks

352   [Gossip Joan.]
                    IN:
                    The Musical Miscellany...Vol. IV (London: John
                        Watts, 1730), p. 36-39. An EPITHALIUM on the
                        MARRIAGE of a Young Gentleman with an Old
                        Lady. [To the Tune of Gossip Joan.] "Whence
                        comes it, Neighbour Dick," (DLC, M1738.A2M81.)

113   Hail Albion, fam'd Albion &c.
                    IN:
                    The American Musical Miscellany...(Northampton:
                        Andrew Wright, 1798), p. 122-25. "Hail America
                        Hail! unrival'd in Fame," (DLC, M1628.A5.Copy 3.

380; 547;   [Hail Americans.]
692   IN:
                    [Timothy Dwight], COLUMBIA: An ODE. "Columbia!
                        Columbia! to glory arise," (MWA, Broadside.)

298; 508   [The Happy Life.]
                 IN:

                 HARK! HARK! THE JOY INSPIRING HORN

50; 372;   Hark! Hark! The joy inspiring Horn.   ("COME
525; 606   soldiers all in chorus join")

842   Hark! Hark! The joy inspiring Horn.   ("Hark!
                 hark! the bugle's lofty sound")

                 IN:
                 A Choice Collection of Favorite Hunting Songs,
                 Book II (London: C. & S. Thompson, 1770?),
                 p. 6-7. A Favorite Hunting Song. Sung by Mr.
                 Dearl at the Grotto Gardens. Set by Rd. Bride.
                 "Hark! hark the joy inspiring Horn."
                 (GB/Lbm, G.302.)

                 HE COMES! HE COMES!
                    See: The Temple of Minerva.

                 HE COMES! HE COMES!   ("He comes! he comes! the
                    Monarch comes!")
                    See: March in Rinaldo. On their Majesties
                       Approach to Portsmouth.

146; 1292;   He comes! He comes!   ("THEY come! they come!
366; 417   the Heroes come!")
                 IN:
                 Clio and Euterpe, or, British Harmony, Vol. I
                    (London: John Welcker, n.d.), p. 72.   (DLC,
                 M1619. A2C6.)

                          HEARTS OF OAK

865   Hearts of Oak.   ("COME chear up my Lads, let us
                 haste to the Main,")

1437   Hearts of Oak.   (COME cheer up, my lads, to our
                 country be firm;")

                                                      (cont.)

James Johnson, ed., The Scots Musical Museum,
Vol. 6 (Edinburgh: J. Johnson, 1803), p. 577.
Hey my Kitten my kitten. "Hey! my kitten, my
kitten," (DLC, M1746.A2J67.)

A New Song. For Young Mother's, & Nurses. (n.p.:
n.p., n.d.). "Oh my Kitten, a Kitten," [A
Collection of Old English Ballads, p. 100.]
(DLC, M1740.A2C69.)

See: Come my kitten, my kitten; and, O my kitten,
my kitten.

297; 630   The Highland March.
IN:
Laurence Ding, The Songsters Favourite: Or,
A New Collection (Edinburgh: J. Johnson, [1785]),
p. 12. The Highland March. "In the garb of
Old gaul," (DLC, M1549.D58S5.Case.)

The Musical Miscellany, or A Collection of Songs,
(Edinburgh: n.p., 1786), p. 180-181 [words],
p. 178-179 [music]. Song XCIV. "In the garb
of Old Gaul," (DLC, M1619.M95.Case.)

HOPE THOU NURSE.
See: The Temple of Minerva

HOSIER'S GHOST: or, Cease rude Boreas; or, The
Storm; or, The Tempest; or, Welcome, welcome
brother debtor.

HOSIER'S GHOST

1107; 1326;   Hosier's Ghost. ("AS near beauteous Boston lying,")
309; 454;
493; 421;
722; 616;
462; 81;
10

348   [Hosier's Ghost.] ("AS near Boston's Township
lying")

IN:
Hosier's Ghost, (n.p.: n.p., n.d.). "Near to
Porto Bello lying." (GB/Lbm, G.310.(164).)
                                    (cont.)

The Muses Delight..(Liverpool: John Sadler,
1754), p. 190. Hosier's Ghost. Set by Mr.
Handel. (DLC, M1619.A2M9.)
See: The Tempest.

HOSIER'S GHOST. ("Mark yon wretch submissive
bending,")
See: A MEDLEY for the LIGHT INFANTRY.

HOSIER'S MILL.
See: Hosier's Ghost.

989
The hounds are all out, &c.
IN:
The British Musical Miscellany, Vol. I (London:
I. Walsh, 1734), p. 145. A Hunting Song. "The
Hounds are all out," (DLC, M1738. B864.)
A Choice Collection of Favorite Hunting Songs,
Book I (London: C. & S. Thompson, 1770?),
p. 15. The Chase is Begun. "The Hounds are
all out," (GB/Lbm, G.302.)
A Choice Collection of Favorite Hunting Songs,
Book I (London: C. & S. Thompson, 1770?),
p. 22. The Hounds are all out. A Favorite
Hunting Song. "The Hounds are all out and the
morning does peep," (GB/Lbm, G. 302.)

HOW HAPPY ARE WE.
See: When you censure the age.

HOW MUCH SUPERIOR BEAUTY AWES.
See: The Sacrifice.

HOW PLEASANT A SAILOR'S LIFE PASSES.
See: A light heart and a thin pair of breeches...

I WINNA MARRY ONY LAD, BUT SANDY O'ER THE LEE.
See: Scots Song.

798
[If fortune would smile, and I cannot complain.]
IN:

IF YOU CAN CAPER AS WELL AS YOU MODULATE.
  See: The Sacrifice.

IN LOVE SHOULD THERE MEET A FOND PAIR.
  See: The Temple of Minerva

888   [In Memory of Mr. James Bremner.]
            IN:
            In Memory of Mr. James Bremner (Paul G. and
              Henry C. Woehlcke, 1931). (DLC, M1621.H.
              Copy 2. Case.)

276   ["In story we're told how our Monarchs of old"]
            IN:
            A Song in THE FAIR, Sung by Mr. Beard (n.p.:
              n.p., n.d.). "In story we're told how our
              Monarchs of old."   (DLC, M1526.S.Case.)

1322; 1355; [The Inn.]
746; 566   IN:

1395   Jenny Dang the Weaver.
            IN:
            Compleat Instructions for the Violin..by Geminiani
              (London: G. Goulding, n.d.), p. 14? JANNIE
              dang the weaver. (DLC, MT356.C62.)
            O Mother dear. Jenny Dang the Weaver. (GB/Lbm,
              Add.Ms. 25074, f. 21r.)
            Whittier Perkins, Collection of Dancing Tunes,
              Marches & Song Tunes, p. 15. Jenny Dang the
              Weaver. (NNC, Hunt/Berol Music.)
            See: Over the Water.

          KITTY FELL: or, Blubber-Hall.

                      KITTY FELL

800   Kitty fell. ("SOME Muse assist me to relate,")

285   Kitty Fell. ("WITH hearts, at York, as light as
            cork,")

IN:
[Thomas Augustine Arne], A Favourite Collection
of English Songs (n.p.: I. Walsh, 1757). Kitty
Fell. "While Beaus to Please the Ladies write"
(DLC, M1620.A2A74.)
Clio and Euterpe, or, British Harmony, Vol. I
(London: John Welcker, n.d.), p. 150. Kitty
Fell. Sung by Mr. Beard at Ranelagh. (DLC,
M1619.A2C6.)

LARRY GROGAN: or, Larry Crogan.

925; 1249;   Larry Grogan.
633   IN:
James Aird, ed., A Selection of Scotch, English,
Irish and Foreign Airs..., Vol. I (Glasgow:
n.p., 1782-94), p. 54. Larry Grogan. (GB/Lbm,
a.27.)
Thomas Augustine Arne, Love in a Village (London:
Longman & Broderip, n.d.), p. 21. Sung by Mr.
Blanchard. "Well, well, say no more" [Larry
Grogan.]   (DLC, M1503.A74.L61.)
Larry Grogan. (GB/Lbm, Add. Ms. 29371, #35.)

1420   Last Sunday morning we sail'd from Cork.
IN:
Whittier Perkins, Collection of Dancing Tunes,
Marches and Song Tunes, p. 21. "Last Sunday
Morning I sail'd from Cork."   (NNC, Hunt/
Berol Music.)

1012; 1238;   A Late worthy old lion, etc.
198; 532;   IN:
624

LET THE BRIGHT SERAPHIM IN BURNING ROW.
See: The Temple of Minerva.

1136; 207;   Let the Toast Pass.
400   IN:
A Collection of New and Favorite Songs
(Philadelphia: B. Carr, n.d.), A General
Toast. "Here's to the Maiden of bashfull
fifteen" (DLC, M1.A1C.)
Thomas Linley, The Camp, An Entertainment
(cont.)

(London: S. & A. Thompson, n.d.), p. 26-27.
THE SONG in the SCHOOL for SCANDAL. "Here's
to the Maiden of bashful fifteen" (DLC,
M1503.L757.C3.Case.)
New General Toast. (n.p.: n.p., n.d.). Words
by Mr. Oakman. Set by Mr. T. Smart. (GB/Lbm,
G.313.(213).)

LEXINGTON MARCH: or, As Jack the Brisk Young
Drummer; or, My Daddy was in the Rebellion; or,
Yankee Doodle.

262; 350;   Lexington March.
526; 914;   IN:
1024; 53   YANKEE DOODLE, or (as now Christened by the
                  Saints of New England) THE LEXINGTON MARCH.
                  "Brother Ephraim sold his Cow." (MB.)
                  (DLC, M1630.3.Y2.Case.)
              See: Yankee Doodle.

670; 969   [Liberty Hall.]
              IN:
              Liberty Hall (n.p.: n.p., n.d.).   (GB/Lbm,
                  H1994.a.(76).)

751; 1438   A light heart and a thin pair of breeches goes
              through the world, brave boys.
              IN:
              [J.C. Pepusch], The Sailor's Ballad. Sung by
                  Mr. Legar in Perseus and Andromeda (n.p.:
                  n.p., n.d.). "How pleasant a Sailors life
                  passes," (DLC, M1508.Case.)

230   The Lilies of France.
              IN:
              Clio and Euterpe, or, British Harmony, Vol. III
                  (London: John Welcker, n.d.), p.26-27.
                  The Fair English Rose. A Favourite Song.
                  (DLC, M1619.A2C6.)
              Francis Hopkinson, His Book, p. 153. "The Lilies
                  of France & the fair English Rose," (DLC,
                  ML96.H83.)

              LILLIBULERO.
              See: Nottingham Ale.

LILLIBURLERRO. ("But since independence we lately
have got,")
See: Medley.

250   [Love and Glory]
IN:
Benjamin Carr, Musical Journal for the Piano
Forte, Vol. V (Philadelphia: B. Carr, n.d.),
p. 53. Love and Glory. "Young Henry was as
brave a youth." (DLC, Ml.AlM98.Vol.V.)
J. Wilson, Love and Glory (N.Y.: J. & M. Paff,
n.d.), "When love and peace, and Fanny Smiling."
(DLC, Ml.AlW.)

511   Low Dutch
IN:
Daniel Bayley, ed., The GENTLEMAN AND LADY'S
MUSICAL COMPANION (Newburyport: Daniel Bayley,
1774), p. 104. Low Dutch, Hymn 3d. "Why do
we mourn departing Friends," (DLC, M2116.S86.
G5.1774.)

LUMPS OF PUDDING.
See: A MEDLEY for the LIGHT INFANTRY.

1148; 405;   Maggie Lauder.
1247; 61   IN:
Dale's Collection of Sixty favorite Scotch Songs,
...Vol. 2 (London: J. Dale, n.d.), p. 104.
Maggie Lawder. "O wha wad na be in love,"
(DLC, M1746.D2.Case.)
Moggie Lawther or Margaret Lowther. (GB/Lbm,
Add. Ms. 29371, #530.)
Whittier Perkins, Collection of Dancing Tunes,
Marches, & Song Tunes (1790), p. 13?. Maggy
Lawder. (NNC, Hunt/Berol Music.)

394; 395   March in Rinaldo. On their Majesties Approach to
Portsmouth.
IN:
March in Rinaldo.
Dr. Pepusch, The Excellent Choice being a
collection of the most favourite old Song
Tunes...(London: I. Walsh, n.d.), p. 13.
Air 23. "Let us take the road, hark!"
(DLC, M1578.W28.Case.)

(cont.)

Warlike Musick, Book II (London: I. Walsh,
1760?), p. 37. March in Rinaldo. "Let us
take the road." (DLC, M63.W28.Case.)
He comes! He comes!
Clio and Euterpe, or British Harmony, Vol. I
(London: John Welcker, n.d.), p. 72. A Two
Part Song. "He comes! He comes!" (DLC,
M1619.A2C6.)

THE MASQUERADE SONG.
See: Ye Medley of Mortals.

1296; 1297; [Medley.]
1298; 1299; IN:
1300 [Return enraptur'd Hours.]
Major Andre, Return enraptur'd Hours (London:
Longman & Broderip, n.d.). "Return enraptur'd
hours," (DLC, M1621.A.Case.)
[Lilliburlerro.]
Apollo's Banquet..., The 2nd Book (London:
H. Playford, 1691), #45. Lilliburlero.
(DLC, M1490.P6A5.Case.)
The Beggar's Opera...(London:n.p., 1729),
p. 33-34. Lillibulero. (DLC, ML50.5.B3.
1729.)
[Cupid god of soft persuasion.]
Thomas Augustine Arne, Love in a Village
(London: Longman & Broderip, n.d.), p.20-21.
[Set by Mr. Giardini.] Sung by Mrs.
Mountain. "Cupid God of soft persuasion,"
(DLC, M1503.A74.L61.)
[Those daughters (most charming and young)(?).]

[Nor in summer, when softly breezes are playing(?).]

850; 851; A MEDLEY for the LIGHT INFANTRY.
852; 853; IN:
854 Over the Hills and far away.
A Favorite Medley for the Light Infantry
(London: n.p., 1780?). "Soldier, whilst the
flowing Bowl". (GB/Lbm, G.311.(152), incomplete)

By the gayly circling Glass.
Thomas Augustine Arne, The Musick in the
Masque of Comus (London: William Smith, n.d.),
p. 15. Sung by Mr. Beard in Comus. "By
the gaily circling Glass" (DLC, M1520.
A2A74.)
Away to the Copse.
A Choice Collection of Favorite Hunting
Songs set for the Voice...Book I (London:
n.p., 1770?), p. 18-19. A Hunting Song
Sung by Mr. Andrews at Sadlers Wells.
"Away to the copse lead away" (GB/Lbm,
G.302.)
Hosier's Ghost.
Apollo's Cabinet: or the Muses Delight..,
Vol. II (Liverpool: John Sadler, 1757),
p. 190. Hosier's Ghost. Set by Mr. Handel.
"As near Portobello lying" (DLC, M1738.
A2A65.)
Hosier's Ghost (n.p.: n.p., n.d.). "As
near Portobello lying" (GB/Lbm, G.310.
(164).)
Lumps of Pudding.
The Beggar's Opera...(London: n.p., 1729),
p. 45-46. Air LXIX. Lumps of Pudding.
"Thus I stand like the Turk, with his
Doxies around:" (DLC, ML50.5.B3.1729.)

MEDLIES.
See: Medley.

MOURN, HAPLESS CALEDONIA.
See: The Tears of Scotland.

MY DADDY WAS IN THE REBELLION.
See: Lexington March.

956 My fond shepherds of late were so bless'd, &c.
IN:
Clio and Euterpe, or British Harmony, Vol. II
(London: John Welcker, n.d.), p. 52-53.
A Favourite Song in the Opera of Eliza.
"My fond Shepherds of late were so bless'd,"
(DLC, M1619.A2C6.)

NANCY DAWSON

971; 1202;   Nancy Dawson. ("OF all the leaders in the state")
70

1007   Nancy Dawson. ("YE Tories all rejoice and sing")

           IN:
           Whittier Perkins, Collection of Dancing Tunes,
              Marches and Song Tunes (1790), p. 38. Nancy
              Dawson. (NNC, Hunt/Berol Music.)

NOR IN SUMMER, WHEN SOFTLY THE BREEZES ARE PLAYING.
    See: Medley.

NOTTINGHAM ALE: or, Lillibulero.

877; 884   Nottingham Ale.
           IN:
           Apollo's Banquet:..., The 2nd Book (London:
              H. Playford, 1691), #45. Lilli Burlero.
              (DLC, M1490.P6A5.Case.)
           The Beggar's Opera...(London: n.p., 1729),
              p. 33-34. Lillibulero. (DLC, ML50.5.B3.1729.)

O MOTHER DEAR JERUSALEM: or, Diana and her darlings
    deare; or, Rogero.

875   O Mother dear Jerusalem.
           IN:

O MY KITTEN, MY KITTEN: or, Come my kitten, my
    kitten; or, Hey my kitten, my kitten.

1109; 1412;   O my kitten, my kitten.
739; 95;   IN:
443; 164;   Convivial Songster..(London: John Fielding, 1782),
1223; 1188   p. 26-7. Song XII. "Hey my kitten, my kitten."
              (DLC, M1738.A2.C76.)

(cont.)

James Johnson, ed., The Scots Musical Museum,
   Vol. 6 (Edinburgh: J. Johnson, 1803), p. 577.
   Hey my kitten my kitten. "Hey! my kitten, my
   kitten," (DLC, M1746.A2J67.)
A New Song. For Young Mother's, & Nurses. "Oh
   my Kitten, my Kitten," [A Collection of Old
   English Ballads, p. 100.] (DLC, M1740.A2C69.)
   See: Come my kitten, my kitten; and, Hey my
   kitten, my kitten.

1281; 979	[Ode for his Majesty's Birth-Day, June 4, 1773.]
	   IN:
	   William Boyce, Manuscripts.(GB/Ob3, Ms. Mus.
	      Sch. D.330^a.)

1267; 227;
736
	[Ode for His Majesty's Birth-Day, June 4, 1774.]
	   IN:
	   William Boyce, Manuscripts. (GB/Ob3, Ms. Mus.
	      Sch.D.332^a.)

1269; 1075;
228; 1442
	[Ode for His Majesty's Birth-Day, 1775.]
	   IN:
	   William Boyce, Manuscripts. (GB/Ob3, Ms. Mus.
	      Sch.D.333^a.)

707	[Ode for his Majesty's Birth-Day, June 4, 1776.]
	   IN:
	   William Boyce, Manuscripts. (GB/Ob3, Ms. Mus.
	      Sch. D.335^a.)

1259; 835; 229	[Ode for his Majesty's Birth-day, June 4, 1781.] IN:

974; 975;
1386; 1387;
1388; .1389;
1390; 1391;
1392; 1393;
1394
	Ode for the Festival of St. John Evangelist in
	   South Carolina 5772.
	   IN:

567	[ODE for the New-Year, 176-.]
	   IN:
	   William Boyce, Manuscripts. (GB/Ob3, Ms. Mus.
	      Sch.D.320^a.)

225   [Ode for the New Year, 1774.]
                       IN:
                       William Boyce, Manuscripts. (GB/Ob3, Ms. Mus.
                          Sch. D. 331ᵃ.)

712; 1170   [Ode for the New Year, 1777.]
                       IN:

528   [Ode for the NEW YEAR, 1778.]
                       IN:
                       William Boyce, Manuscripts. (GB/Ob3, Ms. Mus.
                          Sch. D. 325ᵃ.)

1105; 1174   [Ode for the New Year, January 1, 1778.]
                       IN:
                       William Boyce, Manuscripts. (GB/Ob3, Ms. Mus.
                          Sch. D. 338ᵃ.)   .

1156; 681;   [Ods' blood who's the noodle.]
415; 141   IN:
                       Ods' Blood who's the Noodle (London: Bland, 1780),
                          "I sing of George's Golden Days," (GB/Lbm,
                          G.309.(105).)

422   [Old Ballad composed and sung by some of the first
                      settlers of New England.]
                       IN:

346; 987;   An old Courtier of the Queen's and the Queen's
704   old Courtier.
                       IN:
                       The Old and New Courtier of the Queen's (n.p.:
                          n.p., n.d.). "With an Old Song made by an Old
                          ancient Pate." (Dfo, Ml497.C42.Vol.3.Cage,
                          f.485.)

                   OLD TUNE.
                      See: Derry Down. ("What a Court hath old England
                         of folly and sin,")

                   ONCE THE GODS OF THE GREEKS: or, The Gods of the
                      Greeks.

ONCE THE GODS OF THE GREEKS

961; 1063;   [Once the Gods of the Greeks.] ("In a chariot of
340   light from the regions above,")

306   Once the Gods of the Greeks. ("ONCE the Court
                     of Great-Britain in parliament sat (?).")

455; 424;   Once the Gods of the Greeks.   ("WHEN the Foes of
1184   the Land, our Destruction had plan'd")

                 IN:
                 The Origin of English Liberty. The Words by
                     G. A. Stevens. Sung by Mr. Hudson. (n.p.:
                     n.p., n.d.). "Once the Gods of the Greeks,
                     at ambrosial feast," (GB/Lbm, H.1994.a.(189).)
                 See: The Gods of the Greeks.

685; 324;   One night as Ned stept into bed.
205   IN:
                 KATE and NED (n.p.: n.p., n.d.). "One night as
                     Ned Crept into bed." (GB/Lbm, G.310.(229).)

                 OVER THE HILLS AND FAR AWAY.
                     See: A MEDLEY for the LIGHT INFANTRY.

1395   Over the water.
                     IN:
                 James Johnson, ed., The Scots Musical Museum,
                     Vol. II (Edinburgh: J. Johnson, 1788), p. 195.
                     O'er the water to Charlie. "Come boast me
                     o'er, come row me o'er," (DLC, M1746.A2J67.)
                 Edward Murphy, Manuscript (Newport, October 26,
                     1790), p. 5. Over the water to Charley. [Bound
                     with Entire new and compleat Instructions
                     for the Fife (London: Longman & Broderip, n.d.)]
                     (DLC, MT356.062.)
                 O'er the water to Charlie. "Come boat me o'er,
                     come row me o'er," (GB/Lbm, Add. Ms. 25074,
                     f. 27v.)
                 Over ye Water to Charley. (GB/Lbm, Add. Ms.
                     29371, #265.)
                 Whittier Perkins, Collection of Dancing Tunes,
                     Marches and Song Tunes (1790), p. 16. Over the
                     river to Charley. (NNC, Hunt/Berol Music.)
                 See: Jenny Dang the Weaver.

1026; 918;   [Pepperell and Pumpkinshire People.]
1009   IN:

PITCHER.
   See: 'Tis not yet day.

1157   [Poll of Plymouth.]
            IN:
            [Michael Arne, composer; J. O'Keefe, words]
               Sweet Poll of Plymouth, Sung by Mrs. Kennedy...
               (London: Longman and Broderip, [1782]). (GB/Lbm,
               G.383.h.(3).)

PRINCE EUGEANE'S MARCH.
   See: Eugeane's March.

1424   Prussian Hero.
            IN:

638; 874   [Psalm.]
            IN:

PUSH ABOUT THE JORUM; or, Push about the Forum.

411; 937;   Push about the Jorum.
680; 666   IN:
            James Aird, ed., A Selection of Scotch, English,
              Irish and Foreign Airs, Vol. I (Glasgow: n.p.,
              1782-94?), p. 39. #111. Push about the Jorum.
              (GB/Lbm, a.27.)

THE RAP AT THE DOOR.
   See: [A CATCH in 4 Parts.]

663; 689;   [Restoration March.]
949; 1251;   IN:
562; 337;   Henry Brown, Manuscript Book of Poetry and Songs
139   (1789), p. 42-43. The Dauphin. "Ye sons of
             Mars attend," (NHi.)

RETURN YE ENRAPTUR'D HEARTS;or,Return enraptur'd Hours
See: Medley.

THE ROAST BEEF OF OLD ENGLAND

890   The Roast Beef of Old England. ("On this day our Countrymen, ages before ye,")

1350; 437; 619; 100   [The Roast Beef of Old England.] ("WHEN mighty Roast Beef was the Englishman's Food,")
IN:
Clio and Euterpe, or British Harmony, Vol. I (London: John Welcker, n.d.), p. 43. English Roast Beef. Set by Mr. Leveridge. (DLC, M1619.A2C6.)

ROGERO
See: O Mother dear Jerusalem.

1262   [The Royal Disaster.]
IN:
The Royal Disaster, European Magazine, 1782. "Twas at the Birth-night Ball, Sir" (GB/Lbm, 2117.c.)

RULE BRITANNIA: or, When Britain first, at Heaven's Command.

RULE BRITANNIA

901   Rule Britannia. ("AS bending o'er the azure tide,")
See: The Watry God.

809   Rule Britannia. ("Blest cause of genial life, arise,")

210   Rule Britannia. ("SINCE Heav'n has bless'd us with a soil,")

868   Rule Britannia. ("When Britain, by Divine command,")

470; [1173; 1094]   [Rule Britannia.] ("When Britain first at Heaven's command,")

1021; 156; 436; 466; 97; 1415; 742   Rule Britannia. ("WHEN Britons first, by Heaven's Command,")

(cont.)

879   Rule Britannia. ("When rival nations first descried,")

1006   Rule Britannia. ("WHILE rebel sons with ruffian
              hand")

              IN:
              Thomas Arne, Alfred; A Masque (London: Harrison
                & Co., n.d.), p. 42-3. "When Britain first at
                Heav'ns Command." (DLC, M1543.A74.A5.)
              Clio and Euterpe, or British Harmony, Vol. I
                (London: John Welcker, n.d.), p. 20-21. Rule
                Britannia. Set by Mr. Arne. (DLC, M1619.A2C6.)

845; 846;   The Sacrifice
847   IN:
              The Prophet became a Reverend Seer. [Recitative.]
              How much superior beauty awes.
                Thomas Augustine Arne, Love in a Village
                (London: Longman & Broderip, n.d.), p. 56. "How
                much superior beauty awes." (DLC, M1503.A74.L61.)
              Daphne in Midas. ("If you can caper as well as
                you modulate")
                Midas, A Comic Opera (London: I. Walsh, n.d.),
                  p. 30. "If you can Caper as well as you
                  modulate." (DLC, M1503.M644.Case.)

              THE SAILORS BALLAD.
                See: A light heart and thin pair of Breeches

614   [A Sale.]
              IN:
              N. Thompson, ed., A CHOICE COLLECTION of 180
                LOYAL SONGS, 3rd ed. (London: N. Thompson, 1683),
                p. 149-52. A General Sale of Rebellious House-
                hold Stuff. "Rebellion hath broken up House."
                [Tune: Old Symon the King.] (DLC, M1740.C623.
                Case.)

1095   A Scotch Ballad. ("AND are you sure the news is
              true?")
              IN:
              There's nae Luck about the House. A favorite
                Scotch Song. (London: R. Bremner, 1770?). "And
                are ye sure the news is true." (GB/Lbm, G.306.
                (224).)

1110; 514;   Scots Song, I winna marry ony Lad, but Sandy o'er
755   the Lee.
                 IN:
                 The Vocal Enchantress... (London: J. Fielding,
                    1783), p. 284-5. Song CXLI. "I winna marry
                    ony mon but Sandy o'er the Lee" (DLC, M1738.
                    A2.V84.)

              SEE THE CONQUERING HERO COMES.
                 See: The Temple of Minerva.

              THE SILVER MOON THAT SHINES SO BRIGHT
                 See: 'Tis not yet Day.

1001   [Sing-Song.]
                 IN:

                          SMILE BRITANNIA

889   Smile Britannia. ("ALL hail! Britannia Hail!")

596   Smile Britannia. ("RISE, rise, bright genius rise,")

307   Smile Britannia. ("SHOUT, shout America,/ Thy
                 guardian God appears,")

123   Smile Britannia. ("SMILE, Massachusetts Smile,")

495; 435   Smile Britannia. ("YE Sons of Freedom smile!")

                 IN:
                 Clio and Euterpe, or British Harmony, Vol. I
                    (London : J. Welcker, ca. 1778), p. 1. Smile
                    Britannia. A Favourite Song. (DLC, M1619.
                    A2.C6.)
                 Song. Sung at Vauxhall. "Smile, smile, Britannia,
                    smile," (GB/Lbm, Add.Ms. 37522, f. 21v-21r.)

1155   [A Song for Ranelagh?]
                 IN:
                 A Song for Ranelagh. [Words by W. Whitehead]
                    (London: n.p., 1750?). "Ye Belles and ye Flirts"
                    (GB/Lbm, G.314.(27).)

716; 219   [A Soldier, A Soldier, A Soldier for me!]
               IN:
               A Soldier for me, A Favourite Song. Sung by
               Mrs. Wrighton, in Best Bidder, at the Theatre
               Royal in Drury Lane. Composed by Mr. Hook.
               (London: S. A. & P. Thompson, n.d.). (GB/
               Lbm, H.1994d(27).)

             THE STORM
               See: Hosier's Ghost; and, The Tempest.

             SWEET POLL OF PLYMOUTH.
               See: Poll of Plymouth.

                       THE SWEETS OF LIBERTY

995; 259   [The Sweets of Liberty.] ("HOW blest is he, who
               unconstrain'd")

1443; 954   [Sweets of Liberty.] ("WHO'D know the sweets of
               Liberty?")

               IN:
               Clio and Euterpe, or British Harmony, Vol. III
                 (London: John Welcker, n.d.), p. 12-13. A
               Favourite Song in the Opera of Eliza.
               (DLC, M1619.A2C6.)

             THE TEARS OF SCOTLAND: or, Mourn, Hapless Caledonia.

448   [The Tears of Scotland.]
               IN:
               The Tears of ·Scotland (n.p.: n.p., n.d.).
               "Mourn hapless Caledonia," [A Collection
               of Old English Ballads, p. 1-2.]
               (DLC, M1740.A2C69.)

             THE TEMPEST: or, Cease rude Boreas; or, Hosier's
               Ghost; or, The Storm; or Welcome, welcome brother
               debtor.

933; 216;   The Tempest.
335   IN:
               Hosier's Ghost. (n.p.: n.p., n.d.). "Near to
                 Porto Bello lying." (GB/Lbm, G.310.(164).)
               The Muses Delight. (Liverpool: John Sadler,
                 1754), p. 190. Hosier's Ghost. Set by Mr.
                 Handel. (DLC, M1619.A2M9.)
               See: Hosier's Ghost.

895 [The Temple of Cloacina: An Ora-whig-ial Entertainment.]
See: The Temple of Minerva.

924; 894; The Temple of Minerva. An Oratorial Enter-
329; 504; tainment.
1250; 557; IN:
215 Overture
[He Comes! He Comes!]
Keppel A Favourite Song for 3 Voices (n.p.:
n.p., n.d.). "He Comes He Comes! Brave
Keppel Comes!" (GB/Lbm, G. 308.(123).)
[Ask if yon damask rose.]
Handel's Songs...Vol. II (London: I. Walsh,
n.d.), #105. (DLC, M2006.H15.W32.)
[Yet a While.]
Michael Arne, Cymon (London: Longman &
Broderip, n.d.), p. 28. (DLC, M1523.A73C4.
Case.)
[See the Conquering Hero Comes.]
Handel's Songs...Vol. III (London: I. Walsh,
n.d.), p. 398-99. (DLC, M2006.H15.W32.)
[With solemn rites approach the shrine.]

[Hope! Thou nurse of young desire.]
Thomas Augustine Arne, Love in a Village (London:
I. Walsh, n.d.), p. 7-8. (DLC, M1503.A74.L61.)
[In love should there meet a fond pair.]
Thomas Augustine Arne, Love in a Village (London:
I. Walsh, n.d.), p. 45. (DLC, M1503.A74.L61.)
[Water parted from the sea.]
Thomas Augustine Arne, The Overture, Songs.....
in the Opera of Artaxerxes (London: J.
Johnson, n.d.), p. 47-8. (DLC, M1503.
A74.A7.Case.)
[Thou like the glorious sun.]
Thomas Augustine Arne, The Overture, Songs....
in the Opera of Artaxerxes (London: J. Johnson,
n.d.), p. 43-45. (DLC, M1503.A74.A7.Case.)
[Let the bright seraphim in burning row.]
Handel's Songs...(London: I. Walsh, n.d.),
p. 39. (DLC, M2006.H15.W32.)
[See the Conquering Hero Comes.]
George Friedrich Handel, Judas Macchabeus
(n.p.: n.p., 1746), p. 162-63. (DLC, M3.
H21.[39-43].)

THANKSGIVING OF 1781.
  See: Who would have thought it?

1272   [That Power who form'd the unmeasured Seas.]
              IN:

930   [There was a little man/ and he woo'd a little
                maid.]
              IN:
              The Musical Miscellany...(Perth: J. Brown, 1786),
                p. 154-5. Song LXXXII. The Little Man and
                Maid. "There was a little man" (DLC, M1738.
                M798.Case.)

1323   [Think not lewd Jove.]
              IN:
              Midas, A Comic Opera (London: I. Walsh, n.d.),
                p. 8. Sung by Mrs. Stevens. "Think not
                lewd Jove." (DLC, M1503.M644.Case.)

              THOSE DAUGHTERS MOST CHARMING AND YOUNG (?)
                See: Medley.

              'TIS NOT YET DAY; or, Friend and Pitcher; or,
                Pitcher; or, The Silver Moon that shines so bright.

844   'Tis not yet Day.
              IN:
              THE PITCHER [London: Straight & Skillern, 1770?].
                "The Silver Moon that shines so bright,"
                [Miscellaneous Collection of 18th Century Songs
                Published at London, etc., #93.] (DLC,
                M1619.A2A1.)

1027; 919;   ['Tis Washington's Health, fill a bumper all
75; 1010   round.]
              IN:
              The Toast, composed by F. H. Esq. "'Tis
                Washington's Health, fill a Bumper all round;"
                [Copyright, 1931, Paul G. and Henry Woehlke.]
                (DLC, M1659.W384.Case.)
              A Toast Written and Composed by Fras. Hopkinson
                Esqr. (Philadelphia: B. Carr's Musical
                Repository, 1799?), p. 2. "'Tis WASHINGTONS
                Health fill a bumper all round." (DLC, M1639.
                W38.Case.)

1135; 1246	To all you ladies Now At Land.
	    IN:
	    The Merry Musician; or, A Cure for the Spleen,
	    Vol. I (London: I. Walsh, 1730), p. 38–40.
	    A Ballad by the late Lord Dorset, when at
	    Sea. "To you, fair Ladies, now at Land."
	    (DLC, M1740.M62.Case.)

903; 300	[The Tobacco Box: or, the Soldier's Pledge of
	    Love.]
	    IN:
	    [Samuel Arnold], The Tobacco Box or Soldier's
	    Pledge of Love, A Favorite Dialogue (n.p.:
	    n.p., n.d.). "Tho' the fate of Battle on
	    tomorrow waits" (GB/Lbm, G.297.(16).)

TRUE BLUE: or, From the East breaks the Morn.

425	True Blue.
	    IN:
	    The Muses Delight,...(Liverpool: John Sadler,
	    1754), p. 197. TRUE BLUE. The Words by Mr.
	    S.S. "I hope there's no Soul" (DLC,
	    M1619.A2M9.)
	    See: From the East breaks the Morn.

TURNCOAT: or, The Vicar of Bray.

318	Turncoat.
	    IN:
	    The Merry Musician; or, A Cure for the Spleen,
	    Vol. I (London: I. Walsh, 1730), p. 313–15.
	    The TURN-COAT. "Alack the Times so hard are
	    grown," (DLC, M1740.M62.Case.)
	    See: The Vicar of Bray.

524	[Vicar and Moses.]
	    IN:
	    CALLIOPE: or, The MUSICAL MISCELLANY (London:
	    C. Elliot & T. Kay, 1788), p. 60–62. The
	    Vicar and Moses. Song XXXIII. "At the sign
	    of the horse," (DLC, M1738.A2C2.)

THE VICAR OF BRAY: or, The Vicar of Brae; or,
    The Turncoat.

THE VICAR OF BRAY

319   [The Vicar of Bray.]   ("FOR George the Third I
              turn'd my coat,")

438; 101   [The Vicar of Bray.]   ("In George the second's
              golden days,")

1134   The Vicar of Bray.   ("IN good King George's
              golden days,")

1295; 1162   The Vicar of Bray.   ("In our dependent golden
              days,")

859   The Vicar of Bray.   ("WHEN Royal George rul'd
              o'er this land,")

              IN:
              The British Musical Miscellany, Vol. I (London:
                  I. Walsh, 1734), p. 30-32. The Vicar of Bray.
                  "In good King Charles's golden days." (DLC,
                  M1738.B864.)
              Henry Brown, Manuscript Book of Poetry and
                  Songs (1789), p. 28-31. The Vicar of Bray.
                  "Of Bray the Vicar long I've been" (NHi.)
              CALLIOPE: Or, The MUSICAL MISCELLANY (London:
                  C. Elliot & T. Kay, 1788), p. 284-86. The
                  Vicar of Bray. Song CLI. "In good King
                  Charles golden days,") (DLC, M1738.A2C2.)
              The Merry Musician; or, A Cure for the Spleen,
                  Vol. I (London: I. Walsh, 1730), p. 313-15.
                  The TURN-COAT. "Alack the Times so hard are
                  grown," (DLC, M1740.M62.Case.)
              The Merry Musician: or, A Cure for the Spleen,
                  Vol. IV (London: n.p., 1733), p. 5-7. The
                  Vicar of Bray. "In Charles the Second's Golden
                  Days," (DLC, M1738.A2.M4.)
              See: The Turncoat.

WATER PARTED FROM THE SEA.
    See: The Temple of Minerva.

THE WATRY GOD; or, The Watery God.

THE WATRY GOD

901   The WATRY GODS. ("AS bending o'er the azure
            tide,")
            See: Rule Britannia. ("As bending o'er the
              azure tide,").

305; 580;   [Watry God.] ("AS Mars, great God of battles! lay,")
599

892   The Watry God. ("KING Hancock sat in regal state")

581; 370   Watry God. ("The Stygian God, great Beelzebub.").

125; 44;   The Watry God. ("THE Watry God, great Neptune, lay")
517; 710

1382   The Watry God. ("WHEN Britain first, without a
            cause,")

            IN:
            The WATRY GOD &c. A Song Written on Lord Hawkes
              Victory over Conflans in 1759 (Dublin: John
              Lee, n.d.). "The Wat'ry God great Neptune lay"
              (GB/Lbm, H.1601.a.(102).)

283; 46;   Well met Brother Tar.
1047; 186;   IN:
258; 1383;
1234; 522;
603; 582

WELCOME WELCOME BROTHER DEBTOR.
       See: Hosier's Ghost; and, The Tempest.

WHEN BRITAIN FIRST, AT HEAVEN'S COMMAND.
       See: Rule Britannia. ("When Britain first,
        at Heaven's Command.)

1161   [When rous'd by the Trumpet's loud clangor to arms.]
        IN:

1098   [When the sheep were in the fauld, and the Ky
               were a' at hame.]
               IN:
               The Musical Miscellany (Edinburgh: n.p., 1786),
                  p. 10-11. Song VI. AULD ROBIN GRAY. "When
                  the sheep are in the fauld," (DLC, M1619.
                  M95.Case.)

1276   [When 'tis night, and the mid-watch is come.]
               IN:
               Fred. Aug. Hyde, A Miscellaneous Collection of
                  Songs, Ballads, Canzonets, Duets, Trios,
                  Glees & Elegies, Vol. 2? (London: Longman,
                  Clementi & Comp., n.d.), p. 108-110. The Mid
                  Watch. "When 'tis Night and the mid-watch is
                  come," (DLC, M1620.A2.H97.)
               The Vocal Enchantress...(London: J. Fielding,
                  1783), p. 110-111. Song LII. "When 'tis
                  night and the mid watch is come," (DLC,
                  M1738.A2.V84.)

1400   [When you censure the age.]
               IN:
               Mr. Gay and Dr. Pepusch, The Beggar's Opera
                  (London: W. Strahan, T. Lowndes, T. Caslon,
                  et al., 1777), p. 26, words, and p. 25-26,
                  music. Air XXX. How happy are we, &c.
                  "When you censure the age," (DLC. M1500.P39.
                  B3.)
               Dr. Pepusch, The Excellent Choice being a
                  Collection of the most favourite Old Song
                  Tunes...(London: I. Walsh, n.d.), p. 27.
                  Air 52. "When you censure the age." (DLC,
                  M1578.A2.P42.)

1361; 1072;   [Whilst happy in my native land.]
586   IN:
               F. H. Barthelemon, The Songs in the ELECTION
                  an Interlude...(London: J. Johnston, n.d.),
                  p. 10-11. "Whilst happy in my native land"
                  (DLC, M1513.B28.E5.)
               The Vocal Enchantress..(London: J. Fielding,
                  1783), p. 334-335. Song CLXVI. "Whilst
                  happy in my native land," (DLC, M1738.A2V84.)

77; 1218;   Who has e'er been at Baldock must needs know the
1176   mill.
                  IN:
                  Clio and Euterpe, or British Harmony, Vol. II
                     (London: John Welcker, n.d.), p. 1. The
                     Lass of the Mill. Sung by Mr. Beard. (DLC,
                     M1619.A2.C6.)

               WHO WOULD HAVE THOUGHT IT?: or, The Thanksgiving
                  of 1781.

213   Who would have thought it?
                  IN:

               WILKES'S WRIGGLE.
                  See: Abbot of Canterbury, or Wilkes's Wriggle.

881   [The Wooden Walls of England.]
                  IN:
                  AMUSEMENT for the LADIES.., Vol. II (London:
                     Longman & Broderip, 179-), p. 65-71. The
                     Wooden Walls of England. By Dr. Arne. "When
                     Britain on her sea girt shore," (DLC,
                     M1578.A56.Case.)

                              WORCESTER

967; 1253   [Worcester.] ("BEHOLD, array'd in light")

145   Worcester. ("THE Lord of Glory Reigns,")
                  IN:
                  Andrew Law, Select Harmony (Farrington: n.p.,
                     1779), p. 8. [Abraham Wood]. Worcester.
                     "How beauteous are their feet," (DLC, M2116.
                     L41.S9.)

488   ["THE world's a bubble and the life of man/ Less
                  than a span"]
                  IN:
                  VINCULUM SOCIETATIS, or the Tie of good Company...
                     The Second Book (London: T. Moore and J.
                     Heptinstall, 1688), p. 24. "The World's a
                     bubble" Mr. Richard Brown. (DLC, M1619.A2.V77.)

805   Would you have a young virgin of fifteen years.
                  IN:
                  The Beggar's Opera..(London: n.p., 1729), p. 21.
                     Air XXI. Would you have a young Virgin, &c.
                     (DLC, ML50.5.B3.1729.)

                  YANKEE DOODLE: or, Lexington March.

                              YANKEE DOODLE

1150; 407;   Yankee Doodle. ("CORNWALLIS led a country dance,")
62; 555

838   [Yankee Doodle.] ("From Lewis, Monsieur Gerard came")

872   [Yankee Doodle?] ("GOOD neighbors, if you'll give
                  me leave,")

840   [Yankee Doodle.] ("It was on Mr. Peroy's land,")

654; 1149;   [Yankee Doodle.] ("Ye loyalists all, within the
358; 212   town")

                  IN:
                  James Aird, ed., A Selection of Scotch, English,
                     Irish and Foreign Airs...Vol. I (Glasgow: n.p.,
                     1782), p. 36. #102. Yanky Doodle. (GB/Lbm, a.27.)
                  Edward Murphy, Manuscript (Newport, October 26,
                     1790), p. 1. Yanky Doodle. [Bound with Entire
                     new and Compleat Instruction for the Fife..
                     (London: Longman and Broderip, n.d.)].
                     (DLC, MT356.C62.)
                  Whittier Perkins, Collection of Dancing Tunes,
                     Marches and Song Tunes (1790), p. 4. Yankey
                     doodle. (NNC, Hunt/Berol Music.)
                  Thomas Walter, ed., The Grounds and Rules of
                     Musick Explained..(Boston: Barry Mecom, 1760),
                     p. 56. Yankey Doodle. (MB, M2116.W23.)
                  [Yankee Doodle.] (GB/Lbm, Add. Ms. 29371, #163.)
                  See: Lexington March.

825   [Ye hearts of Oak who wish to try.]
                  IN:
                  The British Tars (n.p.: n.p., n.d.). "Ye hearts
                     of Oak who wish to try." (GB/Lbm, H.1601.a.
                     (101).)

1263   [Ye lads of true Spirit.]
              IN:
              The Convivial Songster (London: John Fielding,
                 1782?), p. 172-3. Song LXXXV. "Ye lads of
                 true Spirit" (DLC, M1738.A2.C76.)
              The Songster's Museum (Northampton: Andrew
                 Wright, 1803), p. 90-1. The Toper. By G. A.
                 Stevens. "Ye lads of true spirit" (DLC,
                 M1628.S96.S6.Case.)

           YE MEDLEY OF MORTALS: or, The Masquerade Song.

                      YE MEDLEY OF MORTALS

342   [Ye Medley of Mortals.] ("COME rouse, brother
              Tories, the loyalists cry,")

1029; 1237; Ye Medley of Mortals. ("GIVE ear to my song, I'll
55; 572;   not tell you a story,")
611; 621;
529

              IN:
              William Defesch, Six NEW ENGLISH SONGS for the
                 Year 1749...(London: n.p., n.d.), p. 6.
                 The Masquerade Song. "Ye Medley of Mortals that
                 make up this Throng," (DLC, M1613.3.F41.
                 Case.)
              The Masquerade Song. Sung by Mr. Beard at
                 Ranelagh (n.p.: n.p., n.d.). "Ye Medley of
                 Mortals that make up this Throng," [A
                 Collection of Old English Ballads, p. 81.]
                 (DLC, M1740.A2C69.)
              The Muses Delight...(Liverpool: John Sadler,
                 1754), p. 201. The Masquerade Song. "Ye
                 Medley of Mortals" (DLC, M1619.A2.M9.)

           YET A WHILE.
           See: The Temple of Minerva.

512

Index of Eighteenth Century Sources from Which
Lyrics Were Reprinted
Numbers are main entry not page numbers. .
This list only includes those sources whose attribution
occured in the colonial newspapers.
Entry numbers are in chronological not numerical order.

206   American Journal. ("I'm not high church nor low
church, nor tory, nor whig,")

1211   American Magazine. ("PITY the sorrows of a poor
old man,")

1153; 334   Antigua Gazette. ("QUIDNUNC, my cronie, thou dost
look")

1284   Basseterre (in St. Christophers) February 5. ("WHEN
heaven, indulgent, bless'd this land,")

21   BINGLEY's London Journal. ("N[OR]th: THOU canker
wedded to my Breast,")

608   Boston. ("In a mouldering Cave, where th'
oppressed retreat,")

497; 166   Boston Evening Post, Feb. 13. ("THERE is a Nation
on the Earth,")

1060   BOSTON INDEPENDENT CHRONICLE. ("SWEET Billy,
precious, royal boy.")
             See: Rivington's Gazette
Independent Chronicle

505; 1200 British Publication. ("WELCOME, one Arnold, to
our shore;")
             See: [LONDON, A NEWSPAPER.]

111   Cambridge News-Paper. ("HARK! 'tis FREEDOM
that calls, come Patriots awake!")

1059; 503 Camp, Peeks-Kill, Oct. 18, 1781. ("While scenes of
transport, ev'ry breast inspire,")

387   Camp, White Plains, Sept. 1, 1778. ("COME and listen
my lads to sweet Liberty's lay,")

341   CHRONICLE of FREEDOM. ("FROM Heaven descends
sweet Smiling Peace.")
             See: Independent Gazetter.
Philadelphia Paper.

499   Connecticut Courant, Feb. 13. ("FAIR Ladies, 'tis
not very arch,")

517   Connecticut Courant. ("THE watry God, great Neptune,
lay")

Entry No.

216; 335	Freeman's Journal. ("O'ER the waste of waters cruising,")
412	FREEMAN's JOURNAL. ("THE dog that is beat has a right to complain,")
1311	Freeman's Journal, Philadelphia, July 10, 1782. ("OLD Judas the traitor (nor need we much wonder)")
564	Freeman's Journal. ("YOUR golden dreams, your flattering schemes,") See: (Pennsylvania) FREEMAN's JOURNAL.
690	Freeman's Journal. ("NO more my friends, of vain applause,")
568	Freeman's Journal. ("THE Indian Chief who, fam'd of yore,")
679; 714	Freeman's Journal. ("THE great unequal conflict past,")
1002	Gentleman's Magazine. (for April last.) ("LIKE a Newton sublimely he soar'd')
1209	Gentleman's Magazine. (London, June, 1778). ("THrice hallowed grace! that keep'st thy pow'r,")
15	Great-Barrington, 9th July, 1774. ("BEneath fair FREEDOM's banner, waving high,")
589	Halifax Paper. ("YE Yankies who Mole-like still throw up the Earth,")
561	INDEPENDENT GAZETTER. ("To years far distant, and to scenes more bright,")
509	Independent Gazetter. ("FROM heaven descends sweet smiling peace,") See: Chronicle of Freedom. Philadelphia Paper.
221	Independent Gazetteer, or the Chronicle of Freedom, Philadelphia. ("The old Tory rout")
201	Independent Ledger. ("YE Farmers all, with one accord,")
925; 1249; 633	[IRISH.] "A late Irish Paper." ("BY your leave, gossip John;")

Eighteenth Century Source Index

Entry No.

451   [LONDON, A NEWSPAPER.] ("Twelve struck the
                clock, Sedition's trump blew high")

456; 1186   [LONDON, A NEWSPAPER.] ("THE expences of war,
159; 1421   and corruptions of peace,")

749; 36;   [LONDON, A NEWSPAPER.] ("COME listen my cocks,
173; 513;   to a brother and friend,")
1436; 1226;   See: LONDON EVENING POST of March 14.
1190

1368   [LONDON, A NEWSPAPER.] ("WE came, we saw,
                but could not beat,")

988   [LONDON, A NEWSPAPER.] ("YE poor silly
                people, who foolishly think,")

578   [LONDON, A NEWSPAPER.] ("What discontents,
                what dire events")

521   [LONDON, A NEWSPAPER.] ("With Christmas Mirth,
                and Christmas Cheer,")

1273; 1028   [LONDON, A NEWSPAPER.] (of December 2, 1777.)
                ("GAGE nothing did, and went to pot,")

1118   [LONDON, A NEWSPAPER.] ("Behold! the Cerberus
                the Atlantic plough,")

394   [LONDON, A NEWSPAPER.] ("LET us take the road*!)
                (*Road of Spithead.)

825   [LONDON, A NEWSPAPER.] ("YE Hearts of Oak,
                who wish to try")

401   [LONDON, A NEWSPAPER.] ("THE Ministers bad,")

887   [LONDON, A NEWSPAPER.] ("AS for his Religion he
                could mix,")

1146   [LONDON, A NEWSPAPER.] ("OH! Old England,
                Old England;")

1215; 651   [LONDON, A NEWSPAPER.] ("Our troops by Arnold
                thoroughly were bang'd,")

552   [LONDON, A NEWSPAPER.] ("AS the papers inform
                us, a person of note,")

935; 217;   [LONDON, A NEWSPAPER.] ("WELCOME one Arnold
563   to our Shore,")
                See: [BRITISH, "Late British Publication."]

300   [LONDON, A NEWSPAPER.] ("THO' the fate
of battle on to-morrow wait;")

141   London Advertiser. ("I Sing of George's golden days,"
See: London General Advertiser.

411; 937   London Courant. ("OF great and glorious names to
speak,")

294   London Daily Advertiser. ("In vain BELLONA mounts
the Gallic Gun.")

293   London Daily Advertiser. ("Strange paradox among
the fowl;")

733   London Evening Post. ("And whither then is British freedom fled,")

737   London Evening Post. ("HARK! or does the indignant ear")
See: LONDON MAGAZINE.

738; 155   London Evening Post. ("GOD prosper long our
liberty,")

983   LONDON EVENING POST of March 14. ("COME listen, my
cocks, to a brother and friend,")
See: London Paper.

758   London Evening Post. ("OUR political wrong
heads, to shew themselves frantic,")

127   London Evening Post. ("SCOTCH Machiavel, in Tory
spleen grown old,")

129   London Evening Post, March 20. ("COME, my boys,
let us sing")

1029; 1237; London Evening Post. ("GIVE ear to my song, I'll
55; 572;   not tell you a story,")
611; 621;
529

635   London Evening Post of February 12. ("FROM Parlia-
ments venal, who barter our laws,")

131; 196   LONDON EVENING POST. ("ONCE more our Rulers call
a Fast,")

Eighteenth Century Source Index

Entry No.

1008; 1121; 1239; 574; 623; 613	London Evening Post.	("WHEN North first began,")
1122; 199	London Evening Post.	("YE poor simple people, who foolishly think.")
533; 291	London Evening Post.	("LET croaker's croak, for croak they will,")
388	London Evening-Post.	("IS there a word of magic found,")
390; 636	London Evening Post.	("TRUE Britons give o'er,")
295	London Evening Post.	("The common soldier who has broke") See: LONDON PACKET.
1133	LONDON EVENING POST.	("LOUD rumour speaks, "The French and Spaniards steer"")
1134	LONDON EVENING POST.	("IN good King George's golden days,")
1135; 1246	LONDON EVENING POST.	("TO all our countrymen at land,")
1147	LONDON EVENING POST (of July.)	("THEY, who content on earth to stay,")
402	London Gazette.	("YE Patriots, go on,")
1031	London General Advertiser of Jan. 6, 1778.	("WHY towards two Georges good, humane and great,")
393	London General Advertiser.	("'TWAS at the royal show, and grand display")
1156; 415	London General Advertiser.	("I Sing of George's golden days,") See: London Advertiser.
1254	London General Advertiser.	("LONG now has the God of Arms")
1022; 743; 165; 105; 1353	London Magazine.	("LOST is our old simplicity of times,")

1015; 315; 536	LONDON MAGAZINE. ("BRITANNIA was sick, for a sick, for a doctor they sent,")
471; 106	London Magazine, The, Oct., 1774. ("BRITONS, if you pant for glory,")
445	LONDON MAGAZINE. ("HARK! or does the indignant ear") See: London Evening Post.
945; 693	London Magazine, Jan., 1783. ("YE nations hear th' immortal tale---")
729; 152	London Mercury. ("Peace to thy royal shade, illustrious [KING]!")
162; 103	London Morning Chronicle. ("BY art and surprize, my Lord swears he'll succeed,")
1050	LONDON PACKET. ("The common soldier who has broke") See: London Evening Post.
1018	London Packet, or New Lloyd's Evening Post, of March 3, 1779. ("When our master, God bless him, ascended the throne,")
304	London Public Advertiser. ("HONOURS, like Sulpher, cure all Stains,")
913; 263	London Public Advertiser, May 21. (May 28?) ("TAX'D as we are beyond our strength,")
47; 996; 604; 1235; 1451; 190; 1271	(London) PUBLIC LEDGER. ("YE wrong heads, and strong heads, attend to my strains;")
1166	Londoner Morgen-Zeitung, vom 14ten May. ("Wofern ihr Obern Maechte")
949	Loudon's NEW-YORK PACKET, printed at Fishkill. ("YE sons of Mars attend,")
260	Maryland Gazette. ("The Morning air, my senses chear,")
144; 224	Maryland Gazette. ([Dearly beloved brethren], "JOYFUL days at length have come!")

Eighteenth Century Source Index

Entry No.

1160; 777   Maryland Gazette, July 4. ("AT length WAR's sanguine
             scenes are o'er;")
             See: New-Jersey Journal.

296; 545   Maryland Journal. ("I AM glad my dear John, now to
             find that some laws,")

630   Maryland Journal. ("WHEN Alcides, the son of Olym-
             pian Jove,")

82   Massachusetts Spy. ("E'Er since the day that Adam
             fell,")

85   Massachusetts Spy. ("PERMIT a giddy trifling girl,")

428; 494;   Massachusetts Spy (June 2, 1774.) ("O! 'twas a
617; 465   joyful sound to hear")

20; 1185;   MASSACHUSETTS SPY. ("YOUR Colonel H[ancoc]k by
1040   neglect,")

101   Massachusetts Spy. ("IN George the second's
             golden days,")

109   Massachusetts Spy. (March 17.) ("WHEN party-spirit
             prevail'd a pace,")

             Massachusetts Spy. ("SEVEN marks the trifle of the
             rising States,")
             See: Thomas's Massachusetts Spy.

             Massachusetts Spy. ("POOR Fellow - surely thou'rt
             an Ass,")
             See: Thomas's Massachusetts Spy.

169   MIDDLESEX JOURNAL. ("B[ute]! M[ansfield]! and N[orth]!
             need I point out the men,")

67   MIDDLETOWN, December, 1783.

450   MORNING CHRONICLE. ("YE Cliffs, where wide-
             resounding o'er the main,")

1221   Morning Chronicle. ("A Game Cock once, of English
             breed,")

1111   Morning Chronicle. ("YE stately Sisters!")

1112; 476;   Morning Chronicle, Aug. 3. ("O GREAT reverse of
1228   Tully's coward heart!")

Entry No.

Entry No.

684; 322; 204; 576; 627	Pennsylvania Gazette. ("HARK! hear the Trumpet's pleasing Sound!")
88	Pennsylvania Journal. ("ATTEND, ye Sons of Freedom, to the call,")
491	Pennsylvania Journal. ("AT length with generous indignation fir'd,")
544	Pennsylvania Journal. ("WHILE Nature reclin'd on the bosom of May,")
750; 115; 1192	Pennsylvania Magazine (for May, 1775.) ("BY my faith but I think ye're all makers of bulls,")
309; 454; 493; 421; 722; 616; 462; 81; 10	Pennsylvania Packet, Jan. 3, 1774. ("AS Near beauteous Boston lying,")
1408	Pennsylvania Packet. ("His royal majesty,")
90	Pennsylvania Packet. ("We men of coventry")
1411; 432	Pennsylvania Packet. ("WITH graceful air and vir- tuous mien,")
514	Pennsylvania Packet. ("WE are the troops that ne'er will stoop")
1011	Pennsylvania Packet (April 24, 1778.) ("AS late I travell'd o'er the plain,")
1013	Pennsylvania Packet. ("GALLANTS attend, and hear a friend")
646	Pennsylvania Packet. ("When virtue calls, enraptur'd we obey,")
134	Pennsylvania Packet. ("TWAS Arnold's post, Sir Henry sought,")
135; 328; 556	Pennsylvania Packet. ("'TWAS for the conquest nobly won,")
570	Philadelphia Paper. ("FROM Heaven descends sweet smiling Peace,")

(cont.)

Entry No.

813   Mr. Rivington's paper of 15th May, 1779. ("WITH-
OUT complaisance I appeal,")

1035   Roads-Town, Cumberland County, N.J., April 24.
("LET ev'ry age due honours pay,")

1168   Royal American Gazette. ("CONFINEMENT, hail! in
Honour's justest cause,")

1109; 1412;   St. James's Chronicle. ("OH MY baby, my baby,")
739; 95

1270; 1236   St. James's Chronicle. ("BY the Red Sea the Hebrew
host detain'd,")

   Say's (British) Journal.
   See: The Craftsman, or Say's (British) Journal.

1287   South Carolina Almanack. ("Behold the swift re-
volving Months disclose")

974   SOUTH CAROLINA and AMERICAN GENERAL GAZETTE. ("Behold the SOCIAL BAND appears!")

975   SOUTH CAROLINA and AMERICAN GENERAL GAZETTE.
("Boast not, Mortals, human Skill,")

1063   Talbot Court-House, dated Feb. 11th (letter). ("In
a chariot of light from the regions above,")
   See: Letter (Talbot Court-House, dated Feb. 11th).
Philadelphia, March 4 (Extract from a letter
from Talbot Court-House dated Feb. 12).

133   Thomas's Massachusetts Spy. ("SEVEN marks the trifle
of the rising States,")
   See: Massachusetts Spy.

587   Town and Country Magazine (for Oct., 1774). ("FREE-
MEN, if you pant for glory,")

1014   Town and Country Magazine. ("SINCE all must die as
well as I,")

834   Universal Magazine. ("Freedom, Peace, Plenty, all
in advance,")

Eighteenth Century Source Index

Entry No.

1038; 92   Virginia Gazette.   ("AMERICA! Thou fractious
                 nation,")

674; 403;   Virginia Gazette.   ("THOU who in glory's shining
686; 211;   track,")
1213; 1197;
548; 502

1137; 399;   WESTMINSTER COURANT, 25th January, 1780.   ("THERE
208   was, and a very great fool,")
                 See: London.

650   Westminister Magazine.   ("Of late the urchin God
                 of love")

829   WHITEHALL EVENING POST.   ("WEEP! Gallia, weep! thy
                 crested flow'rs")

73   YORKTOWN, December 20.   ("Genius of Freedom! whether
                 (sic) art thou fled?")

JOHN SHEYBLI,
ORGAN-BUILDER,
At Mr. Samuel Prince's, cabinet-maker, in Horse and
Cart-street, New-York;

MAKES, repairs and tunes all forts of organs,
harpfichords, fpinnets and Fortepianoes, on the
moft reafonable terms.

N. B. He has now ready for fale, one neat chamber
organ, one hammer fpinnet, one common fpinnet.

PART II
SONG BOOK

TABLE OF CONTENTS

Source of music follows title.

33. A SONG COMPOS'D BY A SON OF LIBERTY. 566
  Henry Brown, Manuscript Book of Poetry and Songs
   (1789), p. 15. British Granadier. "Vain Britons
   boast no longer" (NHi.)

1400. ANECDOTE of Sir ROBERT WALPOLE. 568
  Mr. Gay and Dr. Pepusch, The Beggar's Opera (London:
   W. Strahan, T. Lowndes, T. Caslon, et al., 1777),
   p. 26, words, and p. 25-6, music. Air XXX. How
   happy are we, &c. "When you censure the age,"
   (DLC, M1500.P39.B3.)

455. A SONG for the 5th of MARCH. 570
  The Origin of English Liberty. The Words by G. A.
   Stevens. Sung by Mr. Hudson. (n.p.: n.p., n.d.).
   "Once the Gods of the Greeks, at ambrosial feast,"
   (GB/Lbm, H.1994.a.(189).)

1341. The LIBERTY SONG. 574
  Come cheer up my Lads. Sung by Mr. Champness in
   Harlequin's Invasion (London: n.p., c. 1759).
   (DLC, M1526.B.Case.)

431. The glorious SEVENTY FOUR. 578
  Clio and Euterpe, or, British Harmony, Vol. III
   (London: John Welcker, n.d.), p. 66-67. A Choice
   Song sung by Mr. Champness. Set to Music by Dr.
   Boyce. "Come cheer up my Lads," (DLC, M1619.A2C6.)

443. A NEW SONG...Supposed to have been sung by Goody 582
  N---h, by way of Lullaby, to the foundling Popish
  Quebec-Bill.
  A New Song. For Young Mother's, & Nurses. (n.p.:
   n.p., n.d.). "Oh my Kitten, a Kitten," [A
   Collection of Old English Ballads, p. 100.] (DLC,
   M1740.A2C69.)

155. A PARODY on the SONG of CHEVY CHACE. 584
  Robert Bremner, arr., A Second Set of Scots Songs...
   (London: Preston & Son, n.d.), p. 28-29. Chevy
   Chase. "God prosper long our noble King," (DLC,
   M1746.B833T53.Vol. 2.)

436. An AMERICAN PARODY, on the old song, of "RULE 587
  BRITANNIA."
  Clio and Euterpe, or British Harmony, Vol. I (London:
   John Welcker, n.d.), p. 20-21. Rule Britannia. Set
   by Mr. Arne. (DLC, M1619.A2C6.)

435. LIBERTY SONG. 592
  Clio and Euterpe, or British Harmony, Vol. I (London:
   J. Welcker, ca. 1778), p. 1. Smile Britannia. A
   Favourite Song. (DLC, M1619.A2C6.)

757.   A JUNTO SONG.   618
               Thomas D'Urfey, ed., _Wit and Mirth: or, Pills to_
                  Purge Melancholy, Vol. III (London: n.p., 1719-
                  1720), p. 265-6. A SONG. "There was a Jovial Beggar."
                  (DLC, M1740.W78.1876a.)

1069.   A SONG. Composed at a Town-Meeting in Chester,   620
               Burlington county, July, 1774.
               Come cheer up my Lads. Sung by Mr. Champness in
                  Harlequin's Invasion (London: n.p., c. 1759).
                  (DLC, M1526.B.Case.)

36.   The SAILORS ADDRESS.   623
               Clio and Euterpe, or, British Harmony, Vol. III
                  (London: John Welcker, n.d.), p. 66-67. A Choice
                  Song sung by Mr. Champness. Set to Music by Dr.
                  Boyce. "Come cheer up my Lads," (DLC, M1619.A2C6.)

1361.   A SONG. From a new musical interlude called the   626
               ELECTION.
               F. H. Barthelemon, _The Songs in the ELECTION an_
                  Interlude... (London: J. Johnston, n.d.), p. 10-11.
                  "Whilst happy in my native land" (DLC, M1513.B28.E5.)

751.   An EXTEMPORE SONG, Composed in a Jovial Company.   631
               [J.C. Pepusch], _The Sailor's Ballad_. Sung by Mr.
                  Legar in Perseus and Andromeda (n.p.: n.p., n.d.).
                  "How pleasant a Sailors life passes," (DLC,
                  M1508.Case.)

1362.   FISH and TEA. A NEW SONG.   634
               Thomas D'Urfey, ed., _Wit and Mirth: Or, Pills to_
                  Purge Melancholy, Vol. IV (London: n.p., 1719-20),
                  p. 28. The Ballad of King John and the Abbot of
                  Canterbury. (DLC, M1740.W78.1876a.)

514.   The PENNSYLVANIA MARCH.   636
               The Vocal Enchantress... (London: J. Fielding, 1783),
                  p. 284-5. Song CXLI. "I winna marry ony mon but
                  Sandy o'er the Lee" (DLC, M1738.A2V84.)

475.   LIBERTY-TREE. A new song.   638
               The Origin of English Liberty. The Words by G.A.
                  Stevens. Sung by Mr. Hudson. (n.p.: n.p., n.d.).
                  "Once the Gods of the Greeks, at ambrosial feast,"
                  (GB/Lbm, H.1994.a.(189).)

954.   The GENIUS of AMERICA TO HER SONS.   642
               Clio and Euterpe, or British Harmony, Vol. III (London:
                  John Welcker, n.d.), p. 12-13. A Favourite Song in
                  the Opera of Eliza. (DLC, M1619.A2C6.)

120.　　　　A SONG. *Composed by a Soldier in the Continental*　　　646
　　　　　　Army.
　　　　　　A *Choice Collection of Favorite Hunting Songs set for*
　　　　　　the Voice... Book 1 (London: C. & S. Thompson, 1770?),
　　　　　　p. 10. Black Sloven. (GB/Lbm, G.302.)

1776

711.　　　　　　　　　　　　　　　　　　　　　　　　　　　　651

42.　　　　　THE AMERICAN HERO. - *A Saphic Ode.*　　　　654
　　　　　　Andrew Law, A *Select number of Plain tunes*... *(n.p.:*
　　　　　　Joel Allen, sculp., 1775?), p. 8. (DLC, M2116.L41.S5.)

915.　　　　A NEW LIBERTY SONG.　　　　　　　　　658
　　　　　　Henry Brown, Manuscript Book of Poetry and Songs
　　　　　　(1789), p. 15. British Granadier. "Vain Britons boast
　　　　　　no longer" (NHi.)

44.　　　　A *New* SONG. *The* WATRY GOD.　　　　　661
　　　　　　The WATRY GOD &c. *A Song Written on Lord Hawkes*
　　　　　　Victory over Conflans in 1759 (Dublin: John Lee, n.d.)
　　　　　　"The Wat'ry God great Neptune lay" (GB/Lbm, H.
　　　　　　1601.a.(102).)

1087.　　　A SONG.　　　　　　　　　　　　　665
　　　　　　Thomas D'Urfey, ed., Wit *and* Mirth: or, Pills *to*
　　　　　　Purge Melancholy, *Vol. IV (London: n.p., 1719-20),*
　　　　　　p. 28. The Ballad of King John and the Abbot of
　　　　　　Canterbury. (DLC, M1740.W78.1876a.)

991.　　　*New-Year's Verses, Addressed to the* CUSTOMERS *of* THE　668
　　　　　　PENNSYLVANIA EVENING POST, *By the* PRINTER's LADS
　　　　　　who carry it. Wed., Jan. 1, 1777.
　　　　　　The Muses Delight *(Liverpool: John Sadler, 1754),*
　　　　　　p. 152-3. A Loyal Song, for Two Voices. "God save
　　　　　　great George ye King." (DLC, M1619.A2M9.)

1777

1005.　　　A *new* SONG *composed by a prisoner in Boston jail.*　671
　　　　　　A *Choice* Collection *of* Favorite *Hunting* Songs *set*
　　　　　　for the Voice...*Book 1 (London: C. & S. Thompson,*
　　　　　　1770?), p. 10. Black Sloven. (GB/Lbm, G. 302.)

305.　　　A PARODY *on "The* WATRY GOD' --- *occasioned by General* 674
　　　　　　WASHINGTON's *late successes in the Jersies.*
　　　　　　The WATRY GOD &c. *A Song Written on Lord Hawkes*
　　　　　　Victory over Conflans in 1759 (Dublin: John Lee,
　　　　　　n.d.). "The Wat'ry God great Neptune lay" (GB/Lbm,
　　　　　　H.1601.a.(102).)

259.   The *SWEETS of LIBERTY*. *An Ode*.   678
                  Clio and Euterpe, or British Harmony, Vol. III
                      (London: John Welcker, n.d.), p. 12-13. A Favourite
                      Song in the Opera of Eliza. (DLC, M1619.A2C6.)

581.   The *FIERY DEVIL*. *In Imitation of the WATRY GOD*.   682
                  The WATRY GOD &c. A Song Written on Lord Hawkes
                      Victory over Conflans in 1759 (Dublin: John Lee,
                      n.d.). "The Wat'ry God great Neptune lay"
                      (GB/Lbm, H.1601.a.(102).)

47.   THE HEADS, Or, the Year 1776.   686
                  Thomas D'Urfey, ed., *Wit and Mirth: or, Pills to
                      Purge Melancholy*, Vol. IV (London: n.p., 1719-20),
                      p. 28. The Ballad of King John and the Abbot
                      of Canterbury. (DLC, M1740.W78.1876a.)

809.   The following *SONG* was compos'd by a loyal subject, 689
                  for the 4th day of June, 1777.
                  Clio and Euterpe, or British Harmony, Vol. I
                      (London: John Welcker, n.d.), p. 20-21. Rule
                      Britannia. Set by Mr. Arne. (DLC, M1619.A2C6.)

50.   On the Death of *GENERAL MONTGOMERY*.   693
                  A Choice Collection of Favorite Hunting Songs, Book
                      II (London: C. & S. Thompson, 1770?), p. 6-7. A
                      Favorite Hunting Song. Sung by Mr. Dearl at the
                      Grotto Gardens. Set by Rd. Bride. "Hark! hark the
                      joy inspiring Horn." (GB/Lbm, G.302.)

374.   PARODY.   696
                  Britannia or the Death of Wolfe (Edinburg: N. Steward,
                      n.d.). "In a moudering (sic) Cave a wretched retreat,"
                      (DLC, M1621.B.)

53.   A SONG. On the Surrender of Lieutenant-General   700
                  BURGOYNE and his Army, to Major-General GATES.
                  Yankee Doodle, or (as now Christened by the Saints
                      of New England) *THE LEXINGTON MARCH.* "Brother
                      Ephraim sold his Cow." (MB.)

375.   A NEW SONG.   703
                  The Muses Delight (Liverpool: John Sadler, 1754),
                      p. 152-3. A Loyal Song, for Two Voices. "God save
                      great George ye King." (DLC, M1619.A2M9.)

1779

850-854.   A MEDLEY for the LIGHT INFANTRY.   728
           A Favorite Medley for the Light Infantry (London:
             n.p., 1780?). "Soldier, whilst the flowing Bowl."
             (GB/Lbm, G.311.(152), incomplete.)
           A Choice Collection of Favorite Hunting Songs set
             for Voice...Book 1 (London: n.p., 1770?), p. 18-19.
             A Hunting Song Sung by Mr. Andrews at Sadlers Wells.
             "Away to the copse lead away" (GB/Lbm, G. 302.)
           Apollo's Cabinet: or the Muses Delight..., Vol. II
             (Liverpool: John Sadler, 1757), p. 190. Hosier's
             Ghost. Set by Mr. Handel. "As near Portobello lying"
             (DLC, M1738.A2A65.)
           The Beggar's Opera...(London: n.p., 1729), p. 45-46.
             Air LXIX. Lumps of Pudding. "Thus I stand like
             the Turk, with his Doxies around:" (DLC, ML50.5.
             B3.1729.)

324.   A NEW SONG.   744
           KATE and NED (n.p.: n.p., n.d.). "One night as Ned
             Crept into bed." (GB/Lbm, G.310.(229).)

1780

642.   The TIMES.   748

500.   A SONG, written by a Dutch Lady at the Hague, for   750
           the Americans at Amsterdam, July 4, 1779.
           The Muses Delight (Liverpool: John Sadler, 1754),
             p. 152-3. A Loyal Song, for Two Voices. "God save
             great George ye King." (DLC, M1619.A2M9.)

501.   Another Song written by a Dutch Gentleman, at   753
           Amsterdam, July 4, 1779.
           The Muses Delight (Liverpool: John Sadler, 1754)
             p. 152-3. A Loyal Song, for Two Voices. "God save
             great George ye King." (DLC, M1619.A2M9.)

1135.   SONG. Written by an Officer on board Sir CHARLES   755
           HARDY's Fleet.
           The Merry Musician; or, a Cure for the Spleen, Vol.
             I (London: I. Walsh, 1730), p. 38-40. A Ballad
             by the late Lord Dorset, when at Sea. "To you, fair
             Ladies, now at Land." (DLC, M1740.M62.Case.)

877.   THE LORDS OF THE MAIN.   757
           The Beggar's Opera... (London: n.p., 1729), p. 33-4.
             Lillibulero. (DLC, ML50.5.B3.1729.)

358.   A NEW-YORK ADDRESS.   793
         James Aird, ed., A Selection of Scotch, English,
             Irish and Foreign Airs...Vol. I (Glascow: n.p., 1782),
             p. 36. #102. Yanky Doodle. (GB/Lbm. a.27.)

383.   NEW SONG. Occasioned by the surrender of Earl Corn- 797
         wallis and his whole army, to General Washington.
         Thomas D'Urfey, ed., Wit and Mirth: or, Pills to
             Purge Melancholy, Vol. IV. (London: n.p., 1719-20),
             p. 28. The Ballad of King John and the Abbot of
             Canterbury. (DLC, M1740.W78.1876a.)

61.   CORNWALLIS Burgoyn'd. A SONG.   800
         Moggie Lawther or Margaret Lowther. (GB/Lbm, Add.
             Ms. 28371, #530.)

62.   THE DANCE, A Ballad.   805
         James Aird, ed., A Selection of Scotch, English,
             Irish and Foreign Airs...Vol. I (Glascow: n.p.,
             1782), p. 36. #102. Yanky Doodle. (GB/Lbm, a.27.)

660.   A NEW SONG.   808
         The Muses Delight (Liverpool: John Sadler, 1754),
             p. 152-3. A Loyal Song, for Two Voices. "God save
             great George ye King." (DLC, M1619.A2M9.)

925.   PADDY's ADDRESS to JOHN BULL, A new Ballad.   810
         Larry Grogan. (GB/Lbm, Add. Ms. 29371, #35.)

                          1782

335.   814
         The Muses Delight (Liverpool: John Sadler, 1754),
             p. 190. Hosier's Ghost. Set by Mr. Handel. (DLC,
         M1619.A2M9.)

411.   The GEORGES, a Song. On LORD GERMAIN's Promotion.   819
         James Aird, ed., A Selection of Scotch, English,
             Irish and Foreign Airs, Vol. I (Glascow: n.p.,
             1782-94?), p. 39. #111. Push about the Jorum.
             (GB/Lbm, a.27.)

337.   SONG On the celebration of the birth of the DAUPHIN. 822
         Henry Brown, Manuscript Book of Poetry and Songs
             (1789), p. 42-43. The Dauphin. "Ye sons of Mars
             attend," (NHi).

1263.   MORRIS's VOLUNTEERS. A NEW SONG.   824
         The Convivial Songster (London: John Fielding, 1782?),
             p. 172-3. Song LXXXV. "Ye lads of true Spirit"
             (DLC, M1738.A2C76.)

538

141.   WHO's the NOODLE. A NEW SONG.   826
              Ods' Blood who's the Noodle (London: Bland, 1780),
              "I sing of George's Golden Days," (GB/Lbm,
              G.309.(105).)

903.   The MUSICAL INTERLUDE of the TOBACCO-BOX: Or, The   830
            SOLDIER's PLEDGE of Love.
              [Samuel Arnold], The Tobacco Box or Soldier's Pledge
              of Love, A Favorite Dialogue (n.p.: n.p., n.d.).
              "Tho' the fate of Battle on tomorrow waits" (GB/
              Lbm, G.297.(16).)

                              1783

961.   835
              The Origin of English Liberty. The Words by G. A.
              Stevens. Sung by Mr. Hudson. (n.p.: n.p., n.d.).
              "Once the Gods of the Greeks, at ambrosial feast,"
              (GB/Lbm, H.1994.a.(189).)

967.   A HYMN on PEACE.   840
              Andrew Law, Select Harmony (Farrington: n.p., 1779),
              p. 8. [Abraham Wood]. Worcester. "How beauteous
              are their feet," (DLC, M2116.L41.S9.)

969.   New LIBERTY-HALL: A SONG.   845
              Liberty Hall (n.p.: n.p., n.d.). (GB/Lbm, H.1994.a.(76).)

971.   A SONG. On the wise Coalition compleated the 1st   849
            of April, 1783.
              Whittier Perkins, Collection of Dancing Tunes, Marches
              and Song Tunes (1790), p.38. Nancy Dawson. (NNC,
              Hunt/Berol Music.)

1162.   851
              The Merry Musician: or, A Cure for the Spleen, Vol.
              IV (London: n.p., 1733), p. 5-7. The Vicar of Bray.
              "In Charles the Second's Golden Days," (DLC,
              M1738.A2M4.)

716.   A favourite SONG in the new Farce called the BEST   854
            BIDDER.
              A Soldier for me, A Favourite Song. Sung by Mrs.
              Wrighton, in Best Bidder, at the Theatre Royal in
              Drury Lane. Composed by Mr. Hook. (London: S. A.
              & P. Thompson, n.d.). (GB/Lbm, H.1994d (27).)

146.   ODE, On the Arrival of their Excellencies General   861
            WASHINGTON and Governor CLINTON in New York, on the
            25th November, 1783.
              Clio and Euterpe, or, British Harmony, Vol. I (London:
              John Welcker, n.d.), p. 72. (DLC, M1619.A2C6.)

ABOUT THESE EDITIONS

    Editorial additions to the following songs have been made in order to facilitate modern performance. However, an attempt has been made to keep them to a minimum. Old cleffs and time signatures have been replaced by their modern counterparts. B♯ and E♯'s have been replaced by B♮ and E♮'s. Note and rhythm errors have been corrected and are so noted where they occur. Brackets have been used around words that have been added by the editor. Because the lyrics originally appeared without the music to which they were sung, text underlay is often a problem and sometimes a matter of personal choice. Extra musical notes have not been added to accomodate extra syllables but space has been left should the performer wish to add them. Specific changes in the music, not otherwise noted, are as follows:

Entry
No.

614.   *A SALE.*
       The repeat of the last four measures has been written out.

1323.   *PARODY...*
       The first repeat has been written out.

443.   *A NEW SONG.*
       The first repeat has been written out.

803.   *...jeu d'esprit...*
       The first repeat has been written out.

751.   *An EXTEMPORE SONG...*
       Music for lines 1-4 has been written out for lines 5-8 and chorus.

809.   *The following SONG...*
       The last four measures of music have been repeated.

850-4.   *A MEDLEY for the LIGHT INFANTRY.*
       The music for all the extra verses has been written out. The music missing from the defective British Museum copy has been supplied from other sources where and as noted.

877.   *THE LORDS OF THE MAIN.*
       The last four measures have been repeated.

925.   *PADDY's ADDRESS to JOHN BULL...*
       The first repeat has been written out.

411.   *The GEORGES.*
       The first repeat has been written out.

    Proper names are identified in the index, beginning on page 863.

May 10	*Parliament passes the Tea Act. The East India Company is allowed to export tea to the colonies without paying a regular duty.*
October 16	*Philadelphia citizens resolve that the tea duty is taxation without representation.*
November 30	*New York Sons of Liberty meet to consider the Tea Tax.*
December 16	*Boston Tea Party.*
December 17	*A New York city meeting votes that British Tea should not be landed.*
December 28	*Philadelphia "Tea Party." A large mass meeting in the city resolved that the tea ship, Polly should return to England with the tea. The captain "agreed," reloaded, and started back.*

1386-1394. ODE for the festival of St. JOHN EVANGELIST,
in South Carolina, 5772. By the Most Worshipful the Honourable Sir
EGERTON LEIGH, BARONET, GRAND MASTER, &c. &c. &c.
Set to music by brother PETER VALTON.

RECITATIVE.

BEHOLD the SOCIAL BAND appears,
Imparting joy, dispelling fears,
And wak'd by duty, and by choice,
Command the SONS of FREEDOM to rejoice.

SONG.

Boast not, mortals, human skill,
*   If the sculptur'd dome you raise,*
Works of art, by fancy's will,
*   Lead us oft through folly's maze.*
What if Phidias' chissel guide,
*   What if Titian's pencil grace,*
Marble flatters but our pride,
*   Bane of all the human race!*

RECITATIVE.

'Tis from the watchful culture of the mind,
A well directed soul, a sense refin'd,
That heav'nly virtues spring to grace the man;
This be our noble conflict, and our plan!

AIR.

Let the di'mond's lustre blaze,
*   Call its water bright and clear,*
But confess the greater praise
*   Rests on pity's tender tear.*
May the social virtues bind,
*   Tune each sympathetic heart,*
Raise the feeble, lead the blind,
*   Wipe the tear that swells to part.*

RECITATIVE.

Ye blessed MINISTERS above,
Who guard the good with purest love,
Propitious hear the notes of praise,
Whilst Britain's sons their voices raise.

(cont.)

542

AIR.

Blessings await this western land,
Blessings o'erflow with lib'ral hand,
Commerce uprears our infant state,
And golden currents make us great:
Fair science lifts her head, and cries
"I come to make you good and wise."
These be the glories of each day,
Marking our Monarch's gentle sway.

RECITATIVE.

Our SOCIAL BAND, by love and honour join'd,
Unite their zeal, as friends to human kind;
The mystic sense is out, the sign does move,
Behold the SIGN! peace, harmony, and love.

DUETTO.

Let the day be ever prais'd
When the ROYAL CRAFT was rais'd,
Let the SOCIAL VIRTUES shine,
Doing good is sure divine.

CHORUS.

Give the heroes all their due,
Twine their brows with laurels too;
But shall we no laurels find
For our love to human kind?
Let the SOCIAL VIRTUES shine,
DOING GOOD is sure DIVINE.

614. A SALE.

DAME Liberty's breaking up House,
  Rent and Taxes unable to pay,
The Fixtures and Goods to be sold,
  And the Premises clear'd in a Day.
She long for a Housewife was known,
  Kept the Furniture tidy and sound;
But the Servants so careless were grown,
  There's scarce a whole Thing to be found.
But right them and put them together,
  They'll save the next Comer Expence;
At least they'll do some Way or other;
  So, Neighbours, come lay out your Pence.
Here's the Chair that the Stewards have sat in,
  Who held the Court Leet in the Hall;
'Twill serve when the Star-Chamber's painted,
  To set up against the old Wall.
There's the *Clock & the Bell in the Tow'r,
  Old Graham ne'er finish'd a better;
So Time points the Hand to the Hour,
  So just is the Hour to the Letter.
This Lot, in such excellent Order,
  Should serve the great Man at Hayes,
To put him in Mind of his Nurse,
  And toll upon all hanging Days,
Or since, by unalter'd Records,
  It points out the Passage of Time;
It may go to C-------d, at my Lord's,
  And call up the Servants to dine.
Does none buy the Roll, **or great Chart,
  The Dame held most precious of all?
Take it then to the Son of her Heart,
  It may paper his Prison Wall.
Her Settlement Deed lies here too,
  When she wedded the Brittish King;
Set that up to Don Saltero,
  'Twill suit him like any Thing.
Here's a Cask of Virginia Tobacco,
  The last we may have of the Weed;
It's Ashes will heal in a Cracko,
  The Scab from beyond the Tweed.
Thus the Lotts are open before ye,
  And what may the Price of them be?
Why for Ridance and ready Money,
  Take the Lump at a Scotch Baubee.
                 R. D. C**LINGTON.

*This Clock and Bell was a Fine of Judge Ingham for altering a Record.
**Magna Charta.

614. A SALE

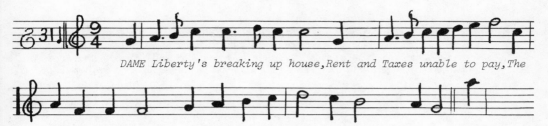

DAME Liberty's breaking up house, Rent and Taxes unable to pay, The

Fixtures and Goods to be sold, And the Premises clear'd in a Day. She

long for a Housewife was known, Kept the Furniture tidy and sound; But the

Servants so careless were grown, There's scarce a whole Thing to be found, But

right them and put them together, They'll save the next Comer Expence; At

least they'll do some Way or other; So, Neighbours, come lay out your Pence.

* ♪ in original

1176-1178.

LONDON. June 24. MUSICAL INTELLIGENCE EXTRAORDINARY.

In commemoration of the alliance between England, France and Spain a CONCERT of Vocal and Instrumental Music will speedily be performed at the COCKPIT, WHITEHALL.
          First Fiddle, Lord North.
          Concerto on the HUMSTRUM, Lord Apsley.
          A bloody March to St. George's Fields, on
             the TRUMPET, Lord Barrington.
          Solo on the JEWS HARP, Jerry Dyson.
          Royal Solo on the BAGPIPE, by the ----.

After the first Act, a Song in Praise of the King of France, set to Music by the late Duke of Bedford, will be sung by Hans Stanley. The Song is set to the Tune of "Who has e'er been at Baldock must needs know the Mill."

The first Stanza is as follows:

Who has e'er been at Versailles must needs know the King;
He's a very swarthy man, wears a very brilliant ring;
He has snuff-boxes in plenty and pictures to bestow,
As the Ministers of George the Third do very well know.

    After Act II. the following Air will be sung.

    AIR IN PRAISE OF HANOVER.

    Hanover, thou Land of Pleasure,
    Seat of ev'ry earthly Treasure,
Thou fost'ring Nurse of British Kings,
    To thee we owe our great Georgius,
    To thee his GRANNY not so pious,
Nor yet so much in LEADING-STRINGS.

    After Act III. there will be a grand Chorus, by all the Persons in Administration; the words as follow:

    Then here's to thee my Boy Jack,
    And here's to thee my Boy Gill;
    If we've plunder'd the Nation,
    To secure our Salvation,
We'll plunder her more and more still,
    Brave ROGUES,
We'll plunder her more and more still.

(cont.)

*When the Concert is over, Lord North will dance a HORNPIPE, in
order to exercise his limbs, in case he should ever be obliged
to cut capers in the air, for protecting an infamous alliance with
a state infamous in the annals of history, for its perfidy and
scandalous breach of faith.*

1176. MUSICAL INTELLIGENCE EXTRAORDINARY.

Who has e'er been at Versailles must needs know the King; He's a

very swarthy man, wears a very brilliant ring; He has

snuff-boxes in plenty and pictures to bestow, As the

548

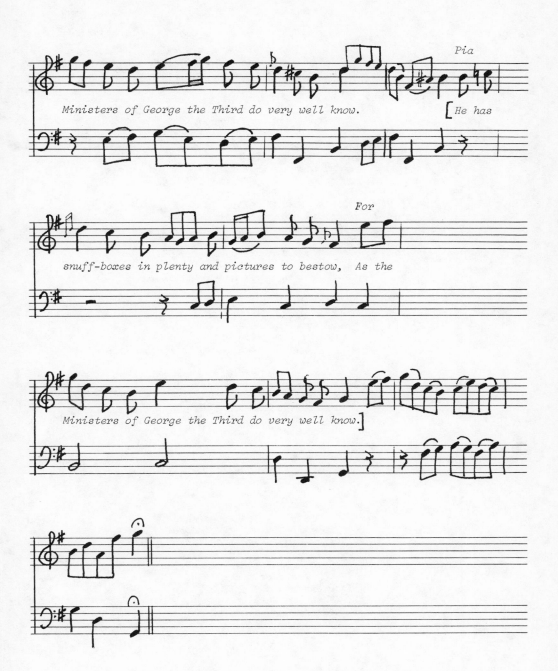

Ministers of George the Third do very well know.   Pia   [He has

snuff-boxes in plenty and pictures to bestow,   As the

Ministers of George the Third do very well know.]

1395. The CONSULTATION; a new BALLAD,
to the tunes of OVER THE WATER, &c JENNY DANG THE WEAVER,
and others, of equal dignity with the metre.

A NOISE was heard thro' all the land,
  Too loud to pass unheeded,
That put good people to a stand
  To think whence it proceeded.
Opinions were divided; men
  About it made the clatter
They make, in all discussions, when
  They're ignorant of the matter.
Coutts swore that, for a choice surloin,
  Th'Apollo was in pother;
But Shaw suppos'd that hounds and swine
  Were cursing one another.
Stark said old Nick was in the fowls;
  But Baker did assure us
It was an anthem of screech-owls,
  With ganders for a chorus.
Jones thought ten scissars-grinders come,
  To keep awake their betters,
Or serjeant, with a kettle drum,
  To beat for regulators.
M'Robert groan'd, that --- 'twas doomsday ---
  Woe, woe, to all deceivers!
But Gerard---holy brother, nay;
  'Tis marrowbones and cleavers.
A miller, with an ell of nose,
  Alarm'd at such a riot,
Conceiv'd his cogs and rounds at blows,
  Tho' late he left them quiet.
The clapboardman (that stopp'd his load
  To take a glass) with wonder
Imagin'd, on the stony road,
  His waggon acting thunder.
The Botetourt-men, they did freeze,
  And eke those of New London;
They whooping heard the Cherokees,
  And gave themselves for undone.
Two ships were thought, by those of York,
  Hot, off the Spit, in battle;
The ladies dropp'd their needle work,
  And oh! the cars did rattle.
As others had their notions, Sir,
  Forefend, in this dominion,
That even Lucian shou'd demur
  To hear my own opinion.--
                              (cont.)

That dulness, gorg'd with black ey'd peas,
  And feeling foul air rack her,
To give her suffering bowels ease,
  Did volley forth a cracker.
As echo, without bone or skin,
  Exists in verse Nasonian,
So does that fundamental din,
  Baptis'd the Muskitonian.
His great descent still in his mind,
  He deals in matters squalid,
And sedulous, at each behind,
  Announces births more solid.

                    D.C.

1395. THE CONSULTATION; a new BALLAD

A NOISE was heard thro' all the land, Too loud to pass un-

heeded, That put good people to a stand To think whence it proceeded.   O-

pinions were divided; men About it made the clatter They make, in all dis-

cussions, when They're ignorant of the matter.   [Opinions were divided Men a-

bout it made a clatter They make, in all discussions, when They're

ignorant of the matter.]

A PARAPHRASE of the LATIN POEM in the week before last paper, attempted.
To the TUNE of the ARCHBISHOP of CANTERBURY.

ALACK-a-day my muse has stray'd,
Good people, tell me, saw ye her?
  I'll sing ye how, if sh'ell but aid,
A poet trick'd a lawyer.

  The busy lawyer bawl'd aloud
To draw the people round him,
  Small jests he had to please the croud,
And truths he could confound 'em.

  For pelf and anarchy he roar'd,
(For lawyer's make a farce on-'s,)
  And government abus'd, and lord!
How ill he us'd the parsons.

  A poet in a corner sat
A fav'rite with Apollo,
  He shot his wit, and hit him pat,
And made the lawyer hollow.

  The lawyer saught another bard
That writes you songs and verses,
  He begs for help, and cries so hard,
And all the tale rehearses.

  Ten pounds I'll give O lend the muse,
I'll pay you and employ her,
  With biting satire pray abuse
Yon poet, says the lawyer.

  The muse was nettled to the quick,
More vex'd than I describe her,
  And whisper'd straight the bard a trick,
And bad him bite the briber.

  Says bard when I bring you the rime,
But pay the price before it,
  If there be fault in sense or chime
The price I will restore it.

  Agreed say both, the bard withdrew,
And brings unspotted paper,
  Here's nothing wrong, I told you true,
So you may bounce and caper.

(cont.)

> Duke Wharton sung the law so high
> That nought could e'er annoy her,
>   But here we find it all a lie,
> A poet tricks a lawyer.

236.

A PARAPHRASE of the LATIN POEM in the week before last paper, attempted.

ALACK-a-day my muse has stray'd, Good people, tell me,

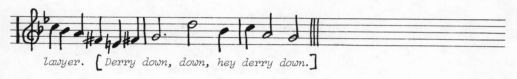

saw ye her? I'll sing ye how, if sh'ell but aid, A poet trick'd a

lawyer. [Derry down, down, hey derry down.]

1323. *PARODY of the first Song in MIDAS.*

GEORGE on his Throne,
Of the Seas great Don,
  With his Frown
  Fort and Town
  Shall subdue;
When on Board, with his Sword,
When on Deck, with his Beck,
He stand confess'd True Blue.

  Lord of the Main,
  He humbles France and Spain;
His Fleet, should it meet
With their Crew,
To the Deep, Man and Ship,
In a Heap, fast asleep, he would sweep,
Till they cry'd out---Morblieu!
  Squab Hollandeers,
  And lean Monsieurs,
He'd souce in briny Dew.

1323. PARODY of the first Song in MIDAS.

GEORGE on his Throne, Of the Seas great Don, With his Frown Fort and Town Shall subdue; When on Board, with his Sword, When on Deck, with his Beck, He stand confess'd True Blue. [The] Lord of the Main, He humbles France and Spain, His

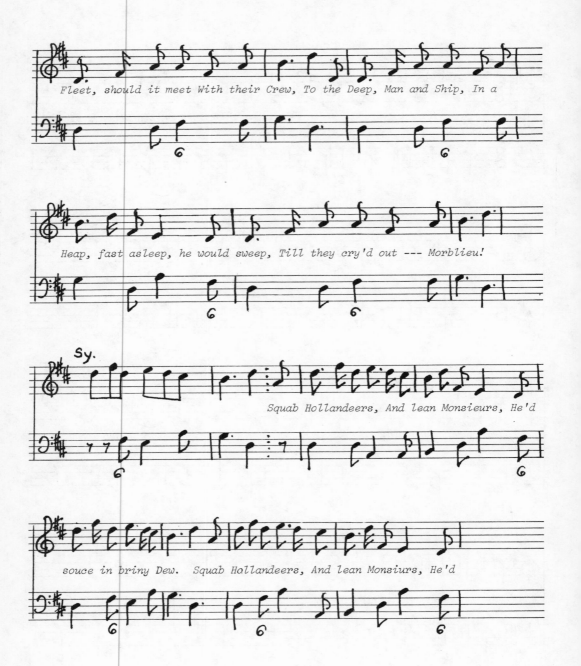

Fleet, should it meet With their Crew, To the Deep, Man and Ship, In a

Heap, fast asleep, he would sweep, Till they cry'd out --- Morblieu!

Sy.

Squab Hollandeers, And lean Monsieurs, He'd

souce in briny Dew. Squab Hollandeers, And lean Monsiurs, He'd

souce in briny Dew.

March 30   *Governor Hutchinson dissolves the Massachusetts General Assembly.*

March 31   *Boston Port Act. Parliament closes Boston Harbor until the city pays for the "Tea Party." First of the "Coercive" or "Intolerable Acts."*

April 22   *New York Sons of Liberty dump tea into harbor. This is the London Incident.*

May 13   *General Thomas Gage arrives in Boston to supplant Thomas Hutchinson as governor.*

May 17   *Freemen of Providence, Rhode Island call for an inter-colonial convention. This is the first such recommendation.*

May 20   *Massachusetts Government Act, part of the "Intolerable Acts." Virtually annulled Massachusetts Charter and prohibited town meetings without prior written consent of the Governor.*

                Quebec Act, regarded by the colonies as one of the "intolerable" measures. Centralized government of Canada under British control, granted religious toleration to Catholics (regarded in "Puritan" New England as a threat), and extended Canada's boundaries to the Ohio River, an area in which Virginia, Connecticut and Massachusetts had claims, thus reaffirming the Procla-mation of 1763's restriction of settlement west of the Appalachia.

June 1   *Boston Port Bill goes into effect. Boston harbor closed; General Court moved to Salem. Many of the colonies solemnized this day with fasting and prayer.*

June 2   *Quartering Act applied to all the colonies. It legalized the quartering of troops not only in taverns and deserted buildings, but also in occupied dwellings.*

September 1   *British troops under General Gage march out to Charlestown and Cambridge and seize powder and cannon belonging to the province.*

September 5   *First Continental Congress convenes in Philadelphia.*

September 9   *Suffolk Resolves (calling for immediate revolutionary activity) drawn up; in response to General Gage's recent fortifications and troop additions in and around Boston.*

September 22 *Congress votes for non-importation of British goods.*

December 14 *Patriots seize Fort William and Mary at Portsmouth, N.H.*

432.

From the Pennsylvania Packet.

Having fixed up a little poetical lath, I send you a few of the shavings that were last turned off, that you may see what sort of materials I work up, and if you have any orders for anything in my way I hope to supply you on the most reasonable terms, in any form, whether political, moral, whimsical, physical, or lovesical, at my lodgings in Garret-lane, towards Sky-hill, where constant attendance and kind words will be given by

TOM GINGLE.

1.
WITH graceful air and virtuous mein,
  AMERICA rises to the view;
Expands her arms, invites the swain
  To bid BRITANNIA's shore adieu.
2.
She points where tow'ring forests wave;
  Where boundless tracts yet unexplor'd
Await the landing of the brave;
  Where food and shelter she'll afford.
3.
HIBERNIA's sons, in shackled state,
  With all the woes of abject slaves,
Receive from her a new-born fate,
  And tempt the danger of the waves,
4.
The Highland lads with bonnets blue
  And Tartan plads, attend her call;
Whole clans embark'd, their Lairds may rue,
  Her Western climes invite them all.
5.
The sons of TAFFY too shall hear,
  That fertile Welch like mountains rise;
That Leeks will grow and Goats appear
  Beneath her distant western skies.
6.
The main shall foam, the billows yield
  To plowing barks from every coast.
The thing's decreed, and fate has seal'd
  That here shall land a num'rous host.
7.
Aghast BRITANNIA shall descry
  The Western tow'rs and stately piles,
Which rise expandant to her eye,
  And spread beneath fair fortune's smiles.

(cont.)

8.

Extensive plains and green-grown meads;
  Golden crops and luscious fruit;
Lowing herds and gallant steeds;
  The lofty horn and softer lute.

9.

These, these shall meet BRITANNIA's eye:
  These, these shall strike BRITANNIA's ear.
And will my native sons, too, fly!
  Behold BRITANNIA drops a tear.

10.

My hamblets(sic) thin, my cities mourn;
  My fields and plains remain untill'd;
My flocks they bleat---remain unshorn,
  And wander round the bry'r-grown field.

11.

The vale which once the oaten reed,
  The pleasing sound, pass'd sweetly thro';
Where shepherds taught their flocks to feed--
  Where milk-maids sought the friendly dew---

12.

These, these are still--no notes are heard---
  A solemn silence reigns around--
These scenes, by love so oft endear'd,
  Shall hear no more the plaintive sound.

13.

With painful step, in anxious mood,
  She bends her sad and mournful way,
To view yon ground where Sheffield stood---
  Sheffield, where Vulcan bore the sway.

14.

But ah! behold a sky serene!
  No sulph'rous cloud o'er hangs the vale;
No swarthy race compose the scene;
  No hammer's sound disturbs the dale.

15.

No more shall Donn's obstructed flood
  Dash thro' the rattling whirling wheel:
Unseen, unheard, its torrent rude
  No more shall pond'rous burthen feel.

16.

Distress'd she turns her wat'ry eye,
  From scenes like these so big with woes,
To Leeds--to Wakefield--still a sigh
  Swells from her heart where'er she goes.

                              (cont.)

562

17

The weavers beam---the shuttle too,
  Alike forlorn neglected stand;
The busy throng no more in view;
  No more the fleecy rolls expand.

18.

All, all deserted--all are fled--
  Alas, BRITANNIA must resign;
'Tis Heaven's vengeance on thy head,
  For some black crime--some fault of thine.

10. *From the PENNSYLVANIA PACKET. A NEW SONG.*
To the plaintive tune of Hosier's Ghost.

As near beauteous BOSTON lying
   On the gentle swelling flood,
Without jack or pendant flying
   Three ill fated Tea ships rode:
2. Just as glorious Sol was setting,
   On the wharf a numerous crew,
SONS of FREEDOM, fear forgetting,
   Suddenly appear'd in view.
3. Arm'd with hammer, ax and chissels,
   Weapons new for warlike deed,
Towards the herbage freighted vessels,
   They approach'd with dreadful speed.
4. O'er their heads aloft in mid sky,
   Three bright Angel forms were seen;
This was HAMPDEN, That was SIDNEY,
   With fair LIBERTY between.
5. "Soon they cry'd, your foes you'll banish,
   "Soon the triumph shall be won;
"Scarce shall setting Phoebus vanish,
   "'Ere the deathless deed be done."
6. Quick as thought the ships were boarded,
   Hatches burst and chests display'd;
Axes, hammers, help afforded;
   What a glorious crash they made!
7. Squash into the deep descended
   Cursed weed of China's coast---
Thus at once our fears were ended;
   British rights shall ne'er be lost.
8. Captains! once more hoist your streamers,
   Spread your sails, and plow the wave!
Tell your masters they were dreamers,
   When they thought to cheat the BRAVE.

BRITTANNO AMERICANUS
Philadelphia, January 1, 1774.

10. A NEW SONG.

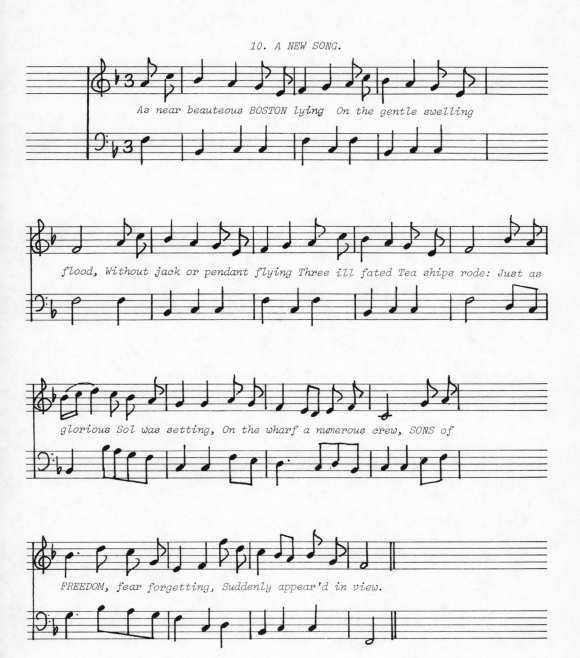

As near beauteous BOSTON lying On the gentle swelling

flood, Without jack or pendant flying Three ill fated Tea ships rode: Just as

glorious Sol was setting, On the wharf a numerous crew, SONS of

FREEDOM, fear forgetting, Suddenly appear'd in view.

33. A SONG COMPOS'D BY A SON OF LIBERTY.
FEBRUARY 13, 1770. (To the tune of the BRITISH GRANADIER.)

THAT Seat of Science Athens, and Earths great Mistress Rome
Where now are all their Glories, we scarce can find their Tomb:
Then guard your Rights, AMERICANS! nor stoop to lawless Sway,
Oppose, oppose, oppose, oppose---my brave America.

Proud Albian bow'd to Caesar, & num'rous Lords before,
To Picts, to Danes, to Normans, & many masters more:
But we can boast Americans! we never fell a Prey;
Huzza, Huzza, huzza, huzza, for a brave America.

We led fair Freedom hither, when lo the Desart, smil'd,
A Paradise of pleasure, was open in the Wild;
Your Harvest bold Americans! no power shall snatch away,
Assert yourselves, yourselves, yourselves, my brave America.

Torn from a world of Tyrants, beneath this western Sky,
We form'd a new Dominion, a Land of Liberty;
The World shall own their Masters here, then hasten on the Day,
Huzza, huzza, huzza, huzza for brave America.

GOD bless this maiden Climate, and thro' her vast Domain,
Let Hosts of Heroes cluster who scorn to waer(sic) a chain:
And blast the venal sycophants who dares our rights betray,
Preserve, preserve, preserve, preserve my brave America.

Lift up your heads my Heroes! and swear with proud disdain,
The Wretch who would enslave you, shall spread his snares in vain;
Should Europe empty all her force, wou'd meet them in array,
And shout, and shout, and shout, and shout for brave America.

Some future day shall crown us the masters of the main,
And giving laws and freedom, to subject France & Spain,
When all the Isles o'er Ocean spread, shall tremble and obey,
Their Lords, their Lords, their Lords, their Lords of brave America.

33. A SONG COMPOS'D BY A SON OF LIBERTY.

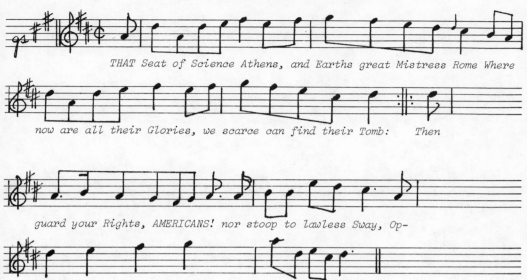

THAT Seat of Science Athens, and Earths great Mistress Rome Where

now are all their Glories, we scarce can find their Tomb: Then

guard your Rights, AMERICANS! nor stoop to lawless Sway, Op-

pose, oppose, oppose, oppose --- my brave America.

1400. ANECDOTE of Sir ROBERT WALPOLE.

DURING the run of the Beggar's Opera, soon after its first representation, Sir Robert sat in the stage box; and when Lockit came to the masterly song,

> (When you censure the age
> Be cautious and sage,
>   Lest the courtiers offended should be;
> If you mention vice or bribe,
> 'Tis so pat to all the tribe,
>   That each cries that was levell'd at me)

An universal encore attended the performance, and the eyes of the audience were immediately fixed upon Sir Robert, against whose conduct Gay is said to have taken up his pen. The courtier, however, with great presence of mind, joined heartily in the plaudit, and encored it a second time, with his single voice; which not only blunted the poet's shaft, but gained a general huzza from the audience.

1400. ANECDOTE of Sir ROBERT WALPOLE.

(When you censure the age Be cautious and sage, Lest the

courtiers offended should be;   If you mention vice or bribe, 'Tis so

pat to all the tribe, That each cries that was levell'd at me.)

455. A SONG for the 5th of MARCH.
To the Tune of Once the Gods of the Greeks, &c.

I.

WHEN the Foes of the Land, our Destruction had plan'd
  They sent ragged TROOPS for our Masters:
But from former Defeat they must now understand,
  Their Wolves shall not prowle in our PASTURES.

II.

Old History shows, and AMERICA knows,
  That Tyrants make Carnage their Food;
But that we will oppose all such insolent Foes;
  Experience hath wrote it in Blood.

III.

No Traitor to come, as we dare to presume,
  Will solicit an Army for BOSTON;
New-England's brave HEROES denounce their sad Doom
  That Britain will mourn she has lost one.

IV.

By the Banner of Freedom determin'd we'll stand,
  Waving high o'er our Countrymens Graves;
From the deep Vault of Death they give forth the Command
  "Revenge us, or live to be Slaves."

V.

Awaken'd; we learn, 'tis a common Concern,
  All AMERICA swarms to the Field;
Not a Coward that wastes one mean Tho't on his Life
  Not a Wretch that has Life, and would yield.

VI.

Blest FREEDOM's the Prize, thither bend all their Eyes
  Stern Valour each Visage inflames;
The Lands they have won, and still Claim as their own,
  And no tyrant shall ravish their Claims.

VII.

A Ray of bright Glory now Beams from afar,
  Blest dawn of an EMPIRE to rise;
The AMERICAN Ensign now sparkles a Star,
  Which shall shortly flame wide thro' the Skies.

VIII.

Strong knit is the Band, which unites the blest Land,
  No Daemon the Union can sever;
Here's a Glass to fair Freedom, come give us your Hand;
  May the ORATOR flourish for ever.

570

455. A SONG for the 5th of MARCH.

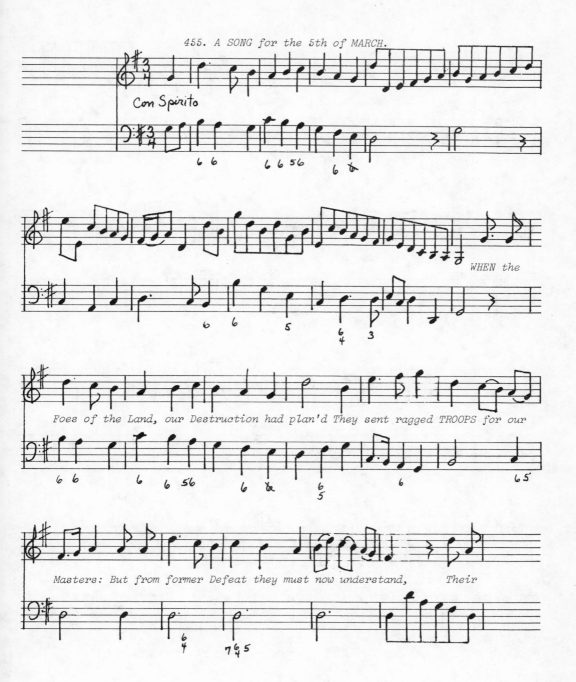

Con Spirito

WHEN the Foes of the Land, our Destruction had plan'd They sent ragged TROOPS for our Masters: But from former Defeat they must now understand, Their

571

Wolves shall not prowle in our PASTURES. *Sy*

Old History shows, and AMERICA knows, That Tyrants make Carnage their

Food; But that we will oppose all such insolent Foes; Experience hath

wrote it in Blood. [Ex-

perience hath wrote it in Blood.]

1341. The LIBERTY SONG.

COME join Hand in Hand, brave Americans all,
And rouse your bold Hearts at fair Liberty's call;
No tyrannous Act shall suppress your free Claim,
Nor stain with Dishonour America's Name.
In Freedom we're born, and in Freedom we'll live;
  Our Purses are ready,
  Steady, Friends, steady,
Not as Slaves but as Freemen, our Money we'll give,

Our worthy Forefathers (let's give them a Cheer)
To Climates unknown did courageously steer,
Through Oceans to Deserts for Freedom they came,
And dying bequeath'd us their Freedom and Name.
  In Freedom, &c.

Their generous Bosoms all Dangers despis'd,
So highly, so wisely, their Birthrights they priz'd:
We'll keep what they gave, we will piously keep,
Nor frustrate their Toils on the Land and the Deep.
  In Freedom, &c.

The Tree their own Hands had to Liberty rear'd
They liv'd to behold growing strong and rever'd;
With Transport they cry'd, now our Wishes we gain,
For our Children shall gather the Fruits of our Pain.
  In Freedom, &c.

Swarms of Placemen and Pensioners soon will appear,
Like Locusts, deforming the Charms of the Year;
Suns vainly shall rise, Showers vainly descend,
If we are to drudge for what others shall spend.
  In Freedom, &c.

Then join Hand in Hand, brave Americans all,
By uniting we stand, by dividing we fall;
In so righteous a Cause let us hope to succeed,
For Heaven approves of each generous Deed.
  In Freedom, &c.

All Ages shall speak with Amaze and Applause,
Of the Courage we'll show in Support of our Laws;
To die we can bear, but to serve we disdain,
For Shame is to Freemen more dreadful than Pain.
  In Freedom, &c.

(cont.)

This Bumper I crown for our SOVEREIGN's Health,
And this for BRITANNIA's Glory and Wealth;
That Wealth and that Glory immortal may be,
If she is but just, and AMERICANS free;
* In Freedom we're born, and in Freedom we'll live;*
*   Our Purses are ready,*
*   Steady, Friends, steady,*
* Not as Slaves, but as Freemen, our Money we'll give.*

1341. The LIBERTY SONG.

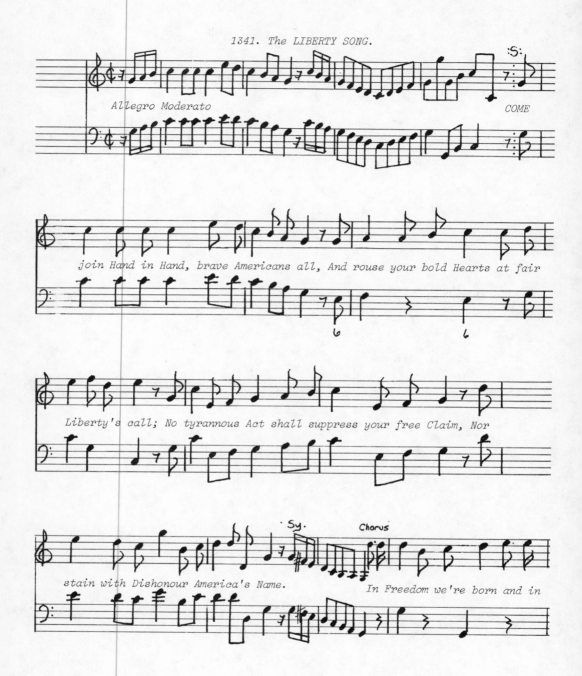

Allegro Moderato

COME

join Hand in Hand, brave Americans all, And rouse your bold Hearts at fair

Liberty's call; No tyrannous Act shall suppress your free Claim, Nor

stain with Dishonour America's Name.

In Freedom we're born and in

576

Freedom we'll live; Our Purses are ready, Steady, Friends, steady, Not as

Slaves but as Freemen, our Money we'll give,

From the NEW-YORK JOURNAL. The glorious SEVENTY FOUR.
A NEW SONG. Tune of Hearts of Oak.

1.

COME, come, my brave boys, from my song you shall hear,
That we'll crown seventy-four, a most glorious year;
We'll convince Bute and Mansfield, and North, though they rave,
Britons still like themselves, spurn the chains of a slave.
                    CHORUS.
    Hearts of oak were our sires,
    Hearts of oak are their sons,
    Like them we are ready, as firm and as steady,
    To fight for our freedom with swords and with guns.

2.

Foolish elves to conjecture by crosing of mains,
That the true blood of freemen would change in our veins,
Let us scorch, let us freeze, from the line to the pole,
Britain's sons still retain all their freedom of soul.
                        Hearts of oak were our sires, &c.

3.

See--our rights to invade, Britain's dastardly foes,
Sending Hysons and Congoes, did vainly suppose,
That poor shallow pates, like themselves were grown,
And our hearts were as servile and base as their own.
                        Hearts of oak were our sires, &c.

4.

Their tea still is driven away from our shores,
Or presented to Neptune, or rots in our stores;--
But to awe, to divide, till we crouch to their sway,
On brave Boston, their vengeance--they fiercely display.
                        Hearts of oak were our sires, &c.

5.

Now, unask'd, we unite, we agree to a man,
See our stores flow to Boston, from rear and from van;
Hark, the shout, how it flies, freedom's voice, how it sounds!
From each country, each clime; hark, the echo rebounds!
                        Hearts of oak were our sires, &c.

6.

Across the Atlantick,--so thund'ring the roar,
It has rous'd Britain's genius, who dos'd on his shore---
Who has injur'd my sons, my brave boys o'er the main;
Whose spirits to vigour it renews me again!
                        Hearts of oak were our sires, &c.

(cont.)

7.

With sons whom I foster'd and cherish'd of yore,
Fair freedom shall flourish till time is no more;
No tyrant shall rule them,---'tis Heaven's decree,
They shall never be slaves, while they dare to be free.
   Hearts of oak were our sires,
   Hearts of oak are their sons,
   Like them we are ready, as firm and as steady,
   To fight for our freedom with swords and with guns.

431. The glorious SEVENTY FOUR.

Allegro Moderato

COME, come, my brave boys, from my song you shall hear, That we'll crown seventy-four, a most glorious year; We'll convince Bute and Mansfield & North, though they rave, Britons still like themselves, spurn the

chains of a slave. Hearts of oak were our sires, Hearts of

oak are their sons, Like them we are ready, as firm and as steady, To

fight for our freedom with swords and with guns.

To the Tune of---O my Kitten, my Kitten.
Supposed to have been sung by Goody N---h, by way of Lulla-by,
to the foundling Popish Quebec-Bill.

I.

O MY baby, my baby,
    And O my baby, my deary,
And was its papa ashamed
    To own this bantling here-e;
My dear little Popish puppet,
    So like its dad Lord B---te-e,
O naughty papa to drop it,
    And the B----ps all sit mute-e.
        Then up with the Papists, up, up,
            And down with the Protestants down-e;
        Here we go backwards and forwards,
            And all for the good of the crown-e.

II.

And we will have gossops in store,
    And Reverend B----ps to bless it,
Lord Chatham shall teaze it no more,
    But let my majority dress it;
That you shall have plenty of clouts,
    The Bishops will tear their lawn sleeve-e,
Then be no more child in the pouts,
    Hush, hushy my baby, what grieve-e?
        Then up with, &c.

III.

Then down with the fam'd reformation,
    Each church, each chapel and meeting;
While I'm overseer of the nation,
    I'll cherish and foster my sweeting;
Then heigh for the fine wooden shoes,
    And heigh for cock-horse to ride-e,
And heigh for processions and shews,
    And heigh for a Smithfield fire-side-e.
        Then up with, &c.

IV.

Then heigh for the penance and pardons,
    And heigh for the faggots and fires,
And heigh for the Popish church wardens,
    And heigh for the Priests and the friars,
And heigh for the Raree-shew relicts,
    To follow my Canada bill-e,
With all the Pope's Mountebank tricks,
    So prithee my baby lie still-e,
        Then up with, &c.

443. A NEW SONG...*Supposed to have been sung by Goody N---h, by way of Lulla-by, to the foundling Popish Quebec-Bill.*

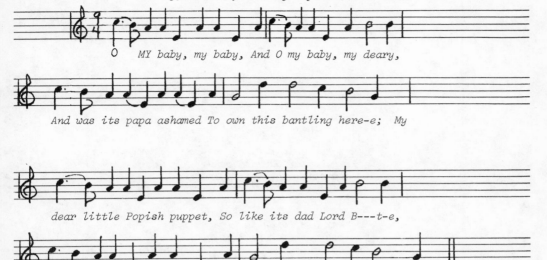

O MY baby, my baby, And O my baby, my deary,

And was its papa ashamed To own this bantling here-e; My

dear little Popish puppet, So like its dad Lord B---t-e,

O naughty papa to drop it, And the B----ps all sit mute-e. Then

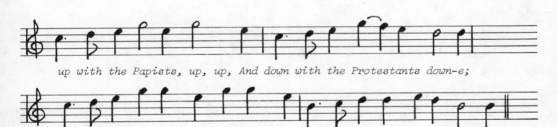

up with the Papists, up, up, And down with the Protestants down-e;

Here we go backwards and forwards, And all for the good of the crown-e.

155. *From the LONDON EVENING POST.*
A PARODY on the SONG of CHEVY CHACE.

GOD prosper long our liberty,
  Our lives and safeties all;
A woeful statute once there did
  In Parliament befal.
To drive true faith out of the land,
  Lord M--sf---d plann'd the way;
The child may rue that is unborn,
  The voting of that day.
Also the Thane, or Earl B---e,
  A vow to God did make,
His pleasure in tyrannic deeds,
  Three summer days to take:
The dearest rights of Englishmen
  To seize and take away.
The tidings to Earl Chatham came,
  In th'country where he lay.
Who sent his Lordship present word
  He would prevent his sport,
The Scottish Thane, not fearing this,
  Did to the house resort:
With fifteen score of placemen bold,
  All chosen rogues of power,
Who knew full well by ways and means,
  Their country to devour.
They swiftly ran unto the house,
  Our liberties to take;
And with their noise and babbling there,
  An echo shrill did make.
Earl Chatham enter'd then the doors,
  Much like a baron bold;
Came foremost of his company,
  With conscience pure as gold.
Shew me, said he, the reason why
  You vote so boldly here
Away the rights of Englishmen,
  Their liberties so dear:
Before you shall enthral us all,
  With arbitrary power,
And popish acts of Parliament,
  In an ill-fated hour;
We'll surely spend our dearest blood,
  Your party chiefs to slay;
And on the block their destin'd heads,
  Most certainly will lay.
                              (cont.)

He ceas'd: --- *They put it to the vote,*
  If popery should be
Th' establishment, and carried it;
  So did the fates decree.
O Christ! it was a grief to see,
  And likewise for to hear,
The groans of men when this was past,
  By George our King so dear.
A future Parliament we hope,
  On them will vengeance take;
And be revenged on them all,
  For true religion's sake.
God save the King, and bless the land,
  In plenty, joy, and peace;
And grant henceforth that popery
  And slavery may cease.

155. A PARODY on the SONG of CHEVY CHACE.

GOD prosper long our liberty, Our lives and safeties all; A

woeful statute once there did In Parliament befal. To drive true faith out

of the land, Lord M--sf---d plann'd the way; The child may rue that

is unborn, The voting of that day.

436.
Parnassian Packet. An AMERICAN PARODY, on the old song,
of "RULE BRITANNIA."

I.
"WHEN Britons first, by Heaven's command,
"Arose from out the azure main,
"This was the charter of the land,
"And guardian angels sung this strain:
"Rule Britannia, rule the waves,
"Britons never will be slaves."
II.
To spread bright freedom's gentle sway,
Your isle too narrow for its bound,
We trac'd wild Ocean's trackless way,
And here a safe asylum found.
Rule Britannia, rule the waves,
But rule us justly--not like slaves.
III.
While we were simple, you grew great;
Nor swell'd with luxury and pride,
You pierce our peaceful free retreat,
And haste t'enslave with Giant-stride.
Rule Britannia, rule the waves,
But rule us justly--not like slaves.
IV.
"Thee haughty tyrants ne'er could tame;
"All their attempts to pull thee down,
"Did but arouse thy gen'rous flame,
"And work their woe and thy renown.
"Rule Britannia, rule the waves,
"Britons then would ne'er be slaves.
V.
Let us, your sons, by freedom warm'd,
Your own example keep in view,--
'Gainst TYRANNY be ever arm'd,
Tho' we our TYRANT find--in you.
Rule Britannia, rule the waves,
But never make your children slaves.
VI.
With justice and with wisdom reign,
We then with thee will firmly join,
To make thee mistress of the main,
"And every shore it circles, thine.
Rule Britannia, rule the waves,
But ne'er degrade your sons to slaves.

(cont.)

VII.

When life glides slowly through thy veins,
  We'll then our filial fondness prove,
Bound only by the welcome chains
  Of duty, gratitude, and love.
    Rule Britannia rule the waves,
    But never make your children slaves.

VIII.

Our Youth shall prop thy tott'ring age;
  Our vigour nerve thy feeble arm:
In vain thy foes shall spend their rage---
  We'll shield thee safe from ev'ry harm.
    Rule Britannia, rule the waves,
    But never make your children slaves.

IX.

For thee we'll toil with cheerful heart,
  We'll labour---but we will be free
Our growth and strength to thee impart,
  And all our treasures bring to thee.
    Rule Britannia, rule the waves,
    Were subjects --- But we're not your slaves.

436. An AMERICAN PARODY, on the old song, of "RULE BRITANNIA."

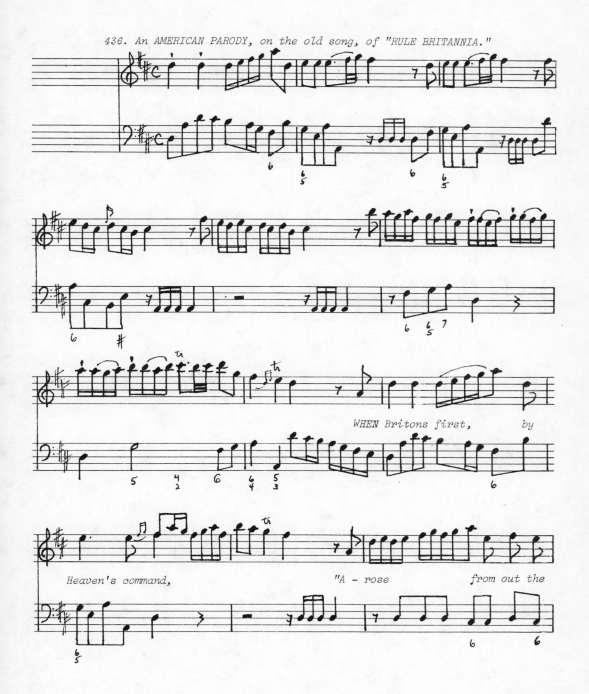

WHEN Britons first, by

Heaven's command,   "A - rose   from out the

589

a - zure main   [Arose, arose from out the azure main,]

"This was the charter [the

char-ter] of the land,   "And guar - dian an - gels

sung this   strain: "Rule Britannia, [Bri - tannia], rule the Waves,

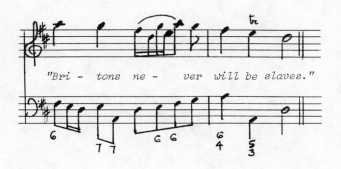

"Bri - tons ne - ver will be slaves."

435. LIBERTY SONG.
Tune, Smile Britannia.

I.

Ye Sons of Freedom smile!
    America unites!
And Friends in Britain's Isle
    Will vindicate our Rights;
In spite of Ga--'s hostile Train,
We will our Liberties maintain.

II.

Boston be not dismay'd,
    Tho' Tyrants now oppress;
Tho' Fleets and Troops invade:
    You soon will have redress:
The resolutions of the brave
Will injur'd Massachusetts save.

III.

The Delegates have met;
    For Wisdom all renown'd;
Freedom we may expect
    From Politicks profound.
Illustrious Congress, may each Name
Be crowned with immortal Fame!

IV.

Tho' Troops upon our Ground
    Have strong Entrenchments made,
Tho' Ships the Town surround,
    With all their Guns display'd,
'Twill not the free-born Spirit tame
Or force us to renounce our Claim

V.

Our Charter-Rights we claim,
    Granted in ancient Times,
Since our Forefathers came
    First to these Western Climes:
Nor will their Sons degenerate,
They Freedom love--Oppression hate.

VI.

If Ga-e shou'd strike the Blow,
    We must for Freedom fight,
Undaunted Courage show,
    While we defend our Right;
In spite of the oppressive Band,
Maintain the Freedom of the Land.

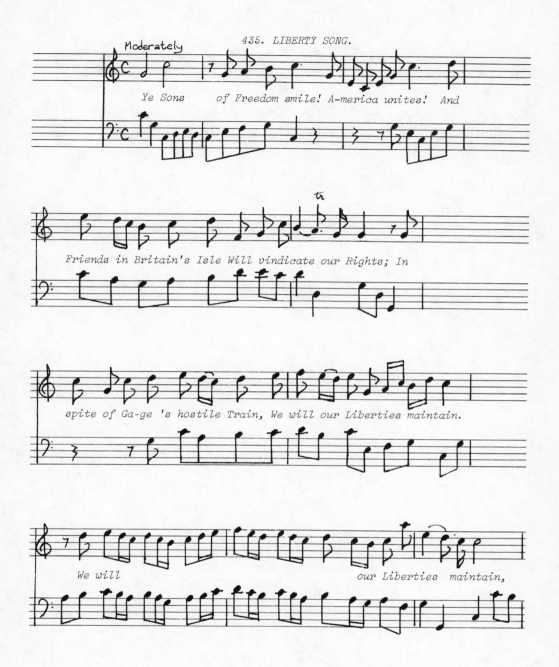

435. LIBERTY SONG.

Moderately

Ye Sons of Freedom smile! A-merica unites! And Friends in Britain's Isle Will vindicate our Rights; In spite of Ga-ge 's hostile Train, We will our Liberties maintain. We will our Liberties maintain,

We will   our Liberties maintain.

594

437. The ROAST BEEF of OLD ENGLAND.

WHEN mighty Roast beef was the Englishman's food,
It ennobled our veins, and enliven'd our blood,
Our soldiers were brave, and our courtiers were good.

When good Queen Elizabeth sat on the throne,
Ere coffee and tea, and such slip-slops were known,
The world was in terror if ere she did frown.

Our lawyers were virtuous, ne'er sought for applause,
By confounding with purport and tenour the laws,
Nor framing of bills against liberty's cause.

Our Bishops were zealous, religion their care,
And honestly spoke when in senate they were,
That no Traitor dar'd offer a Popish bill there.

They boldly asserted, the Prince on the Throne,
If he broke through the oath that he took with the Crown,
'Twas no act of justice, but one of his own.

Our nobles had honour in records of fame;
Their sons are but shadows, and know but the name,
Their fathers eat beef, their sons whore and game.

With beef and their charters, how happy and free!
Their sons, if they've charters, must live upon tea,
And cringe to a venal majority.

The Britons, that once were inured to fight,
Now tamely sit down their petitions to write;
Which serve for a laugh, and the boys for a kite.

The return of the seasons are settled by fate,
The Tories may tremble, though now so elate,
And freedom revive with the new eighty-eight.

437. The ROAST BEEF of OLD ENGLAND.

WHEN mighty Roast beef was the Englishman's food, it en-

nobled our veins, and enliven'd our blood, Our soldiers were brave, and our

Chorus.

courtiers were good. [Oh the Roast beef of old England And old English Roast

beef.

From a late London Paper. SONG, to the Tune of Derry Down.

I.

THE expences of war, and corruptions of peace,
Are the same to all people, their taxes near(sic) cease;
That the poor are distrest, we all know to be true:
So damn the old Parliament, heigh! for a new!
                    Derry down.

II.

To pay the King's debts (how they came the Lord knows)
We were fleec'd of our Cash, as the ministers chose;
New taxes were rais'd, we all know to be true;
So damn the old Parliament, heigh! for a new!
                    Derry down.

III.

The people's complaint was the cause of their mirth,
They call'd honest freemen the skum of the earth;
That they wish'd for to starve us, we know to be true;
So damn the old Parliament, heigh! for a new!
                    Derry down.

IV.

That the customs of France is the thing they must choose,
Such as arbitrary power and curs'd wooden shoes;
That they made Popish laws, we all know to be true;
So damn the old Parliament, heigh! for a new!!
                    Derry down.

456. SONG.

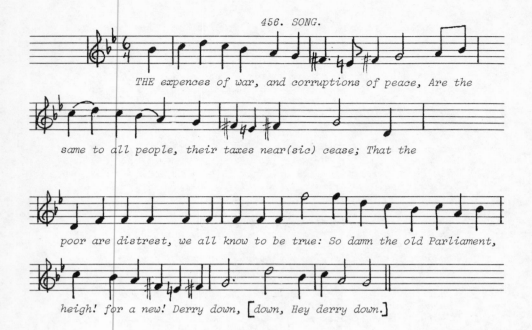

THE expences of war, and corruptions of peace, Are the

same to all people, their taxes near(sic) cease; That the

poor are distrest, we all know to be true: So damn the old Parliament,

heigh! for a new! Derry down, [down, Hey derry down.]

January 20   Lord Chatham's proposal to withdraw British troops
              from Boston defeated in parliament.

March 30   New England Restraining Act receives royal assent. It
              forbids the New England colonies to trade with any nation
              but Britain and the British West Indies, and bars them from
              the North Atlantic fisheries.

April 13   The provisions of the New England Restraining Act applied
              to New Jersey, Pennsylvania, Maryland, Virginia, and South
              Carolina after news is received in London that these colonies
              had ratified the Continental Association.

April 14   Gage receives a letter from Lord Dartmouth ordering him
              to use force if necessary to execute the Coercive and
              other acts, to strike at once, even if it means bringing
              on hostilities, rather than permit the rebellious
              faction time to perfect their organization.

April 18   "Midnight Ride" of Paul Revere, Samuel Prescott, and
              William Dawes begins. They alert patriots between Boston
              and Concord of British plans.

April 19   Skirmish at Lexington. First military action of the
              American Revolution.

              Skirmish at Concord. The "shot heard round the world."
              British retreat from Concord; seige of Boston begins.

April 20   British seize patriot gunpowder at Williamsburg, Virginia.

May 4   William Pitt's speech in Parliament calling for the
              withdrawing of troops from Boston reprinted in the
              Virginia Gazette. This speech was to go through numerous
              editions and reprints in the colonies, with Pitt adopted
              as American advocate in Parliament.

May 9   Capture of Fort Ticonderoga. Ethan Allen demands and
              receives the surrender of Fort Ticonderoga and its garrison,
              "in the name of the Great Jehovah and the Continental
              Congress."

May 10   Second Continental Congress convenes at Philadelphia.

May 12   Green Mountain Boys seize Crown Point.

May 14   Benedict Arnold leads an expedition against St. John's,
              Canada.

May 24   John Hancock elected president of the Second Continental
              Congress.

June 12   *General Gage proclaims martial law in Massachusetts.*
Declares those in arms to be rebels and traitors, offers
pardon to all who return to allegiance, except for
Samuel Adams and John Hancock.

June 17   *Battle of Bunker Hill.*

June 27   *Congress authorizes invasion of Canada.*

July-March *Siege of Boston*

July 3   *Washington assumes command of all Continental forces on*
Cambridge Common.

July 31   *Congress rejects Lord North's plan for reconciliation.*

August 23 *Proclamation of Rebellion. George III declares the*
American colonies to be in open rebellion.

August 30 *Lord William Campbell, governor of South Carolina,*
dissolves the assembly, and flees to a British warship.

September 12 *The Second Continental Congress reconvenes.*

October 5 *Continental Congress orders the arrest of all dangerous*
loyalists.

November 13 *Americans under General Montgomery occupy Montreal.*

December 3 *First official American flag raised aboard* Alfred. *Flag*
raised by Lieutenant John Paul Jones.

December 6 *Congress answers the royal proclamation of rebellion of*
August 23. Disclaims intention to deny the King's
sovereignty but disavows allegiance to Parliament.

December 11 *Governor Dunmore and loyalists defeated at Great Bridge;*
evacuates Norfolk.

December 22 *American Prohibitory Act. This act put a complete stop*
to trade and commerce in the colonies.

December 31 *Battle of Quebec. Americans repulsed and Canada lost to*
colonists. Montgomery was killed and Arnold wounded.

273.
BALTIMORE.
ON LIBERTY

Americans be men, espouse the glorious cause,
'Tis in defence of liberty and laws!
Think of your hopes, your fortunes, all your care,
Your wives, your infants, and your parents share;
Think of each living father's rev'red head,
Think of each ancestor, with glory dead.
Absent alas! they sigh, and now they sue;
They ask their safety and their fame of you.
Now seize th'occasion, on! on! without delay,
To war, and glory, when Heav'n directs the way
Death is the worst, a fate we all must try
And for our country 'tis a bliss to die!
The gallant man, though slain in fight he be,
Yet leaves his nation safe, his children free;
Entails a debt on all the grateful state,
His own brave friends shall glory in his fate
His wife live honor'd, all his race succeed,
And late posterity enjoy the deed!
                    CORIO LANUS

101.

From the MASSACHUSETTS SPY. The following parody on the Ballad of the
Vicar of Bray, contains the same Sentiments which have always actuated
a Provincial General Officer, who in September last most shamefully
deserted his colours.

I.
IN George the second's golden days,
  When mod'rate men look'd big Sir;
My country's rights I did maintain,
  (Of course I was a Whig Sir;
And so preferment I procur'd
  By our true faith's defender,
And always ev'ry day abjur'd
  The Pope and the Pretender.
    And this is law I will maintain
      Until my dying day Sir,
    That whatsoever King shall reign,
      I will receive my pay, Sir.

II.
When his Successor mounts the throne,
  The R----h C----s glory,
Another face of things is seen,
  And I'm become a Tory,
New fangled Counsellors I praise,
  And love their moderation
Nor think the state in...
  From their administration.
    And this is law, &c.

III.
The illustrious Throne of Hanover,
  And C-----k succession?
To these I do allegiance swear,
  While they can keep possession:
For by my faith and loyalty,
  I never more will faulter;
And George my lawful King shall be ---
  Until the time shall alter,
    And this is law, &c.

IV.
But if the Colonies revolt,
  And liberty maintain Sir;
I then will steer another course,
  And turn a Whig again Sir.
And thus my house I will preserve
  Against a confiscation:
For if I can outwit them all --
  Ne'er mind prevarication.

And this is law I will maintain
   Until my dying day Sir.
Which ever Part their Point shall gain,
   I will receive my pay Sir.

101. ... parody on the Ballad of the Vicar of Bray...

IN George the second's golden days, when mod'rate men look'd

big Sir; My country's rights I did maintain, (Of course I was a Whig Sir;)And

so preferment I procur'd By our true faith's defender, And always ev'ry

day abjur'd The Pope and the Pretender. And this is law I will maintain un-

til my dying day Sir, That whatsoever King shall reign I will receive my

pay, Sir.

Baltimore, December 19.
Sir,

    HAPPENING lately to be at Annapolis, I enquired for certain Pamphlets, advertised by you, Free Thoughts on the Proceedings of the Congress, &c. but was disappointed; being told these Pamphlets had not yet appeared there:---You really Sir, would serve this Province, by sending a Number here, which I believe would readily sell. You, no doubt, have seen the Resolves of certain MAGNATES of our Province, naming themselves a Provincial Congress: I will not say these Worthies are under the Influence of the Moon, or are proper Subjects for Confinement, but one of their Resolves is exactly calculated for the Meridian of the Inquisition, and the others smell furiously of Bedlam. I would gladly contribute my humble mite, to ridicule the folly, ingratitude, and violence of our deluded patriots: If therefore, Sir, you think that the subjoined jeu d'esprit, worth a place in your most useful paper insert it, and oblige
                        Your very humble servant,
                          AGRICOLA.

Tune Abbot of CANTERBURY, or WILKES's Wriggle.

I.

ON Calvert's plains new faction reigns,
Great-Britain---we defy, Sir;
True liberty---lies gag'd in chains,
Tho' freedom is the cry, Sir:
The Congress, and their factious tools,
Most wantonly oppress us,
Hypocrisy triumphant rules,
And sorely does distress us.

II.

The British bands with glory crown'd,
No longer shall withstand us;
Our martial deeds loud fame shall sound,
Since mad LEE--now commands us:
Triumphant soon, a blow he'll strike,
That all the world shall awe, Sir,
And General GAGE, Sir, Perseus like,
Behind his wheels, -- he'll draw, Sir.

III.

When Galic hosts, ungrateful men,
Our race meant to extermine,
Pray, did COMMITTEES, save us THEN,
Or H-----k, or such vermin?
Then faction spurn, think for yourselves,
Your parent-state, believe me,
From REAL GRIEFS, from FACTIOUS ELVES,
Will speedily relieve ye.

803. ....jeu d'esprit...

ON Calvert's plains new faction reigns, Great-Britain---we de-

fy, Sir; True liberty---lies gag'd in chains, Tho' freedom is the cry,Sir:The

Congress, and their factious tools, Most wantonly oppress us, Hypocrisy tri-

umphant rules, And sorely does distress us.

606

Mr. *RIVINGTON*

As I am one of those people who believe implicitly every article they meet with in Mr. Holt's paper; and as I find, by his last, that he intends to present his readers, in the next, with the picture of a WHIG: an Irish one, I suppose, by its being copied from a Dublin print; I request the favour of your reprinting the portrait of an American Whig; as I presume it must be, from its having been printed in the very time of the American Whigs, and in good Mr. Holt's own very impartial paper; and which, from the known verity of the publisher, I could not but look upon as genuine and unsophisticated. I am glad that I happened to keep so great a curiosity till the present time; especially as among other good effects, it will evidence to the world, that Mr. Holt, is a man of too much integrity ever to change his principles, or to say one thing when he means another.

THE WHIG: A SONG.
To the tune of "Would you have a young virgin of fifteen years."

WOULD you know what a WHIG is, and always was,
I'll shew you his face, as it were in a glass,
He's a rebel by nature, a villain in grain,
A saint by profession, who never had grace:
Cheating and lying are puny things,
Rapine and plundering venial sins;
His great occupation is ruining nations,
Subverting of Crowns, and murdering Kings.
2.
To shew that he came from a wight of worth,
'Twas Lucifer's pride that first gave him birth,
'Twas bloody Barbarity bore the elf,
Ambition the midwife that brought him forth:
Old Judas was tutor, until he grew big,
Hypocrisy taught him to care not a fig
For all that is sacred,---and thus was created,
And brought in the world, what we call a WHIG.
3.
Spew'd up among mortals by hellish jaws,
To strike he begins at religion and laws,
With pious inventions, and bloody intentions,
And all for to bring in the good of cause*.
At cheating and lying he plays his game,
Always dissembling, and never the same;
Till he fills the whole nation with sins of d--n-t--n,
Then goes to the d-v-l, from whence he came.

*The present editor would humbly recommend, at this particular time, to the lovers of melody, the following little alteration, "And all for the good of the common cause;" which, however, was a liberty he durst not take in transcribing.

607

805. THE WHIG; A SONG.

WOULD you know what a WHIG is, and always was, I'll

shew you his face, as it were in a glass, He's a rebel by nature, a

villain in grain, A saint by profession, who never had grace:

Cheating and lying are puny things, Rapine and plundering venial sins, His

608

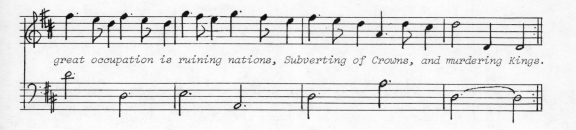

great occupation is ruining nations, Subverting of Crowns, and murdering Kings.

1448.

LONDON, ...Dec. 2.....
    We are informed, that on Friday last, at a meeting of the tradesmen
of his Royal Highness the Duke of Gloucester, to celebrate his birthday,
at the King's Arms tavern, in Bond street, Mr. Showell, whip maker, of
Oxford street, and Mr. Pinchbeck, of Cockspur street, stewards, the
following stanza was added to the song of God save the King:

> *"May each unkind report,*
> *"Which keeps our Duke from Court,*
>   *"Quickly be o'er;*
> *"And the whole family*
> *"Live from all discord free,*
> *"In love and harmony,*
>   *"Till time's no more."*

    Many loyal toasts, besides the Royal Family, were drank; among which
was, "A happy reconciliation between Great Britain and her Colonies!"
The whole day was spent with the utmost spirit and decency.

610

1448.

"May each unkind report, "Which keeps our Duke from Court,

"May each unkind report, "Which keeps our Duke from Court,

"Quickly be o'er; "And the whole family "Live from all discord free,

"Quickly be o'er: "And the whole family "Live from all discord free,

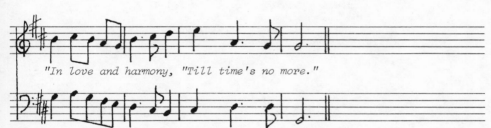

"In love and harmony, "Till time's no more."

"In love and harmony "Till time's no more."

271.

Baltimore, May 17.
ON LIBERTY

Curs'd be the Wretch, that's bought and sold
And barters LIBERTY for Gold;
For when Elections are not free,
In vain we boast our Liberty.
And he who sells his single Right,
Would sell his Country if he might.
When LIBERTY is put to Sale
For Wine, for Money, or for Ale,
The Sellers must be abject Slaves,
The Buyers vile designing Knaves,
[And't has a proverb been of old,
* The Devil's bought, but to be sold.]*
This Maxim, in the Statesman's School
Is always taught, divide and rule.
All Parties are to him a Joke;
While Parties foam, he fits the Yoke.
When Men their Reason once Resume,
He in his turn begins to fume.
Learn then AMERICANS to unite;
Leave off the old exploded Bite,
Henceforth let Feuds and Discords cease,
And turn all party Rage to Peace:
Rouse, and maintain your ancient GLORY;
UNITE, as Power can then oppose YE.

                    A MARYLANDER

271. ON LIBERTY

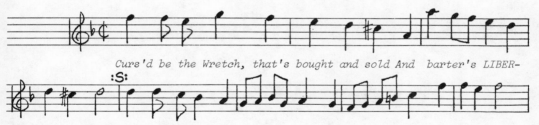

Curs'd be the Wretch, that's bought and sold And barter's LIBER-

TY for Gold; For when Elections are not free, In vain we boast our Liberty.

And he who sells his single Right, Would sell his Country if he might.

[:S: - When the first singer reaches this point, the second begins. When the second singer reaches this point, the third begins, thus realizing this 3 voice round.]

111.

From the Cambridge News-Paper.
To the Tune of "The ecchoing Horn."

HARK! 'tis FREEDOM that calls, come Patriots awake!
  To arms my brave Boys, and away:
'Tis Honour, 'tis Virtue, 'tis Liberty calls,
  And upbraids the too tedious Delay.
What Pleasure we find in pursuing our Foes,
  Thro' Blood and thro' Carnage we'll fly;
Then follow, we'll soon overtake them, Huzza!
  The Tyrants are seiz'd on, they die.
                II.
Triumphant returning with Freedom secur'd,
  Like MEN, we'll be joyful and gay---
With our Wives, and our Friends, we will sport, love and drink,
  And lose the Fatigues of the Day.
'Tis Freedom alone gives a Relish to Mirth,
  But Oppression all Happiness sours;
It will smooth Life's dull Passage, 'twill slope the Descent,
  And strew the Way over with Flowers.

111. A SONG.

HARK! 'tis FREEDOM that calls, come Patriots a-

wake! To arms my brave Boys, and a-way: 'Tis Honour, 'tis Virtue, 'tis

Liberty calls, And upbraids the too tedious Delay. What Pleasure we

find in pursuing our Foes, Thro' Blood and thro' Carnage we'll fly; Then

follow, we'll soon overtake them, Huzza! The Tyrants are seiz'd on, they

die. [they die   The Tyrants are seiz'd on, they die.

CHORUS.

Then follow, we'll soon overtake them, Huzza! The Tyrants are

Then follow, we'll soon overtake them, Huzza! The Tyrants are

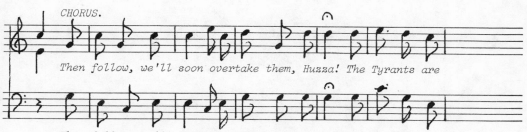

seiz'd on, they die.

seiz'd on, they die.]

617

757. A JUNTO SONG
To the tune of a begging we will go, we'll go, &c.

'TIS money makes the member vote,
  And sanctifies our ways;
It makes the patriot turn his coat,
  And money we must raise.
        And a taxing we will go, we'll go, &c.
More taxes we must sure impose,
  To raise the civil list;
Also to pay our ayes and noyes,
  And make opposers hist.
        And a taxing, &c.
One single thing untax'd at home,
  Old England could not shew;
For money we abroad did roam,
  And thought to tax the new.
        And a taxing, &c.
The pow'r supreme of Parliament,
  Our purpose did assist,
And taxing laws abroad were sent,
  Which rebels do resist,
        And a taxing,. &c.
Shall we not make the rascals bend
  To Britain's supreme power?
The sword shall we not to them send,
  And leaden balls a shower?
        And a taxing, &c.
Boston we shall in ashes lay,
  It is a nest of knaves:
We'll make them soon for mercy pray,
  Or send them to their graves,
        And a taxing, &c.
But second thoughts are ever best,
  And lest our force should fail,
What fraud can do, we'll make a test,
  And see what bribes avail.
        And a taxing, &c.
Each Colony, we will propose,
  Shall raise an ample sum;
Which we'll(sic) applied, under the rose,
  May bribe them---as at home.
        And a taxing, &c.
We'll force and fraud in one unite,
  To bring them to our hands;
Then lay a tax on the sun's light,
  And King's tax on their lands.
        And a taxing, &c.

757. A JUNTO SONG.

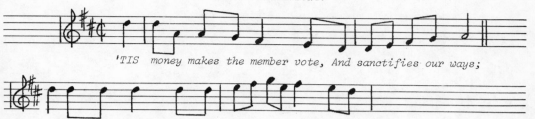

'TIS money makes the member vote, And sanctifies our ways;

It makes the patriot turn his coat, And money we must

raise. And a taxing we will go, we'll go, we'll go And a ta-xing we will go.

1069. A SONG.
Composed at a Town-Meeting in Chester, Burlington county, July, 1774.

COME join hand in hand all ye true, loyal souls,
'Tis Liberty calls, let's fill up our bowls,
We'll toast all the lovers of Freedom's good cause;
America's Sons will support all our laws:
 Our firelocks are good; let fair Freedom ne'er yield;
  We're always ready,
   Steady, boys, steady
 By Jove we'll be free, or we'll die in the field.

Tho' the Lords and the Commons may rail in the House
At our patriot Assemblies, we don't care a souse,
We'll keep chearful spirits, nor mind their commands,
The sun of fair Liberty will shine o'er our lands.
 Our firelocks are good, &c.

The bright Star of Empire begins to arise,
The Genius of Freedom expands thro' the skies;
On her head we will place the imperial Crown,
America's the spot where she fixes her Throne.
 Our firelocks are good, &c.

To Wedderburne and North now confusion we'll Drink,
Their dastardly souls, we will cause them to shrink;
Then join hand in hand, here's a full flowing bowl,
'Tis FRANKLIN and LIBERTY enlighten the Soul.
 Our firelocks are good, &c.

1069. A SONG. Composed at a Town-Meeting in Chester, Burlington county, July, 1774.

Allegro Moderato

COME join hand in hand all ye true, loyal souls, 'Tis

Liberty calls, let's fill up our bowls, We'll toast all the lovers of

Freedom's good cause; A-merica's Sons will support all our laws:

Chorus.

Our firelocks are good; let fair Freedom ne'er yield; We're

always ready,   Steady, boys, steady   By Jove we'll be free, or we'll

Sy.

die in the field.

622

From a London Paper.
The SAILORS ADDRESS.

I.

COME listen my cocks, to a brother and friend,
One and all to my song, gallant sailors attend,
Sons of Freedom ourselves, let's be just as we're brave
Nor America's freedom attempt to enslave.
 Firm as oak are our hearts, where true glory depends,
  Steady, boys steady,
  We'll always be ready
 To fight all our foes, not to murder our friends.

II.

True glory can ne'er in this quarrel be won,
If New England we conquer, Old England's undone;
On brethren we then should assist to fix chains,
For the blood of Great-Britain flows warm in their veins.
 Firm as oak, &c.

III.

Shall Courtier's fine speeches prevail to divide
Our affection from those who have fought by our side?
And who often have join'd to sink in the main
The proud boasting natives of France and of Spain?
 Firm as oak, &c.

IV.

Near relations of some who at Court now do thrive,
The Pretender did join in the year forty-five;
And many in favour, disguis'd with foul arts,
While they roar out for George, are for James in their hearts.
 Firm as oak, &c.

V.

Of such men as these let us scorn to be tools,
Dirty work to perform---do they take us for fools?
Brave sailors are wiser than thus to be bamm'd,
Let them turn out themselves, lads, and fight and be damm'd.
 Firm as oak, &c.

VI.

To the ground may disputes with our Colonies fall,
And George long in splendor reign King of us all;
And may those who would set the two lands by the ears,
Be put in the bilboes, and brought to the jears.
 Firm as oak are our hearts, where true glory depends,
  Steady, boys, steady,
  We'll always be ready
 To fight all our foes, not to murder our friends.

36. The SAILORS ADDRESS.

Brisk

COME listen my cocks, to a brother and friend, One and
all to my song, gallant sailors attend, Sons of Freedom ourselves, let's be
just as we're brave Nor America's freedom attempt to enslave.

624

Chorus.

Firm as oak are our hearts, where true glory depends, Stea-

dy, boys steady, We'll always be ready To fight all our foes, not to

murder our friends.

1. ♩ 𝄽 =in original

From a new musical interlude called the ELLECTION.

WHILST happy in my native land,
  I boast my country's charter,
I'll never basely lend my hand
  Her liberties to barter.

The noble mind is not at all
  By poverty degraded;
'Tis guilt alone can make us fall,
  And well I am persuaded,
Each free-born Briton's song should be,
  "Or give me DEATH or LIBERTY!"

Tho' small the power which fortune grants,
  And few the gifts she sends us,
The lordly hireling often wants
  That freedom which defends us.

By law secured from lawless strife,
  Our house is our castellum:
Thus bless'd with all that's dear in life,
  For lucre shall we sell 'em?
No; every Briton's song should be,
  "Or give me DEATH or LIBERTY!"

1361. A SONG. From a new musical interlude called the ELECTION.

MAESTOSO

UNISON

WHILST happy in my native land, I

boast my country's charter, I'll never basely lend my hand Her liberties to

bar - ter. The no - ble mind is not at all by

poverty de - graded;   'Tis guilt a-lone can make us fall, And well I am per-

suaded,   Each free-born Briton's song should be, "Or give me DEATH or

LIBERTY!" "Or give me DEATH or LIBERTY!" ["Or give me DEATH or LIBERTY!" "Or

give me DEATH or LIBERTY!"]   Tho'

small the power which for-tune grants, And few the gifts she sends us, The

UNISON

lord-ly hireling of-ten wants, That freedom which de--fends us.

By law se - cur'd from lawless strife, Our house is our cas-

tellum; Thus bless'd with all that's dear in life, For lu-cre shall we

sell 'em? No; every Briton's song should be, "Or give me DEATH or LIBERTY!""Or

give me DEATH or LIBERTY!""Or give me DEATH or LIBERTY!"Or give me DEATH or

LIBERTY!"

630

751. *An EXTEMPORE SONG, Composed in a Jovial Company.*
To the tune of A light heart and a thin pair of breeches goes
through the world, brave boys.

YE sons of true freedom and spirit,
  Who, firmly your rights would support,
May now secure honour by merit,
  And property--spite of the court.
First sing of our Congress and leaders;
  Then, toast all our friends, far and near,
Determined, no foreign invaders,
  Shall with tyrannic pow'r reign here.
The blessing of God will attend us,
  Tho' thousands against us combine:
Deserted by those should defend us,
  Our cause to Heaven we resign.
Oppression's dire tools, and their masters,
  Promoters of slaughter and strife,
In the end will be proved but impostors,
  And Bute lose his forfeited life.
While freedom's our motto, my heroes,
  Intire will support it till death;
Great rascals, Gage, North, and all Nero's,
  Like traitors shall yield up their breath.
Then, here is success to our forces,
  True honour, and honesty's sons,
Our Congress will plan out our courses;
  We cheerfully take up our guns.

751. *An EXTEMPORE SONG, Composed in a Jovial Company.*

YE sons of true freedom and spi-rit, Who, firmly your

rights would sup-port, May now se-cure ho--nour by me-rit, And property---

spite of the court. First sing of our Congress and leaders; Then,

toast all our friends, far and near, de-termined,no foreign in -

va -ders, Shall with tyrannic pow'r reign   here. [Then why should we

quarrel for Riches, or any such glittering toy,   A light heart & a

thin pair of breeches, Goes through the world brave boys.]

1362. FISH and TEA. A NEW SONG.--To an Old Tune.

WHAT a Court hath Old England of folly and sin,
Spite of Chatham and Camden, Barre, Burke, Wilkes, and Glyn!
Not content with the game-act, they tax fish and sea,
And America drench with hot water and tea.
        Derry down, &c.
Lord S--------, he swears they are terrible cowards,
Who can't be made brave by the blood of the Howards;
And to prove there is truth in America's fears,
He conjures Sir Peter's poor ghost 'fore the Peers,
        Derry down, &c.
Now indeed if these poor people's nerves are so weak,
How cruel it is their destruction to seek!
Dr. Johnson's a proof, in the highest degree,
His soul and his system were changed by tea.
        Derry down, &c.
But if the wise Council of England doth think
They may be enslaved by the power of the drink,
They're right to enforce it; but then do you see?
The colonies too may refuse, and be free.
        Derry down, &c.
There is no knowing where this oppression will stop;
Some say---there's no cure but a capital chop;
And that I believe's each American's wish,
Since you've drenched 'em with tea, and depriv'd 'em of fish.
        Derry down, &c.
The birds of the air and the fish of the sea,
By the Gods for poor Dan Adam's use were made free,
Till a man with more power than old Moses would wish,
Said--Ye wretches, she shan't touch a fowl or a fish.
        Derry down, &c.
Three Gen'rals these mandates have borne' cross the sea,
To deprive them of fish, and to make them drink tea;
In turn, sure these freemen will boldly agree
To give them a dance upon Liberty Tree.
        Derry down, &c.
Then freedom's the word both at home and abroad,
And d--n ev'ry scabbard that holds a good sword!
Our forefathers gave us this freedom in hand,
And we will die in defence of the rights of the land.
        Derry down, &c.

1362. FISH and TEA. A NEW SONG.

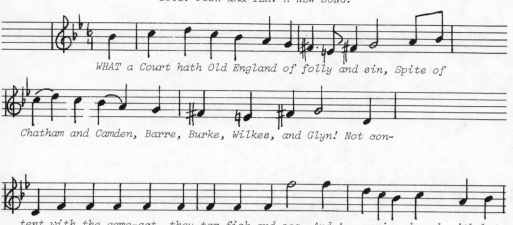

WHAT a Court hath Old England of folly and sin, Spite of

Chatham and Camden, Barre, Burke, Wilkes, and Glyn! Not con-

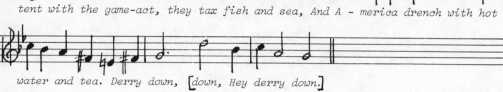

tent with the game-act, they tax fish and sea, And A - merica drench with hot

water and tea. Derry down, [down, Hey derry down.]

From the PENNSYLVANIA PACKET. The PENNSYLVANIA MARCH.
To the Tune of the SCOTS SONG,
I winna Marry ony Lad, but Sandy o'er the Lee

WE are the troops that ne'er will stoop
  To wretched slavery.
Nor shall our seed, by our base deed,
  Despised vassals be.
Freedom we will bequeath them,
  Or we will bravely die;
Our greatest foe, e'er long shall know,
  How much did Sandwich lie.
            CHORUS.
    And all the world shall know,
      Americans are free;
    Nor slaves nor cowards, will we prove,
      Great Britain soon shall see.
            II.
We'll not give up our birth right,
  Our foes shall find us men:
As good as they in any shape,
  The British troops shall ken.
Huzza brave boys, we'll beat them,
  On any hostile plain;
For freedom, wives, and children dear,
  The battle we'll maintain.
            CHORUS.
    What? Can those British Tyrants think
      Our fathers cross'd the main;
    And savage foes, and dangers met,
      To be enslav'd by them?
    If so, they are mistaken,
      For we will rather die;
    And since they have become our foes,
      Their forces we defy.

514. The PENNSYLVANIA MARCH.

WE are the troops that ne'er will stoop To wretched slaver-y. Nor
shall our seed, by our base deed, De - spised vassals be.   Freedom we will
bequeath them, Or we will bravely die;   Our greatest foe, e'er
long shall know, How much did Sandwich lie. And all the world   shall
know, A-me - ri - cans are free; Nor slaves nor cowards, will we prove, Great
Britain soon shall see.

475. LIBERTY-TREE. A new song.
Tune. The Gods of the Greeks

IN a chariot of light from the regions of day,
  The Goddess of Liberty came,
Ten thousand celestials directed the way,
  And hither conducted the dame.
A fair budding branch from the gardens above,
  Where millions with millions agree,
She brought in her hand, as a pledge of her love,
  The plant she nam'd, Liberty Tree.

The celestial exotic stuck deep in the ground,
  Like a native it flourish'd and bore,
The fame of its fruit drew the nations around,
  To seek out this peaceable shore.
Unmindful of names or distinctions they came,
  For freemen like brothers agree,
With one spirit endu'd, they one friendship pursu'd,
  And their temple was Liberty Tree.

Beneath this fair tree, like the patr'archs of old
  Their bread in contentment they eat,
Unvex'd with the troubles of silver and gold,
  The cares of the grand and the great.
With timber and tar they old England supply'd
  And supported her pow'r on the sea,
Her battles they fought, with out getting a groat,
  For the honour of Liberty Tree.

But hear O ye swains, ('tis a tale most profane)
  How all the tyrannical pow'rs,
King, Commons, and Lords, are uniting amain,
  To cut down this guardian of ours.
From the east to the west, blow the trumpet to arms
  Thro' the land let the sound of it flee,
Let the far and the near, unite with a cheer,
  In defence of our Liberty Tree.

475. LIBERTY-TREE. A new song.

Con Spirito

IN a chariot of light from the regions of day, The Goddess of Liber-ty came, Ten thousand ce - lestials di - rec-ted the way, And

639

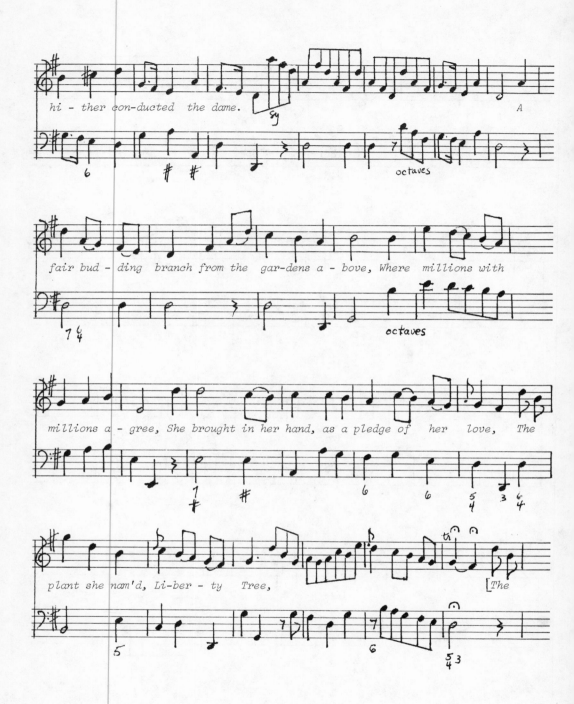

hi - ther con-ducted the dame.

A fair bud - ding branch from the gar-dens a - bove, Where millions with

millions a - gree, She brought in her hand, as a pledge of her love, The

plant she nam'd, Li-ber - ty Tree, [The

octaves

octaves

640

plant she nam'd Li- ber - ty Tree.

954. *The GENIUS of AMERICA TO HER SONS.*

WHO'D know the sweets of liberty?
'Tis to climb the mountain's brow,
Thence to discern rough industry,
At the harrow or the plough;
'Tis where my sons their crops have sown,
Calling the harvest all their own;
'Tis where the heart to truth ally'd,
Never felt unmanly fear;
'Tis where the eye with milder pride,
Nobly sheds sweet pity's tear;
Such as AMERICA yet shall see,
These are the sweets of Liberty.

954. *The GENIUS of AMERICA TO HER SONS.*

WHO'D

know the sweets of li-ber-ty? 'Tis to climb the mountain's brow,

Thence to dis-cern rough in - dus-try, At the har - row or the plough;

1. ♩ = in original 2. ♩ = in original

[Thence to dis - cern rough in-dus-try At the har - row or the

plough; At the har - row or the plough;]

'Tis where my sons their crops have

sown, Cal-ling the har - vest all their own; ['Tis where my

644

sons their crops have sown Cal-ling the har - vest all their

own; Cal - ling the har-vest all their own.

120. *A SONG. Composed by a Soldier in the Continental Army.*
To the Tune of the Black Sloven.

THO' some folks may tell us, it is not so clever
To handle a musket in cold frosty weather;
By yonder bright Congress,* In spite of all such,
I'll tarry this season, and take t'other touch.
  Let poltoons and tories retire from our lines,
We're stronger without them above fifty times;
Their infamous characters none will begrutch
Who tarry with us, boys, to take t'other touch.
  Tho' Haldimand, Gage, and the big talker** too,
Think fusty old pork and our sauce will not do;
My brave fellow soldiers, we can't think it much,
On the strength of raost beef, t'give Howe t'other touch.
  Our raiment, provision and pay, is quite good;
We've sea coal from Scotland, and plenty of wood:
How the country must laugh, if our folly is such
As to let the militia obtain t'other touch.
  Shall they have our posts, when we've all the works done,
Who for them ha'nt labour'd - no, none of this fun;
I'll see next campaign out - if 'tis on a crutch;
And here's to the lads, who will take t'other touch.
  When North by brave Manly has sent, one wou'd think,
A vessel, whose bottom had all we want in't;
Do ye think I wont stay when th'prizes we clutch?
Yes, faith, that I will - and so here's t'other touch.
  The conquering Gen--, I've forgot his hard name,
Has made Fort St. John, and Chamblee very tame;
And Montreal also -- 'twill sweat Bute & Hutch--
When they hear that Qu'bec too has got t'other touch.
  And besides all the mortars, bombs, cannon and shells,
And bullets and guns -- as the new-paper tells,
Our cargoes of meat, drink and cloaths beat the Dutch:
Now who wou'd not tarry, and take t'other touch?

*The mortar so called.
**Alluding to Burgoyns speech and letters.

646

120. A SONG. *Composed by a Soldier in the Continental Army.*

THO' some folks may tell us, it is not so clever To handle a mus-ket in cold fro-sty weather; [Fa la la, fa la la, fa la la, fa la la,] By yonder bright Con-gress; in

spite of all such, I'll tar-ry this season, and take t'o-ther touch. [Fa la

la, fa la la, fa la la, fa la la, fa la la, fa la la, fa la la.]

1776

January 10 — Thomas Paine's *Common Sense* published in Philadelphia. This converted thousands to the idea of independence.

January 24 — Colonel Henry Knox reaches Cambridge with 43 cannon and 16 mortars from Fort Ticonderoga.

February 27 — Battle of Moore's Creek Bridge. Patriots defeat Scottish loyalists from upper North Carolina taking 900 prisoners.

April 13 — Washington and main army arrive in New York from Cambridge.

April 17 — Navy Captain John Barry, commanding the *Lexington*, makes first capture in actual battle of a British warship by a regularly commissioned American cruiser.

May 2 — French clandestine support to colonies begins. Charles III of Spain makes similar arrangements soon afterward.

May 3 — General Henry Clinton is joined by General Charles Cornwallis with troops from Britain and decides to attack Charleston, South Carolina.

King appoints General Howe and Admiral Lord Richard Howe peace commissioners.

May 21 — Congress learns that Britain has hired German troops.

June 1 — British forces under Generals Clinton and Cornwallis appear off Charleston, where defense preparations are well under way.

June 8 — Battle of Trios Rivieres, Canada.

June 10 — Louis XVI approves loans to America.

June 11 — Riot in New York City. Tories are stripped, ridden on rails and put in jail by mob.

June 28 — Thomas Jefferson presents his draft of the Declaration to Congress.

(Battle of Sullivan's Island) Repulse of British at Charleston, South Carolina. This ended active British operations in the South for over two years.

June 30 — General Howe and his 9,000 troops from Halifax disembark on Staten Island.

July 2 — Arrival of the British fleet and army in New York harbor.

July 4 — Declaration of Independence approved and signed.

July 12   Howe brothers join forces. Admiral Lord Richard Howe arrived off Staten Island from England with over 100 ships and 11,000 soldiers.

July 29   American invasion of Cherokee County, North Carolina. American General Griffith Rutherford with 2,400 men begin a long invasion which will destroy 32 Indian villages.

August 27   Battle of Long Island. Continental army defeated by General Howe.

September 15   Occupation of New York City by the British.

               Battle of Kips Bay, New York.

September 16   Battle of Harlem Heights, New York.

September 22   Nathan Hale executed by the British as an American spy.

September 26   Congress appoints three commissioners to negotiate with European nations: Silas Deane, Franklin, and Jefferson; Jefferson declines and Arthur Lee named in his place.

October 11   Naval battle on Lake Champlain; Arnold defeated by British.

October 12-13   Battle of Throg's Neck, New York.

October 18   Battle of Pell's Point, New York.

October 28   Battle of White Plains, New York.

November 16   Fort Washington captured by British.

November 30   Howe brothers issue proclamation of pardon. Pardon is promised, with few exceptions, to all those who declare allegiance to the King within 60 days.

December 8   British General Clinton takes possession of Newport, Rhode Island.

December 12   Congress flees from Philadelphia to Baltimore. Invests Washington with virtually dictatorial powers.

December 17   Action at Springfield, New Jersey.

December 25   Washington crosses the Delaware.

December 26   Washington defeats Hessian garrison at Trenton; most captured.

I.

FAIR LIBERTY came o'er,
Through her Britannia's Aid,
And on this savage Shore
With sweet Complacence stray'd:
Britannia's Standard was her own;
For Liberty by her was known.

II.

Happy she liv'd a while,
And all the Welkin round
Was jocund in her Smile,
And rang with gladdest Sound:
Her Swains increased through ev'ry Year,
And blest the Hand that plac'd her here.

III.

Joy never beat so high,
In her Britannia's Breast,
As when fair Liberty
Appear'd so much caress'd:
Defence with gen'rous Hand she gave,
And conquer'd ev'ry adverse Slave.

IV.

At length three Suitors came,
To take her for a Bride,
Presented each their Claim,
And scorn'd to be denied:
Each thought himself supremely sure
To catch the Maiden in his Lure.

V.

With Names of diff'rent Sound,
All three were near of Kin,
And fled Britannia's Ground
Because they could not win
Her Crown, her Mitres, and her Trade,
And ev'ry Bound of Law invade.

VI.

John Presbyter was first,
And, with a lank Grimace,
All Opposition curst
Beyond the Help of Grace:
He Bishops pass'd to Hell alive---
That he on Earth might better thrive.

VII.

Though Honour to the KING
God strictly has enjoin'd;
John said, 'Twas no such thing,
For God had chang'd his Mind,
That now he'd prove it just and right,
To kill the King; and, ergo, fight.

(cont.)

VIII.

"Fair Maiden, thou art mine,
"Quoth John, I take my Vow;
"For I have Right divine,
"To which all Flesh should bow."
The Maiden turn'd her Head aside,
Hating his sly Deceit and Pride.

IX.

Will Democrack came next,
Who swore all Men were ev'n,
And seem'd to be quite vext,
That there's a King in Heav'n:
Will curst the hilly Country round,
Because it made---unequal Ground.

X.

It gave him vast Surprize,
That Beasts, and Birds, and Fishes
Were form'd not of a Size,
Like Wedgewood's earthen Dishes:
With wise Alphonso, he'd have taught
His God t'have made things, "as he ought."

XI.

To him the Virgin said,
"That on an equal Claim,
"If she no Diff'rence made,
"He none could justly blame:
"But yet she could not bear the Rule,
"Of ev'ry vulgar Knave or Fool."

XII.

Though last in his Pretence,
Brisk Nathan Smuggle came,
Yet for sound Impudence
He had as good a Name:
Urg'd by illicit Spirit's Fire,
Nathan profess'd his warm Desire.

XIII.

Resenting with Disdain
The Plea of such a Brute,
She told him, "'Twas in vain
"To teize her with his Suit;"
That Rascal turn'd about and swore,
That Liberty was but a Whore.

XIV.

He veaw'd, a Cask of Rum,
Or contraband Molasses,
Was better worth at home
Than twenty such nice Lasses:
Yet still he felt an angry Pride,
Because so perfectly denied.

(cont.)

XV.

He therefore told the Town,
That the pert Minx was free,
And to each Scoundrel known,
And ev'ry dirty He;
That she imported rank Disease,
And swarm'd with "Vermin," Bugs, and Fleas.

XVI.

Each Whore and Rogue re-told
Our Nathan's lying Tale,
And ev'ry Dunce "felt bold"
At the poor Girl to rail:
In short, to act the basest Shame,
To Slavery they chang'd her Name.

XVII.

Britannia heard the News
Of her dear Sister's Fate:
But, wond'ring at th' Abuse
And undeserved Hate,
She mildly ask'd, "Who states a Cause
"Against my LIBERTY and Laws?"

XVIII.

John answer'd, "Thou art proud,
"Britannia, mad, and rich:"
Will d----d her, with his Croud,
And call'd her, "Tyrant B---h:"
While Nathan his Effusions bray'd,
And veaw'd, "She ruin'd all his Trade."

XIX.

This heard, her gen'rous Mind,
With Indignation fir'd,
Her warlike Sons combin'd,
By mutual Flame inspir'd:
She bade their antient Ardor rouze,
Conducted by her fav'rite Howes.

XX.

"Go, Sons, said she, and show
"That LIBERTY I love,
"And teach her Foes to know,
"Their deeds I disapprove;
"Patient, to Reason make appeal,
"Ere ye my awful Vengeance deal.

XXI.

"While Error ye reclaim,
"Let ev'ry Foe perceive,
"That none, who wound my Fame,
"Without my Terrors live;
"And that my Thunders can be hurl'd
"For LIBERTY around the World."

42. THE AMERICAN HERO. - A Saphic Ode.

I.
WHY should vain Mortals tremble at the sight of
Death and Destruction in the field of Battle,
Where blood & Carnage clothe the Ground in Crimson,
Sounding with Death-groans?

II.
Death will invade us by the Means appointed,
And we must all bow to the king of Terrors!
Nor am I anxious, if I am prepared,
What shape he comes in.

III.
Infinite Wisdom teacheth us Submission;
Bids us be quiet under all his dealings:
Never repining, but forever praising,
GOD our Creator.

IV.
Well may we praise him, all his ways are perfect;
Tho' a Resplendence infinitely glowing,
Dazzles in Glory on the sight of Mortals,
Struck blind by Lustre!

V.
Good is JEHOVAH in bestowing Sunshine,
Nor less his Goodness in the Storm and Thunder:
Mercies and Judgments both proceed from kindness;
Infinite Kindness!

VI.
O then exult, that GOD forever reigneth
Clouds, that around him hinder our Perception,
Bind us the stronger to exalt his Name, and
Shout louder praises!

VII.
Then to the Wisdom of my Lord and Master,
I will commit all that I have or wish for:
Sweetly as Babes sleep will I give my Life up
When call'd to yield it.

VIII.
Now do I dare thee, clad in smoky Pillars
Bursting from Bomb-shells, roaring from the Cannon,
Ratling in Grape-shot, like a storm of Hailstones,
Torturting Aether!

IX.
Up the bleak Heavens, let the spreading flames rise
Breaking like Aetna thro' the smoky Columns;
Louring like Egypt o'er the falling City
Wantonly burnt down.

X.
While all their Hearts quick palpitate for Havock,
Let slip your blood Hounds, nam'd the British Lyons;
Dauntless as Death-stares; nimble as the Whirldwind;
Dreadful as Daemons.

(cont.)

                    XI.
Let Ocean waft on all your floating Castles;
Fraught with Destruction, horrible to Nature;
Then, with your Sails fill'd by a storm of Vengeance,
Bear down to Battle!

                    XII.
From the dire Caverns made by ghostly Miners,
Let the Explosion, dreadful as Vulcanoe's,
Heave the broad Town with all its Wealth and People,
Quick to Destruction.

                    XIII.
Still shall the Banner of the King of Heaven
Never advance where I'm affraid to follow:
While that preceeds me, with an open Bosom,
War, I defy thee.

                    XIV.
Fame and dear Freedom lure me on to Battle,
While a fell Despot, grimer than a Death's-head,
Stings me with Serpents, fiercer than Medusa's,
To the Encounter.

                    XV.
Life, for my Country and the cause of Freedom,
Is but a cheap Price for a Worm to part with;
And if preserved in so great a Contest,
Life is redoubled.---

42. *THE AMERICAN HERO.- A Saphic Ode.*

WHY should vain Mor-tals tremble at the sight of Death and De-

WHY should vain Mor-tals tremble at the sight of Death and De-

WHY should vain Mor-tals tremble at the sight of Death and De-

WHY should vain Mor-tals tremble at the sight of Death and De-

struction in the field of Battle, Where blood & Carnage, Where blood &

struction in the field of Battle, Where blood &

struction in the field of Battle, Where blood &

struction in the field of Battle, Where blood & Carnage, Where blood &

Wagner Music Publishers, 1974

656

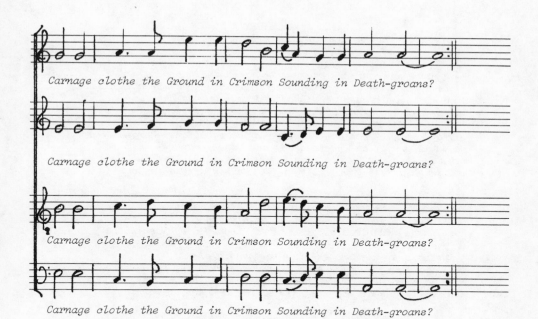

Carnage clothe the Ground in Crimson Sounding in Death-groans?

Carnage clothe the Ground in Crimson Sounding in Death-groans?

Carnage clothe the Ground in Crimson Sounding in Death-groans?

Carnage clothe the Ground in Crimson Sounding in Death-groans?

915. A NEW LIBERTY SONG.
To the tune of the "British Grenadiers."

VAIN Britons boast no longer with proud indignity,
By land your conqu'ring legions, your matchless strength by sea,
Since we your braver sons incens'd, our swords have girded on,
Huzza, Huzza, Huzza, Huzza for war and Washington.

Urg'd on by North and Vengeance, these valiant champions came,
Loud bellowing tea and treason, and George was all on flame,
Yet sacrilegious as it seems, we rebels still live on,
And laugh at all your empty puffs, huzza for Washington.

Still deaf to mild intreaties, still blind to England's good,
You have for thirty pieces, betray'd your country's blood;
Like Aesop's greedy cur, you'll gain a shadow for a bone,
Yet find us fearless shades indeed, inspir'd by Washington.

Mysterious! unexampled! incomprehensible!
The blundering schemes of Britain, their folly, pride and zeal;
Like lions how ye growl, and threat, mere asses have ye shown,
And ye shall share an ass's fate, and drudge for Washington.

Your dark, unfathom'd councils, our weakest heads defeat,
Our children rout your armies, our boats destroy your fleet;
And to compleat the dire disgrace, coop'd up within our own,
You live the scorn of all our host, the slaves of Washington.

Great Heaven! is this the nation, whose thund'ring arms were hurl'd
Thro' Europe, Afric, India, whose navy rul'd the world?
The lustre of your former deeds, whose ages of renown,
Lost in a moment, or transfer'd to us and Washington.

Yet think not thirst of glory unsheaths our vengeful swords,
To rend your bands asunder, and cast away your cords;
'Tis heaven-born freedom fires us all, and strengthens each brave son,
From him who humbly guides the plow, to God-like Washington.

For this, O! could our wishes, your ancient rage inspire,
Your armies should be doubled, in numbers, force and fire;
Then might the glorious conflict prove which best deserves the boon,
America or Albion, a George or Washington.

Fir'd with the great idea, our fathers shades would rise,
To view the stern contention, the Gods desert the skies,
And Wolfe, midst hosts of heroes, superior bending down,
Cry out with eager transport, well done brave Washington.

(cont.)

Should George, too choice of Britons, to foreign realms apply,
And madly arm half Europe, yet still we would defy!
Turk, Russian, Jew, and Infidel, or all those powers in one,
While Hancock crowns our senate, our camp great Washington.

Tho' warlike weapons fail us, disdaining slavish fears,
To swords we'd beat our plow-shares, our pruning-hooks to spears;
And rush all desperate on our foes, nor breathe till th'battle's won,
Then shout, and shout America, and conquering Washington.

915. A NEW LIBERTY SONG.

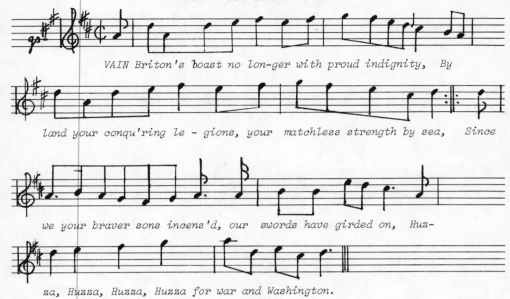

VAIN Briton's boast no lon-ger with proud indignity, By

land your conqu'ring le - gions, your matchless strength by sea,   Since

we your braver sons incens'd, our swords have girded on, Huz-

za, Huzza, Huzza, Huzza for war and Washington.

44. A New SONG. The WATRY GOD.

THE watry God, great Neptune, lay
In Dalliance soft and am'rous Play
    On Amphitritis Breast;
When up he rear'd his hoary Head,
The Tritons shrunk, the Nereids fled,
    And all their Fear confest.
    II.
Loud Thunder shook the vast Domain,
The liquid World was wrapt in Flame,
    The God amazed spoke;
"Go forth, ye Winds, and make it known
"Who dares thus shake my coral Throne
    "And fill my Realms with Smoke."
    III.
The Winds, obsequious at his Word,
Sprung strongly up t'obey their Lord,
    And saw two Fleets away.
Hopkins commanded one brave Line,
The other Navy, Howe, was thine,
    In Terror and Dismay.
    IV.
They view America's bold Sons,
Deal Death and Slaughter from their Guns,
    And strike the dreadful Blow,
That made ill-fated British Slaves
Seek life by flying o'er the Waves,
    Or sink to Shades below.
    V.
Amaz'd they fly and tell their Chief,
That Howe is ruin'd past Relief,
    And Hopkins conquering rode.
"Hopkins!" says Amphy, "Who is he,
"That dares usurp this Pow'r at Sea,
    And thus insult a God?"
    VI.
The Winds reply, "In distant Land
"A Congress sits, whose martial Bands,
    "Defy all Britain's Force.
"And when their floating Castles roll
"From Sea to Sea, from Pole to Pole,
    "Hopkins directs their Course."
    VII.
"And when their winged bullets fly
"To reinstate fair Liberty,
    "Or scourge oppressive Bands,
"Then gallant Hopkins, calm and great,
"Tho' Death and Carnage round him wait,
    "Performs their dread Commands."

(cont.)

VIII.

Neptune with vast Amazement hears,
How great this infant State appears,
          What Feats their Heroes do;
Washington's Deeds and Putnam's Fame,
Join'd to great Lee's immortal Name,
          And cries, "Can this be true?"

IX.

"A Congress! sure they're Brother Gods
"Who have such Heroes at their Nods
          "To govern Earth and Sea:
"I yield my Trident and my Crown
"A Tribute due to such Renown;
          "These Gods shall rule for me."

44. A New SONG. The WATRY GOD.

Moderato THE wat-ry God, great Neptune, lay In

Dalliance soft and am'-rous Play On Am-phi-tritis Breast; When

up he rear'd his hoa-ry Head, The Tri-tons shrunk, the

Ne-reids fled, And all their Fear con-fest, And

all   their Fear con - fest.

1087. A SONG.
Tune Derry down.

I.

SAINT George for their Patron our ancestors chose,
The pride of his friends, and the scourge of his foes;
To separate fiction from truth tho' unable,
Some meaning we all must ascribe to the fable.

II.

His sword might of courage, of justice his spear,
His shield of his faith might the emblem appear,
The white horse he rode on, the truth of his cause,
When engag'd as the champion of freedom and laws.

III.

The Dragon was slavery clad all in mail,
Bright guineas & moidores form'd each shining scale,
His paws were oppression, his pinions were power,
His tongue was deceit dropping lies ev'ry hour.

IV.

The virgin may signify some charter'd right,
To subjects more dear than the blessing of light,
Each day singl'd out by some new fangled laws,
A feast for the monster, to cram his vile jaws.

V.

The conquest he gain'd o'er fair Liberty's dread,
With ever-green laurels adorned his head;
What pity his children, forgetful of fame,
Should sully his trophies, dishonour his name.

VI.

What daemon suggested a voyage to make
Across the Atlantic to worry a snake,
To harass her covert with fury accurst?
She never opposes unless stricken first.

VII.

No boasts doth she utter, nor threat'nings bring,
Tho' nature with venom hath furnish'd her sting,
Had you not provok'd her, and urg'd her to battles
You had ne'er been disturb'd with the noise of her rattles.

VIII.

Take warning in time, and return home again,
Your cause is unjust, and your forces are vain;
If sever'd in pieces a dozen or more,
Again shall unite with more strength than before.

IX.

Remember Saint George, to each Englishman dear,
Mix courage with justice--his sword with his spear--
A fair silver ground wide emblazon'd his shield.
The bloody cross now only covers the field.

(cont.)

665

X.

Let pride yield to justice, resentment to reason,
Defence of our Liberty, cannot be treason;
We both may have err'd--grant us yet but our right
And then as one people we'll ever unite.

1087. A SONG.

SAINT George for their Pa-tron our ancestors chose, The
pride of his friends, and the scourge of his foes; To separate fiction from

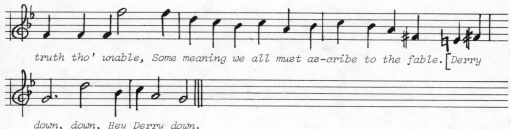

truth tho' unable, Some meaning we all must as-cribe to the fable. [Derry
down, down, Hey Derry down.

991. New-Year's Verses, Addressed to the CUSTOMERS of
THE PENNSYLVANIA EVENING POST, By the PRINTER's LADS who carry it.
Wednesday, January 1, 1777.

Hail! O America!
Hail now the joyful day!
　Exalt your voice
Shout, George is king no more,
Over this western shore;
Let him his loss deplore,
　While we rejoice.
Now in thy banner set,
Transtulet sustinet*;
　God is our King,
Who does in mercy deign,
Over us for to reign,
And our just rights maintain,
　His praises sing.
O may he deign to bless,
The great and each Congress,
　Of this our land,
With wisdom from on high,
And unanimity,
To save our liberty,
　Nobly to stand.
And on the virt'ous head,
Abundant blessings shed,
　Of Washington;
Give him to know thy will,
Fill him with martial skill,
His station to fill,
　'Till glory's won.
And may our Gen'rals all,
Officers great and small,
　Be Heaven's care:
Within the hostile field,
Guard them with thine own shield,
While they the sword do wield,
　In this great war.
O may our men be spar'd,
If not for death prepar'd;
　Lord hear our cry.
Let us behold thy face,
And taste of thy rich grace,
While we this earth do trace,
　Before we die.
And to thee th'Lord of host,
Father, Son and Holy Ghost,
　We'll give all praise,
And ever magnify,
Honor and glorify,
To all eternity,
　And never cease.
*He who transplanted us hither will support us.

991. *New-Year's Verses, Addressed to the CUSTOMERS of THE PENNSYLVANIA EVENING POST, By the PRINTER's LADS who carry it. Wed., Jan. 1, 1777.*

Hail! O A - me-rica! Hail now the joyful day! Exalt your voice

Hail! O A - me-rica! Hail now the joyful day! Exalt your voice

Shout, George is King no more, O-ver this western shore; Let him his

Shout George is King no more, O-ver this western shore; Let him his

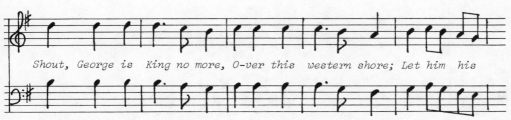

loss de-plore, While we re-joice.

loss de-plore, While we re-joice.

January 3	Battle of Princeton, New Jersey.
April 26	British raid Danbury, Connecticut.
May 1	Arthur Lee named to represent the U.S. at the Spanish court.
July 6	British occupy Fort Ticonderoga, New York, which fell later that day.
July 7	Battle of Hubbardton, Vermont.
July 20	Treaty of Long Island. The Overhill Cherokees defeated by frontier militia, cede disputed lands to Virginia and North Carolina.
August 3	Colonel Barry St. Leger reached and beseiged Fort Stanwix, New York.
August 16	Battle of Bennington.
September 11	Battle of Brandywine. Americans thrown back, and retreat to Philadelphia.
September 18	Congress flees Philadelphia.
September 19	Daniel Morgan checks Burgoyne at the Battle of Freeman's Farm. (First Battle of Saratoga).
September 20	American's routed by surprise bayonet attack at Paoli, Pennsylvania.
September 26	Howe occupies Philadelphia.
October 4	Battle of Germantown, Pennsylvania.
October 6	British General Clinton captures Forts Clinton and Montgomery, New York.
October 7	Burgoyne again checked, at Bemis Heights. (Second Battle of Saratoga).
October 16	British raid on Esopus (Kingston), New York.
October 17	Burgoyne surrenders at Saratoga.
October 22	Americans successfully defend Fort Mercer against a force of Hessians four times their size.
November 15	Articles of Confederation formally adopted by Congress.
December 17	The French inform American envoys that the King will recognize the independence of the U.S.

1005. *A new SONG composed by a prisoner in Boston jail.*
Tune, Black Sloven.

AMericans swarming by thousands on shore,
Grew mighty in mischief, were subjects no more, Fa la, &c.
Held George in defiance, his friends they trepann'd,
The loyal imprison'd, and rav'd through the land. Fa la, &c.

They boasted Great Britain no more dare oppose,
And those who dissented, they treated as foes. Fa la, &c.
Independance proclaimed, each tailor look'd big,
Flung his measure aside, became colonel and Whig. Fa la, &c.

His majesty frown'd at their folly and rage,
But his pity prevail'd, he was loth to engage. Fa la, &c.
Be easy and happy, my children, he cried,
Their madness was boundless, his mercy defy'd. Fa la, &c.

Go forth then brave HOWE, and the rebels chastise,
He spoke while soft pity sat drench'd in his eyes. Fa la, &c.
Go bear provok'd vengeance, but rather forgive,
Should the rebels submit, then spare and let live. Fa la, &c.

HOWE fled o'er the ocean, and bounc'd on his prey,
Whole colonies swarm'd, as assur'd of the day, Fa la, &c.
But what are e'en numbers, when Britons arise?
They run on sure ruin: Who meets them but dies? Fa la, &c.

Each port was a fortress, their armies secure,
Whilst lock'd in their trenches, of conquest quite sure, Fa la, &c.
The valour of Britons, when absent, despise,
And laugh'd till her levell'd artillery flies. Fa la, &c.

A'ghast they cry out, "Sure Old Harry is here;
"What thunders, what earthquakes burst full on my ear? Fa la, &c.
"Are these British regulars? 'Zounds I'll away;
"They shoot at our mans; I'll be damn'd if I stay." Fa la, &c.

The rebels retreat and their bulwarks they shun,
To the woods nimbly skulk with their brave Washington. Fa la, &c.
HOWE boldly advances, and tempts them to fight;
The rebels know better, their safety's in flight, Fa la, &c.

Their impregnable fortress, Long-Island, is taken,
And York and Kingbridge are forever forsaken. Fa la, &c.
Now where will the Yankies retreat in their flight?
To Jemina, be sure, better bundle than fight. Fa la, &c.

Come on ye brave heroes, proceed, Boston assail,
Relieve the poor Tories, who languish in jail. Fa la, &c.
To brave HOWE they their grateful oblations will bring,
And shout for the army, the navy, and king. Fa la, &c.

1005. A new SONG composed by a prisoner in Boston jail.

A-Me-ri-cans swarming by thousands on shore, Grew mighty in mischief, were subjects no more, Fa la la, fa la la, fa la la, fa la la, Held

George in de-fiance, his friends they trepann'd, The loyal imprison'd, and

rav'd through the land. Fa la la, fa la la, fa la la, fa la la, fa la

la, fa la la, fa la la.

Sy

305. *A PARODY on "The WATRY GOD"--occasioned by*
General WASHINGTON's late successes in the Jersies.

AS Mars, great GOD of battles! lay,
In dalliance soft and amorous play,
  On fair Bellona's breast;--
Surpris'd he rear'd his hoary head,
The conscious Goddess shook with dread,
  And all her fears confess'd.

Loud thunder roll'd thro' Heaven's domain,
Th' aetherial world was wrapt in flame,
  The God amazed spoke,
Go forth, ye powers and make it known
Who dares thus boldly shake my throne,
  And fill my realms with smoke.

The Gods obsequious to his word,
Sprung swiftly forth to 'bey their Lord,
  And saw two hosts away;--
The one great WASHINGTON was thine,
The other How's disorder'd line,
  In sorrow and dismay.

Appal'd they view COLUMBA's sons
Deal death and slaughter from their guns,
  And strike a dreadful blow,
Which made ill-fated British slaves,
On distant shores to find their graves,
  And sink to shades below.

Amaz'd they tell of battles won,
That Britain's ruin'd, WASHINGTON
  Alone triumphant rode:--
Ha! cries the fair, pray who is he
That dares reverse e'en JOVE's decree,
  And thus insult a GOD.

The GOD's reply, in yonder lands,
Great LIBERTY alone commands,
  And gives the Hero force;
And when his thund'ring cannons roar,
And strike with dread earth's distant shore,
  'Tis SHE directs their course.

And when HER winged bullets flie,
To check a tyrant's treachery,
  And lay his glories low,--
Then WASHINGTON serenely great,
Tho' death and carnage round him wait,
  Performs the dreadful blow!

                  (cont.)

The GOD with wonder heard the story,
Astonish'd view'd COLUMBA's glory,
  Which time can ne'er subdue,
Great WARREN's deeds and GATES's fame,
Join'd to great LEE's immortal name,
  And cried can this be true!

Britain shall cease to plague mankind,
With sister tyrants strive to bind,
  And check the freeborn soul:
To WASHINGTON her trophies yield,
FREEDOM shall triumph in the field,
  And rule from pole to pole.

305. A PARODY on "The WATRY GOD"--occasioned by General WASHINGTON's
late successes in the Jersies.

AS Mars, great GOD of battles! lay, In dalliance soft and
amorous play, On fair Bel - lo - na's breast;-- Surpris'd he rear'd his hoa - ry head, The con - scious God - dess
shook with dread, And all her fears con - fess'd, [And

all her fears con - fess'd.]

259. The SWEETS of LIBERTY. An Ode.

---sic deiur vincere, sic moriar.

How blest is he, who unconstrain'd
  Obeys kind nature's equal laws;
Who fears no power, by might maintain'd,
  And boldly vindicates his country's cause.

Fortune's attacks secure he braves,
  Firmly prepar'd for any chance;
None tremble at her frowns but slaves,
  Whose dastard fears their abject hopes enhance.

With thee --- who treads th'eternal snows
  Of distant Greenland's icy coast;
Or scorch'd beneath the line he glows,
  By adverse deities unkindly tost.

His roving steps uncurb'd by dread,
  From clime to clime can freely roam;
He goes where choice or fortune lead,
  Freedom his guide, and all the world his home.

The face of war he nobly dares,
  In freedom's cause prepar'd to bleed;
And, soldier-like, desires all cares
  But such as bounteous heav'n hath long decreed.

Conscious of worth, his gen'rous soul
  To stoop to lawless power disdains;
No threats his principles controul,
  He e'en enjoys his liberty in chains.

'Tis not ambition's giddy strife,
  But justice feeds the hero's fire;
Th'emblazon'd joys of public life
  May please his fancy, not his breast inspire.

Hail Genius of our bleeding land!
  (Whose smiles confer a deathless name)
Thy glorious cause nerves ev'ry hand,
  To pluck the laurel from the brow of fame.

              P

259. *The SWEETS of LIBERTY. An Ode.*

How blest is he, who unconstrain'd O-beys kind nature's e -qual laws; Who fears no po - wer, by might main - tain'd,

(1) ♪ in origenal (2) ♪ in original

coun - try's cause, vin-di - cates his coun - try's cause.]

581. The FIERY DEVIL.
In Imitation of the WATRY GOD.

The Stygian God, great Beelzebub
With Bute and North his fav'rite Club,
    In Pandemonium met;
Where they, with all th'infernal Host,
Who Heav'nly Liberty had lost,
    Foam'd with invideous Sweet.

The dreary Cavern rang Applause
Obedience to old Belial's Laws
    Combin'd the Demons stood:
And all the fierce Cerberean Breed
Who Hell in hideous Forms exceed,
    Howl'd for Columba's Blood.

Then rose the grim Tartarean God,
Bespoke Attention with a Nod,
    And thus tremendous spake;
(Which burst Hell's burning Vaults intwain,
Rais'd Billows on the burning Main;
    And made the Concave shake)

"Hail damn'd Associates" let us all
Conspire to plan Columba's Fall,
    See I here's the sily Bute;
Vulcan shall in his bellowing Forge,
Cast Thunder-Bolts for minion George
    Who waits to execute.

The grisly Fiends all grin'd Assent,
Bute on the dark Embassage went
    To Albion's bloody Court;
There to confer with British Power,
And at the Hell appointed Hour
    Return and make Report.

George to the Scot, Attention paid
Thank'd the kind Monarch for his Aid
    In such laborious Task;
I form'd th'infernal Prince of Night
This Craft and his Satannic Might
    With Deference should ask.

This done---the red sulphurean Breed,
Were all commission'd for the Deed,
    With Britains Myrmidons;
Who brib'd the hoary God of Sea
Their murd'ring Legions to convey,
    And crush Columba's Sons.
                              (cont.)

Next an enormous Fleet appears
(The Effect of Albion's Golden Year)
  Full fraught with missle Death;
To storm her fair Mercantile Towns,
Spread dismal Carnage without bounds
  By foul Pandora's Breath.

But HE who rides upon the Sph-es,
With bright Angelic Charioteer's,
  Spake with the Thunder's Voice;
Columba! hear th'Almighty Lord!
Defend your Birthright! grasp the Sword,
  Make this your happy Choice!"

The heavenly Edict spread alarm,
--A Universal Shout "to Arm--"
  Was heard from Sea to Sea.
"We'll front the haughty Tyrant Foe,
And let all HELL and Albion know,
  Columba will be free.

581. *The FIERY DEVIL. In Imitation of the WATRY GOD.*

The Stygian God, great Beelzebub With Bute and North his

fav' - rite Club, In Pan - de - mo - nium met; Where

they, with all th'in - fer - nal Host, Who heav'n - ly Li - ber -

ty had lost, Foam'd with in - vi - deous Sweet. Foam'd

with in - vi - deous Sweet.

From the (LONDON) PUBLIC LEDGER.
THE HEADS, Or, the Year 1776.

YE wrong heads, and strong heads, attend to my strains;
Ye clear heads, and queer heads, and heads without brains;
Ye thick skulls, and quick skulls, and heads great and small;
And ye heads that aspire to be heads over all.
                    Derry Down, &c.
Ye ladies--(I would not offend for the world)
Whose bright heads, and light heads, are feather'd and curl'd,
The mighty dimensions dame Nature surprize,
To find she'd so grosly mistaken the size.
                    Derry down, &c.
And ye petit maitres, your heads I might spare,
Encumber'd with nothing---but powder and hair;
Who vainly disgrace the true monkey race,
By transplanting the tail from its own native place.
                    Derry down, &c.
Enough might be said, durst I venture my rhymes,
On crown'd heads, and round heads, of these modern times;
This slipery path let me cautiously tread---
The neck else may answer, perhaps for the head.
                    Derry down, &c.
The heads of the church, and the heads of the state,
Have taught much, and wrought much, too much to repeat;
On the neck of corruption uplifted 'tis said,
Some rulers, alas! are too high-- by the head.
                    Derry down, &c.
Ye schemers and dreamers of politic things,
Projecting the downfall of kingdoms and kings;
Can your wisdom declare how this body is fed,
When the members rebel and wage war with the head.
                    Derry down, &c.
Expounders, confounders, and heads of the law,
I bring case in point, do not point out a flaw,
If reason is treason, what plea shall I plead?
To your chief I appeal -- for your chief has a head.
                    Derry down, &c.
On Britania's bosom sweet liberty smil'd,
The parent grew strong while she foster'd the child:
Neglecting her offspring, a fever she bread,
Which contracted her limbs, and distracted her head.
                    Derry down, &c.

                              (cont.)

Ye learned state doctors, your labours are vain,
Proceeding by bleeding to settle her brain;
Much less can your art the lost members restore,
Amputation must follow---perhaps something more.
                    Derry down, &c.

Pale Goddess of whim! when with cheeks lean or full,
The influence seizes an Englishman's skull,
He blunders yet wonders his schemes ever fail,
Tho' often mistaking the head for the tail.
                    Derry down, &c.

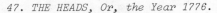

47. THE HEADS, Or, the Year 1776.

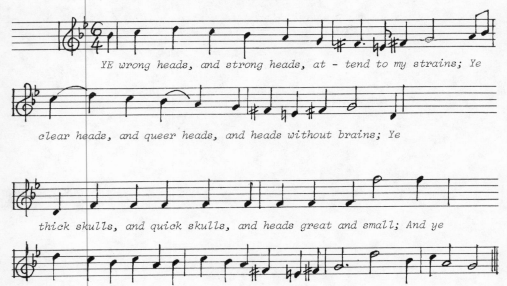

YE wrong heads, and strong heads, at - tend to my strains; Ye

clear heads, and queer heads, and heads without brains; Ye

thick skulls, and quick skulls, and heads great and small; And ye

heads that aspire to be heads over all. Derry down, down, Hey Derry down.

809.

The following SONG was compos'd by a loyal subject, for the 4th day of
June, 1777. Tune,-- Rule, Britannia.

Blest cause of genial life, arise,
Illume the wide, unbounded skies;
Propitious smile, and chear the morn,
This day illustrious GEORGE was born.
CHORUS:
Rule, Great GEORGE! thy injur'd rights regain,
And Britannia's glory long maintain,
Hail! happy day, Oh glorious priod come,
When Traitors meet their final doom.

Britannia on triumphant car,
Hails her intrepid sons of war;
Suspend, this day, the glorious strife,
Which gave my darling Monarch life.

Hark! Freedom from her parent isles,
Demands a respite from our toils;
She bids obedient song be gay,
And own her Guardian's natal day.

Commerce and Arts exalt their plume,
The brow of culture joys assume;
The sorrow'd heart meets sweet allay,
On their Protector's natal day.

Sure bulwark of the best of Kings,
See Loyalty extend her wings;
Embody'd legions catch the flame,
And sing aloud their Monarch's name.

Fame, with thy trump, on high proclaim,
His worth, his virtues, and his name:
Ne'er ceasing, sound from shore to shore,
'Till Time and Kingdoms are no more.

809. The following SONG was compos'd by a loyal subject, for the 4th day of June, 1777.

Blest cause of ge - - - nial

690

life, a - rise, Il-lume the wide, un-

boun - - ded skies; [illume, illume the wide, un-

boun - ded skies;]

Pro - pi - tious smile, [smile,] and chear the morn, This

691

day il - lu - - - - strious GEORGE was born.

Rule, Great GEORGE! thy in - jur'd rights re-gain,

And Bri - tan - - - nia's glory long maintain, Hail! happy day, Oh

glo-rious pri - od come, When Trai - tors meet their final doom.

692

50.

To the tune of FAVORITE HUNTING SONG, sung by Mr. Taylor.
Hark! Hark! the joy inspiring Horn.
On the Death of GENERAL MONTGOMERY.

COME soldiers all in chorus join
To pay that tribute at the shrine,
  Of brave Montgomery;
Which to the memory is due
Of him who fought and died that you
  Might live and yet be free.
With chearful and undaunted mind
Domestic happiness resign'd
 He with a chosen band,
Thro' desarts wild with fix'd intent
Canada for to conquer went,
  Or perish sword in hand.
Six weeks before St. John's they lay
While cannon on them constant play,
  In cold and marshy ground,
When Prescot forc'd at length to yield,
Aloud proclaim'd it in the field
  Virtue a friend had found.
To Montreal he wing'd his way
Which seem'd impatient to obey
  And open'd wide its gate,
Convinc'd no force could e'er repel
Troops who had just behav'd so well,
  Under so hard a fate.
With scarce on third part of his force
Then to Quebec he beat his course,
  That grave of heroes slain,
The pride of France the great Montcalm
And Wolf the strength of Britain's arm,
  Both fell on Abraham's Plain.
Having no less of fame requir'd
There too Montgomery expir'd
  With conquest by his side;
Carlton 'tis said his corse convey'd
To earth his all the grand parade
  Of Military Pride.

50. On the Death of GENERAL MONTGOMERY.

COME sol - diers all in cho - rus join To pay   that tri -bute

at   the shrine, Of brave Montgo - me - ry;   [Of brave Montgo - me -

Sy

ry; Which to the me - mo - ry is due Of

him who fought and died that you Might live and yet be

free. [Might live and yet be free.]

Sy

f

695

BOSTON. *HAVING lately seen many Compositions consecrated to the Memory of General MONTGOMERY, I suppose a Parody, which accidentally fell in my Hands, in Honor to Major General WARREN, would not be disagreeable. I should have been happier, was I possessed of it sooner, but General WARREN was too precious to his Countrymen, to have any Thing disagreeable, even in remote Time, that tends to perpetuate his Memory.*

PARODY.

In a mouldring Cave, where th' oppressed retreat,
  COLUMBA sat wasted with Care--
She wept for her WARREN exclaim'd against Fate,
  And gave herself up to Despair.
The Walls of her Cell she had sculptur'd around,
  With the Form of her favourite Son, ---
And even the Dust as it lay on the Ground,
  Express'd the high Deeds he had done.--
The Sire of the Gods from his Chrystalline Throne,
  Beheld the disconsolate Dame,
And mov'd at her Tears, he sent Mercury down,
  And these were the Tidings that came--
COLUMBA, forbear--not a Sigh to alloy,
  For thy WARREN so justly belov'd---
Thy Grief shall be chang'd into Triumphs of Joy,
  Thy WARREN's, not dead, but remov'd---
The Sons of the Earth, the proud Giants of old,
  Have broke from their darksome Abode,
And this is the News---for in Heaven it's told,
  They are marching to War with the Gods.---
A Council was held in the Chambers of Jove,
  And this was the final Decree,
That WARREN should soar to the Armies above,---
  And the Charge was entrusted to me.
To Bunker's tall Heights, with the Orders I flew,
  He beg'd for a Moment's Delay.
Like Wolfe, cry'd forbear, let me Vict'ry hear,
  And then thy Commands I'll obey.--
He spake,---with a film incompass'd his Eyes,
  And bore him away in an Urn,
Lest the Fondness he felt, for the Heroes he left,
  Should tempt him again to return.--

374. PARODY.

In a mouldring Cave, where th' op-pressed re-treat, CO-LUM-BA sat wasted with Care--She wept for her WAR - REN ex-claim'd a - gainst Fate, And gave herself up to Des-pair. The

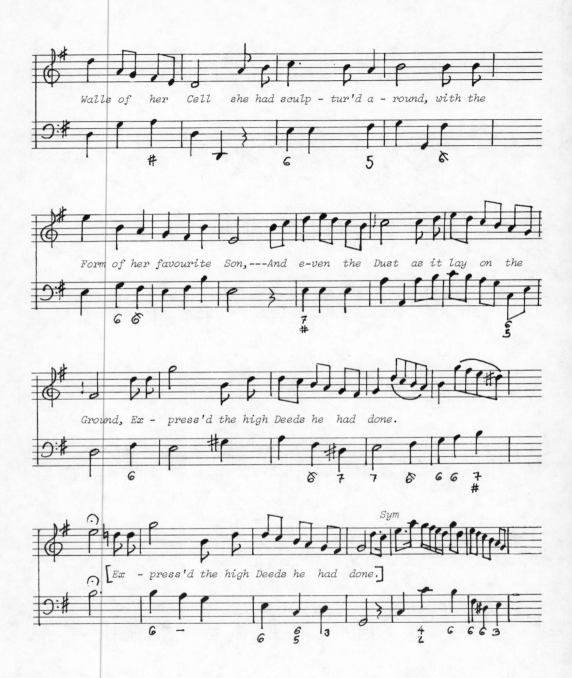

Walls of her Cell she had sculp - tur'd a - round, with the

Form of her favourite Son, ---And e-ven the Dust as it lay on the

Ground, Ex - press'd the high Deeds he had done.

Sym

[Ex - press'd the high Deeds he had done.]

6
4   3

699

53. *A SONG. On the Surrender of Lieutenant-General BURGOYNE*
   and his Army, to Major-General GATES.
   Tune,-My Daddy was in the Rebellion.

AS JACK, the King's commander,
  Was going to his duty,
Thro' all the crowd he smil'd and bow'd
  To every blooming beauty.

The city rung of feats he'd done
  In Portugal and Flanders;
And all the town tho't he'd be crown'd
  The first of Alexanders.

To Hampton court he first repairs,
  To kiss great George's hand, Sir;
Then to harangue on state affairs
  Before he left the land, Sir.

The Lower House sat mute as mouse
  To hear his grand oration;
And all the Peers with loudest cheers
  Proclam'd him thro' the nation!

Then straight he went to Canada,
  Next to Ticonderoga;
And, passing those, away he goes
  Straitway to Saratoga.

With grand parade his march he made
  To gain his wish'd for station,
Whilst far and wide his minions hie'd
  To spread his PROCLAMATION.

"To such as staid he offers made
  "Of Pardon on SUBMISSION;
"But savage bands should waste the lands
  "Of ALL in OPPOSITION."

But ah! the cruel fate of war!
  This boasted son of Britain,
When mounting his triumphal car,
  With sudden fear was smitten.

The sons of Freedom gather'd round,
  His hostile bands confounded;
And when they'd fain have turn'd their backs.
  They found themselves surrounded.

                              (cont.)

700

In vain they fought, in vain they fled,
  Their Chief, humane and tender,
To save the rest soon tho' it best
  His forces to surrender.

Brave St. Clair, when he first retir'd
  Knew what the fates portended;
And Arnold with heroic Gates,
  His conduct have defended.

Thus may America's brave sons
  With honor be rewarded;
And be the fate of all her foes
  The same as here recorded.

53. A SONG. *On the Surrender of Lieutenant-General BURGOYNE and his Army, to Major-General GATES.*

AS JACK, the King's com-man - der, Was going to his du-ty, Thro'
all the crowd he smil'd and bow'd To every blooming beauty. The
ci-ty rung of feats he'd done In Portu-gal and Flan - ders; And
all the town tho't he'd be crown'd the first of A - lex - an-ders.

375. A NEW SONG.
To the Tune of--GOD SAVE THE KING.

FAME, let thy Trumpet sound,
Rouse all the World around,
             With loud Alarms!
Fly hence to Britain's Land,
Tell George in vain his Hand
Is rais'd 'gainst FREEDOM's Band,
             When call'd to Arms!
Each Island of the Main
Free'd from the Tyrant's Chain,
             Shall own our Sway;
Loud Songs of Thankfulness,
Each Bosom shall possess;
Fondly fair FREEDOM's Bliss,
             They shall display!
LEXINGTON's Plains proclaim,
From brazen Trump of Fame,
             Our Strength in Fight;
DEATH shew'd his Arrows round,
And purpl'd all the Ground
Nor one had Safety found,
             But in swift Flight.
Again they bend their Course,
With full united Force,
             To BUNKER-HILL;
Asham'd of their late Flight,
With an envenom'd Spite,
They fiercely rush to Fight,
             Our Blood to spill!
But FREEDOM's Sons once more,
Did Vengeance on them show'r,
             And check their Pride;
Of wounded and of slain,
Full fifteen Hundred Men,
With Blood the Field did stain,
             On BRITAIN's Side!
Where BOSTON's Turrets rear,
Their Heads aloft in Air,
             They fly for rest;
Hem'd in on ev'ry Side,
The Legions vainly try'd,
To stem the rusing Tide,
             Which on them prest!
Behold! those Sons of Shame,
Who falsely boast of Fame,
             In War acquir'd!
Hark!-How our Cannon roar!---
They fly fair BOSTON's Shore!
Nor can resist our Power,
             By FREEDOM fir'd.
                   (cont.)

Come MUSE! fly hence apace,
NEW-JERSEY claims a Place,
           In War's rude Song;
Our March, through Hail and Snow,
To meet the murd'rous Foe!
And sing their overthrow,
           To me belong.
TRENTON and PRINCETON own,
How we in Arms have shone;--
           Heroic Band!
We came--they fled or yield!
In vain their Arms they weild,
Victorious in the Field,
           Confest we stand!
CANADA's restless Sons,
Shall dread our thund'ring Guns
           And fly our Pow'r;
GATES! Virtue's fairest Son,
Has made the Cowards run,
Striving their Fate to shun,
           In luckless Hour!
Pursu'd from Post to Post,
BRITANIA's mighty Host!
           Out-strip'd the Wind!
With coward Fear possesst,
Swiftly they onward prest,
Yet could not ease no rest,
           Nor safety find.
Encircled by our Band,
See! vaunting BURGOYNE stand,
           And madly Rave!
His Strength, so late his Boast,
Is vanish'd hence and lost!
Made Captive by our Host,
           Of PATRIOTS brave!
O' gen'rous Sons of Worth!
Nobly have ye stept forth,
           Your rights to Guard;
On FAME's swift Pinions driv'n,
Th' approving Nod from Heav'n,
To crown You, shall be giv'n,
           Your just Reward.

375. A NEW SONG.

FAME, let thy Trumpet sound, Rouse all the World around,

FAME, let thy Trumpet sound, Rouse all the World around,

With loud A - larms! Fly hence to Britain's Land, Tell George in

With loud A - larms! Fly hence to Britain's Land, Tell George in

vain his Hand Is rais'd 'gainst FREEDOM's Band, When call'd to Arms!

vain his Hand Is rais'd 'gainst FREEDOM's Band, When call'd to Arms!

February 6   Franco-American alliance signed in Paris.

March 21   British adopt defensive strategy in the North and
                begin offensive in the South.

April 28   John Paul Jones, aboard the _Ranger_, executed raids along
                English coast and takes the British sloop _Drake_ off
                the coast of Northern Ireland.

May 5   Baron Friedrich Wilhelm von Steuben appointed inspector
                general by Congress.

June 17   French and British naval forces clash, and France
                enters the war against England.

June 18   Evacuation of Philadelphia by the British.

June 28   Battle of Monmouth Courthouse (Freehold), New Jersey.

July 4-12   Court-martial of General Charles Lee. Guilty of disobedience
                misbehaviour at the Battle of Monmouth; suspended from
                command.

December 29   Capture of Savannah by the British.

For THOMAS's MASSACHUSETTS SPY, &c.
COLLINET and PHEBE. A NEW SONG.
(Wrote by a YOUNG LADY in VIRGINIA, and now first published.)

AS COLLINET and PHEBE sat
  Beneath a poplar grove,
The gentle youth, with fondest truth,
  Was telling tales of love.
Dear blooming maid, the shepherd said,
  My tender vows believe;
These down cast eyes, and artless sighs,
  Can ne'er thy faith deceive!

Though some there are, from fair to fair,
  Delighting like to rove,
Such change thou ne'er, from me canst fear,
  Thy charms secure my love.
Then PHEBE now, approve my vow,
  By truth, by fondness press'd;
A smile assume to grace thy bloom,
  And make thy shepherd bless'd.

A blush o'erspread her cheek with red,
  Which half she turn'd aside;
With pleasing woes her bosom rose---
  And thus the maid replyd:
Dear gentle youth, I know thy truth,
  And all thy arts to please;
But ah! is this a time for bliss,
  Or themes so soft as these.

While all around, we hear no sound,
  But War's terrifick strains!
The drum commands our arming bands,
  And chides each tardy swain;
Our Country's call, arouses all
  Who dare be brave and free!
My love shall crown the youth alone
  Who saves himself and me.

'Tis done! he cry'd, from thy dear side,
  Now quickly I'll be gone;
From Love will I, to Freedom fly,
  A slave to thee alone!
And when I come with Laurels home,
  And all that free men crave,
To crown my love, your smiles shall prove
  The Fair reward the brave.

266. *BRITISH VALOUR DISPLAYED: Or, The BATTLE of the KEGS.*

Gallants attend, and hear a friend
  Trill forth harmonious ditty;
Strange things I'll tell, which late befel
  In Philadelphia city.
'Twas early day, as Poets say,
  Just when the sun was rising:
A soldier stood on a log of wood
  And saw a sight surprising.
As in a maze he stood to gaze,
  The truth can't be deny'd, Sir;
A sailor too in jerkin blue,
  This strange appearance viewing,
First damm'd his eyes in great surprize,
  Then said---"some mischief's brewing:
"These kegs now hold the rebels bold
  "Pack'd up like pickl'd herring,
"And they're come down t'attack the town
  "In this new way of ferrying."
The soldier new, the sailor too,
  And scar'd almost to death, Sir,
Wore out their shoes to spread the news,
  And run 'till out of breath, Sir.
Now up and down throughout the town
  Most frantic scenes were acted;
And some ran here and others there,
  Like men almost distracted.
"Some fire cry'd, which some deny'd,
  But said the earth had quaked;
And girls and boys, with hideous noise,
  Ran thro' the streets half naked.
Sir William he, snug as a flee,
  Lay all this time a snoring;
Nor dreams of harm, as he lay warm
  In bed with Mrs. Loring.
Now in a fright he starts upright,
  Awak'd by such a clatter;
First rubs his eyes, then boldly cries,
  "For God's sake, what's the matter?"
At his bed side he then espy'd
  Sir Erskine at command, Sir.
Upon one foot he had one boot
  And t'other in his hand, Sir.
"Arise, arise," Sir Erskine cries,
  "The rebels---more's the pity!
"Without a boat are all afloat
  "And rang'd before the city.
"The motley crew, in vessels new,
  "With Satan for their guide, Sir,

                                    (cont.)

708

Pack'd up in bags, and wooden kegs,
  "Come driving down the tide, Sir,
"Therefore prepare for bloody war,
  "These kegs must all be routed,
"Or surely we despis'd shall be,
  "And British valour doubted,"
The royal band now ready stand,
  All rang'd in dread array, Sir,
On every slip, in every ship,
  For to begin the fray, Sir.
The cannons roar from shore to shore.
  The small arms make a rattle;
Since wars began I'm sure no man
  E'er saw so strange a battle.
The REBEL dales--the REBEL vales,
  With REBEL trees surrounded.
The distant woods, the hills and floods,
  With REBEL echoes sounded.
The fish below swam to and fro,
  Attack'd from ev'ry quarter;
Why sure, thought they, the De'ils to pay
  'Mong folks above the water.
The kegs, 'tis said, tho' strongly made
  Of REBEL staves and hoops, Sir,
Could not oppose their pow'rful foes,
  The conqu'ring British troops, Sir.
From morn to night these men of might
  Display'd amazing courage;
And when the sun was fairly down,
  Retir'd to sup their porridge.
One hundred men, with each a pen
  Or more, upon my word, Sir,
It is most true, would be too few
  Their valour to record, Sir.
Such feats did they perform that day
  Against these wicked kegs, Sir.
That years to come, if they get home,
  They'll make their boasts and brags, Sir.

266. BRITISH VALOUR DISPLAYED: Or, The BATTLE of the KEGS.

Gal-lants at-tend, and hear a friend Trill forth harmo - nious dit-ty; Strange things I'll tell, which late be-fell in Phila-del-phia ci - ty.

1010. The TOAST.

'Tis Washington's health---Fill a bumper all round,
　For he is our glory and pride;
Our arms shall in battle with conquest be crown'd,
　Whilst virtue and he's on our side.
'Tis Washington's health---Loud cannon should roar,
　And trumpets the truth should proclaim,
There cannot be found, search all the world o'er,
　His equal in virtue and fame.
'Tis Washington's health---Our hero to bless,
　May heaven look graciously down,
O long may he live, our hearts to possess,
　And freedom still call him her own.

1010. The TOAST.

'Tis Washington's health---Fill a bumper all round, For

he is our glo - ry and pride; Our arms shall in bat - tle with

conquest be crown'd, Whilst virtue and he's on our side. [Our

arms shall in bat - tle with conquest be crown'd, Whilst virtue and

he's on our side, and he's on our side.]

From the London Evening Post.
The HALCYON DAYS of OLD ENGLAND; Or, The Wisdom of
Administration demonstrated: A BALLAD.
To the Tune of---Ye Medley of Mortals.

I.
GIVE ear to my song, I'll not tell you a story,
This is the bright aera of Old England's glory!
And tho' some may think us in pitiful plight,
I'll swear they're mistaken, for matters go right!
  Sing tantarrarara wise all, wise all,
  Sing tantararara wise all!

II.
Let us laugh at the cavils of weak, silly elves!
Our Statesmen are wise men! they say so themselves!
And tho' little mortals may hear it with wonder,
'Tis consummate WISDOM that causes each blunder!
  Sing tantarara wise all, &c.

III.
They now are engag'd in a glorious war!
(It began about tea about feathers and tar)
With spirit they push what they've planned with sense!
Forty millions they've spent--for a tax of three pence!
  Sing tantarara wise all, &c.

IV.
The debts of the nation do grieve them so sore,
To lighten our burden--they load us the more!
They aim at th' American's cash, my dear honey!
Yet beggar this kingdom, and send them the money!
  Sing tantararara wise all, &c.

V.
What honours we're gaining by taking their forts,
Destroying batteaux, and blocking up ports!
Burgoyne would have work'd them--but for a mishap
By Gates and by Arnold--he's caught in a trap!
  Sing tantararara wise all, &c.

VI.
But Howe was more cautious and prudent by far,
He sail'd with his fleet up the great Delaware:
All summer he struggled, and strove to undo them,
But the plague of it was, that he could not get to them!
  Sing tantararara wise all, &c.

VII.
Oh! think us not cruel, because our allies
Are savagely scalping men, women and boys!
Maternal affection to this step doth move us--
The more they are scalped--the more they will love us!
  Sing tantararara wise all, &c.

(cont.)

VIII.

Some folks are uneasy, and make a great pother,
For the loss of one army and half of another:
But Sirs, next campaign by ten thousands we'll slay them
If we can but find soldiers, and money to pay them!
   Sing tantararara wise all, &c.

IX.

I've Sung you my song, now I'll give you a pray'r;
May peace soon succeed to this horrible war!
Again may we live with our brethren in concord,
And the authors of mischief all hang in a strong cord!
   Sing tantararara wise all, wise all,
   Sing tantararara wise all.

55. The HALCYON DAYS of OLD ENGLAND; Or, The Wisdom of Administration demonstrated. A BALLAD.

GIVE ear to my song, I'll not tell you a sto - ry, This is the bright ae-ra of Old England's glo-ry! And tho' some may think us in pi-ti-ful plight, I'll swear they're mista-ken for matters go right! Sing tan-tar-ra-ra-ra wise all, wise all, Sing tan-tar-ra-ra-ra wise all!

288.

The following SONG was composed ex Tempore, on receiving the TREATISE from France.

I.

God save America.
Free from despotic Sway,
  Till Time shall cease
Hush'd be the Din of Arms,
Also fierce War's Alarms,
And follow in all her Charms
  Heaven born Peace.

II.

Next in our Song shall be,
Guardian of Liberty,
  Louis the King
Terrible God of War,
Plac'd in victorious Car
Of France and of Navarre,
  Louis the King.

III.

GOD save great Washington,
Fair FREEDOM's chosen Son;
  Long to command.
May ev'ry Enemy,
Far from his Presence fly,
And be grim Tyranny,
  Bound by his Hand.

IV.

Thy Name Montgomery,
Still in each Heart shall lie,
  Prais'd in each Breath:
Tho' on the fatal Plain,
Thou wer't untimely slain,
Yet shall thy Virtues gain.
  Rescue from Death.

288. *The following SONG was composed ex Tempore, on receiving the TREATISE from France.*

God save A - me-ri-ca. Free from des-po-tic Sway,

God save A - me-ri-ca. Free from des-po-tic Sway,

Till Time shall cease   Hush'd be the Din of Arms, Al-so fierce

Till Time shall cease   Hush'd be the Din of Arms, Al-so fierce

War's A-larms, And fol - low in all her Charms Hea-ven born Peace.

War's A-larms, And fol - low in all her Charms Hea-ven born Peace.

56. The TRUE SOLDIER. A NEW SONG.
To the Tune of—BLACK SLOVEN.

WHEN valor directed by motives sincere
Nerves the arm of a soldier; what foe can he fear?
Undaunted he fights, for bright virtue and fame,
And grasps at the lawrel to crown the campaign.

No horrible story of Briton or Hessian,
Will ever incline him to quit his profession,
Which eager to follow his soul's all on flame,
And burns for a part in the next brave campaign.

In fatigue toil and danger he nobly delights,
No station alarms him, no terror affrights;
All the fortune of war he unmov'd can sustain,
To gain his last wish, a triumphant campaign.

Tho'each of his foes were like Hercules brave,
While their efforts were tending a land to enslave,
He'd view their menaces with silent disdain
And court the fierce combat and bloody campaign.

Should their numbers the legions of Xerxes surpass,
Were their limbs of firm steel, and their bodies of brass
He'd attempt to dissolve them in gun powder flame,
And smile at the terror of such a campaign.

The love of his country impassions his breast,
Impels him unequal the field to contest;
To exert ev'ry nerve and distend ev'ry vein,
And a thousand times die in a single campaign.

The wreath shall be twin'd with unfading renown,
His brow to encircle, his actions to crown,
Till clarion immortal in sonorous strain,
Shall transmit to ages the glorious campaign.

56. The TRUE SOLDIER. A NEW SONG.

WHEN valor directed by motives sincere Nerves the arm of a soldier; What foe can he fear? [Fa la la, fa la la, fa la la, fa la la, fa la la,] Un - daunted he fights, for bright

virtue and fame, And   grasps at the lawrel to crown the campaign. [Fa la

la, fa la la, fa la la, fa la la, fa la la, fa la la, fa la la.]

199.

From the LONDON EVENING POST.
Tune---A Cob'er there was, &c.

YE poor simple people, who foolishly think,
That the glory of Britain is likely to sink;
Your affairs will soon prosper, recover your frights,
For the Hero of Minden will set them to rights.
            Derry down, &c.
'Tis true, that we all have some cause to complain,
Of the laurels we got by the summer's campaign,
Henceforward our arms, without doubt, will succeed,
Since so great a commander has taken the lead.
            Derry down, &c.
Our Premier! a peaceable, good kind of man,
Is not over found of his vigorous plan;
But since war is a measure he's oblig'd to pursue,
He has chose a fit person to carry it through.
            Derry down, &c.
His judgment sometimes, if the enemy's near,
Is weaken'd, its true, by the passion of fear;
But having th' Atlantic 'twixt him and his foe,
All his talents for war he'll intrepidly shew.
            Derry down, &c.
'Gainst the foes of Great-Britain, the legions of France,
Price(sic) Ferdinand thought him but loth to advance;
'Gainst his countrymen none can his ardour impeach,
He's ready enough, but they're out of his reach.
            Derry down, &c.
How surpris'd did our Gen'rals his orders receive,
With what joy they attempt what he bids them atchieve;
Since they all must conclude, by his being in place,
To be broke and cashier'd is not thought a disgrace.
            Derry down, &c.
His spirit must soon make the Colonies yield,
He's bold in the council, tho' slack in the field;
And such orders he'll issue, while safe from the storm,
As he'd rather be d---'d, than be forc'd to perform.
            Derry down, &c.
Then droop not, Britannia, but lift up your voice,
And join in applauding this excellent choice;
Tho' Sackville once left on your glory a stain,
Your disgraces will all be repaid by Germain.
            Derry down, &c.

TOMAHAWK.

199.

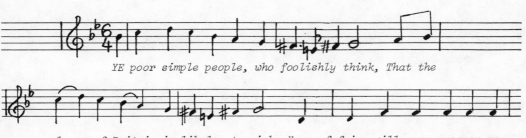

YE poor simple people, who foolishly think, That the

glo-ry of Britain is likely to sink; Your af-fairs will soon prosper, re-

co-ver your frights, For the He-ro of Minden will set them to rights, Derry

down, [down, Hey Derry down.]

Mr. Louden,

Enclosed is a new original camp song, which please to insert in your paper, when convenient. I am,

Your's, &c.
LIBERTY's CALL.
Tune, Black-Sloven

Come and listen my lads to sweet Liberty's lay,
For protected by her nought shall ever dismay;
Fal la, &c.
'Tis dear Liberty's voice! pray attend to her call;
While inspired by her charms we her foes shall appal.
Fa lal lal, &c.
My dear sons who so bravely have fought in my cause,
In defence of your freedom, your country, your laws---
See the goal full in view! but persist for a day,
Wide abroad, o'er your bands, I'll my banner display---
My bright banner! which in a once dear happy isle,
Was rever'd and ador'd, while the virt'ous did smile---
Now they've spurn'd me, I scorn such despisers to sue;
But have left the Old World to reside in the New.
And lo! here my wide empire extended shall be,
From the Pole to the Zone, and the shores of each sea;
For when True-British-Honour, expiring, was slain,
He bequeath'd to his sons, his controul of the main.
Then attend all my vot'ries! revere my decree---
Be their mem'ries still dear, by whose blood you are free:
As you honour to heroes departed perform,
Oh! be grateful to heroes who've weather'd the storm:
See, my brave Standard-bearer encircled with Bays,
Let his praise be rehears'd still in each of your lays;
For enraptur'd with me, the great WASHINGTON came,
And led on my choice sons, both to freedom and fame.
And now hark! all afar! who desire to behold,
Human natures true rights, shine like burnished gold---
To the gen'rous and brave of all nations I call,
Here is Place for the worthy all over the Ball.
Fal lal lal la, &c.

683. LIBERTY's CALL.

listen my lads to sweet Liberty's lay, For pro-tected by her nought shall

e - ver dismay; [Fa la la, fa la la, fa la la, fa la la,] 'Tis

dear Li-ber-ty's voice! pray at- tend to her call; While in-

spired by her charms we her foes shall ap - pal. [Fa la la, fa la la, fa la

la, fa la la, fa la la, fa la la, fa la la.

Sy

July 5	*Plundering of New Haven by William Tryon, Royal Governor of New York.*
July 15	*General Anthony Wayne takes Stony Point.*
August 29	*Generals John Sullivan and James Clinton defeat loyalists and Indians at Newton. Sullivan moves on to destroy 10 Seneca and Cayuga villages.*
September 23	*John Paul Jones' <u>Bonhomme Richard</u> (named after Franklin) defeats the British Warship, <u>Serapis</u>.*
	Siege operations begin against Savannah.

850-854. A MEDLEY for the LIGHT INFANTRY. BY A SOLDIER.

Tune--Over the Hills and far away.

SOLDIER whilst the flowing bowl
Warms your heart and cheers your soul,
Let me to your mind recall
Scenes familiar to us all,
In the gloomy forest's shade
Where your weary limbs you've laid,
Or your parched mouth applied
To the cool refreshing tide.

Think you see the nights again
When, amid the rattling rain,
Some of Britain's light-arm'd troops
Sit around their fires in groupes;
Some, in wigwams seeking rest,
With the toiling march opprest,
Sleep the stormy night away,
Heedless of the coming day.

Tune--By the gayly circling Glass.

Listen to that swelling noise!
'Tis the bugle's warlike voice,
Which, in accents loud and clear,
Warns us that the foe is near.
War to noble minds has charms:--
See the Light-Bobs spring to arms,
Form, and march without delay,
Pleased the summons to obey.

Tune---Away to the Copse.

Behold with what ardor to action they press,
    They dash into cover with glee;
Insulted Britannia they wish to redress,
    And set sad America free;
Thro' thickets and marshes they patiently go,
    'Till day-light anounces the morn.--
Assail'd by a volley---to close with the foe
    They rush----at the sound of the horn.
Past many a bullet and sulphur'ous cloud
    They forward to conquest proceed.
Now flight's the resource of the fanatic crowd,---
    The Britons pursue them with speed:
The boasters who lately their prowess defied
    And vow'd to have gallantly stood,
The well-pointed bayonet humbles their pride,
    And bathes the false rebels in blood.

                                        (cont.)

728

Tune---Hosier's Ghost.

Mark yon wretch submissive bending,
  In whose features shame and grief
Mixt with terror seem contending---
  That was late a Rebel Chief.
  "Give me quarter," hear him crying,
  "I beseech you on my knee!
  "I am not prepar'd for dying
  "Since my country's wrong'd by me.

"For your vows and treaties breaking,
  "Tho' your forfeit life should pay,
"Rise---it is not worth my taking,"
  (Hear the gen'rous victor say.)
"Give this lesson due attention,
  "If you wou'd be truly free,
"Help to quell this dire contention,
  "Take your country's part like me.

Tune---Lumps of Pudding.

We've shewn them full oft' of what stuff we are made,
As often unmerited mercy display'd;
But shou'd they persist, we'll not vengeance restrain,
But probe to the quick the approaching campaign;
Then hence with all thread-bare disputes for this night,
To laugh there's a season, as well as to fight:
And one at a time is enough by my soul,
And so brother Soldier---about with the bowl.

729

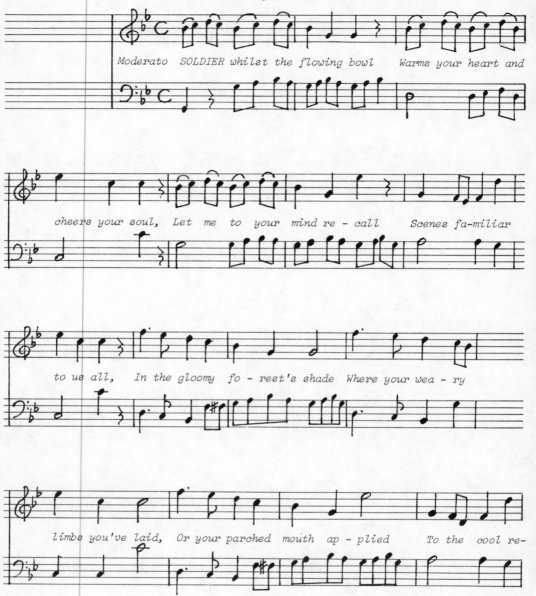

Moderato SOLDIER *whilst the flowing bowl* *Warms your heart and*

cheers your soul, *Let me to your mind re - call* *Scenes fa-miliar*

to us all, *In the gloomy fo - rest's shade* *Where your wea - ry*

limbs you've laid, *Or your parched mouth ap - plied* *To the cool re-*

730

freshing tide. Think you see the nights a-gain When, a-mid the

rattling rain, Some of Bri-tain's light-arm'd troops

Sit a-round their fires in groupes; Some, in wigwams seeking rest,

With the toiling march op-prest, Sleep the stor-my night a-way,

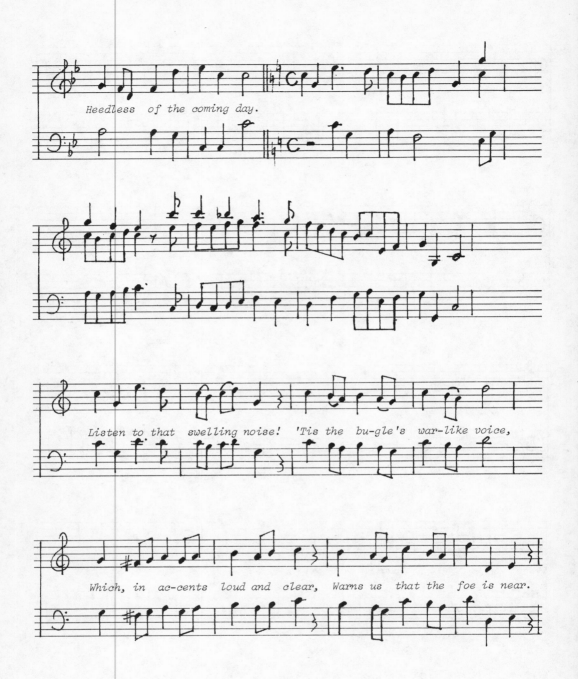

Heedless of the coming day.

Listen to that swelling noise! 'Tis the bu-gle's war-like voice,

Which, in ac-cents loud and clear, Warns us that the foe is near.

[Warns us that the foe is near.]

War to no - ble minds has charms:--See the Light-Bobs spring to arms,

Form, and march with- out de-lay, Pleased the sum-mons to o - bey.

[Pleased the sum-mons to o-bey.]

Be-hold with what ar-dor to action they press, They dash in-to co-ver with glee; In-sulted Bri- tannia they wish to re- dress, And set [sad A- me - ri - ca,] sad A- me-ri-ca free; Thro'

thickets and mar - shes they pa-tiently go, 'Till day -light a-nounces the morn.--- As-sail'd by a vol-ley---to close *with the* foe [*They rush---at the sound of the horn, The sound of the horn, The sound of the horn, The sound of the horn*]····

1. Page missing in GB/Lbm, G.311.(152).

They rush--at the sound of the horn. Past ma-ny a bullet and sulphur'ous

cloud They forward to con-quest pro-ceed. Now flight's the re-

source of the fa-na-tic crowd,---The Bri-tons pur - sue them with

speed: [pur-sue them with speed:]

The boasters who late - ly their

prowess de - fied And vow'd to have gallant-ly stood, The

well-pointed ba-yo-net humbles their pride, And bathes the false

re - bels in blood. [false re-bels in blood. false re-bels in blood. false

re-bels in blood. . . . .

. . . . And bathes the false re - bels in blood.]

Mark yon wretch submissive bending, In whose features shame and

grief Mixt with ter-ror seem con-tending--That was late a Rebel

Chief. "Give me quarter," hear him crying, "I be-seech you on my

knee! I am not prepar'd for dying Since my country's wrong'd by

me. "For your vows and treaties breaking, Tho' your forfeit life should

pay, Rise--it is not worth my taking," (Hear the gen'rous victor

say.) "Give this les - son due attention, If you wou'd be truly

free, Help to quell this dire con-tention, Take your

country's part like me."   We've   shewn them full oft' of what

stuff we are made, As of-ten unme-ri-ted mer-cy display'd; But

shou'd they persist, we'll not vengeance restrain, But

probe to the quick the ap - proaching campaign; Then

hence with all thread-bare dis - putes for this night, To

2. End of missing page in GB/Lbm, G.311. (152).

laugh there's a season, as well as to fight: And

one at a time is e - nough by my soul, And so bro-ther Sol-dier a-

bout with the bowl. [Then hence with all thread-bare dis-

putes for this night, To   laugh there's a season, as well as to fight:And

one at a time is e - nough   by my soul, And so brother Soldier--- a -

bout with the bowl.]

From the NEW-YORK PACKET.
A NEW SONG,
To the tune of "One night as Ned stept into bed," &c.

JULY they say, the fifteenth day,
In glitt'ring arms arrayed,
That Gen'ral WAYNE, and his brave men,
The British lines essayed;
Just twelve at night, if I am right,
And honestly informed,
Both wings at once, they did advance,
And Stony-Point they stormed.
    With ascents steep, morasses deep,
This boasted place abounded,
Strong abettees, of forked trees,
Was doubly plac'd around it;
"In this strong place, the rebel race,
"Us never dare come night Sir,
"Great WASHINGTON, and all his train,
"I JOHNSON do defy Sir."
    But mark the fate of JOHNSON's bate,
How quickly he was humbled,
When light'ning like, bold WAYNE did strike,
His pride and glory tumbled;
See FLEURY brave, the standard wave,
Which strongly was defended,
And from his foes, 'midst of their blows,
Most gallantly did rend it.
    Let STEWART's name in books of fame,
Forever be recorded,
Through show'rs of balls, he scal'd their walls,
And danger disregarded;
O'er stones and rocks, heroic Knox,
To charge the foe he pushed,
In gallant fight, with eagles' flight,
O'er their strong ramparts rushed.
    And GIBBONS, gay as chearful May,
His duty well discharged,
He dealt his foes, such deadly blows,
That left their walls unguarded.
May wars alarms, still rouse to arms,
The gallant sons of brav'ry,
Who dare withstand, a tyrant's band,
And crush infernal slav'ry.

324. A NEW SONG.

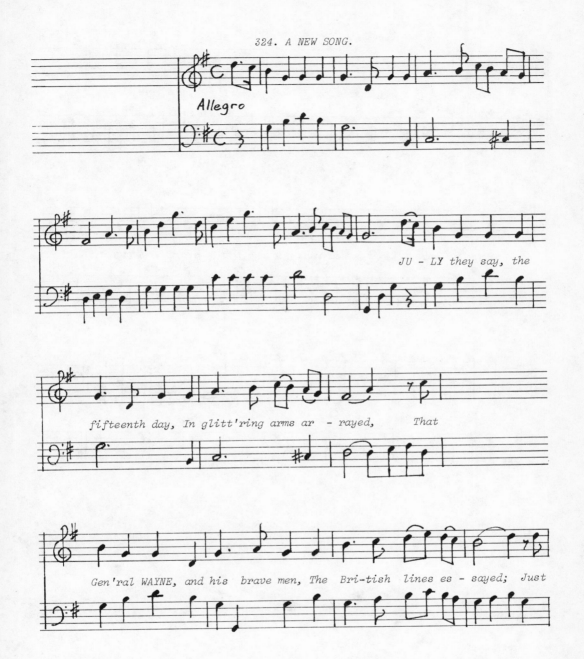

JU - LY they say, the
fifteenth day, In glitt'ring arms ar - rayed,   That
Gen'ral WAYNE, and his brave men, The Bri-tish lines es - sayed;   Just

twelve at night, if I am right, And honestly in - formed, Both

wings at once, they did ad-vance, And Sto-ny-Point they stormed.

April 11   Siege of Charleston, South Carolina.

May 12   Fall of Charleston, South Carolina. Clinton captures the 5,400 men garrison and four American ships. Heaviest American defeat of the war.

June 2-9   Lord George Gordon Riots. Religious fanatic Mad Lord George instigates week-long riot in London, causing hundreds of deaths, and hundreds of pounds in property damage. The English leadership suspect that Benjamin Franklin, known to control a "fifth column" in England, might have had a part in this, but there was never any evidence linking Franklin with the wanton destruction.

June 13   American Daughters of Liberty established Philadelphia Women organized to provide clothing for soldiers.

June 20   Action at Ramsour's Mills, North Carolina.

June 23   Battle of Springfield, New Jersey.

July 10-11   Count de Rochambeau and 6,000 French troops arrive in Newport, Rhode Island.

July 12   Actions at Stallins, South Carolina, and Brandon's Camp, South Carolina; Civil War in the Carolinas. Skirmishes between local patriot militia and tories in bitter civil war.

July 12   Arnold's treasonable secret offer to surrender West Point, New York.

August 16   General Gates defeated by Cornwallis at Camden, South Carolina.

August 18   Defeat of Americans at Fishing Creek, North Carolina. This prepared the way for invasion of North Carolina.

September 21   Benedict Arnold delivers plans of War to the British.

September 23   Andre's capture; Arnold's treason.

October 7   Battle of King's Mountain. Frontiersmen under Shelby and Campbell overwhelmingly defeat a loyalist troop: This stymied Cornwallis' invasion of North Carolina.

642. The TIMES.

No more, my friends, of vain applause,
  Nor complimental Rhymes;
Come muse let's call another cause,
  And sing about the times.
For all the ages ever known,
  The present is the oddest;
As all the men are honest grown,
  And all the women modest.
No lawyers now are fond of fees,
  Nor clergy of their dues;
Few people at the play one sees,
  At church what crowded pews,
No courtiers now their friends deceive,
  With promises of favour;
For what they make 'em once believe,
  They faithfully endeavour.
Our Congress, Heaven defend us all!
  I'll nothing say about them,
For they are great, and I'm but small,
  So muse jog on without 'em
The ladies dress so plain indeed,
  You'd think them Quakers all;
Witness the wool packs on their heads,
  So comely and so small.
What tradesman now forsakes his shop
  For politicks or news;
Or takes his dealer at a hop,
  Through interested views.
No soaking sot his spouse neglects,
  · For mugs of mantiling nappy;
For madly squanders his effects,
  To make himself quite happy.
Our frugal taste the states secure,
  Whence then can woe begin;
For luxury's turn'd out of doors,
  Frugality's took in.
Hence all the plenty of the times,
  Hence all provision cheap;
Hence dearth of follies and of crimes,
  Hence all complaints asleep.
Happy the nation thus endowed,
  So void of wants and crimes;
All zealous for their neighbour's good,
  Oh! these are glorious times.

                    (cont.)

Your characters, with wond'ring stare,
   Says Tom, is mighty high, Sir,
But pray forgive me, if I swear,
   I think 'tis all a lie, Sir.
Hah! think you so, my honest clown,
   Then take another sight on't;
Just turn the picture upside down,
   I fear you'll see the right on't.

500. *A SONG, written by a Dutch Lady at the Hague,*
for the Americans at Amsterdam, July 4, 1779.

1.

God save the Thirteen States!
Long rule th' United States;
  God save our States!
Make us victorious,
Happy and glorious,
No tyrants over us;
  God save our States!

2.

Oft did America
Foresee with sad dismay,
  Her slavery near:
Oft did her grievance state,
But Britain, falsely great,
Urging her desp'rate fate,
  Turn'd a deaf ear.

3.

Now the proud British foe
We've made, by vict'ries know,
  Our sacred right:
Witness at Bunker's Hill,
Where Godlike WARREN fell,
Happy his blood to spill
  In gallant fight.

4.

To our fam'd WASHINGTON,
Brave STARK, at Bennington,
  Glory is due:
Peace to Montgomery's shade,
Who, as he fought and bled,
Drew honors round his head,
  Numerous as true.

5.

Look to Sar'toga's plain,
Our captures on the main,
  MOULTRIE's defence:
Our catalogue is long
Of heroes yet unsung,
Who noble feats have done,
  For Independence.

6.

The melting mother's moarns,
The aged father's groans,
  Have steel'd our arms.
Ye British Whigs beware!
Your chains near formed are,
In spite of Richmond's care
  To sound alarms.

(cont.)

750

7.

Come join your hands to ours;
No royal blocks, nor tow'rs;
  God save us all!
Thus in our country's cause,
And to support our laws,
Our swords shall never pause
At freedom's call.

8.

We'll fear no tyrant's nod,
Nor stern oppression's rod,
  Till time's no more:
Thus Liberty, when driv'n
From Europe's States is giv'n
A safe retreat and heav'n
  On our free shore.

9.

O Lord! thy gifts in store,
We pray, our CONGRESS pour,
  To guide our States.
May union bless our land,
While we with heart and hand,
Our mutual rights defend.
  God save our States!

10.

(in full chorus)
God save the Thirteen States!
Long watch the prosp'rous fates
  Over our States!
Make us victorious,
Happy and glorious;
No tyrants over us;
  God save our States!

God save the Thirteen States! Long rule th' U-ni-ted States;

God save the Thirteen States! Long rule th' U-ni-ted States;

God save our States! Make us vic-to-rious, Hap-py and glo-rious,

God save our States! Make us vic-to-rious, Hap-py and glo-rious,

No ty - rants o - ver us; God save our States!

No ty - rants o - ver us; God save our States!

752

501. *Another written by a Dutch Gentleman, at Amsterdam, July 4, 1779.*

1.
GOD bless the Thirteen States!
And save for e'er our fates
    From tyranny!
This is the joyful day,
Whereon we glory may,
We saw the glitt'ring ray
    Of Liberty.
2.
When we King George abjur'd,
We first all wrong endur'd
    From Parliament.
It push'd with violence
Its stamp act's foul pretence,
But lost all influence
    On government,
3.
Now are our only laws
Those God and nature have
    Laid on mankind,
To those our chiefs adhere;
Our people those revere;
To those alone we here
    All Statesmen bind.
4.
As of our family,
All of the mind must be,
    We'll ever sing:
We fought for Liberty;
Be Independency
But hereditary,
    We want NO KING.

The foregoing are true copies of two songs, written at the Hague and Amsterdam; with a most hearty wish, that they may add fuel to the precious fire which is burning in every true American heart.   Attest.
THE STEADY FRIENDS OF AMERICA AT THE HAGUE.   Endure, dear brethren, what remains of labour, To get the port of freedom's heav'nly favour.

501. Another Song written by a Dutch Gentleman, at Amsterdam, July 4, 1779.

GOD bless the Thirteen States! And save for e'er our fates

GOD bless the Thirteen States! And save for e'er our fates

From ty - ran-ny! This is the joy-ful day, Whereon we glo-ry may,

From ty - ran-ny! This is the joy-ful day, Whereon we glo-ry may,

We saw the glitt'ring ray Of Liberty.

We saw the glitt'ring ray Of Liberty.

1135.

From the LONDON EVENING POST.

SONG.

To the tune of--"To all you ladies now at land."

Written by an Officer on board Sir CHARLES HARDY's Fleet.

TO all our countrymen at land,
We men at sea indite,
And hope they will not understand,
That we're afraid to fight.
We'll never flinch, by all the Gods,
Though two to one are fearful odds.
    With a fal,lal,lal,la,la.
Had we our fav'rite Kepple here,
Or gallant Viscount Howe,
Their presence would our spirits cheer,
Which are but drooping now:
But doubtless fellows such as they,
To Jemmy Twitcher must give way.
    With a fal, lal, &c.
In winter Jemmy makes his boasts,
He'll equal all our foes;
In summer they insult our coasts,
And he a fishing foes:
Whilst our Commanders are disgrac'd,
That Jemmy may not be displac'd.
    With a fal,la,&c.
Can Britain's sons unmov'd remain,
Whose navy was her pride,
And see the fleets of France and Spain
Within her Channel ride?
And must her foes unpunish'd brag,
That they have brav'd the British flag?
    With a fal,lal,&c.
Whene'er we on the ocean find
This proud insulting fleet,
O! should their sixty-six combin'd,
Our nine and thirty beat;
Our injur'd country will, we hope,
For Jemmy's neck provide a rope.
    With a fal,lal,&c.
And now we bid you all adieu,
Friends, children, sweethearts, wives;
For England, for our King, and you,
We freely risk our lives.
But if out-number'd we should fall,
On Jemmy's head revenge us all.
    With a fal, lal, &c.

1135. SONG. *Written by an Officer on board Sir CHARLES HARDY's Fleet.*

TO all our coun-try-men at land, We men at sea in-

dite, And hope they will not under-stand, That we're a-fraid to fight.

We'll ne-ver flinch, by all the Gods, Though two to one are fearful

odds. With a fal, lal, lal, la, la. [We'll never flinch, by all the

Gods, Though two to one are fearful odds. With a fal, la, lal, la la.]

877. THE LORDS OF THE MAIN,
Tune---"Nottingham Ale"

WHEN faction, in league with the treacherous Gaul,
  Began to look big and paraded in state,
A meeting was held at Credulity Hall,
  And Echo proclaim'd their Ally good and great!
    By sea and by land
    Such wonders are plan'd,
No less than the bold British Lion to chain!
  Well hove! said Jack Lanyard,
  French, Congo and Spaniard,
Have at you--remember we're Lords of the Main.
  Lords of the Main,---ay, Lords of the Main.
The Tars of Old England are Lords of the Main.

Though party contention a while may perplex,
  And lenity hold us is doubtful suspence,
If perfidy rouse, or ingratitude vex,
  In defiance of Hell we'll chastise the offence.
    When danger alarms,
    'Tis then that in arms,
United we rush on the foe with disdain;
  And when the storm rages,
  It only presages
Fresh triumphs to Britons, as Lords of the Main.
  Lords of the Main,---ay, Lords of the Main,
Let Thunder proclaim it, we're Lords of the Main.

Then Britons strike home--make sure of your blow,
  The chase is in view, never mind a lee shore,
With vengeance o'ertake the confederate foe;--
  'Tis now we may rival our heroes of yore!
    Brave Anson and Drake,
    Hawks, Russel and Blake,
With ardour like yours we defy France and Spain!
  Combining with treason,
  They're deaf to all reason,
Once more let them feel we are Lords of the Main!
  Lords of the Main.---ay, Lords of the Main,
The first born of Neptune are Lords of the Main.

(cont.)

Nor are we alone in the noble career,
  The Soldier partakes of the generous flame,
To glory he marches to glory we steer,
  Between us we share the rich harvest of fame.
    Recorded on high,
    Their names never die,
Of Heroes by sea and by land what a train!
  To the KING, then, God bless him!
  The World shall confess him
"The Lord of those who are Lords of the Main"
  Lords of the Main, --ay, Lords of the Main,
The Tars of Old England are Lords of the Main.

877. THE LORDS OF THE MAIN.

WHEN faction, in league with the treacherous Gaul, Be-

gan to look big and pa-ra-ded in state, A meeting was held at Cre-[1]

du-li-ty Hall, And E-cho pro-claim'd their Al-ly good and great! By

sea and by land Such won-ders are plan'd, No less than the bold British

1. E in original

759

Li-on to chain! Well hove! said Jack Lan-yard, French,

Con-go and Spaniard, Have at you-- re - member we're Lords of the Main.

Lords of the Main,--ay, Lords of the Main, The Tars of Old

England are Lords of the Main.

* Sic

To the PRINTER.

SIR,

We petty Rhymers are too apt hastily to send our Bantlins forth
into the wide world. But the wee things are so soon forgotten that
we may, with little hazard of detection, give them the benefit of
revocation, and, with some few improvements in their dress and de-
portment, put them off as virgin adventurers, on a second trip; and
possibly, with now and then a little wholesome discipline in the way
of correction, they may stand a chance of arriving, some time or other
in the neighbourhood of the temple of fame.

Give me leave to try the experiment with the following chansonette,
which ought to have appeared on the first of January, Anno D: currente.

ODE for the NEW-YEAR, 1780.

Recitative.
OLD Time flew panting by, in full career,
And turn'd his glass, to mark the dawning year.
The FESTIVE BOARD was met, the Loyal Band
To CHURCH and KING devote each heart each hand
To ratify their vow the bowl goes round,
While songs of triumph to the Skies resound.

AIR.---"Rule Britannia."
I.
When rival nations first descried,
 Emerging from the boundless main,
This land, by tyrants yet untried,
 On high was sung this lofty strain.
  Rise, Britannia, beaming far,
  Rise, bright freedom's morning star!
II.
To distant regions, unexplor'd,
 Extend the blessings of thy sway,
To yon benighted world afford
 The light of thy all cheering ray.
  Rise, Britannia, rise, bright star,
  Spread thy radiance wide and far.
III.
The shoots of science, rich and fair,
 Transplanted from thy fostering isle,
And by thy Genius nurtur'd there,
 Shall reach the wilderness to smile.
  Shine, Britannia, rise and shine,
  To bless mankind the task be thine.

(cont.)

IV.

Nor shall the muses, now, disdain
    To find a new asylum there;
And, ripe for harvest, see the plain,
    Where lately rov'd the prowling bear!
        Plume, Britannia, plume thy wing,
        Teach the savage wilds to sing.

V.

From thee descended, here the swain
    Shall croud the port and spread the sail,
And soon wide Ocean, thy domain,
    Shall waft the wealth in every gale.
        Now, Britannia, now repose,
        Freedom reigns and plenty flows.

IV. (sic VI)

But ah! what frenzy breaks the ties
    Of love and duty held so dear!
Do Sons of Britain madly rise,
    And at their Parent point the spear!
        Rise, Britannia rise to quell
        Frantic sons who dare rebell.

VII.

By thee controul'd for ages past,
    See, now, half Europe in array!
For wise ambition hopes, at last,
    To fix her long projected sway,
        Rise, Britannia, rise again,
        The scourge of haughty France and Spain.

VIII.

The howling tempest fiercely blows,
    And ocean rages in the storm;
'Tis then the fearless pilot shows
    What skill and courage can perform.
        "Rule, Britannia, rule the waves,"
        Fearless, while the tempest raves.

IX.

If but thy native sons were true,
    From faction were thy senate free,
How should'st the proudest nations rue
    Their bold attempts to cope with thee!
        Seize, Brittania, seize thy launce,
        To fame's high summit now advance.

X.

And lo "thy Genius comes again,"
    Rebellion hides her guilty head,
For still thy thunder rules the main,
    And wild ambition's hope is fled.
        Now, Britannia, now repose,
        Freedom triumphs o'er her foes.

                                    (cont.)

If the gentle reader, of tenacious memory, should imagine that he has seen this song before; I beg leave to assure him, that in my opinion, what he saw was only a premature, abortive production. If he replies, that the present edition is no better than the former, I must give up the point. No harm is done, only - "MUCH ADO ABOUT NOTHING."

879. ODE for the NEW-YEAR, 1780.

When ri-val na-tions

first des - cried, E - mer - ging from the

bound - less main, [E-merge, E-merging from the

bound - less main,] This land, [by ty-rants,] by

ty - rants yet un-tried, On high was sung this lof-ty strain.

765

Rise, Britannia, Bri - tan-nia, beam-ing far,

Rise, bright free - dom's morning star!

1210.

To the PRINTER of the AMERICAN JOURNAL.

SIR,

    By inserting the following lines in your next paper you'll greatly oblige, your's, &c.

                J.R.
                Newport, April 13, 1780.

I'M not high church nor low church, nor tory, nor whig,
Nor flatt'ring young coxcomb, nor formal old prig;
I can laugh at a jest if not told out of time,
And excuse a mistake though not flatter a crime.
Unbias'd I view things around as they pass,
Nor squint at the great through a blackening glass;
The faults of my friends I would scorn to disclose,
And detect private scandal tho' cast at my foes.
I put none to the blush on any pretence,
For immodesty shocks both good breeding and sense.
No man's person I hate, though his conduct I blame,
I censure a crime without naming a name.
To amend, not expose is the will of my mind,
But reproof must be lost, if ill nature is joined.
When merit appears, tho' in rags, I respect it,
And will plead virtues cause tho' the world should reject it.
Cool reason I bow to, wherever 'tis found,
And rejoice when true learning with honor is crown'd.
No party I serve, in no quarrels I join,
Nor damn the opinions that differ from mine.
No corruption I screen, tho' no treason I sing,
I'm a friend to my country, not to a bad king.

1210.

I'M not high church nor low church, nor to-ry, nor whig, Nor

flatt'ring young coxcomb, nor for-mal old prig; I can

laugh at a jest if not told out of time, And ex-cuse a mistake though not

flatter a crime. [Derry down, down, Hey Derry down.]

I.

HENCE with the Lover who sighs o'er his wine,
Cloe's and Phillis's toasting.
Hence with the Slave who will whimper and whine,
Of Ardour and Constancy boasting;
Hence with Love's Joys
Follies and noise,
The Toast that I give is the VOLUNTEER BOYS.

II.

Nobles and beauties and such common Toasts
Those who admire may drink, Sir,
Fill up the Glass to the VOLUNTEER Hosts
Who never from danger will shrink, Sir,
Let Mirth appear,
Ev'ry heart chear,
The Toast that I give is the brave VOLUNTEER.

III.

Here's to the Squire who goes to Parade,
Here's to the Citizen Soldier,
Here's to the Merchant who fights for his Trade,
Whom danger increasing makes bolder,
Let Mirth appear,
Union is here,
The Toast that I give is the brave VOLUNTEER.

IV.

Here's to the Layer who leaving the bar
Hastens where Honour doth lead, Sir,
Changing the gown for the Ensigns of War,
The Cause of his Country to plead Sir,
Freedom appears,
Ev'ry heart cheers,
And calls for a health to THE LAW VOLUNTEERS.

V.

Here's to the Soldier tho' battered in Wars
And safe to his farm retired,
When called by his Country ne'er thinks of his Scars
With ardour to join us inspired;
Bright Fame appears,
Trophies Uprears,
To Veteran Chiefs who became VOLUNTEERS.

VI.

Here's to the Farmer who dares to advance
To Harvests of Honour with pleasure,
Who with a slave the most skilful in France,
A Sword for his would measure:
Hence with cold fear,
Heroes rise here,
The Ploughman is changed to the Stout VOLUNTEER.

(cont.)

VII.

Thus the bold bands for IERNE's defence,
The Muse has with rapture Review'd Sir,
With our VOLUNTEER BOYS as our verse commence,
With our VOLUNTEER BOYS they conclude Sir.
Discord or Noise,
Ne'er damp our Joys.
But health and success to the VOLUNTEER BOYS.

VIII.

Here's to the Peer first in Senate and Field,
Whose Actions to Titles add Grace, Sir,
Whose Spirit undaunted wou'd never yet yield
To a Foe, to a Pension, or Place, Sir,
Gratitude here
Toasts to the Peer,
Who adds to his Titles THE BRAVE VOLUNTEER.

1136. The VOLUNTEER BOYS.

HENCE with the Lo-ver who sighs o'er his wine,

Cloe's and Phillis's toasting. Hence with the Slave who will

whimper and whine, Of Ardour and Constancy boas-ting;

Hence with Love's Joys Follies and noise, The Toast that I give is the

CHORUS:

VO-LUNTEER BOYS. [*Hence with Love's Joys Fol-lies and noise, The*

Sy

Toast that I give is the VO-LUNTEER BOYS.]

825.

The following new Song is taken from a late London paper:

> YE Hearts of Oak, who wish to try
>   Your fortunes on the sea,
> And Britain's enemies defy,
>   Come enter here with me:
> Here's five pounds bounty, two months pay,
>   And leave to go ashore,
> With pretty girls to kiss and play--
>   Can British tars wish more?
>
> Our ship is stout, and sails like wind,
>   To chace a hostile foe:
> To fight like Britons we're inclin'd,
>   We'll let the Monsieurs know.
> Our Captain's generous, brave and good,
>   Of grog we'll have good store;
> Of prizes rich we'll sweep the flood---
>   Can British tars wish more;
>
> And when from driving Bourbon's fleet
>   Victorious we arrive,
> With music, dance, and jovial treat,
>   To please our girls we'll strive;
> Both Spanish silver, and French gold,
>   We'll count in plenty o'er;
> Which we have won, my shipmate bold---
>   Can British tars wish more?

825.

YE Hearts of Oak, who wish to try Your for-tunes on the sea, And Bri - tain's e - ne- mies de-fy, Come en-ter here with me: Here's

five pounds boun-ty, two months pay, And leave to go a - shore, With

pret-ty girls to kiss and play --- Can Bri-tish tars wish more.

545.

From the MARYLAND JOURNAL.

To the PRINTER,

By inserting the following **NEW SONG**, which I lately met with in the Maryland Journal, you will gratify several of the sons of St. Patrick, besides your friend, &c.

YOUNG PADDY.
Baltimore, June 5, 1780.

PADDY speaking to English JOHN.
(To the tune of Ballanamona oro.)

I.

I AM glad my dear John, now to find that some laws,
Were lately repeal'd for a very good cause,
You know what they are, tho' you wear a cockade;
By my love, 'twas Shilelagh that fot a free trade.
  For Ballanamona oro
  And the sight of the bold volunteers.

II.

I went to your country to open my case,
But North Sir he huff'd and star'd full in my face,
With an air of disdain and a strut of parade,
He bid me go home for I'd get no free trade.
  For Ballanamona oro,
  Which fill'd me all over with pain.

III.

To look for a Scotchman I stroll'd to the Mews:
My brogues on my back as you saw by the News:
A label for fun, on my rump Sir they laid,
With words arrah Paddy sure wants a free trade.
  For his Ballanamona oro,
  Nabocklish, come listen to me.

IV.

And when I came home, Sir, I heard of the game,
They made of my brogues, myself and my name,
I then cry'd Nabocklish, which made them afraid,
And rather than vex me they gave me free trade.
  For my Ballanamona oro,
  I appeal to Shillelagh for truth.

V.

I think I may laugh now, as you did at me,
I'll drink and I'll sing, and by Jove I'll be free;
And fight for my country, come Jack who's afraid,
Not I by St. Patrick, since I've got a free trade.
  For my Ballanamona oro,
  If more you should want call for me.

(cont.)

VI.

I'm made of true metal, I never met fear;
I'll wear not your cloth, nor taste of your beer,
Good cloth, and good beer, myself, Sir, has made,
Much better than your's for to toast a free trade.
  For my Ballanamona oro,
  The land of Shillelagh for me.

VII.

If ever I'm wanting upon a good cause,
I'll out in a moment to support all just laws,
The laws, Sir, of freedom like each volunteer,
I'm ready to stand by Shillelagh, look here.
  And my Ballanamona oro,
  The land of old Sheelah for
                PADDY.

545. PADDY speaking to English JOHN.

I AM glad my dear John, now to find that some laws,

Were late-ly re- peal'd for a ve-ry good cause, You

know what they are, tho' you wear a cock-ade; By my

love, 'twas Shilelagh that fot a free trade   For

Bal-la-na-mo - na o - ro And the sight of the bold vo-lunteers, the

sight of the bold vo- lun-teers.

MR. PRINTER,

  The enclosed lines (said to be written by a young gentleman in Connecticut) lately fell into my hands, and if you think proper you may give them a place in your paper.

         Your humble servant,
         A SOLDIER.

HAIL AMERICANS:

I.

COLUMBIA! Columbia! to glory arise,
The queen of the world, and the child of the skies;
Thy genius commands thee, with raptures behold,
While ages on ages thy splendors unfold:
Thy reign is the last and the noblest of time,
Most fruitful thy soil, most inviting thy clime;
Let the crimes of the east ne'er incrimson thy name,
Be freedom, and science, and virtue thy fame.

II.

To conquest and slaughter, let Europe aspire,
Whelm nations in blood, wrap cities in fire;
Thy heroes the rights of mankind shall defend,
And triumph pursue them and glory attend;
A world is thy realm, for a world be thy laws,
Enlarg'd as thy empire and just as thy cause;
On freedom's broad basis, that empire shall rise,
Extend with the main and dissolve with the skies:

III.

Fair science her gate, to thy sons shall unbar,
And the east see thy morn hide the beams of her star;
New Bards and new ages unrival'd shall soar,
To fame unextinguished when time is no more;
To thee the last refuge of virtue design'd,
Shall fly from all nations, the best of mankind;
There grateful to Heaven, with transports shall bring,
Their incense more fragrant than odours of spring.

IV.

Nor less shall thy fair ones to glory ascend,
And genius and beauty in harmony blend;
The graces of form shall awake pure desire,
And the charms of the soul still enliven the fire;
Their sweetness unmingled, their manners refin'd,
And virtue's bright image instamp'd on the mind;
With peace and sweet rapture shall teach life to glow,
And light up a smile in the aspect of woe.

         (cont.)

V.

Thy fleets to all regions, thy power shall display,
The nations admire, and the ocean obey;
Each shore to thy glory its tribute unfold,
And the East and the South yield their spices and gold;
As the day spring unbounded thy splendors shall flow,
And earth's little kingdoms before thee shall bow;
While the ensigns of union in triumph unfurl'd,
Hush the tumult of war, and give peace to the world.

VI.

Thus as down a lone valley with cedars o'erspread,
From wars dread confusion I pensively stray'd;
The gloom from the face of fair Heaven retir'd,
The winds ceas'd to murmour, the thunders expir'd;
Perfumes as of Eden flow'd sweetly along,
And a voice as of Angels enchantingly sung,
Columbia! Columbia! To glory arise,
The queen of the world, and the child of the skies.

380. HAIL AMERICANS.

CO-LUMBIA! Co - lumbia! to glo-ry a - rise, the queen of the world, and the child of the skies; Thy ge-nius commands thee, with raptures be-hold, While a-ges on a-ges thy splendors un-fold: Thy reign is the last and the no-blest of time, Most

fruit-ful thy soil, most in - vi-ting thy clime; Let the

crimes of the east ne'er in-crimson thy name, Be freedom, and science, and

virtue thy fame. [And virtue thy fame, And virtue thy fame. Be

freedom, and science, and virtue thy fame.]

January 17	Morgan's victory at Cowpens, South Carolina.
March 1	Ratification of Articles of Confederation.
March 15	Cornwallis' phyrric victory over Greene and Morgan at Guilford Courthouse, North Carolina.
May 22	Greene begins siege of the British stronghold at Ninety-Six, South Carolina.
June 5	Surrender of Augusta, Georgia to Americans.
July 5	French army under Rochambeau joins Washington above New York.
August 26	Cornwallis occupies Yorktown, Virginia.
	Comte De Grasse with French fleet arrives in Chesapeake Bay.
August 31	French troops land near Jamestown. De Grasse sends 3,000 troops under Marquis de Saint-Simon to join Lafayette.
September 5-9	French fleet drives British fleet away from Chesapeake Bay, leaving the French in command of the sea off Yorktown. (Battle of the Capes)
September 8	Battle of Eutaw Springs, South Carolina.
September 28	Siege of Yorktown begins.
October 19	Cornwallis surrenders at Yorktown.

229. ODE for his MAJESTY's BIRTH-DAY, June 4, 1781.
Written by William Whitehead, Esq. Poet Laureat,
and set to Musick by Mr. Stanley,
Master of the King's Band of Musicians.

STILL does the Rage of War prevail,
Still thirsts for blood th' insatiate Spear?
Waft not, ye Winds, th' invidious Tale,
Nor let th' untutor'd Nations hear
That Passion baffles Reason's boasted Reign,
And Half the peopled World is civiliz'd in vain.
What are Morals, what are Laws.
What Religion's sacred Name?
Nor Morale soften, nor Religion awes;
Pure tho' the Precepts flow, the Actions are the same.
Revenge and Pride, and deadly Hate,
And Av'rice tainting deep the Mind,
With all the Fury Fiends that wait
As tort'ring Plagues on human Kind,
When shown in their own native Light,
In Truth's clear Mirror, heav'nly bright,
Like real Monsters rise;
But let Illusion's pow'rful Wand
Transform, arrange, the hideous Band,
They cheat us in Disguise;
We dress their horrid Forms in borrow'd Rays,
Then call them Glory, and pursue the Blaze.
O blind to Nature's social Plan,
And Heaven's indulgent End!
Her kinder Laws knit Man to Man
As Brother and as Friend.
Nature intent alone to bless,
Bids Strife and Discord cease;
"Her Ways are Ways of Pleasantness,
And all her Paths are Peace."
E'en this auspicious Day would wear
A brighter Face of Joy serene;
On lighter Wings would Zephyrs move,
The Sun with added Lustre shine,
Did Peace, descending from above,
Here fix her earthly Shrine;
Here to the Monarch's fondest Pray'r
A just Attention yield,
And let him change the Sword of War
For her protecting Shield.

649. The ORPHAN

I.

An Orphan's woes I sing, ye Great, attend;
  Ye Sons of Folly, lend a listening ear,
Draw nigh, and tho' refusing to befriend,
  Sure woes like his will force one pitying tear.

II.

No father o'er the Babe complacent smil'd,
  No tender mother clasp'd him to her breast,
Hung fondly prattling o'er her darling child,
  Sooth'd when awake, or guarded while at rest.

III.

His Sire (but ah! he never knew the name,
  Ne'er knew the pleasures that the name bestows)
Snatch'd from his Consort --- in the field of fame
  Fell, bravely fighting 'gainst his Country's foes.

IV.

Shocked by the fatal blow, his Mother died
  Ere yet two Moon sh'ed felt a mother's throes;
Far happier he had Fate his life denied,
  And bade him with his kindred clay repose.

V.

But Heaven reserv'd for future ills and pain,
  And Heaven's a witness he's enjoyed his share;
Toss'd to and fro o'er Life's tempestuous main,
  Chil'd by each blast, and rack'd by every care.

VI.

No relative his parents loss supplied,
  Virtue to cherish, growing Vice restrain,
His infant feet his erring steps to guide,
  And curb his passions with a prudent rein.

VII.

None when by youthful follies led astray,
  The friendly caution whisper'd in his ear;
His thoughts directed to a future day,
  By hope encourag'd or deterr'd thro' fear.

VIII.

Cheerless he roams, a prey to every woe,
  To Poverty, and all her meagre train;
To every ill that human Life can know,
  Distracting care, and agonizing pain.

IX.

Thus fares some vessel by the tempest toss'd,
  At night when not a star illumes the sky,
Unknowing how to steer (the pilot lost),
  The storm increasing, and no succours nigh!

Misericors

630.

BALTIMORE, Feb. 20
To the Printer of the Maryland Journal.

    This being the Birth Day of our illustrious military Chief, you
will much oblige many Friends of Freedom, and can offend none of
that Denomination, by the insertion of the following Lines in your
next paper. Yours, &c.

                A SOLDIER.   February 11, 1781.

On GENERAL WASHINGTON.
Tune, The Highland March.

WHEN Alcides, the Son of Olympian Jove,
Was call'd from the Earth to the Regions above,
The Fetters grim Tyranny burst from his Hand,
And with Rapine & Murder usurp'd the Command;
While peace, lovely Maiden, was scar'd from the Plains,
And Liberty, Captive, sat wailing in Chains;
Her once gallant Offspring lay bleeding around,
Nor on Earth cou'd a Champion to save her be found.

The Thun'er'r, mov'd with Campassion(sic), look'd down
On a World so accurst, from his Chrystaline Throne,
Then open'd the Book, in whose mystical Page
Were enrolled the heroes of each future Age;
Read of Brutus, and Sidney, who dar'd to be free,
Of their Virtues approv'd & confirm'd the Decree;
Then, turn'd to the Annals of that happy Age,
When Washington's Glories illumin'd the Page.

'When Britania shall strive with tyranical Hand
'To establish her Empire in each distant Land,
'A Chief shall arise in Columbia's Defence,
'To whom the just Gods shall their favours dispense:
'Triumphant as Mars, in the glorious Field,
'While Minerva shall lend him her wisdom & Shield
'And Liberty, freed from her Shackles, shall own
'Great Washington's Claim as her favorite Son.'

630. On GENERAL WASHINGTON.

WHEN Al-ci-des, the Son of O-lym-pi-an Jove, Was call'd

from the Earth to the Re - gions a - bove, The Fetters grim Ty-ranny

burst from his Hand, And with Ra - pine & Mur - der u -

surp'd the Com-mand; While peace, love-ly Mai - den, was

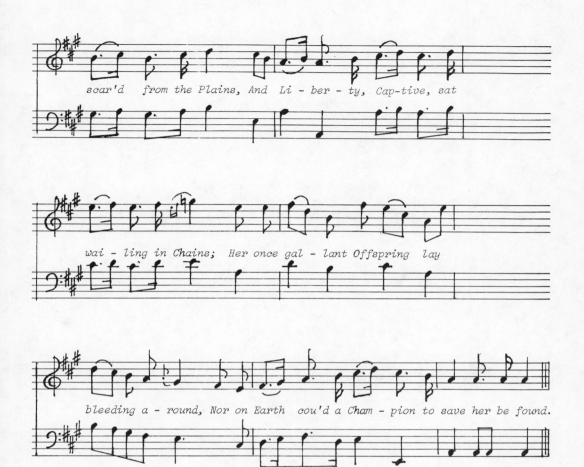

scar'd from the Plains, And Li - ber - ty, Cap-tive, sat

wai - ling in Chains; Her once gal - lant Offspring lay

bleeding a - round, Nor on Earth cou'd a Cham - pion to save her be found.

230. The VOLUNTEERS of AUGUSTA, A NEW SONG.
To the Tune "The Lilies of France."

I.
COME join, my brave lads, come all from afar,
We're all Volunteers, all ready for war;
  Our service is free, for honour we fight,
  Regardless of hardships by day or by night.
Chorus. Then all draw your swords, and constantly sing,
        Success to our Troop, our Country, and King.

II.
The Rebels they murder,---Revenge is the word,
Let each lad return with blood on his sword;
  See Grierson's pale ghost point afresh to his wound,
  We'll conquer, my boys, or fall dead on the ground.
        Then brandish your swords, and constantly sing,
        Success to our Troop, our Country, and King.

III.
They've plunder'd our houses, attempted our lives,
Drove off from their homes our children and wives;
  Such plundering miscreants no mercy can crave,
  Such murdering villains no mercy shall have.
        Then chop with your swords, and constantly sing,
        Success to our Troop, our Country, and King.

IV.
Then think not of plunder, but rush on the foe,
Pursue them, my boys, with blow after blow,
  Till in their own blood we see them all welter,
  Or behind the Blue Mountains retreat for a shelter,
        Then chop with your swords, and constantly sing,
        Success to our Troop, our Country, and King.

V.
There the Indians to them that mercy will owe,
Which they, when victorious, to others did show:
  But we will return our estates to enjoy,
  In rooting out Rebels our time we'll employ.
        Then sheath, boys, your swords, and constantly sing,
        Success to our Troop, our Country, and King.

VI.
When back through Augusta our horses shall prance,
We'll dismount at the Captain's, and there have a dance,
  We'll toss off full bumpers of favourite grog,
  Be merry all night, in the morning drink knog.
        Then rest on your swords, and constantly sing,
        Success to our Troop, our Country, and King.

VII.
Here's a health to our Governor, Peace at our homes,
Honour to Ingram, to Douglass, and Holmes,
  A wife to each soldier, and other good cheer,
  And victory for ever to each Volunteer.
        Then lay by your swords, and constantly sing,
        Success to our Troop, our Country, and King.

230. The VOLUNTEERS of AUGUSTA, A NEW SONG.

COME join, my brave lads, come all from a-far, We're all Vo-lunteers, all rea-dy for war; Our service is free, for

ho - -nour we fight, Re - gard - less of hardships by

day   or by night.   Then all draw your swords,   and

con - stant-ly sing,   Suc-cess to our Troop, our

Instru.

Coun - try, and King.

358. A NEW-YORK ADDRESS.
"To all honest hearts and sound bottoms."

YE loyalists all, within the town,
  Attend unto my ditty,
You know how oft', with great renown,
  I have harang'd the city.
                    Yankee doodle, &c.
You know full well, from rostrum high,
  With seeming genuine zeal, Sir,
I help'd to raise the patriot cry,
  And propt the rebel weal, Sir.
But conscious of my former crimes,
  And greatly dreading Howe, Sir,
I snugly turn'd my coat, by turns,
  And gently made a bow, Sir.
Since, hard I've laboured in the cause,
  And strove with might and main, Sir,
To aid an injured Prince's laws,
  And help him out again, Sir.
For this I'm call'd a traitor now,
  And held in great contempt, Sir,
And if I'm caught, I fear, I vow,
  From danger not exempt, Sir.
As this, perchance, may be our fate,
  From which good heaven defend us,
We need to fear the rebel hate,
  But HARRY will befriend us.
On British Clinton we rely,
  And hope to be rewarded,
The rebel Clinton we defy,
  We loyalists are recorded.
You know we told you th'other day,
  How what we fear'd was doing,
The French and rebels, in their way,
  Great mischiefs were a brewing.
Since certain things have come to pass,
  Which prowess could not hinder,
It is our duty, now, -- alas!
  To dread one more surrender.
Hence one advice I wish to give,
  We know not what may hap, Sir,
Loyal we are, and wish to live,
  But not in rebel trap, Sir,
We all should keep a sharp look-out,
  Nor trust to time or chance, Sir,
For WASHINGTON may be about
  Another York-Town dance, Sir.
With Count De GRASSE and ROCHAMBEAU,
  And all the rebel route, Sir,

                              (cont.)

That HARRY himself may hardly know
  How safely to get out, Sir.
If this should be our wretched state,
  And this our cruel lot, Sir,
The "civil resort" may fix our fate,
  And send us all to pot, Sir,
Better it were to quit the shore,
  And go beyond the sea, Sir,
In Britain they will love us more
  Than here we e'er can be, Sir.
A gentle Prince upon his throne,
  With goodness looking down, Sir,
Will give us each some beef and bone,
  And call us all his own, Sir.
There we may, with Galloway Joe,
  Partake of royal bounty,
And ministry too, for aught we know,
  May give us each a county.
Should we cross the India seas,
  And undertake the job, Sir,
We may return when e'er we please,
  As rich as great Nabob, Sir.
With all these prospects, hopes and fears,
  This varied scene before us,
It is enough to draw forth tears,
  And make good men deplore us.
As we have join'd the noble cause,
  And laboured in the royal,
We all should feel for Britain's laws,
  With hearts most truly loyal.
We should deplore the fatal day,
  Which makes us all so sober,
And so we should, as well we may,
  The rebel month October.
For in one day, the rebels tell,
  How fell the great BURGOYNE, Sir,
On the same day, we know full well,
  CORNWALLIS did resign, Sir.
Eight thousand men, they say, and more,
  Of British--Hessian---mould, Sir,
And Anspach too the like before
  In Story ne'er was told, Sir
Heroes and chiefs, of great renown,
  The glory of the nation,
Were forc'd to lay their laurels down,
  And march in humble station.
What dire disgrace!--What fatal day!
  Does fortune thus deride us?--
And will not Europe, wond'ring say,
  Unfriendly stars do guide us.

                              (cont.)

With France and Spain, and eke the Dutch,
   And all the rebels round, Sir,
Alack-a-day!--It is too much-
   Rejoicings will abound, Sir.

YE loyalists all, with-in the town, At-tend un-to my ditty, You

know how oft', with great re-nown, I have harang'd the city.

Yankee doodle, [*keep it up, Yankee doodle dan - dy, Mind the music*

and the step, And with the girls be handy.]

383. NEW SONG. Occasioned by the surrender of Earl Cornwallis
and his whole army, to General Washington.
Tune "Derry down, &c"

When southward Cornwallis first enter'd the land
Commander in chief, with the sword in his hand,
He swagger'd and boasted, and threaten'd the fates
In spite of their teeth, he would ravage the States.
Derry down, &tc.
No longer he sits, with his thumb in his mouth,
Like prudent Sir Harry---but conquers the south--
And soon having victory bound in his chain--
Inclos'd her in letters, he sent to Germain.
Derry down, &c.
The hero of Minden each packet displays,
St. James's resounds, and the Tower cannon blaze;
The King and his Parliament make an oration,
Protesting this Peer, had no Peer in the nation.
Derry down, &c.
Thus deck'd with the plumage of eagle-winged fame
He swore there was conquest annex'd to his name;
For fortune the wanton voluptuous Gypsey---
Had pledg'd him her cup 'till his Lordship was tipsey.
Derry down, &c.
So rising in wrath like Achilles at Hector,
He swore he wou'd turn every whig to a Spectre;
And bloodily threaten'd to peirce Mr. Greene,
And shiver more rebels than ever were seen.
Derry down, &c.
But ah what a pity! The hero of Britain,
On fame's highest pinacle loftily sitting;
Should ever be stung by the serpant--mischance!
Or Morgan teach Tarleton the Lexington dance.
Derry down, &c.
Yet the heroic Earl of invincable spunk--
Determine to finish us, sober or drunk;
He foams and he raves, and he marches severe,
'Till Greene sends him off, with a flea in his ear.
Derry down, &c.
Now quitting the loyal, deserting whole nations,
Subdu'd and protected by brave Proclamations;
Again he moves victor, for bright glory shows him
Now triumphs wherever no mortals oppose him.
Derry down, &c.
'Till Washington cloath'd in the potence of might,
Resistless as Jove, hurl'd the thunders of fight;
The hands of bold freemen surrounded the shore,
And 'tis said the Earl never will conquer us more.
Derry down, &c.

(cont.)

Thus still may the triumph of freedom expand,
Her laurels forever embellish the land;
And all whom oppose her, in fetters await,
Disgraces, defeats, and Cornwallis's fate,
                    Derry down, &c.

383. NEW SONG. *Occasioned by the surrender of Earl Cornwallis and his whole army, to General Washington.*

When southward Cornwallis first en - ter'd the land Com-

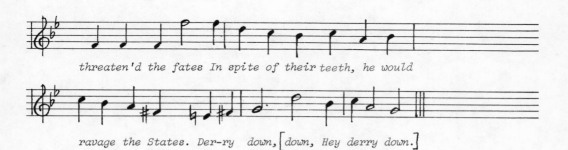

mander in chief, with the sword in his hand, He swagger'd and boasted, and

threaten'd the fates In spite of their teeth, he would

ravage the States. Der-ry down, [down, Hey derry down.]

61. CORNWALLIS Burgoyn'd. A SONG.
To the Tune of "MAGGIE LAUDER."

I.
WHEN British troops first landed here,
   With HOWE Commander o'er them,
They thought they'd make us quake for fear,
   And carry all before them:
With thirty thousand men, or more,
   And she without assistance,
AMERICA must needs give o'er,
   And make no more resistance.
                    Fol, lol, fol, lol, &c.
II.
But WASHINGTON, her glorious son,
   Of British hosts the terror,
Soon, by repeated overthrows,
   Convic'd(sic) them of their error:
Let PRINCETON and let TRENTON tell,
   What gallant deeds he's done, Sir;
And MONMOUTH's plains, where hundreds fell,
   And thousands more have run, Sir,
III.
CORNWALLIS too, when he approach'd
   Virginia's old dominion,
Thought he would soon her conqu'rer be;
   And so was NORTH's opinion:
From State to State, with rapid stride,
   His troops had march'd before, Sir,
'Till quite elate with martial pride,
   He thought all dangers o'er, Sir.
IV.
But our ALLIES, to his surprise,
   The CHESAPEAKE had enter'd;
And now, too late, he curs'd his fate,
   And wish'd he ne'er had ventur'd:
For WASHINGTON no sooner knew
   The visit he had paid her,
Than to his parent State he flew,
   To crush the bold invader.
V.
When he set down before the town*,
   His Lordship soon surrender'd:
His martial pride he laid aside,
   And CAS'D the British standard.
GODS! How this stroke will North provoke,
   And all his thoughts confuse, Sir!
And how the PEERS will hang their ears,
   When first they hear the news, Sir!
                              (cont.)

800

VI.
Be PEACE, the glorious END OF WAR,
  By this event effected:
And the name of WASHINGTON
  To latest times respected:
Then let us toast AMERICA,
  And FRANCE in union with her;
And may GREAT-BRITAIN rue the day,
  Her hostile bands came hither.

*YORK

61. CORNWALLIS Burgoyn'd. A SONG.

WHEN British troops first landed here, With
HOWE Com-man-der o'er them, They thought they'd make us quake for fear, And
car-ry all be - fore them: With thirty thousand men, or more, And
she without as - sis-tance, A-ME-RI-CA must needs give o'er, And

make no more re-sistance. But WASHINGTON, her glorious son, Of

Bri-tish hosts the ter-ror, Soon, by re-pea-ted o-verthrows, Con-

vi [n] c'd them of their er-ror: Let PRINCETON and let TRENTON tell, What

gallant deeds he's done, Sir; And

MONMOUTH's plains, where hundreds fell, And thousands more have run, Sir,

62. THE DANCE, A Ballad,
to the Tune of "Yankey Doodle."

CORNWALLIS led a country dance,
  The like was never seen, sir,
Much retrograde, and much advance,
  And all with General Greene, sir.
II.
They rambled up, they rambled down,
  Join'd hands, then off they run, sir,
Our general Greene to Charlestown,
  The earl to Wilmington, Sir.
III.
Greene, in the south, then danc'd a set,
  And got a mighty name, sir,
Cornwallis jigg'd with young Fayette,
  But suffered in his fame, sir.
IV.
Then down he figur'd to the shore,
  Most like a lordly dancer,
And on his courtly honour swore,
  He would no more advance, sir.
V.
Quoth he--my guards are weary grown,
  With footing country dances,
They never at Saint James's shone,
  At capers, kicks or prances.
VI.
Though men so gallant ne'er were seen,
  While saunt'ring on parade, sir,
Or wriggling o'er the park's smooth green,
  Or at a masquerade, sir.
VII.
Yet are red heels, and long lac'd skirts,
  For stumps and briars meet, sir,
Or stand they chance with hunting shirts,
  Or hardy veteran feet, sir.
VIII.
Now hous'd in York he challeng'd all,
  At minuet or all'mande,
And lessons for a courtly ball,
  His guards by day and night conn'd.
IX.
This challenge known, full soon there came,
  A set who had the bon ton,
De Grasse and Rochambeau, whose fame,
  Fut brillant pour un long tems.

(cont.)

X.

And Washington, Columbia's son,
  Whom easy nature taught, sir,
That grace, which cant by pains be won,
  Or Plutus' gold be bought, sir.

XI.

Now hand in hand they circle round,
  This ever dancing peer, sir,
Their gentle movements soon confound,
  The earl as they drew near, sir.

XII.

His music soon forgets to play--
  His feet can move no more, sir,
And all his bands now curse the day,
  They jigg'd it to our shore, sir.

XIII.

Now tories all what can ye say?
  Come--Is not this a griper?
That while your hopes are danc'd away,
  'Tis you must pay the piper.

FINIS.

62. THE DANCE, A Ballad.

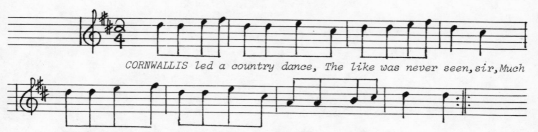

CORNWALLIS led a country dance, The like was never seen, sir, Much

re-trograde, and much advance, And all with General Greene, sir.

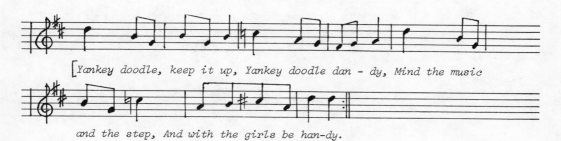

[Yankey doodle, keep it up, Yankey doodle dan - dy, Mind the music

and the step, And with the girls be han-dy.

660.
For the New Jersey Journal.
A NEW SONG.

From the Americ shore,
The vast Atlantic o'er,
   Shout--"Washington!"
Americans all unite
To do the hero right,
Our glory--boast--delight--
   High in renown
See o'er the British Peer
He rides the grand career
   Of Victory.
At his advance the foe
Lay their proud standards low,
And, by these tokens, show
   America's free.
An army in parade
Captives, at length, are made;
   The deed is done.
America triumphs free;
Laws, Rights, and Liberty,
Next God, we owe to thee, Great Washington.
Prophetic truths of yore,
Of thee their import bore;
   Events explain.
How born to save this land,
You, 'neath th'almighty hand,
Deliverance should command,
   And break it's chain.
Thou, the chief object--choice
Of our united voice,
   Mak'st tyrants bleed.
By thy heroic flame,
See ev'ry kindred name
Rescu'd from want and shame---
   From slav'ry freed!
Be earthly honours thine!
Health to thy life's decline;
   Enlargement give;
And when thy course is run,
In Heav'n, Great WASHINGTON,
Beaming bright as the sun, Evermore live.

660. A NEW SONG.

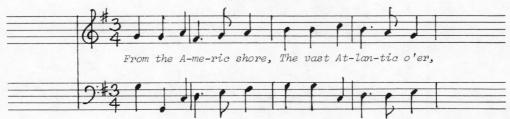

From the A-me-ric shore, The vast At-lan-tic o'er,

From the A-me-ric shore, The vast At-lan-tic o'er,

Shout - "Washing-ton!"   A-me-ri-cans all u-nite To do the He-ro right,

Shout - "Washing-ton!"   A-me-ri-cans all u-nite To do the He-ro right,

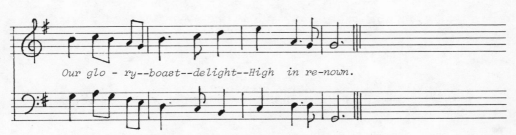

Our glo - ry--boast--delight--High in re-nown.

Our glo - ry--boast--delight--High in re-nown.

From a late Irish Paper.
PADDY's ADDRESS to JOHN BULL, A new Ballad.
Tune, Larry Crogan.

BY your leave, gossip John;
By my faith, it is so long
Since we've play'd you a lilt, the same key on, same key on;
Don't turn the deaf ear,
Since our harp wants repair,
Faith, we've got other music to play on, to play on.
Sixty thousand bold boys
Have contriv'd such a noise,
As now charms the ears of gay France, sir, gay France, sir.
Nay, some folks go further,
(I hope 'tis no murder)
To say it would make a king dance, sir, king dance, sir.

II.

Were you not cursed dull,
When you took off our wool,
To leave us so much of the leather, the leather?
It ne'er enter'd your pate,
That a sheep skin well beat,
Would arouse the whole nation together, together.
One and all, young and old,
None complain of the cold,
Tho' stripp'd to the skin and the bone, sir, the bone sir;
All join the parade,
And shout out, A FREE TRADE,
Or else!!!---you may let it alone, sir, alone, sir.

III.

Now, what signifies
Your pallaver and lies,
Can't you speak the blunt truth, plain and civil, and civil?
Can't you say, gossip patt,
You shall have this or that,
A FREE TRADE, or---the road to the devil, the devil.
By St. Patrick, my namesake,
I wish for the gamesake,
To see how we'd take this last answer, last answer,
Not the cowardly Yankies
E'er gave you such thank ye's,
Or the thundering Armadas of France, sir, of France sir,

(cont.)

IV.
Our commons made wise,
Have open'd their eyes,
And perceive their rent in a stew, sir, a stew, sir;
Some steps must be taken
For saving their bacon,
As hanging or starving won't do, sir, won't do, sir;
A HALF YEAR's MONEY BILL--
Arrah can't you sit still?
Bless your stars that 'tis more than a quarter, a quarter:
Then grant our request--
By my faith, you had best--
Or, by Patrick, the next shall be shorter, be shorter.
V.
But make me your friend,
And let all squabbles end,
My old heart will be light as a feather, a feather;
While our joyful hearts sing,
And drink healths to the king,
Oagh, we'll dance bolthyourgh together, together,
But remember the drum,
And take care how you hum,
For, we teagues are damn'd nice in our booze, sir, booze, sir;
We'll make friends, or fight,
Just as we see right;
So I leave you at leisure to chuse, sir, to chuse, sir.

925. PADDY's ADDRESS to JOHN BULL, A new Ballad.

BY your leave, gossip John; By my faith, it is so long Since we've

play'd you a lilt, the same key on, same key on; Don't

turn the deaf ear, Since our harp wants repair, Faith, we've

got other music to play on, to play on. Sixty thousand bold boys have con-

triv'd such a noise, As now charms the ears of gay

France, sir, gay France, sir. Nay, some folks go further, (I

hope 'tis no murder) To say it would make a king

dance, sir, king dance, sir.

February 23   *Sir Guy Carleton appointed commander-in-chief to replace Clinton.*

February 27   *Britain decides to end war.*

March 5   *Parliament passes a bill authorizing the King to make peace with his former colonies.*

March 10   *Lord North resigns.*

March 22   *Rockingham succeeds North.*

July 1   *Death of Lord Rockingham; formation of the ministry of Lord Shelburne.*

July 11   *Savannah evacuated by British.*

November 30   *Signing by America of the preliminary Articles of Peace between Great Britain and America.*

December 14   *Charleston, South Carolina evacuated by British.*

From the FREEMAN's JOURNAL, of May 8, 1782.
   Reading Capt. Barney's late gallant exploit in your and other
newspapers, I could not restrain myself from scribbling the few
following stanzas relative to that affair; and descriptive not of
what was really said or done in the more minute particulars, but
of what might be supposed to have passed in similar circumstances.
                                    Yours,
                                          RUSTICUS.
          To the tune of The Tempest; or, Hosier's Ghost.

          OE'R(sic) the waste of waters cruising,
            Long the General Monk had reign'd;
          All subduing, all reducing,
            None her lawless rage restrain'd:
          Many a brave and hearty fellow
            Yielding to his warlike foe
          When her guns began to bellow,
            Struck his humbled colours low.

          But grown bold with long successes,
            Leaving the wide watry way,
          She, a stranger to distresses,
            Came to cruise within Cape May:
          "Now we soon (said Captain Rogers)
            Shall their men of commerce meet:
          In our hold we'll have them lodgers,
            We shall capture half their fleet.

          Lo! I see their van appearing:--
            Back our topsails to the mast--
          They toward us full are steering
            With a gentle western blast;
          I've a list of all their cargoes,
            All their guns, and all their men;
          I am sure these modern Argo's
            Can't escape us one in ten:

          Yonder comes the Charming Sally,
            Sailing with the General Greene;---
          First we'll fight the HYDER ALI,
            Taking her is taking them;
          She intends to give us battle,
            Bearing down with all her sail:---
          Now, boys, let our cannon rattle!
            To take her we cannot fail.
                                    (cont.)

Our eighteen guns, each a nine pounder,
  Soon shall terrify this foe;
We shall maul her, we shall wound her,
  Bringing rebel colours low."----
While he thus anticipated
  Conquests that he could not gain,
He in the Cape May channel waited
  For the ship that caus'd his pain.

Captain Barney then preparing,
  Thus address'd his gallant crew,----
"Now, brave lads! be bold and daring,
  Let your hearts be firm and true;
This is a proud English cruiser,
  Roving up and down the main,
We must fight her--must reduce her,
  Tho' our decks be strew'd with slain.

Let who will be the surviver,
  We must conquer or must die,
We must take her up the river,
  Whate'er comes of you or I:
Tho' she shows most formidable
  With her eighteen pointed nines,
And her quarters clad in sable,
  Let us baulk her proud designs.

With four nine pounders, and twelve sixes,
  We will face that daring band;
Let no dangers damp your courage,
  Nothing can the brave withstand.
Fighting for your country's honor,
  Now to gallant deeds aspire;
Helmsman, bear us down upon her,
  Gunner, give the word to fire!"

Then yard arm and yard arm meeting,
  Strait began the dismal fray,
Cannon mouths, each other greeting,
  Belch'd their smoky flames away:
Soon the langrage, grape and chain shot
  That from Barney's cannon flew,
Swept the Monk, and clear'd each round top,
  Kill'd and wounded half her crew.

(cont.)

Captain Rogers strove to rally
  His men, from their quarters fled,
While the roaring Hyder Ali
  Cover'd o'er his decks with dead.
When from their tops their dead men tumbled
  And the streams of blood did flow,
Then their proudest hopes were humbled
  By their brave inferior foe.

All aghast, and all confounded,
  They beheld their champions fall,
And their Captain sorely wounded,
  Bade them quick for quarters call.
Then the Monk's proud flag descended,
  And her cannon ceas'd to roar;
By her crew no more defended,
  She confess'd the contest o'er.---

Come, brave boys, and fill your glasses,
  You have humbled one proud foe,
No brave action, this surpasses,
  Fame shall tell the nations so.---
Thus be Britain's woes completed,
  Thus abrid'g her cruel reign,
Till she ever, thus defeated,
  Yields the sceptre of the main.

OE'R(sic) the waste of waters cruising, Long the

General Monk had reign'd; All sub-du-ing, all re-du-cing, None her

law-less rage re-strain'd: Many a brave and hear-ty fellow Yielding

to his warlike foe When her guns be-gan to bellow, Struck his

humbled colours low.

From the LONDON COURANT.
The GEORGES, a Song. On LORD GERMAIN's Promotion,
Tune---"Push about the Forum"

OF great and glorious names to speak,
  Since fame the subject urges,
In fighting times a pride I take,
  To sing about the Georges.
For Gordon George whose life was spar'd,
  The mob may rant and tear-o,
He's nothing in the scale compar'd
  To George the Minden Hero.

When Statesmen of unsulli'd fame,
  With honours were invested,
By Britons never was a name,
  Than Sackville more detested:
But now to England's mighty boast,
  So much revers'd the case is;
The very man is honour'd most,
  Who most the Crown disgraces.

Alive had brave Duke William been,
  He, like old George, when fretted,
Would kick his hat about to've seen,
  This noble deed gazetted:
The public prints his fame shall spread,
  And make the world acquainted,
That George Germain a peer is made,
  By George the Lord's Anointed.

George Brydges Rodney, Fortune's son
  Of property tenacious,
Amongst the many wonders done,
  He conquer'd St. Eustatius!
The Auction o'er---the British Don,
  Beheld himself a Noodle,
Who lost the place, whilst he and Vaughan,
  Were singing Yankee-Doodle.

Paul Jones may well prick up his ears,
  For so it is reported,
He'll rank amongst the new-made Peers,
  The moment he's converted.
And when America's re-took,
  And George for joy get groggy,
One Arnold shall be made a Duke,
  The Duke of Saratoga.
                              (cont.)

The surly sons of Britain's isle,
  May ridicule the matter;
I'll lay my life 'twill make 'em smile,
  On t 'other side the water:
"Then shout, my boys, at George's name,
  "And drink his health till mellow;
"Old Time may travel till he's lame,
  "Before he finds his fellow."

411. The GEORGES, a Song. On LORD GERMAIN's Promotion.

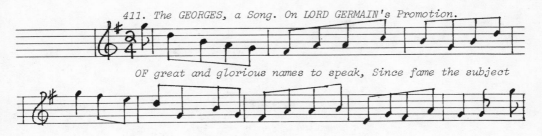

OF great and glorious names to speak, Since fame the subject

ur-ges, In fighting times a pride I take, To sing about the Georges. For

Gordon George whose life was spar'd, The mob may rant and tear-o, He's

nothing in the scale compar'd to George the Minden Hero. When

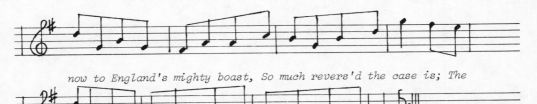

Statesmen of un-sulli'd fame, With honours were in-vested, By

Britons never was a name, Than Sackville more de-tested: But

now to England's mighty boast, So much revers'd the case is; The

very man is honour'd most, Who most the Crown disgraces.

337. *SONG on the celebration of the birth of the DAUPHIN.*
To the restoration march.

YE sons of Mars attend
Come join the festive throng
In loftiest strains exult
For Jove approves the song.
Let gladness every heart expand,
Let gratitude inspire
Each patriot breast with joy unfeigned
To hail the royal Sire.
  CHORUS. A Dauphin's born let cannons loud
  Bid echo rend the sky
  Long life to Gallia's King
  Columbia's great Ally.
             2.
Hark! hark! a feu de joie
Makes trembling AEther ring,
Whilst shouting armies hail
A Prince, a future King,
On whom may heaven with liberal hand
Its choices gifts bestow,
May peace and wisdom bless his reign
And laurels grace his brow.
  CHORUS. A Dauphin's born let cannons loud
  Bid echo rend the sky
  Long life to Gallia's King
  Columbia's great Ally.
             3.
To visit earth once more
Lo! Lo! Astrea deigns,
The golden age returns
How truth with justice reigns,
See proud oppression hide its head
Fell tyranny expire,
For Independence heaven's fair gift
Lights Freedom's sacred fire.
  CHORUS. A Dauphin's born let cannons loud
  Bid echo rend the sky
  Long life to Gallia's King
  Columbia's great Ally.

337. SONG On the celebration of the birth of the DAUPHIN.

YE sons of Mars at ~ tend Come join the fes - tive throng in

loftiest strains ex - ult For Jove ap - proves the song.   Let

gladness every heart ex-pand, Let gra-ti-tude in-spire Each

pa-triot breast with joy un-feigned To hail the ro-yal Sire. A

Dauphin's born let cannons loud Bid e-cho rend the sky Long

life to Gal - lia's King Co - lum - bia's great Al - ly.

1263. MORRIS's VOLUNTEERS. A NEW SONG.

I.
YE Lads of true Spirit,
  Who wish to inherit,
A Fame to increase with your Years;
  And the King and his Laws,
    Come join in the Cause,
  With Morris's bold Volunteers, brave Boys,
  With Morris's York Volunteers.
II.
An Example so glorious!
  Heaven send them victorious;
May they ever be strangers to fears;
  May the Trumpet of Fame
    Ever give them the Name,
  Of Morris's bold Volunteers, brave Boys,
  Of Morris's, &c.
III.
May they ever oppose
  Great-Britain's proud Foes,
And make them confess, e'en with Tears,
  'Tis in Vain to withstand
    So united a Band,
  As Morris's bold Volunteers, brave Boys,
  As Morris's, &c.
IV.
Then let us unite,
  'Gainst REBELLION to fight;
Come, Lads, then assist with three Cheers;
  And let each hearty Soul,
    Drink a Health in a Bowl,
  To Morris's bold Volunteers, brave Boys,
  To Jack Morris's York Volunteers.
                              C

824

1263. MORRIS's VOLUNTEERS. A NEW SONG.

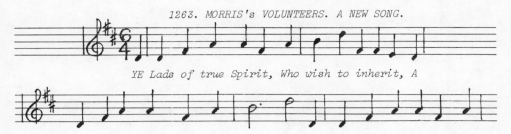

YE Lads of true Spirit, Who wish to inherit, A

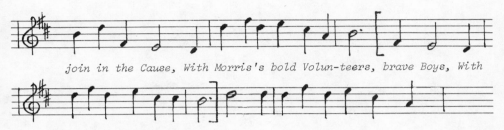

Fame to increase with your Years; And the King and his Laws,   Come

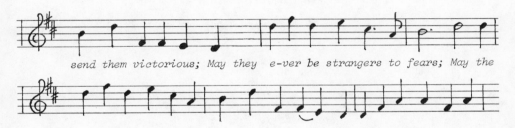

join in the Cause, With Morris's bold Volun-teers, brave Boys, With

Morris's York Volun-teers   An Ex-am-ple so glorious! Heaven

send them victorious; May they e-ver be strangers to fears; May the

Trumpet of Fame E-ver give them the Name,   Of Morris's bold Volun-

teers, brave Boys, Of Morris's bold Volun - teers.

[ ] Music within brackets not in original.

141.

From the London Advertiser.
WHO's the NOODLE. A NEW SONG.

I Sing of George's golden days,
  Not George the first or second;
Tho' they deserve the nation's praise,
  With this they can't be reckon'd:
For he beyond compare is known,
  God bless him he so wise is,
That every day he fills the throne,
  His wisdom higher rises.
    Yankee doodle, who's the noodle?
      Bonny Scotchmen boast him;
    Every tory sings his glory,
      And in bumpers toast him.

The rebels over yonder main,
  Who play the very devil;
Who fire and prime, and load again
  With rifles most uncivil;
Who dare refuse a paultry tax,
  And swear he shall not cheat them,
Will all be glad to turn their backs,
  When mighty George has beat them.
    Yankee doodle, &c.

What tho' Britannia, sees her sons
  Confounded and divided,
And by monsieurs and Spanish dons
  Insulted and derided;
Tho' taxes rise and trade decays,
  And millions are expended,
On George with gratitude we gaze,
  By his right arm defended.
    Yankee doodle, &c.

And see Hyde Park, and Tiptree too,
  Display their hostile banners;
Who dare invade? od's blood, par bleu!
  We'll teach them better manners:
He comes, he comes, the man of might!
  His gallant troops reviewing;
"Oh! Amherst, what a heavenly sight,"
  Who fears the storm that's brewing?
    Yankee doodle, &c.

(cont.)

Then here's a health to George the third,
  Who brightens England's glory!
(If you will take a Poet's word,
  Or trust a loyal tory:)
Then halloo, boys, at George's name,
  And drink his health 'till mellow;
Old time may travel 'till he's lame,
  Before he finds his fellow.
    Yankee doodle, &c.

141. WHO's the NOODLE. A NEW SONG.

Majestic

I Sing of George's golden days, Not George the first or se-cond; Tho' they de-serve the nations praise,With this they can't be reckon'd: For he be-yond com-pare is known, God

828

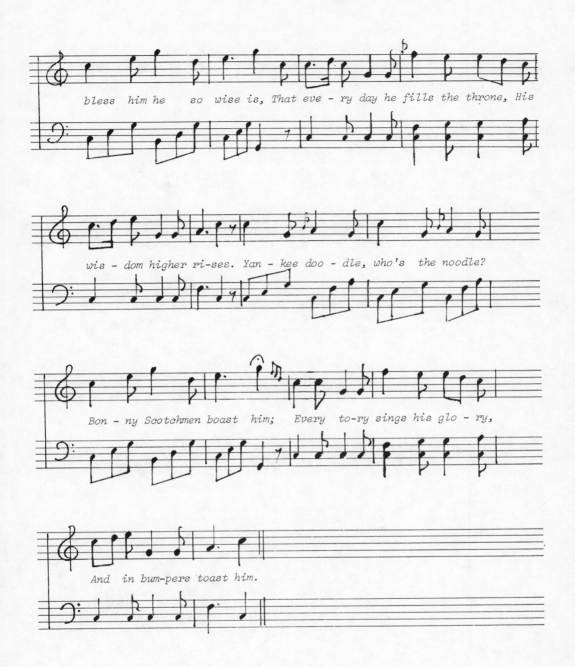

bless him he so wise is, That eve - ry day he fills the throne, His

wis - dom higher ri-ses. Yan - kee doo - dle, who's the noodle?

Bon - ny Scotchmen boast him; Every to-ry sings his glo - ry,

And in bum-pers toast him.

903.

The MUSICAL INTERLUDE of the TOBACCO-BOX: Or, The SOLDIER's PLEDGE of LOVE.
As performed at the HAY MARKET THEATRE.

Thomas,....................Mr. BRETT.
Kate,......................Miss MORRIS.

THOMAS.
THO' the fate of battle on to-morrow wait,
Let's not lose our prattle now, my charming Kate;
Till the hour of glory love should now take place,
Nor damp the joys before you with a future case.

KATE.
Oh, my Thomas, still be constant, still be true,
Be but to your Kate as Kate is still to you;
Glory will attend you, still will make us blest,
With my firmest love, my dear, you're still possest.

THOMAS.
No new beauties tasted, I'm their arts above,
Three campaigns are wasted, but not so my love;
Anxious still about thee thou art all I prize,
Never Kate without thee will I bung these eyes.

KATE.
Constant to My Thomas I will still remain,
Nor think I will leave thy side the whole campaign,
But I'll cherish thee, and strive to make thee bold,
May'st thou share the victory, mayst thou share the gold.

THOMAS.
If by some bold action I the halbert bear,
Think what satisfaction when my rank you share;
Drest like any Lady, fair from top to toe,
Fine lac'd caps and ruffles then will be your due.

KATE.
If a Serjeant's lady I should chance to prove,
Clean linen shall be ready always for my love;
Never more will Kate the Captain's laundress be,
I'm too pretty Thomas, love, for all but thee.

THOMAS.
Here Kate, take my 'bacco box, a soldiers all,
If by Frenchmen's blows your Tom is doom'd to fall;
When my life is ended, thou may'st boast and prove,
Thou'd'st my first, my last, my only pledge of love.
(cont.)

830

KATE.

Here take back thy 'bacco box, thou'rt all to me,
Nor think but I will be near thee, love, to see,
In the hour of danger let me always share;
I'll be kept no stranger to my soldier's fare.

THOMAS.

Check that rising sigh, Kate, stop that falling tear,
Come, my pretty Comrade, entertain no fear;
But may heav'n befriend us--hark! the drums command,
Honour I obey you. Love, I kiss your hand.

KATE.

*I can't stop these tears, tho' crying I disdain,
But must own, 'tis trying hard the point to gain:
May good Heav'ns defend thee; conquest on thee wait,
One kiss more, and then I'll give thee up to fate.

*Both repeat this verse, only Thomas says,--"Conquest on me wait;"
and "Yield myself to fate."

The above petit piece has been universally admired for its melody,
and the simplicity of the dialogue. The original music is French,
and the accompanyments are Dr. Arnold's.

903: The MUSICAL INTERLUDE of the TOBACCO-BOX: Or, The SOLDIER's PLEDGE of Love.

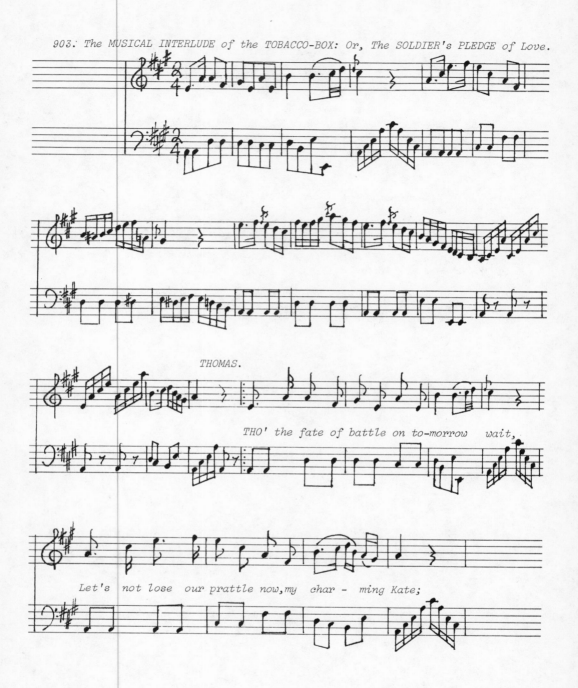

THOMAS.

THO' the fate of battle on to-morrow wait,

Let's not lose our prattle now, my char - ming Kate;

Till the hour of glo - ry love should now take place, Nor

damp the joys be - fore you with a fu - ture case.

January 20	Articles of peace signed between Britain and France, and Britain and Spain. The U.S. - British accord could not go into effect until a settlement was reached in Europe.
April 11	Congress proclaims end of war.
April 15	Articles of Peace ratified by Congress.
April 26	7,000 loyalists sail from New York. This was the last of a total of almost 100,000 who left the U.S. for Europe or Canada.
June 13	Army disbands.
November 25	British evacuate New York City.
December 4	Washington bids farewell to his officers at Frances Tavern, New York.
December 23	Washington resigns his commission as Commander-in-Chief.

961.

PHILADELPHIA, March 4.

Extract of a letter from Talbot Court-House, dated Feb. 11.

"This being the first year that the birth day of our great and worthy General hath been announced to the Public, Henry Hooper, Esquire, Lieutenant of Dorchester county, Maryland, with a respectable body of the truly patriotic officers and gentlemen of that county, and also several officers of the Maryland line, assembled at Cambridge, to celebrate the auspicious day which gave birth to the great Defender of American Liberty; where a public dinner being provided, the company assembled at noon, and after dinner drank the following toasts:

1. General Washington, long may he live the boasted hero of liberty.
2. Congress.
3. Governor and state of Maryland.
4. Lewis XVI. the Protector of the Rights of Mankind.
5. Continental army.
6. Maryland line.
7. May trade and navigation flourish.
8. The Seven United Provinces, our allies.
9. The Count Rochambeau and French army.
10. May the union between the powers in alliance ever continue on the basis of justice and equity.
11. May the friends of freedom prove the sons of virtue.
12. Conversion to the unnatural sons of America.
13. May the union of the American States be perpetual.

The evening being spent with the utmost festivity, gladness filled the hearts of all that were present, and joy sparkled in their eyes. The entertainment was concluded with the following song, composed by an American.

> In a chariot of light from the regions above,
> The Goddess of Freedom appear'd;
>   The sun beams of day,
>   Emblazon'd her way,
> And empire America rear'd.
>
> To sustain the vast fabric her offspring were taught,
> She smil'd on each patriot birth;
>   But shielded her charms,
>   Secure in the arms
> Of the Chieftain celestial on earth.
>
> This guardian exalted, the trumpet of fame
> Resounding from hence to the skies--
>   All the deities bend,
>   And list'ning attend,
> In silent delight and surprise.

(cont.)

835

But fir'd at his glories the fierce power of war,
Disturbing aetherial repose--
  Exclaim'd--Thrones divine,
  "See an hero of mine---
How matchless and god-like he glows!"

"Your hero!--Minerva indignant replies,
'Twas I from his birth did preside,
  Form'd, finish'd his mind,
  The great talents design'd,
His Goddess, Preceptress, and Guide!"

Their accents scarce ended, Apollo arose-
If intuitive knowledge, he cries,
  Makes him great, ye must own
  The free gifts of my throne--
He's mine, Gods, as sure as the skies!

Next the fair pow'r of virtue serene and severe,
Intreats they'd a moment be mute,
  Her laws she'd protest,
  Alone rul'd his breast;
So Heav'n was all in dispute.

Jove hear'd it, and summon'd the Synod supreme,
Which met in the chambers of day,
  Obedient Fate
  Then hush'd the debate,
And thus did the Thunderer say,

"Minerva, Mars, Phoebus and Virtue attend!
T'oblivion this clamour resign,
  For just is each claim,
  And in Washington's name,
For ever your laurels combine!"

961.

Con Spirito

In a chariot of light from the regions a - bove, The God - dess of

Freedom ap - pear'd; The sun beams of day, Em - blazon'd her

way,　　And　em - pire　A - me - ri-ca rear'd.

6　　　6　　　# #

To sus-tain the　vast　fa-bric her

octaves

7　6
　　4

offspring were taught, She smil'd on　each　pa-tri-ot birth;　But

octaves

shielded her charms,　Se-cure in　the arms ⌈Of the　Chieftain ce-

7　　　#　　　　　6　　　6　5　3　6　　　5
#　　　　　　　　　　　　　　4　　4

les-tial on earth,]   Of the

Sy

Chieftain ce - lestial on earth.

967. A HYMN on PEACE.

1.

BEHOLD, array'd in light
And by Divine Command,
Fair Peace, the child of Heav'n, descends
  To this afflicted land,
Like the bright morning star
She leads a glorious day,
And o'er this western world extends
  Her all reviving ray.

2.

Your swords to plough shares turn'd,
Your fields with plenty crown'd,
Shall laugh and sing---and freedom spread
  The voice of gladness round.
Oh, sing a new made song!
  To God your hymns address.
He rul'd the hearts of mighty Kings,
  And gave our arms success.

3.

He check'd our haughty foe,
  And bad the contest cease;
"Thus and no farther, shalt thou go,
  Be all the world at peace.
No more shall Savage war
  Lead on the hostile band;
No more shall suff'ring captives mourn,
  Or blood pollute the land.

4.

Confess Jehovah's pow'r,
  And magnify his name,
Let all the world with one accord,
  His wondrous work proclaim,
Let us with hearts devout,
  Declare what we have seen,
And to our children's children tell,
  How good the Lord hath been.

967. A HYMN on PEACE.

And by Di - vine Command,

BE-HOLD, ar - ray'd in light And by Di - vine Command,

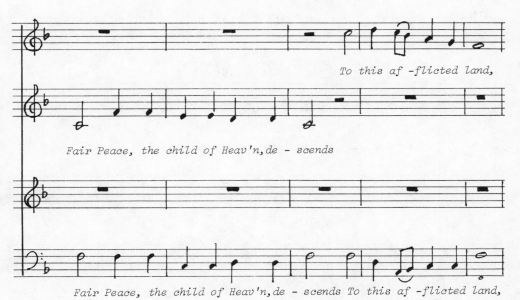

To this af -flicted land,

Fair Peace, the child of Heav'n, de - scends

Fair Peace, the child of Heav'n, de - scends To this af -flicted land,

Music Publishers, 1973

Fair Peace, the child of Heav'n, de - scends To this af-flicted land,

Fair Peace, the child of Heav'n, de - scends To this af-flicted land,

Fair Peace, the child of Heav'n, de - scends To this af-flicted land,

Fair Peace, the child of Heav'n, de - scends To this af-flicted land,

Like the bright morning star She leads a glorious day,

Like the bright morning star She leads a glorious day,

Like the bright morning star She leads a glorious day,

Like the bright morning star She leads a glorious day,

tends Her all re- vi- ving ray,

vi- ving ray, Her all re- vi-ving

And o'er this wes- tern world ex- tends Her all re-vi-ving

world ex- tends Her all re-vi-ving

And o'er this western world ex - tends Her all reviving ray.

ray, And o'er this western world ex - tends Her all reviving ray.

ray, And o'er this western world ex - tends Her all reviving ray.

ray, And o'er this western world ex - tends Her all reviving ray.

969. *New LIBERTY-HALL: A SONG.*

OLD Homer--but what have we with him to do,
What are Grecians or Trojans to me or to you;
Such Heathenish heroes no more I'll invoke,
Choice spirits assist me, attend hearts of oak.

2.

Perhaps my address you may premature think,
Because that I mention no toast as I drink---
There are many fine toasts, but the best of them all
Is the toast of the times, lads, Liberty-Hall.

3.

This fine British building by Alfred was fram'd,
It's grand corner stone, Magna Charta was nam'd;
Fair freedom then came at integrity's call,
And fram'd the front pillars of Liberty-Hall.

4.

The manor our forefathers bought with their blood
And their sons and their son's sons have prov'd the deed good;
By the title we'll live, by the title we'll fall,
For life is not life out of Liberty-Hall.

5.

There's your sweet smiling courtiers, of ribband and lace,
Those Spaniels of power and country's disgrace,
So suple, so servile, so passive they fall,
'Twas passive obedience lost Liberty-Hall.

6.

Now this English building is gone to decay,
The master's turn'd tyrant,---his slaves in dismay;
The foundation's gone, superstructure and all,
And naught but despair's in Old Liberty-Hall.

7.

The artists would there have fain built it again,
But found no materials excepting a chain:
They left it, and came to America all,
And here they have finish'd New Liberty-Hall.

8.

Happy asylum! we've thrown off the Crown,
And natural reason keeps tyranny down;
No threats, arm'd by despots, appear to appal
The doors are thrown open of Liberty-Hall.

9.

In the mantle of honor, each star spangled fold,
Playing bright in the sunshine, the burnish of gold,
Truth beams on her breast, see! at Washington's call,
America's genius in Liberty-Hall.

(cont.)

10.

Our ships, with our allies, they now sweep the sea,
Their standard is justice, their watch word be free:
The Congress we've chosen, they're our countrymen all,
God bless them, and bless us in Liberty-Hall.

11.

But where is this building; Lord Bute fain would know?
It's neither at Richmond, St. James's, or Kew;
'Tis a place of no mortal architect's art,
For Liberty Hall's an American's heart.

969. New LIBERTY-HALL: A SONG.

OLD Ho - mer -- but what have we with
him to do, What are Grecians or
Tro-jans to me or to you; Such Heathen-ish he - roes no
more I'll in - voke, Choice spi-rits as-sist me, at - tend hearts of

847

oak.   [Choice spi - rits as - sist me, at - tend hearts of oak.

971. A SONG. On the wise Coalition compleated the 1st of April, 1783.
To the Tune of Nancy Dawson.

OF all the leaders in the state
That in the House of Commons prate,
And make our Sov'reign scratch his pate,
  There's none like twisting Charley.
On Shelburne's peace he made a rout,
Sore vex'd he had in wrath gone out,
But nimbly turn'd him North-about,
  And in popp'd subtle Charley.

The noble Lord of high renown,
The champion firm of England's crown,
By Reynard frighten'd, knuckles down
  To patriotic Charley.
This canting changeling now will swear,
That "no opponent was so fair,"
"No friend so warm," so worth his care
  As honest little Charley.

The snake that in the grass did lurk,
That artful Jesuit, Ed--d B---e,
Now sets his only tongue at work
  To puff off worthy Charley,
He vows that things will quickly mend,
No two such men the state defend
As Tory N--th and his new friend,
  That upright Whig, sweet Charley.

What wonder-workings shall we see
Atchiev'd by these united Three,
Who in fair promises agree
  To raise Britannia's glory!
But if their Party-Spirit bring
Disgrace on England and her King,
On Tyburn-tree then let them swing;
  Hang Jesuit, Whig, and Tory!

971. A SONG. On the wise Coalition compleated the 1st of April, 1783.

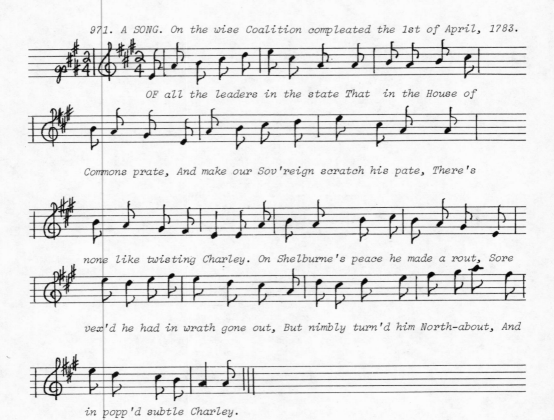

OF all the leaders in the state That   in the House of

Commons prate, And make our Sov'reign scratch his pate, There's

none like twisting Charley. On Shelburne's peace he made a rout, Sore

vex'd he had in wrath gone out, But nimbly turn'd him North-about, And

in popp'd subtle Charley.

1162.

"To keep in place"
"Is no disgrace."
ANON.

IN our dependent golden days,
  When loyalty no harm meant;
A zealous courtier then I was,
  By which I got preferment.
To flatter the great I never miss'd,
  Or those in power or station,
And curs'd all those who did resist,
  The rulers of the nation.
    And this is law I will maintain,
    (I hold it no disgrace sirs)
    That whatsoever power shall reign,
    I'll keep myself in place sirs.

When Gage in Boston first arriv'd,
  And committees assembled,
We were of government depriv'd,
  And then I own, I trembled.
But always having power in view,
  (The British being far distant)
I join'd the noisy whiggish crew,
  And to them became assistant.
    And this is law, &c.

When to New-York the Howes first came,
  With hosts prepar'd to maul us,
I lost my patriotic flame,
  While rebels they did call us.
I independence then abjur'd,
  In hopes to 'scape the halter,
But kept my sentiments obscur'd,
  In case the times should alter.
    And this is law, &c.

Next when the Burgoynade took place,
  I strutted and look'd big sirs,
My countenance clear'd up apace,
  And I stood confess'd a whig sirs!
When Charleston fell, and the British host,
  Were marching unmolested,
I thought the American cause was lost,
  And against all whigs protested.
    And this is law, &c.

(cont.)

When York in pudding time was ta'en,
  And British arms were grounded,
I turn'd about, it then was plain,
  All tories were confounded.
That dastard race no more are seen,
  But are to whigs converted!
To Aristocratic whigs, I ween,
  As is by some asserted.
    And this is law, &c.

These freeborn states, in all thirteen,
  Or more if in succession,
To them I'll cleave as shall be seen,
  While they can keep possession.
And in my mind no one can say,
  I any way do flatter,
For Congress shall my rulers be,
  Until the times do alter.
    And this is law, &c.

1162.

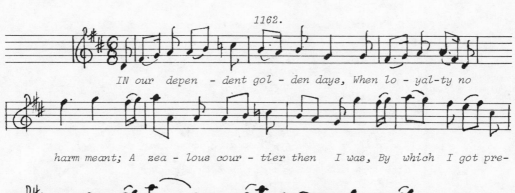

IN our depen - dent gol - den days, When lo - yal-ty no

harm meant; A zea - lous cour - tier then I was, By which I got pre-

ferment. To flat - ter the great I ne - ver miss'd, Or

those in power or station, And curs'd all those who did re-sist,The

ru - lers of the nation. And this is law I will maintain, (I

hold it no dis-grace sirs) That what - so-e -ver

power shall reign, I'll keep my-self in place sirs.

716. *A favourite SONG in the new Farce called the BEST BIDDER.*

A Soldier, a Soldier, a Soldier for me!
  His arms are so bright,
  And he stands so upright,
  So gallant and gay,
  When he trips it away,
Who is so nice and well powdered as he?
  Sing rub a dub, dub a dub, whe, whe, whe, fe, fe, fe,
  Thunder and plunder, a soldier, a soldier, a soldier, for me.

Each morn when you see him upon the Parade,
  He cuts such a flash,
  With his gorget and sash,
  And makes such a do
  With his gaiter and queue,
Sleeping or waking, who need be afraid?
  Sing rub a dub, &c.

Or else when he's mounted so trim and so tall,
  With broad sword in hand,
  The whole town to command,
  Such capers, such prances,
  Such ogling, such glances,
Our hearts gallop off, and are left at Whitehall.
  Sing tara-tan-tara-tan, too too too, too too too,
  Trumpet and thump it--a soldier, a soldier, a soldier for me.

854

Vivace

Fife

Drum

tutti

A Soldier, a Soldier, a Soldier for me! [*A Soldier, a Soldier, a*

855

Soldier for me, His arms are so bright, And he stands so upright, So

gal-lant and gay, When he trips it a-way, Who is so nice and well

powdered as he? Sing rub a dub, dub a dub,

Pizzicato

whe, whe, whe, fe, fe, fe, Thunder and plunder,

a soldier, a soldier, a soldier, for me.   A

soldier, a soldier, a soldier for me.

Each morn when you see him upon the Parade,
   He cuts such a flash,
   With his gorget and sash,
   And makes such a do
   With his gaiter and queue,
Sleeping or waking, who need be afraid?
         Sing rub a dub, &c.

Or else when he's mounted so trim and so tall, Or

else when he's mounted so trim and so tall, With

broad sword in hand, The whole town to command, Such

capers, such prances, Such ogling, such glances, Our

hearts gallop off, and are left at Whitehall. Sing tara-tan-tara-tan

Too too too, too too too,

Trumpet and thump it— a soldier, a soldier, a

soldier for me, a soldier, a soldier, a soldier for me.

859

146. ODE, On the Arrival of their Excellencies General WASHINGTON
and Governor CLINTON in New York, on the 25th of November, 1783.
Tune --- "He comes! He comes!"

THEY come! they come! the Heroes come!
With sounding fife, and thund'ring drum,
Their ranks advance in bright array.
The Heroes of AMERICA.
He comes! 'tis mighty WASHINGTON!
Words fail to tell all he has done;
Our Hero, Guardian, Father, Friend!
His fame can never, never end.
He comes! he comes! 'tis CLINTON comes'
Justice her ancient seat resumes.
From shore to shore let shouts resound,
For Justice comes with Freedom crown'd.
She comes! the white rob'd Virgin, Peace.
And bids grim War his horrors cease.
Oh! blooming Virgin, with us stay,
And bless, oh! bless AMERICA.
Now freedom has our wishes crown'd,
Let flowing goblets pass around;
We'll drink to Freedom's fav'rite Son,
Health, Peace, and Joy to WASHINGTON.

146. *ODE, On the Arrival of their Excellencies General WASHINGTON and Governor CLINTON in New York, on the 25th November, 1783.*

THEY come! they come! the He-roes come! With sounding fife,

they come! the He-roes come! With sounding fife,

and thund'ring drum, Their ranks ad-vance in bright array. The

and thund'ring drum, Their ranks ad-vance in bright array. The

Heroes of A-ME-RI-CA Heroes, heroes, heroes, heroes, heroes of A-

Heroes of A-ME-RI-CA heroes, heroes, heroes of A-

ME - RI-CA.

ME - RI-CA.

Page No.	Main Entry No.	
550 553; 836	1395; 236; 961	Apollo
546	1176-8	Lord Apsley
814	335	Argo
701; 714; 819	53; 55; 411	Arnold - Benedict Arnold (1741-1801), Continental General, hero and traitor. May 10, 1775, captured Ticonderoga, May 17 raided St. Johns, Canada, April, 1776, surrendered outside of Quebec. Battle of Saratoga won by Americans against Burgoyne September 19 and October 7, 1777. Arnold seriously wounded. Awarded Major General rank November 29, 1777.
819	411	Arnold, Duke of Saratoga - See above.
822	337	Astrea
566	33	Athens, Seat of Science
665	1087	Atlantic
790	230	Augusta, Georgia

B

550	1395	Baker
546	1176-78	Baldock
814-15	335	Captain Barney
634	1362	Barré - Isaac Barré (1726?-1802), British officer and politician who championed American rights. First used the term Sons of Liberty, referring to Americans.
546	1176-78	Lord Barrington
546	1176-78	Duke of Bedford - John Russell, fourth Duke of Bedford (1710-71) negotiated peace settlement at end of French and Indian War, a settlement generally regarded as having lost at the peace table what had been won by Britain on the battlefield.

682   581   Beelzebub, Stygian God.

568   1400   Beggar's Opera - ballad opera, written by John Gay;
                      a satire on high life at court and in parliament.
                      All the main characters were thieves, whores, etc.

682   581   Belial

674   305   Bellona

750   500   Bennington - Vermont, location of battle, August 16, 1777,
                      between German force under Lieutenant Colonel
                      Friedrick Baum and American Brigadier General John
                      Stark. Americans won, contributing to ultimate defeat
                      of British force under General John Burgoyne at
                      Saratoga, New York.

623   36   bilboes - foot shackles

582   443   B[isho]ps

653   711   B---h [Bitch?]

757   877   Blake - famous British naval commander

790   230   Blue Mountains

811   925   bolthyourgh

564;   10; 455;   Boston - Massachusetts
570;   431; 435;
578;   1005; 374;
592;   757; 375;
671;   1162
696;
618;
703;
851

671   1005   Boston jail

550   1395   Botetourt-men - supporters of Royal Governor of Virginia,
                      Norborne Berkeley Bottetourt (c.1718-1770).

773   825   Bourbon's fleet - French fleet

757   877   British Lion

671   1005   British regulars

C

866

Page No.	Main Entry No.	
550	1395	Cherokees
800	61	Chesapeake Bay - French fleet sailed into Chesapeake in campaign that led to defeat of British at Yorktown in 1781.
564	10	China
793	358	Clinton (British) - Henry Clinton (1738?-1795), British Commander in Chief, 1778-82.
793; 861	358; 146	Clinton, (Governor) - George Clinton (1739-1812), first governor of New York state; Continental General.
849	971	Coalition compleated the 1st of April, 1783 - See: Charley
546	1176-8	COCKPIT
674-5; 682-3; 696	305; 581; 374	COLUMBA - alternate name for thirteen Colonies
780-1; 787; 806; 822	380; 630; 62; 337	Columbia - alternate name for thirteen Colonies
638	475	Commons (House of)
757	877	Congo - Continental Congress
578	431	Congoes - members of Continental Congress.
592; 605; 631; 646; 661-2; 668; 751; 835; 846; 851	435; 803; 751; 120; 44; 991; 500; 961; 969; 1162	Congress - Continental Congress
794; 797; 800; 805	358; 383; 61; 62	CORNWALLIS Earl Cornwallis - Charles Cornwallis (1738-1805), British General who surrendered at Yorktown, October 19, 1781.

F

G

| 592 | 435 | Ga--'s (Gage) |

605;	803; 751;	GAGE (General) - Thomas Gage (1719?-87), British
631;	120; 1162	Commander in Chief in America (1763-75)
646;		
851		

| 605 | 803 | Galic - French |

| 822 | 337 | Gallia's King - French King Louis XVI |

| 794 | 358 | Galloway Joe - Joseph Galloway (c.1731-1803) Prominent Philadelphia loyalist and lawyer, in charge of civil government in Philadelphia during British occupation there. Roundly hated by American rebels. |

| 634 | 1362 | game-act |

675;	305; 53;	GATES (Major-General) - Horatio Gates (1728-1806),
700-1;	375; 55	Continental General in charge of forces that
704;		defeated Burgoyne at Saratoga in 1777. Fled
714		the British at Camden in 1780.

| 568 | 1400 | Gay - John Gay, composer and writer of Beggar's Opera. |

| 646 | 120 | Gen-- |

| 819 | 411 | Gordon George - In London June 2-9, 1780, Lord George Gordon led a mob protesting the Catholic Relief Act. Riots followed. British public rallied to support George III. |

| 819 | 411 | George the Minden Hero |

| 826 | 141 | George the I - King of England |

| 602; | 101; 141 | George the II - King of England |
| 826 | | |

556;585;	1323; 155;	George the III
602;623;	101; 36;	Georgius - King of England
658-9;	915; 991;	
668;671;	1005; 581;	
689;700;	309; 53;	
703;753;	375; 501;	
827	141	

646	120	Hutch--
826	141	Hyde Park - park near London
814	335	HYDER ALI - a capable buccaneer in Mysore, India, who challenged British control of India for 24 years in the middle of the 18th century. In this case, HYDER ALI is the name of a ship.
578	431	Hysons

I

658;794	915; 358	India
790	230	Indians
770	1136	IERNE
659	915	Infidel
790	230	Ingram
607	805	Irish

J

700	53	Jack, the King's commander - See: Burgoyne, John.
757	877	Jack Lanyard
623	36	James
671	1005	Jemina
674	305	Jersies, late successes in - New Jersey Campaign of General George Washington, November 1776 - January 1777. Defeat of British almost completely drove Howe out of New Jersey.
849	971	Jesuit, Ed[war]d B[ut]e - See: Bute, Edward
659	915	Jew
634	1362	Dr. Johnson - Dr. Samuel Johnson, British tory leader.
744	324	Johnson - Henry Johnson (1748-1835), British Officer captured at Stony Point, New York, October 8, 1778. Court martialed and apparently acquitted.

M

646	120	Manly - John (Manley) (1734-93). American naval officer. Took first and last prizes of war.
578; 584	431; 155	Mansfield Lord M--sf---d - William Murray, first Earl of Mansfield (1705-93), judge who in 1772 in the Somerset case declared slavery to be illegal in England.
674; 787; 822; 836	305; 630; 337; 961	Mars
835	961	Maryland line
592	435	Massachusetts
814-15	335	Cape May
696	374	Mercury
776	545	Mews
722; 797	199; 383	Hero of Minden - George Germain (?) accused of misconduct, Battle of Minden, August 1, 1759. Decisive battle in Seven Years' War. British beat French. LaFayette's father killed on French side.
787; 836	630; 961	Minerva
546	1176-8	Ministers of George the Third
814	335	General Monk
800	61	MONMOUTH - New Jersey Battle, June 28, 1778, Washington vs. Clinton - militarily a draw, last important battle in the North.
556; 773; 826	1323; 825; 141	Monsieurs - French
693	50	Montcalm - Marquis Louis-Joseph de Montcalm (1712-59), French General killed in Battle of Quebec during Seven Years' war.

880

884

U

V

Page No.	Main Entry No.	
		Y
793	358	Yankee
819; 826-7	411; 141	Yankee-Doodle
671; 810	1005; 925	Yankies
800; 805; 851	61; 62; 1162	York - See: Yorktown
550; 671	1395; 1005	York - See: New York
793	358	York-Town - North Carolina. On October 2, 1781, Cornwallis surrendered to Washington, effectively ending the British military effort against the Americans.
824	1263	York Volunteers

DATE DUE

MAR 03 1998	